Social Marketing

Social Marketing

Lynne Eagle, Stephan Dahl,

Susie Hill, Sara Bird,

Fiona Spotswood and Alan Tapp

PEARSON

Harlow, England • London • New York • Boston • San Francisco • Toronto • Sydney
Auckland • Singapore • Hong Kong • Tokyo • Seoul • Taipei • New Delhi
Cape Town • São Paulo • Mexico City • Madrid • Amsterdam • Munich • Paris • Milan

Pearson Education Limited
Edinburgh Gate
Harlow CM20 2JE
Tel: +44 (0)1279 623623
Website: www.pearson.com/uk

First published 2013

Pearson Education is not responsible for the content of third-party internet sites.

ISBN: 978-0-273-72722-4 (print)
       978-0-273-72723-1 (PDF)
       978-0-273-78099-1 (eText)

British Library Cataloguing-in-Publication Data
A catalogue record for this book is available from the British Library

Library of Congress Cataloging-in-Publication Data
Eagle, Lynne.
   Social marketing / Lynne Eagle, Stephan Dahl, Susie Hill, Sara Bird, Fiona Spotswood and Alan Tapp. — First Edition.
      pages cm
   Includes bibliographical references and index.
   ISBN 978-0-273-72722-4 (print) — ISBN (invalid) 978027372723 (PDF) — ISBN (invalid) 978-0-273-78099-1 (eText)   1. Social marketing.   I. Title.
   HF5414.E1794 2013
   658.8—dc23
                                                                    2012034833

10 9 8 7 6 5 4 3 2 1
16 15 14 13 12

Typeset in 9.5/12.5 pt Charter ITC Std by 75.
Print edition printed and bound in country by Ashford Colour, Gosport

NOTE THAT ANY PAGE CROSS REFERENCES REFER TO THE PRINT EDITION

Brief contents

Contents

Companion Website

For open-access **student resources** specifically written to complement this textbook and support your learning, please visit **www.pearsoned.co.uk/eagle**

Lecturer Resources

For password-protected online resources tailored to support the use of this textbook in teaching, please visit **www.pearsoned.co.uk/eagle**

Contributors

Sara Bird is Senior Lecturer in Marketing at University of the West of England, and member of the Bristol Social Marketing Centre there. Her research focuses on social marketing and the role it can play in sexual health, but she also has a keen interest in emotional versus rational decision-making processes, particularly amongst adolescents and older people. She lectures in public relations and research methods.

Dr Stephan Dahl is Senior Lecturer in Marketing at Hull University Business School. His research interests include social media, and the role social marketing and marketing communication can play to prevent health problems, and especially to increase physical activity in a cross-cultural and diverse context.

Professor Lynne Eagle is Professor of Marketing at James Cook University. Her research interests centre on marketing communication effects and effectiveness, including the impact of persuasive communication on children; the impact of new, emerging and hybrid media forms and preferences for/use of formal and informal communications channels and trans-disciplinary approaches to sustained behaviour change in social marketing/health promotion/environmental protection campaigns.

Susie Hill has led health improvement programmes and campaigns in the NGO and corporate sectors since 1994. She has a Masters in Health and Social Marketing and has a professional interest in wellness and human performance. Susie is currently the Global Adviser on health behaviour change and health promotion for Shell.

Dr Fiona Spotswood is Lecturer in Marketing and Social Marketing at Bristol Social Marketing Centre, University of the West of England. Her research interests include the implications of contemporary British 'working class' culture on physical activity participation and the use of marketing techniques to improve utility cycling as a transport mode.

Professor Alan Tapp is Professor of Marketing at the University of the West of England and Director of the Bristol Social Marketing Centre. He has worked in commercial and academic marketing for 25 years, and is interested in applying marketing ideas to solve social problems. Alan is also interested in social and cultural changes and how these are influenced by commercial marketing, politics and other macro forces.

Preface

Social marketing is a rapidly evolving field that will continue to change and adapt in line with the evolution of new technologies and communication interfaces between social marketers and their target groups. New ways of measuring the effects and effectiveness of interventions will also impact on the design and implementation of social marketing activity.

In this text we have tried to address the learning needs of students who will go on to careers in this dynamic and challenging sector, while at the same time acknowledging the need for additional research, critical evaluations of existing concepts and theories and a communications landscape that will look very different in five years, let alone in the next decade.

We stress critical evaluation throughout the text for several reasons. Social marketing deals with a number of complex issues for which no single solution exists. There is a need to synthesise and evaluate data, often of variable quality, from a range of sources in order to understand a problem. Our knowledge in the field is growing exponentially; however, there are still a number of gaps in the extant knowledge base and many concepts and theories have not been fully tested across wide ranges of population segments or situations. In areas such as communications, theories need to evolve and adapt to take into account the rapidly changing communications environment.

While there is a growing body of evidence that interventions based on sound theoretical foundations are more effective than those made on judgement alone, most theories provide only partial explanations or predictors of behaviour. Judgement will always be an important component in social marketing decisions. Environmental, social and economic forces can act as enablers or inhibitors of behaviour change and interventions need to be framed for the context in which the behaviours occur. Budgetary constraints also force limitations on the scope or duration of interventions – there is, unfortunately, no ideal world.

For all interventions, there are always multiple potential solutions and a critical approach ensures that all available data and other forms of information are not just passively accepted, but rather evaluated, with judgements being made where other forms of data do not exist. A critical perspective also ensures that the input and the points of view of a range of stakeholders are considered, together with the likely impact of intervention decisions upon them.

We have tried to provide definitions of all significant terms throughout the text. Real-world 'vignettes' and detailed case studies drawn from a range of countries provide insights into the approaches used by practitioners to address actual social marketing challenges. The cases also link to key chapter concepts. We acknowledge the valuable contribution that access to these cases has made to illustrating key concepts throughout the text and for helping to make the link between concepts and real-world implementation very vivid. Space prohibits the inclusion of more than a small number of cases from the resource. You are encouraged to visit the websites of the organisations featured, together with those of policy makers and regulators, in order to gain a deeper understanding of real-world issues facing social marketers.

The text is organised into three separate parts, with multiple themes running through all chapters. A list of recommended additional resources is provided at the end of each chapter and a detailed glossary at the end of the book.

Part 1: The principles of social marketing

The chapters in this initial part of the text introduce social marketing concepts and principles, providing an overview of the intervention planning process, upstream, policy and partnership issues and ethical considerations.

Chapter 1 What is social marketing?

This chapter introduces social marketing as a field and discusses its evolution and the differences between it and related activity such as health education. The scope of social marketing and the relative complexities of potential interventions across the range of areas in which social marketing currently operates, or could potentially operate in the future, are then examined, followed by a discussion of the potential for unintended impacts of social marketing interventions in each of these areas.

Chapter 2 The core principles of social marketing

The core principles of social marketing are reviewed in this chapter, together with debates such as the use of commercial marketing theory in a social marketing context, the strengths and weaknesses of specific tools and techniques of commercial marketing in a social marketing context, and the value of alternative theories and tools. Tensions regarding whether social marketing should adopt a more service-driven approach versus the traditional product-driven approach are also considered.

Chapter 3 The social marketing intervention planning process

This chapter outlines the stages required in planning a social marketing intervention and methods for conducting a critical review of competitors whose activity may impact on the planning process. The potential of partnership development as part of the intervention planning process is also discussed. The role of research in the planning process, including commercial marketing techniques which may be helpful, is examined.

Chapter 4 Upstream, policy and partnerships

Chapter 4 focuses on the evaluation of external, environmental and policy factors that may act as facilitators of, or barriers to, social marketing interventions. The complexities of developing collaborative partnerships within communities, particularly when establishing public – private partnerships, and the particular challenges presented by some sectors of commercial marketing, are reviewed.

Chapter 5 Ethical issues in social marketing

In this chapter, the strengths and weaknesses of the main ethical frameworks featured in the business literature are discussed in the context of the relevance of each to social marketing activity. Ethical dilemmas that may occur in social marketing activity in relation to these frameworks are considered. The role of codes of ethics in ensuring ethical behaviour from all participants in social marketing interventions is then discussed in the context of the structure of codes that might be successfully implemented among social marketing practitioners.

Part 2: Understanding the consumer

This second part of the book focuses on the role of theory in developing interventions, complemented by research and segmentation tools.

Chapter 6 Understanding the consumer: the role of theory

This chapter focuses on the role of theory in planning, implementing and evaluating social marketing interventions. It provides an overview of key theories used in social marketing and their potential applications and provides guidance on how to critically evaluate these theories, taking into consideration both their flaws and strengths. Guidance is also given for comparing theoretical concepts across different types of social marketing interventions.

Chapter 7 Conducting research in social marketing

The focus of Chapter 7 is on the principles and practice of research within a social marketing context, and ethical challenges that may apply to research on a range of topics and across a range of population segments. This is followed by a discussion of the processes and techniques for designing and justifying research projects for specific interventions, evaluating the design and outputs of research projects and research programmes to evaluate the effects and effectiveness of an intervention.

Chapter 8 Segmentation

In this chapter, the strengths and weaknesses of different forms of segmentation used in social marketing activity are discussed and guidance is provided for evaluating possible segmentation frameworks for different types of social marketing interventions. The reasoning behind the segmentation strategies used in past interventions is also examined, together with strategies for improving future segmentation processes.

Chapter 9 Social forces and population-level effects

This chapter discusses the influence of social groups on individual and collective behaviours, the impact of conformity on social marketing activity and the concept of tipping points for a range of behaviours. The impact of social norms on individual and group behaviours is considered and guidance provided as to how these factors should be evaluated and appropriate action incorporated into social marketing interventions.

Part 3: Designing effective social marketing solutions

In this third section of the text, the chapters focus on key intervention design and evaluation issues.

Chapter 10 Designing social marketing interventions: products, branding, channels and places

In this chapter, different levels of 'products' are considered in the context of the development of social marketing campaigns. The role of branding in social marketing is then discussed, including techniques for evaluating appropriate branding strategies and developing suitable brand images for interventions. The role of channels and distribution in social marketing product development are then examined.

Chapter 11 Message framing

We focus on the role of message framing in developing social marketing interventions, including the use of positive or negative framing, and rational or emotional messages. Guidance is provided for decisions as to which of these forms of framing may be effective for specific circumstances or population segments and on assessing and making reasoned recommendations regarding ways of evaluating framing alternatives for a specific intervention.

Chapter 12 Creativity in social marketing

This chapter discusses the role of creativity in social marketing interventions, focusing on how creative strategy evolves from scoping stages and the identification of insights into possible behaviour change options, and the development of a creative brief for the design of material. Guidance is provided on how the needs of disadvantaged groups should be taken into account when designing interventions. The influence of different media on the development of material is then discussed, along with the unique features of designing material for new media forms and social media.

Chapter 13 Media planning

Chapter 13 explains the principles of planning traditional mass media such as television, radio, newspapers or magazines, and social media integration and the issue of advertising weight versus duration of an advertising schedule across a budget period. The enduring debate over whether advertising (and, by extension, all forms of marketing communication in the current era) is a strong or weak force is then discussed, along with the strengths and weaknesses of major media vehicles, both traditional and new media, and qualitative factors that should also be considered in planning media.

Chapter 14 The challenges of evaluation

This final chapter discusses why evaluations should occur, what should be evaluated and when, and the contribution of evaluation processes at all stages of an intervention programme. Guidance is provided on how to critically evaluate formal and informal evaluative processes and how to develop and justify evaluation programmes for a range of social marketing interventions. The specific challenges involved in evaluating multi-component and multi-partner interventions are considered, followed by a discussion of the way in which the effect of competition on interventions can be evaluated.

Many more useful resources are provided on the companion website to this book. Please visit **www.personed.co.uk/eagle** for more material to support your study.

Acknowledgements

Authors' acknowledgements

We would like to thank our colleagues within the BSMC, especially Simon Jones and Yvette Morey for providing samples of material from recent research projects for use in Chapter 7. We also thank Professor Julia Verne, Director of the South West Public Health Observatory for permission to use samples of epidemiological data.

Publisher's acknowledgements

We are grateful to the following for permission to reproduce copyright material:

Figures

Figure 2.1 adapted from 'Social Marketing and Communication in Health Promotion', *Health Promotion International*, 6 (2), pp 135–45 (Hastings, G. and Haywood, A., 1991), Oxford Journals; Figure 2.6 from 'Ready to Fly Solo? Reducing Social Marketing's Dependence on Commercial Marketing Theory', *Marketing Theory*, 3 (3), pp. 365–85 (Peattie, S. & Peattie, K., 2003); Figure 6.5 from 'Integrative Model of Behavioural Prediction and Change', *Journal of Communication*, 56 (August supplement), S1–S17 (Fishbein, M., & Cappella, J.), John Wiley & Sons; Figure 7.1 from draft of the published report: http://www.swpho.nhs. uk/resource/view.aspx?RID=88928, see Figure 3.2 on page 36, South West Health Observatory, Bristol; Figures 7.2a and 7.2b from *Exploring Marketing Research* 7th edn, The Dryden Press, Orlando FL (Zikmund, W.G.) The Dryden Press, Orlando FL © 2000 South-Western, a part of Cengage Learning, Inc. Reproduced by permission. www.cengage. com/permissions; Figures 7.4, 7.5, 7.6 & 7.7 from NVivo illustration of software package, www.qsrinternational.com/products_nvivo.aspx, QSR International Ltd, Courtesy of QSR International Pty Ltd; Figures 9.3, 9.4 & 9.5 after *The Tipping Point* (Gladwell, M., 2000) Little, Brown & Company, Boston (Hachette Book Group); Figure 10.1 from 'Appreciating brands as assets through using two-dimensional model' (de Chernatony, L. & McWilliam, G., 1990) *Journal of Marketing Management*, 9, pp. 173–88, Taylor & Francis journals; Figure 10.6 from Play Zone logo, www.tht.org.uk/, Copyright © Terrence Higgins Trust; Figure 10.7 from Cabwise logo, http://tfl.gov.uk, Transport for London; Figures 10.9 & 10.10 from 'Transport for London – Cabwise: creating a brand to help prevents rapes' (2008 IPA Effectiveness Awards case history at www.warc.com), www.warc.com, Warc Advertising Agency; Figure 11.2 from 'Fear Control and Danger Control: A Test of the Extended Parallel Process Model (EPPM)', *Communication Mongraphs*, 61 (1), pp. 113–34 (Witte, K., 1994), Taylor & Francis; Figure 11.4 from Texting Skills: Road Safety Authority (Republic of Ireland) and the Department of the Environment (Northern Ireland) – Road safety campaign: 'Pay attention, or pay the price', www.rsa.ie/, Crown copyright

Screenshots

Figure 2.3: Facebook; Figure 2.4: Twitter; screenshot on p. 81 from http://webarchive. nationalarchives.gov.uk/+/www.dh.gov.uk/en/Publichealth/Publichealthresponsibility deal, Crown copyright

Tables

Table 1.2 from *Social Marketing. Improving the Quality of Life,* Sage Publications Inc (Kotler, P., Roberto, N. & Lee, N., 2002) Sage Publications Thousand Oaks, CA; Table 2.1 adapted from 'The Marketing Mix Revisited: Towards the 21st Century Marketing,' *Journal of Marketing Management,* 22, pp. 407–38 (Constantinides, E. 2006), Routledge/Taylor & Francis; Table 5.1 from 'Unintended Effects of Health Communication Campaigns', *Journal of Communication,* 57 (2) (Cho, H., & Salmon, C. T), Wiley journals; Table 14.1 from 'Assessing the Effectiveness of Social Marketing', paper presented at the ESOMAR conference, Berlin. (Varcoe, J., 2004), ESOMAR; Table 14.3 from' ESRC analysis of public understanding of the safety of the MMR vaccine', *Towards a Better Map: Science, the Public and the Media* (Hargreaves, I., Lewis, J., & Speers, T.).

Text

Box 8.4 from Department of Health Segmentation description, http://www.dh.gov. uk/prod_consum_dh/groups/dh_digitalassets/documents/digitalasset/dh_086291.pdf, Department of Health. Crown copyright.

Photographs

Front cover images: Getty Images; photographs on pp. 11, 27, 238: Advertising Archives; Figure 9.6: Collaborative Change/Steven Johnson; Figure 10.2: Alamy/SS Studios; Figure 10.3: NHS; Figure 10.4: 56 Dean Street; Figure 10.5: Rescuescg.com; Figure 11.3: NHS Branding; Figure 12.1: Alamy/Gabbro; Figure 13.1: Alamy/MBI.

All other images © Pearson Education

In some instances we have been unable to trace the owners of copyright material, and we would appreciate any information that would enable us to do so.

PART 1

The principles of social marketing

Chapter 1

What is social marketing?

Chapter objectives

On completing this chapter, you should be able to:

- critically discuss the evolution of social marketing and the differences between it and related activity such as health education;
- critically discuss the scope of social marketing and debate the relative complexities of potential interventions across the range of areas in which social marketing currently operates or could potentially operate in the future;
- critically evaluate the potential for unintended impacts of social marketing interventions in each of these areas;
- critically evaluate the role of government and other stakeholders in interventions in each of these areas;
- critically debate individual personal responsibility when individual actions may result in adverse consequences for others (actual harm to others or costs of medical treatment etc. being borne by others).

Evolution and application of social marketing

Human behaviour is complex, at times apparently irrational and, as a result, often unpredictable. Our behaviours have consequences, both positive and negative, that impact the individual, the community and the environment. With so much resting on our behaviours, encouraging us to modify or change what we do for the common or individual good has become an important strategic objective for governments, NGOs and civil society. Social marketing techniques have been deployed to help achieve these objectives: be it for health improvement, disease prevention, accident or crime reduction or environmental responsibility, social marketing is being used to facilitate voluntary behaviour change. This tool has been used with varying degrees of success, and sometimes delivers unintended consequences, but the body of evidence that points to the efficacy of theory-based, well-researched social marketing interventions is growing.

The precise origins of social marketing are hard to pinpoint. For over 40 years, this marketing discipline has been the subject of vigorous academic debate, but there is consensus that its foundation was laid in the early 1950s when Wiebe posed the question 'Why can't you sell brotherhood and rational thinking like you sell soap?'[1] Today, like many other marketing-related concepts, there is no single definition of social marketing; instead the concept has evolved over time from narrow and somewhat simplistic foundations[2] including 'planned social change'[3] and the 'marketing of social causes'[4] to a range of definitions, each emphasising different aspects of social marketing.

The following definition is drawn from the National Social Marketing Centre:

Social marketing is 'the systematic application of marketing concepts and techniques to achieve specific behavioural goals, for a social or public good' and Health-related social marketing is 'the systematic application of marketing concepts and techniques to achieve specific behavioural goals, to improve health and reduce health inequalities'.[5]

A more complete and more managerially useful definition is provided by Andreasen,[6] drawing on a definition originally developed in the late 1980s:[7]

A social change management technology involving the design, implementation and control of programs aimed at increasing the acceptability of a social idea or practice in one or more groups of target adopters. It utilizes concepts of market segmentation, consumer research, product concept development and testing, directed communication, facilitation, incentives, and exchange theory to maximize the target adopter's response.

Andreasen[8] notes that some writers take issue with the phrase 'acceptability of a **social idea**' in the above definition, arguing that the objective of social marketing must be behaviour change. We would add to Andreasen's[9] suggestion that social marketing should be seen not as a specific **theory**, but rather as a **process** that 'is modelled on processes used in private sector marketing' and draws on an interdisciplinary range of concepts and theories, such as psychology, sociology, anthropology and communication as well as marketing itself.

Until the early 1990s, social marketing appears to have been perceived as somewhat apart from 'mainstream marketing'[10, 11] and some academics questioned whether it was legitimate to broaden the focus of **mainstream marketing** to encompass social change.[12] In fact, some of these early writers suggested that broadening the concept of marketing to include **non-commercial activity** would be detrimental to the marketing discipline as a whole.[13] An unforeseen adverse consequence of the drive to precisely define the scope of marketing and thus to be able to articulate a single theory of marketing was an over-emphasis on 'the body of facts which comprise this field'[14] and law-like generalisations that could be empirically tested.[15, 16, 17]

In a seminal paper,[18] it is argued that:

more than most other fields of scientific inquiry, marketing is context dependent; when one or more of the numerous contextual elements surrounding it (such as the economy, social norms, demographic characteristics, public policy, globalization or new communication technologies such as the Internet) change, it can have a significant impact on the nature and scope of the discipline.

Marketing is not, and never will be, an exact science in the way that **natural sciences** are, hence a search for a set of principles that are universally applicable – or at least applicable across a wide range of situations – is futile and counter-productive.[19] Human behaviour is extremely complex and difficult to predict; at times it appears irrational – as when patients do not comply with medical advice, or take medication as prescribed, in spite of severe potential health consequences from failing to do so.[20] A range of **psychosocial variables**, including **attitudes, beliefs** and norms, underpin behaviour. These not only differ across cultures, but change over time.[21] Additionally, the relative importance of the variables varies according to the behaviour targeted as well as the target population.[22]

In addition to the complexity of the above factors, which must be identified before social marketing **interventions** can be developed, there are those who suggest that social marketing may still be perceived as unethical compared to education and law as a tool for changing or maintaining behaviour.[23] In spite of these criticisms, social marketing principles have been applied to a wide range of areas in the past, and current government endorsement is leading to heightened interest in the use of its techniques across a widening range of public health issues.

There is considerable scepticism regarding the application of **commercial marketing** techniques to solving social marketing problems, particularly when risky behaviours such as poor diet, smoking and irresponsible alcohol consumption are all linked, rightly or wrongly, to commercial marketing activity that is claimed to encourage those behaviours[24] and therefore contribute to health problems. Further, critics regard commercial marketing techniques as 'slick and manipulative with a ready inclination to provide simplistic **advertising** solutions to complex **social problems**'.[25]

This is a somewhat defeatist argument as these critics acknowledge that marketing can achieve behaviour change that they do not approve of, yet seem to suggest that this rules out the use of similar techniques to achieve behaviour change that is desirable.

It should also be stressed that social marketing is not simply **selling** – or advertising. Social marketing is a holistic approach to behaviour change that, depending on the target audience and the cause, may use neither. In fact, there is considerable debate as to how far communication/advertising-based social marketing interventions can be successful in achieving change.[26] However, a lack of financial resources may mean a compromise between what is ideal in terms of ways of communicating with a target group and what is achievable within a finite budget.

The publication of a behavioural economics-based text *Nudge*[27] in 2008 led to heightened interest in 'nudging' people towards behaviour change through strategies such as 'choice architecture', i.e. making subtle changes in the environment in which (often habitual, sometimes irrational) behaviour choices are made. A second publication advocated 'steering' people's behaviour towards positive and beneficial behaviour choices in situations where deliberate, conscious choices are being made through increasing knowledge of how judgements are made and habits formed.[28]

The influence of these, and other behavioural science-based publications can be seen in recent government publications such as *MINDSPACE*.[29] These approaches are compatible with social marketing's overall focus and are seen by some as useful additional tools or perspectives for social marketers.[30]

Social marketing has been applied to a wide range of issues and behaviours; some are relatively uncontroversial and others, such as genetic screening, are more controversial and raise significant ethical issues. While the focus is on encouraging sustained, positive behaviour change among individuals and groups, social marketing also encompasses environmental and policy factors 'upstream' of actual behaviour change that may be barriers to, or enablers of, that change.[31] Upstream factors are discussed in more detail in Chapter 4.

VIGNETTE 1.1

Effective social marketing? Push Play

In 1998 in New Zealand, a national Physical Activity Taskforce was set up to combat the rising obesity and physical inactivity in the country and promote the 'thirty minutes, five times a week' message. One of their recommendations was a national media campaign to raise awareness of these new guidelines, called Push Play.

Push Play's television commercials, billboards, radio ads, magazine promotions, and a national Push Play Day tried to encourage people to link physical activity with daily chores and events (such as mowing the lawn or playing with the children) and present it as fun and with a 'kiwi' orientation. The campaign slogan was 'Push Play 30 minutes a day' and the campaign targeted all adults, particularly the middle-aged, and males (30–54 years) across New Zealand. The overall campaign design, development and implementation had an approximate total budget of $3 million between 1999 and 2002.

Annual cross-sectional population surveys (1999–2002) reported that there were substantial increases in awareness of the Push Play message and significant increases in intention to be more active, but no sustained changes in physical activity levels.[32]

Question to consider

The main objective of Push Play was to increase awareness of the benefits of physical activity and to encourage people to think about becoming more physically active, so the campaign could be said to have been a success. However, was Push Play social marketing if there was no measurable behavioural goal and no measurable behaviour change? What mistakes were made?

Table 1.1 provides an indicative list of papers which have reported on the impact of social marketing interventions across a number of health and behavioural areas. What these issues have in common is that they focus on actions by individuals that potentially affect, positively or negatively, both their own well-being and that of others.

It is difficult to compare success (or otherwise) of the factors used in the interventions, due to variations in methodology and reporting procedures. Some critics may challenge whether all of the campaigns are in fact social marketing, rather than **health education**. The latter generally involves the use of a single programme, led by **expert knowledge** and **provider-driven** rather than receiver-driven programmes specifically **customised** to meet user needs.

Evaluating the relative impact of components of social marketing campaigns can be difficult, and understanding how they impact, both individually or in combination, on factors underpinning behaviour can also be challenging.

What social marketing is not

Social marketing focuses on voluntary behaviour change – it is not 'selling', nor is it **coercion;**[33] however, there is a level of confusion between social marketing and activities such as health education and **health promotion**. We therefore briefly describe these other, related activities to illustrate the differences between them.

Table 1.1 Indicative list of social marketing interventions and studies examining impact

Issues/behaviour targeted	Representative sample of authors of studies in this area
Safe sex/condom use/contraception	Dejong, Wolf and Austin, 2001; Fishbein, von Haeften and Appleyard, 2001; Strecher, De Vellis, Becker and Rosenstock, 1986; von Haeften, Fishbein, Kasprzyk and Montano, 2001; Knerr, 2009
Smoking cessation	Bock, Marcus, Rossi and Redding, 1998; Devlin, Eadie, Stead and Evans, 2007; Fishbein and Cappella, 2006; Pechmann, Zhao, Goldberg and Reibling, 2003; Vidrine, Simmons and Brandon, 2007
Responsible drinking	Bock et al., 1998; Goldberg, Niedermeier, Bechtel and Gorn, 2006; Jones and Rossiter, 2002; Powell, Tapp and Sparks, 2007
Seat belt use	B. Smith, 2006; W.A. Smith, 2006
Responsible driving/anti-speeding	Henley and Donovan, 2006; Senserrick, 2006
Sun protection/skin cancer awareness	Eadie and MacAskill, 2007; Peattie, Peattie and Clarke, 2001; Smith, Ferguson, McKenzie, Bauman and Vita, 2002; Walsch, Rudd, Moeykens and Moloney, 1993
Domestic violence	Keller and Otjen, 2007
Immunisation	Fox and Kotler, 1980; Kotler and Zaltman, 1971; McDermott, 2000; Opel, 2009
Medical screening (cancer, cholesterol, etc.)	Lowry, Archer, Howe, Russell, 2009; Briss et al., 2004; Cox and Cox, 2001; Moreno et al., 1997; Pavlik et al., 1993; Sligo and Jameson, 2000
Genetic testing to reduce the occurrence of inherited diseases	Brenkert, 2002
Nutrition	Brug, Campbell and van Assema, 1999; John, Kerby and Landers, 2004; Reinaerts, de Nooijer, van de Kar and de Vries, 2006
Drug education	Fishbein, Hall-Jamieson, Zimmer, Haeften and Nabi, 2002; Jones and Rossiter, 2002; Yzer, Hennessy and Fishbein, 2004
Exercise/physical activity	Marcus et al., 2000; Renger, Steinfelt and Lazarus, 2002; Rudd, Goldberg and Dietz, 1999
Malaria control	Hanson et al., 2003; Rowland et al., 2002
Mental health	Gotham, 2004
Environmental issues, e.g. recycling, energy conservation, pollution	Altman and Petkus Jr., 1994; Brenkert, 2002; Glenane-Antoniadis, Whitwell, Bell and Menguc, 2003; Peattie and Peattie, 2009
Workplace health	Glenane-Antoniadis et al., 2003
Volunteering	Kotler, Roberto and Lee, 2002; Boehm, 2009
Disaster management and preparedness, e.g. hurricanes, earthquakes, volcanic eruptions	Guion, Scammon and Borders, 2007; Johnson et al. 1999

Health education:

'is an activity that seeks to inform the individual on the nature and causes of health/illness and that individual's personal level of risk associated with their lifestyle-related behaviour. Health education seeks to motivate the individual to accept a process of behavioural change through directly influencing their value, belief and attitude systems, where it is deemed that the individual is particularly at risk or has already been affected by illness/disease or disability'.[34]

Health promotion:

'is the process by which the ecologically-driven socio-political-economic determinants of health are addressed as they impact on individuals and the communities within which they interact. This serves to counter social inaction and social division/inequality. It is an inherently political process that draws on health policy as a basis for social action that leads to community coalitions through shared radical consciousness. Health promotion seeks to radically transform and empower communities through involving them in activities that influence their public health – particularly via agenda setting, political lobbying and advocacy, critical consciousness-raising and social education programmes. Health promotion tools look to develop and reform social structures through developing participation between representative stakeholders in different sectors and agencies'.[35]

To show how little clarity there is on terminology, scope or relative areas of expertise, we have included some simpler definitions from Wikipedia in Box 1.1.

Box 1.1 Overly simplistic Wikipedia definitions

Health promotion WHO Ottawa Charter defines Health Promotion as: 'the process of enabling people to increase control over, and to improve their health'.[36] In the USA, health promotion is frequently more narrowly defined as the art of helping people to change their lifestyle in order to move towards a state of optimal health.

Health education is defined as 'the principle by which individuals and groups of people learn to behave in a manner conducive to the promotion, maintenance or restoration of health'.

Cause-related marketing 'refers to a type of marketing involving the cooperative efforts of a "for profit" business and a non-profit organization for mutual benefit. The term is sometimes used more broadly and generally to refer to any type of marketing effort for social and other charitable causes, including in-house marketing efforts by a non-profit organization. Cause marketing differs from corporate giving (philanthropy) as the latter generally involves a specific donation that is tax deductible, while cause marketing is a marketing relationship generally not based on a donation.'

An activity that is at times linked with social marketing but which is totally separate from it is:

Corporate social responsibility (CSR) which 'is a concept that organizations, especially (but not only) corporations, have an obligation to consider the interests of customers, employees, shareholders, communities, and ecological considerations in all aspects of their operation. This obligation is seen to extend beyond their statutory obligation to comply with legislation. CSR is closely linked with the principles of sustainable development, which argues that enterprises should make decisions based not only on financial factors such as profits or dividends, but also based on the immediate and long-term social and environmental consequences of their activities.'

Another term that causes some confusion due to the similarity of names is that of **societal marketing**: the idea that the organisation should determine the needs, wants and interests of target markets and deliver the desired satisfaction more effectively and efficiently than do competitors, in a way that maintains or improves the consumer's and society's well-being.[37]

Box 1.2 Jupiter Media's 'social marketing' service

In 2006, Jupiter Media announced its 'Social Marketing' service, examining social media on behalf of corporate clients. The social marketing community protested over the hijacking of the term – however, Jupiter stuck with the name, despite the approach being more correctly (and commonly) referred to as social media optimisation: http://www.jupitermedia.com/

Note 1: Social media: describes the online technologies and practices that people use to share opinions, insights, experiences and perspectives. Social media can take many different forms, including texts, images, audio and videos. Sites typically use technologies such as blogs, message boards, podcasts, wikis and vlogs to allow users to interact.

Note 2: Social media optimisation (SMO) is a way to optimise websites so they would be more easily connected or interlaced with online communities and community websites, also called 'social media sites'.

To add to the confusion, the term 'social marketing' itself has been hijacked by at least one commercial organisation for activity that most others would classify as social media use (see Box 1.2).

Another misconception is that social marketing equates to **social advertising**, i.e. successful interventions centre around mass media advertising in order to communicate the desired messages. Although interventions may indeed use advertising or other forms of marketing communication where it is appropriate for specific target groups, there are many examples of interventions that do not rely on marketing communication, instead using other ways of reaching the target groups. Intervention design is covered in more detail later in this book.

Current social marketing focus

In 2004 the UK government White Paper *Choosing Health*[38] specifically advocated the adoption of the principles underpinning social marketing in order to promote public health issues more effectively, acknowledging that existing communication strategies were not effective. Subsequently, the Department of Health commissioned an independent study of the scope, and the potential, of social marketing as a tool by which to help improve health and overall quality of life among the wider population. This study notes that the majority of the population distrust or ignore government advice and highlights the fiscal impact of preventable ill health: 'the total annual cost to the country of preventable illness amounts to a minimum of £187 billion. In comparative terms this equates to 19% of total GDP (gross domestic product) for England'.[39]

While it is difficult to compare data across nations due to differences in data collected, the problems of preventable illness are international. In the USA, approximately 1 million deaths per annum are attributable to **lifestyle** and **environmental factors**.[40] Some indications of the magnitude of various health and lifestyle issues in the USA are shown in Table 1.2. We have no reason to believe that, in the absence of more specific data, the figures cannot be used as a crude indicator of the potential magnitude of similar issues in other developed countries.

An example of a specific health-related area which warrants investigation is **medication compliance** (also called adherence). Compliance rates across all medical conditions

Table 1.2 Magnitude (in the USA) of issues social marketing may contribute towards allieviating

Issue	Magnitude
Alcohol use during pregnancy	Estimated 5000 infants born with foetal alcohol syndrome each year
Sexually transmitted diseases	40% of sexually active high school students report not using a condom
Diabetes	About 1/3 of the nearly 16 million people with diabetes are not aware they have the disease
Skin cancer	Approximately 70% of American adults do not protect themselves from the sun's dangerous rays
Breast cancer	More than 20% of females aged 50 and over have not had mammograms in the last two years
Prostate cancer	Only about half of all prostate cancers are found early
Colon cancer	Only about 1/3 of all colon cancers are found early
Seat belts	An estimated 30% of drivers and adult passengers do not always wear their seat belts
Fires	Almost 50% of fires and 60% of fire deaths occur in the estimated 8% of homes with no smoke alarms

Source: Kotler, P., Roberto, N. and Lee, N. (2002) *Social Marketing: Improving the Quality of Life.* Thousand Oaks, CA: Sage Publications.

internationally are generally no better than 50 per cent, and are lower for behaviourally demanding treatment regimes and within some population groups such as adolescents and the elderly.[41] The costs of medicine non-compliance may be more than the cost of the original medicines.[42] The only estimated detailed costings for medication non-compliance originate in the USA and Canada.[43, 44] Extrapolating their data to other markets purely on the basis of relative population size, we estimate the cost in the United Kingdom (population 60.4 million) to be £7.8 billion – and the cost to the total European Union (population 457 million) to be £59 billion. An investigation into ways of improving medication compliance therefore has the potential for significant cost savings and improvements in quality of life.

The leading causes of death in the civilised world could be substantially reduced if medication compliance rates were improved, diets became healthier, cigarette smoking rates were reduced, exercise rates improved and alcohol and drug misuse were reduced.

This suggests that there is considerable scope for improving population health if effective and cost-efficient means of conveying information are used; indeed, the academic literature contains numerous examples of successful social marketing programmes.[45, 46, 47] As a result of government and policy-maker interest in the contribution social marketing might make to issues such as improvement of health-related behaviours, social marketers have moved 'from snake oil salesmen to trusted policy advisors'.[48]

There is, however, a danger that enthusiasts for the concept of social marketing will over-promise what can be achieved; some interventions have not delivered what was optimistically expected of them, leading some observers to question what can realistically be achieved through social marketing techniques.[49, 50] However, even small changes over time can lead to significant shifts in societal norms such as attitudes towards smoking.[51]

Unintended consequences

There is a danger of well-intended campaigns having unintended consequences which may harm the long-term effectiveness of the campaign. An example of this is the UK Department of Health (DoH) 'fishhook' smoking cessation campaign. In May 2007, in response to 774 complaints to the Advertising Standards Authority (ASA), this campaign was deemed to be in breach of advertising regulations and was ordered to be discontinued. The majority of complaints related to children's fear and distress upon seeing the advertisements. The ASA adjudication is summarised in Case Study 1.1.

CASE STUDY 1.1

Department of Health 'fishhook' campaign

'A TV ad showed a woman folding clothes while a child watched TV. She said "Ten more minutes then homework, yeah?" She looked out of the window. A hook appeared in her mouth and she was dragged along the floor and into another room by a wire attached to the hook. As the woman was shown smoking, a voice-over stated "The average smoker needs over 5000 cigarettes a year". The ad cut to a man walking down the street. He was dragged along the ground, over a car bonnet and into a corner shop by a line attached to a hook pulling on the inside of his cheek. The man was shown leaving the shop and putting a cigarette in his mouth while a voice-over and on-screen text stated "Get unhooked. Call 0800 169 0 169 or visit www.getunhooked.co.uk".'

Less graphic follow-up TV ads were used, along with posters, national press ads and magazine ads in TV magazines. These featured 'people with pained expressions; a taut wire was pulling on hooks embedded above their lips . . .' Internet ads featuring similar imagery allowed viewers to click on the line to distort the face and start a clip with a similar message to the original TV ads.

A sample of the graphics used is shown below:

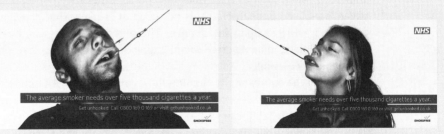

Source: Advertising Archives.

The DoH in their response argued that 'any fear created by the ads would pale into insignificance when compared to the physical and emotional harm caused to smokers (and their families and friends) who became ill or died as a result of smoking . . .'

Case study 1.1 (*continued*)

They said, 'instead of telling smokers about smoking-related illnesses and death, which were commonly perceived by smokers as problems for the future, the ads focused on the controlling nature of addiction to nicotine experienced by smokers every day.'

DoH added that, 'since the launch of the campaign, 83,606 smokers had phoned the NHS Smoking Helpline; 545,564 had visited the gosmokefree website; 195,000 had had interactions with the TV pages and 6743 had made contact via SMS.'

In their judgement, the ASA acknowledged that 'smoking was the UK's single greatest cause of preventable illness and early death, and that promoting NHS services that helped smokers quit was an important public service'. However, the posters, while not placed near schools 'had appeared in places where they could easily be seen by children'. Further, they ruled that, although the initial TV ads had not been placed in children's TV programmes, they were shown at times when children could see them. Both the posters and initial ads were ordered to be discontinued. The less graphic follow-up ads were deemed permissible; the internet, press and magazine ads were considered unlikely to be seen by children and allowed to continue.

Questions

1 Critique the Department of Health 'fishhook' communication campaign. Do you agree with the ASA ruling? Justify your answer.

2 How might the campaign have been pre-tested to identify potential problems such as those that led to the numerous complaints to the ASA about elements of the communication?

3 Find other examples of fear-based social marketing interventions and critique them against the ASA codes of advertising. What lessons can be learned from this?

4 Draw up a checklist for organisations planning social marketing interventions to:

(a) identify any potential adverse effects from the intervention and

(b) decide on the most appropriate way of resolving any problems identified.

Source: Advertising Standards Authority (2007) Adjudication, Department of Health. Retrieved 29 May 2007, from http://www.asa.prg.uk/asa/adjudications/Public/TF_ADJ_42557.htm

We can find no reference to any research that related to **pre-testing** the campaign material or to consideration of the ethics and possible negative consequences of using such a strong **fear-based appeal**. Had this occurred, it is likely that problems would have been identified and acted upon in advance. The outcome of the adjudication may mean that funding will need to be diverted to amending and reproducing material rather than ensuring campaign continuity.

This is not the only example of unintended consequences. An American initiative aimed at increasing the fruit and vegetable intake of low-income and ethnically diverse schoolchildren through changes to school snack food menus achieved an increase in intake of fruit – though not of vegetables – but also resulted in reduced calcium and vitamin A consumption due to lower consumption of dairy products.[52] Again, there is no evidence of potential consequences of dietary change having been considered prior to the menu change being implemented.

Another intervention to have received criticism is the international campaign to highlight the dangers of over-exposure to sun. The interventions have been accused in at least two countries (Australia and the UK) of resulting in too little exposure to sun, leading to vitamin D deficiency, which can cause rickets in children and which has also been linked to cancer, diabetes and multiple sclerosis.[53]

Alongside the success stories and reports of unintended consequences are also reviews of programmes that have not resulted in any significant change in behaviours.[54, 55] Even much-vaunted US interventions in the late 1980s and early 1990s, such as the Stanford Heart Disease project, the Minnesota Heart Health Programme and Community Intervention Trial for Smoking Cessation, all achieved much more modest changes in behaviour than was predicted.[56] While other interventions appear to have been more successful, it is claimed that there is both limited academic and **practitioner** expertise to develop effective interventions based on sound theoretical foundations, and limited examples of successes written up in a way that would enable others to use them as guides in developing future interventions among both practitioners and academics.[57]

Poorly designed or misdirected interventions may result in social marketing being dismissed as yet another management fad before its potential contribution to health and quality of life has been fully recognised. There is also a danger of uncritically adopting interventions that have been successful in one situation only to find that they are not as effective in different situations.[58] There is an additional danger of well-intended interventions having the opposite effect to what was intended.[59] Issues of scepticism and persuasion resistance are addressed in Chapter 11.

Justification of government-sponsored social marketing interventions

Some of the costs of preventable health conditions were noted earlier. In areas such as increased health risk related to obesity, such as type-2 diabetes, hypertension, heart disease, stroke and some cancers, personal choices regarding diet, exercise and other lifestyle factors affect the individual, but medical care costs and indirect costs such as lost productivity are borne by the wider society, raising questions of whether legislation might be justifiable and, if so, how effective it might be in changing behaviours.[60]

Legislation has been used in a number of areas, such as speeding restrictions, the requirement to wear seat belts and sanctions for driving with excess blood alcohol levels.[61] Other mandatory interventions have existed for some considerable time without major current commentary, such as fluoridation of water supplies and the addition of vitamins and minerals to a range of foodstuffs. Examples of these mandatory interventions include, from the early part of the 20th century, the addition of iodine to salt to prevent goitre, the addition of vitamins to fat-based spreads and the addition of niacin (vitamin B3) to a range of foodstuffs to prevent pellagra (a serious illness caused by the lack of niacin and protein). More recently, in the USA folic acid has been added to grain products such as bread, cereals and rice to reduce the risk of some birth defects such as spina bifida.[62] The UK Food Standards Agency recommended in May 2007 that folic acid be added to flour, in spite of industry concerns regarding the practicalities involved and concerns that deficiencies in vitamin B12 might be masked by the folic acid.[63]

Issues arise in relation to potential over-consumption of these additives and in the harmonisation of activity across national borders such as within the European Union where a range of **mandatory inclusions**, voluntary inclusions and inclusion prohibitions exists across member countries.[64] Another point of debate centres on who has the right to decide that entire populations should be subject to these treatments. For example, men (who will never get pregnant) do not require the same levels of folic acid as women who are in the very early stages of pregnancy. These issues are discussed in more detail in Chapter 5.

A further example of mandatory interventions is the recent restriction on smoking in public places which has been introduced across many countries. While there are limits to the amount of legislation aimed at forcing behaviour change deemed acceptable, as noted in the 2004 White Paper *Choosing Health*, the provision of information aimed at aiding consumers to make healthy lifestyle choices has not been effective. As one observer notes: 'If information was all that was needed to change behaviour, cigarette smoking would have declined drastically in the mid-1960s and be nonexistent today, and food consumption and exercise regimens would follow widely publicized government guidelines.'[65]

There is evidence of concern over the role of government in health promotion, with opponents suggesting that 'health promotion is something the **nanny state** (or the Welfare State) forces on us because it is good for us, such as a dose of nasty-tasting medicine that will make us grow big and strong and live longer'.[66] However, although some commentators observe that assertions of '**nannyism**' may be met with 'postures of reticence' on behalf of government, 'in reality, complaints about nannyism have negligible influence. There is virtually no resistance to the advance of government intrusion in lifestyle if it is deemed to be justified in terms of public health.'[67]

As already noted, many health-related interventions have comprised simply information provision in the expectation that this would result in changes to behaviour. There is often frustration evident when well-intentioned health-related programmes do not perform as expected or patients do not follow medical advice.[68] There are myriad reasons, including **complacency**, **indifference** or merely a failure to understand the **relevance** and importance of the messages being sent.

Examples of complacency include a lack of recognition among women aged 16–30 years of the personal risk of HIV infection through unprotected sex, in spite of considerable publicity on the topic.[69] Considerable resources have also been placed behind the promotion of children's knowledge of balanced diets, yet it appears that 'the messages have sometimes become confused'.[70] Furthermore, most children do not read information on food packaging[71] and, dependent on their (age-related) stage of cognitive development, may struggle to make reasoned decisions[72] based on, for example, percentage of recommended daily allowance data for specific ingredients.

Critics question whether the change in emphasis from information provision to persuasion will be effective when, as noted earlier, there is widespread distrust of government advice. A more extreme view suggests that government is perceived, by some sectors of society at least, as 'inherently bad' and many citizens 'want as little to do with it as possible', leading to the somewhat blunt question 'Does government-sponsored health promotion have any chance of success where the government is the enemy?'[73] Indeed, the philosophy behind the government White Paper *Choosing Health* has been criticised as being paternalistic and nannyism.[74]

In addition, the lack of co-ordination and integrated policy, let alone practical application, has been criticised, with the observation that 'atomised initiatives are unlikely to deliver requisite change'.[75] Further, there is evidence that persuasive messages alone have not been successful in changing some behaviours due to the influence of external or environmental factors.[76]

Thus the domain of social marketing can be seen as complex and controversial. However, it can also be tremendously rewarding to observe, let alone participate in, the development and implementation of interventions that do make a genuine positive difference to individuals and society as a whole. In the following chapters, we will expand on many of the issues introduced here and introduce concepts, theories and strategies that will aid the development, testing and implementation of social marketing interventions.

CASE STUDY 1.2

Food Dudes

Background

It is well known that eating a diet rich in fresh fruit and vegetables is vital for health and well-being and yet the UK and Ireland have one of the lowest fruit and vegetable intakes in Europe. Many children, particularly, do not eat enough fruit and vegetables, due to a lack of support for healthy eating at home or in schools, and lack of positive role models. Sometimes fruit and vegetables are not easily available compared to less nutritious, heavily marketed alternatives to which the children become brand loyal. Creating a positive environment for fruit and vegetable consumption and a strong, recognisable brand is an important premise of the Food Dudes programme.

Overview

The Food Dude Healthy Eating Programme is designed for use in primary schools to increase 4–11-year-old children's consumption of fruit and vegetables by targeting the children and their parents, carers and teachers.

The children are shown short daily videos featuring hero figures, the 'Food Dudes', who like fruit and vegetables and are social models for the children to imitate. They are also given small rewards to support their tasting of new foods so they will come to think of themselves as 'fruit and vegetable eaters'. Food Dude letters and Food Dude home packs provide support for teachers and parents to ensure maintenance of the desired behaviour change.

Based on the pilot's success, in 2007 the Irish government made the Food Dudes programme available to every primary school in Ireland, introducing it to the country's 3,300 primary schools over seven years with a budget of 28 million Euros. From 2009, the programme will be rolled out in selected parts of England. Plans are also being developed to introduce Food Dudes in Italy, the USA and Canada. View the Irish Food Dudes website at: www.fooddudes.co.uk).

Started with insight

Like all social marketing, Food Dudes began with a deep understanding of the target audience. The Bangor Food and Activity Research Unit used behavioural psychology to understand how children learn, emulate role models, respond to incentives, and acquire early taste patterns.

Findings showed that children are motivated by rewards, recognition and praise from positive role models. Telling children what to eat is unsuccessful. Children learn most effectively via social networks and modelling.

Behavioural psychology accepts that language locks in specific behaviours. If a parent says repeatedly 'Jenny hates tomatoes', Jenny will categorise herself as a tomato-hater. Food Dudes encourages children to try new foods, and to be proud of their new identity

Case study 1.2 (*continued*)

as fruit and vegetable 'likers'. Children can overcome their preference for sugary snacks by developing a taste for fruit and vegetables.

Research also recognised that peer pressure is a strong influence in schools, so Food Dudes uses peer pressure in its favour, making it 'cool' to eat fruit and veg.

The intervention

Based on this insight, a pilot intervention was designed and trialled on 450 children, aged 2–7. The programme template included two key elements: video adventures featuring the Food Dude hero figures, and small rewards (pencils, toys, stickers etc.) to encourage children to taste the new foods. The rewards are phased out and replaced by the sustainable incentive of enjoyment and preference for the foods. A home pack also encourages changes at home, including changes to parents' own diets.

Two theories helped support the intervention. Reinforcement theory suggests that rewards and positive role-models can reinforce positive behaviour. The Food Dudes programme reinforces positive behaviour by encouraging children to repeatedly taste different fruits and vegetables.

Secondly, taste acquisition theory suggests that repeated tasting of these foods allows children to discover that they actually like the taste, which means the children then become more likely to eat these foods simply for their flavour, rather than for any external reward.

In pilot trials in primary schools, fruit consumption of 5–6 year olds more than doubled from 28% to 59% over six months, whilst vegetable consumption increased from 8% to 32%. Following this, a package was developed for all primary schools and ages. In all schools, children were presented with fruit and vegetables at lunchtime and snack-time. The videos and rewards were then introduced.

Evaluation and results

Food Dudes has been tested with thousands of children and has been shown to be highly successful in getting children to eat fruit and vegetables. Observation was undertaken of each child's fruit and vegetable consumption during and after the programme. Interviews and questionnaires were also used with teachers, parents and children.

Key evaluation findings include:

- Large increases in fruit and vegetable consumption.
- The greatest increases in consumption are shown by those children who ate the least at the start.
- Increases in consumption are long-lasting.
- Increases extend across a wide range of fruit and vegetable varieties.
- The programme works for all children aged 2–11 years old.
- The effects generalise across contexts i.e. school to home.
- The programme is equally effective for boys and girls.
- Effects are highly reliable, regardless of school location and social deprivation.

(Results to support these are available at www.fooddudes.co.uk.)

Although amongst schoolteachers there has been initial resistance to Food Dudes, since its delivery needs commitment of time and energy, the benefits of the programme have been proved, and evaluation demonstrates that teachers and parents come to support it.

Conclusion

The Food Dude programme has wide-ranging impacts on the diets of both boys and girls, including those who suffer social exclusion. The future of Food Dudes is promising, although it has been suggested that problems have arisen when ensuring sufficient funding for the future of the programme beyond its launch. The materials, project co-ordinators and fruit and vegetable provision are all expensive, at an estimated 26 Euros per child per year, excluding the fruit and vegetables. In the Republic of Ireland the programme currently reaches 85,000 children in 625 schools per year. The additional cost of providing fruit and vegetables is 20 Euros per child.

Questions

1 Critique this intervention. What do you believe were the key factors in its success?

2 What is the likely consequence of funding for the programme not being continued?

3 How would you respond to any criticism of the cost of the programme?

4 How do you believe the momentum of the intervention could be maintained with and without ongoing funding?

5 (a) How would you recommend parents could help maintain the momentum?

   (b) What other organisations could help with this?

Source: 'Food Dudes Programme in Ireland', Paper presented by Michael Maloney at 5th International Symposium of the International Fruit and Vegetable Alliance, October 2006.

Lowe, C.F., Dowey, A. and Horne, P. (1998) Changing what children eat, in Murcott, A. (ed.), *The Nation's Diet: The Social Science of Food Choice*. Addison Wesley Longman, London, pp. 57–80.

Further reading

Lowe, C.F., Horne, P.J., Tapper, K., Bowdery, M. and Egerton, C. (2004) Effects of a peer modelling and rewards-based intervention to increase fruit and vegetable consumption in children. *European Journal of Clinical Nutrition*, 58, 510–22.

Horne, P.J., Tapper, K., Lowe, C.F., Hardman, C.A., Jackson, M.C. and Woolner, J. (2004) Increasing children's fruit and vegetable consumption: A peer-modelling and rewards-based intervention. *European Journal of Clinical Nutrition*, 58, 1649–60.

Horne, P.J., Hardman, C.A., Lowe, C.F., Tapper, K., Noury, J Le, Madden, P., Patel, P. and Doody, M. (2009) Increasing parental provision and children's consumption of lunchbox fruit and vegetables in Ireland: the Food Dudes intervention. *European Journal of Clinical Nutrition*, 63, 613–8.

Summary

Social marketing has been recognised for well over 50 years, although its role within the wider marketing sphere has often been debated. This debate will continue, along with discussion about the relationship of social marketing to other behaviour change tools. Criticism and scepticism will also no doubt continue to be levelled at social marketing aims and strategies, while a growing body of evidence shows the success that well-designed and implemented interventions can have.

Social marketing concepts and techniques have been used across a diverse range of issues and behaviours, from sexual health, smoking cessation, responsible drinking, road safety, disease prevention and screening, physical activity and environmental issues through to disaster preparation and management.

Lack of clarity about social marketing's role relative to other behaviour change strategies will continue to generate debate. This is not helped by overly simplistic definitions provided via popular websites such as Wikipedia and confusion between social marketing and social media. Additional concerns are evident when social marketing interventions have achieved unexpected results, such as creating anxiety among groups who were not the target of an intervention.

While the field faces numerous challenges, the effectiveness of well-researched and developed interventions is not in doubt and benefits to society are increasingly recognised, making social marketing a rewarding field of study and practice.

CHAPTER REVIEW QUESTIONS

1 Critically analyse the use of commercial marketing concepts and theories for interventions aimed at improving societal health and well-being.

2 Critically discuss the potential of social marketing activity to impact on genetic testing rates compared to improving exercise levels across the population.

3 Critically discuss the legitimacy of government involvement in social marketing interventions aimed at impacting on individual and cumulative societal behaviours.

4 Critically debate the factors that may lead to social marketing intervention activity achieving less impact on behaviour change than predicted.

5 Discuss the problems of ongoing funding for social marketing interventions such as Food Dudes. What recommendations should be made to policy makers?

Recommended reading

Department of Health (2004) *Choosing Health: Making Healthy Choices Easier* (White Paper). London: Department of Health.

Department of Health (2008) *Healthy Weight, Healthy Lives: A Cross Government Strategy for England*. London: Department of Health.

Donovan, R. and Henley, N. (2003) *Social Marketing Principles and Practice*. Melbourne, Australia: IP Communications.

French, J., Blair-Stevens, C., McVey, D. and Merritt, R. (eds) (2010) *Social Marketing and Public Health: Theory and Practice*. Oxford: Oxford University Press.

Hastings, G. (2007) *Social Marketing: Why Should the Devil Have all the Best Tunes?* Amsterdam: Elsevier/Butterworth-Heinemann.

Kotler, P. and Lee, N. (2007) *Marketing in the Public Sector*. Upper Saddle River, NJ: Pearson Education.

National Social Marketing Centre (2006) *It's Our Health! Realising the Potential of Effective Social Marketing*. London: National Consumer Council.

Note: in reading the Hastings and Kotler and Lee texts, contrast the USA and UK perspectives. How might factors discussed in these texts be expected to vary across the EU?

Notes

1 Wiebe, G.D. (1951) Merchandising commodities and citizenship on television. *Public Opinion Quarterly,* 15 (4), 679.

2 Kotler, P. and Zaltman, G. (1971) Social Marketing: An Approach to Planned Social Change. *Journal of Marketing,* 35 (3), 3–12.

3 Ibid.

4 Ibid.

5 National Social Marketing Centre. (2006) *It's Our Health! Realising the Potential of Effective Social Marketing.* London: National Social Marketing Centre, p. 1.

6 Andreasen, A.R. (2002) Marketing Social Marketing in the Social Change Marketplace. *Journal of Public Policy and Marketing,* 21 (1), 7.

7 Kotler, P. and Roberto, E. (1989) *Social Marketing.* New York: The Free Press.

8 Andreasen, A.R. (2002) op.cit.

9 Ibid., p. 7.

10 Andreasen, A.R. (1997) Prescriptions for Theory-Driven Social Marketing Research: A Response to Goldberg's Alarms. *Journal of Consumer Psychology,* 6 (2), 189–96.

11 Goldberg, M.E. (1995) Social Marketing: Are We Fiddling While Rome Burns? *Journal of Consumer Psychology,* 4 (4), 347–70.

12 Bloom, P.N. and Novelli, W.D. (1981) Problems and Challenges in Social Marketing. *Journal of Marketing,* 45 (2), 79–88.

13 Luck, D.J. (1969) Broadening the Concept of Marketing – Too Far. *Journal of Marketing,* 33 (3).

14 Alderson, W. and Cox, R. (1948) Towards a Theory of Marketing. *Journal of Marketing,* 13 (2), 137–52.

15 Hunt, S.D. (1973) Lawlike Generalizations and Marketing Theory. *Journal of Marketing,* 37 (3), 69–70.

16 Hunt, S.D. (1983) General Theories and the Fundamental Explananda of Marketing. *Journal of Marketing,* 47 (4), 9–17.

17 Leone, R.P. and Schultz, R.L. (1980) A Study of Marketing Generalizations. *Journal of Marketing,* 44 (1), 10–18.

18 Sheth, J.N. and Sisodia, R.S. (1999) Revisiting Marketing's Lawlike Generalizations. *Journal of the Academy of Marketing Science,* 27 (1), 72.

19 Barwise, P. (1995) Good Empirical Generalizations. *Marketing Science,* 14 (3), 29–35.

20 Fogarty, J.S. (1997) Reactance Theory and Patient Noncompliance. *Social Science & Medicine,* 45 (8), 1277–88.

21 Zinkhan, G.M. and Hirschheim, R. (1992) Truth in Marketing Theory and Research: An Alternative Perspective. *Journal of Marketing,* 56 (2), 80–8.

22 Fishbein, M. and Cappella, J. (2006) The Role of Theory in Developing Effective Health Communications. *Journal of Communication,* 56 (August Supplement), S1–S17.

23 Rothman, A.J. (2000) Toward a Theory-based Analysis of Behavioral Maintenance. *Health Psychology,* 19 (1), 64–9.

24 Petty, R.E. and Cacioppo, J.T. (1996) Addressing Disturbing and Disturbed Consumer Behavior: Is It Necessary to Change the Way We Conduct Behavioral Science? *Journal of Marketing Research* 33 (1), 1–8.

25 Anonymous (2004) Positioning Social Marketing. *Social Marketing Quarterly,* 10 (3), 18.

26 Randolph, W. and Viswanath, K. (2004) Lessons Learned from Public Health Mass Media Campaigns: Marketing Health in a Crowded Media World. *Public Health* 25.

27 Thaler, R.H. and Sunstein, C.R. (2008) *Nudge: Improving Decisions About Health, Wealth, and Happiness* New Haven: Yale University Press.

28 Grist, M. (2010) *STEER. Mastering Our Behaviour Through Instinct, Environment and Reason.* London: Royal Society for the Encouragement of Arts, Manufacturing and Commerce.

29 Dolan, P., Hallsworth, M., Halpern, D., King, D. and Vlaev, I. (2009) *MINDSPACE, Influencing Behaviour Through Public Policy.* London: Institute for Government.

30 Smith, B. (2010) Behavioral Economics and Social Marketing: New Allies in the War on Absent Behavior. *Social Marketing Quarterly,* 16 (2), 137–41.

31 Dorfman, L. and Wallack, L. (2007) Moving Nutrition Upstream: The Case for Reframing Obesity. *Journal of Nutrition Education and Behavior,* 39 (2, Supplement 1), S45–S50.

32 Bauman, A., McLean, G., Hurdle, D., Walker, G., Boyd, J., van Aalst, I. and Carr, H. (2003) Evaluation of the national 'Push Play' campaign in New Zealand – creating population awareness of physical activity. *New Zealand Medical Journal,* 116 (1179), 535–46.

33 Stead, M., Gordon, R., Angus, K. and McDermott, L. (2007) A Systematic Review of Social Marketing Effectiveness. *Health Education,* 107 (2), 126–91.

34 Whitehead, D. (2004) Health Promotion and Health Education: Advancing the Concepts. *Journal of Advanced Nursing,* 47 (3), 313.

35 Ibid. 314.

36 WHO (1986) *Ottawa Charter for Health Promotion.* Geneva: World Health Organization.

37 Kotler, P., and Armstrong, G.M. (1994) *Principles of Marketing* (6th edn). Englewood Cliffs, NJ: Prentice-Hall, p. 14.

38 Department of Health (2004) *Choosing Health: Making Healthy Choices Easier* (White Paper). London: Department of Health.

39 National Social Marketing Centre (2006) *It's our Health! Realising The Potential of Effective Consumer Marketing.* London: National Consumer Council.

40 Rothschild, M.L. (1999) Carrots, Sticks and Promises: A Conceptual Framework for the Management of Public Health and Social Issue Behaviors. *Journal of Marketing,* 63, 24–37.

41 Haynes, R.B., McDonald, H. and Garg, A. (2002) Helping Patients Follow Prescribed Treatment. *Journal of the American Medical Association,* 288 (22), 2880–3.

42 Coambs, R.B. (2003) Not Taking Our Medicine Correctly Hurts. *Better Health,* on-line edition. Retrieved 14 January 2004, from http://www.pfizer.ca/betterhealth

43 Cleemput, I. and Kesteloot, K. (2002) Economic Implications of Non-compliance in Health Care. *The Lancet,* 359, 22 June.

44 Sullivan, S.D., Krehling, D.H. and Hazlet, T.K. (1990) Noncompliance with Medication Regimes and Subsequent Hospitalizations: A Literature Analysis and Cost of Hospitalization Estimate. *Journal of Research in Pharmaco-economics,* 2, 19–33.

45 Fishbein, M. and Yzer, M.C. (2003) Using Theory to Design Effective Health Behavior Interventions. *Communication Theory,* 13 (2), 164–83.

46 McDermott, R.J. (2000) Social Marketing: A Tool for Health Education. *American Journal of Health Behavior,* 24 (1), 6–10.

47 Stead, M., Gordon, R., Angus, K. and McDermott, L. (2007) A Systematic Review of Social Marketing Effectiveness. *Health Education,* 107 (2), 126–91.

48 French, J. and Blair-Stevens, C. (2006) From Snake Oil Salesmen to Trusted Policy Advisors: The Development of a Strategic Approach to the Application of Social Marketing in England. *Social Marketing Quarterly,* 12 (3), 29.

49 Malafarina, K. and Loken, B. (1993) Progress and Limitations of Social Marketing: A Review of Empirical Literature on the Consumption of Social Ideas. *Advances in Consumer Research,* 20 (1), 397–404.

50 Thombs, D.L., Dotterer, S., Olds, R.S., Sharp, K.E. and Raub, C.G. (2004) A Close Look at Why One Social Norms Campaign Did Not Reduce Student Drinking. *Journal of American College Health,* 53 (2), 61–8.

51 Bell, S.G., Newcomer, S.F., Bachrach, C., Borawski, E., Jemmott, J.B., Morrison, D., et al. (2007) Challenges in Replicating Interventions. *Journal of Adolescent Health,* 40, 514–20.

52 Cassady, D., Vogt, R., Oto-Kent, D., Mosley, R. and Lincoln, R. (2006) The Power of Policy: A Case Study of Healthy Eating Among Children. *American Journal of Public Health,* 96 (9), 1570–1.

53 Laurance, J. (2005) Too Little Sun Causes Harm, Cancer Specialists Say. *The Independent,* 22 March, electronic edition, from http://www.independent.co.uk/life-style/health-and-families/health-news/too-little-sun-causes-harm-cancer-specialists-say-529482.html

54 Goldberg, M.E., Niedermeier, K.E., Bechtel, L.J. and Gorn, G.J. (2006) Heightened Adolescent Vigilance Towards Alcohol Advertising to Forestall Alcohol Use. *Journal of Public Policy & Marketing,* 25 (2), 147–59.

55 Jones, L.W., Sinclair, R.C., Rhodes, R.E. and Courneya, K.S. (2004) Promoting Exercise Behaviour: An Integration of Persuasion Theories and the Theory of Planned Behaviour. *British Journal of Health Psychology,* 9 (4), 505–21.

56 Goldberg, M.E. (1995) Op. cit.

57 National Social Marketing Centre (2006) Op. cit.

58 Wang, S., Moss, J.R. and Hiller, J.E. (2005) Applicability and Transferability of Interventions in Evidence-based Public Health. *Health Promotion International,* 21 (1), 76–83.

59 Stewart, D.W. and Martin, I.M. (1994) Intended and Unintended Consequences of Warning Messages: A Review and Synthesis of Empirical Research. *Journal of Public Policy & Marketing,* 13 (1), 1–19.

60 Gostin, L.O. (2007) Law as a Tool to Facilitate Healthier Lifestyles and Prevent Obesity. *Journal of the American Medical Association,* 297 (1), 87–90.

61 Brenkert, G.G. (2002) Ethical Challenges of Social Marketing. *Journal of Public Policy & Marketing,* 21 (1), 14–36.

62 Fletcher, R.J., Bell, I.P. and Lambert, J.P. (2004) Public Health Aspects of Food Fortification: A Question of Balance. *Proceedings of the Nutrition Society,* 63 (4), 605–14.

63 BBC News (2007) Experts Back Folic Acid in Flour. Retrieved 29 May, 2007, from http://news.bbc.co.uk/1/hi/health/6648059.stm

64 Serra-Majem, L. (2001) Vitamin and Mineral Intakes in European Children. Is Food Fortification Needed? *Public Health Nutrition,* 4 (1), 101–7.

65 Schneider, T.R. (2006) Getting the Biggest Bang for Your Health Education Buck. Message Framing and Reducing Health Disparities. *American Behavioral Scientist,* 49 (6), 812–22.

66 Callahan, D. (2001) Promoting Healthy Behavior: How Much Freedom? Whose Responsibility? *American Journal of Preventive Medicine,* 20 (1), 83.

67 Fitzpatrick, M. (2004) From 'Nanny State' to 'Therapeutic State'. *British Journal of General Practice,* 54 (505), 645.

68 Fogarty, J.S. (1997) Op. cit.

69 BBC News (2007) Young Women 'Complacent over HIV'. Retrieved 25 January, 2007, from http://news.bbc.co.uk/1/hi/health/6293729.stm

70 Edwards, J.S.A. and Hartwell, H.H. (2002) Fruit and Vegetables – Attitudes and Knowledge of Primary School Children. *Journal of Human Nutrition and Dietetics,* 15 (5), 365–74.

71 Neeley, S.M. and Petricone, B. (2006) Children's (Mis)understanding of Nutritional Information on Product Packages: Seeking Ways to Help Kids Make Healthier Food Choices. *Advances in Consumer Research,* 33 (1), 556–7.

72 Moses, L.J. and Baldwin, D.A. (2005) What Can the Study of Cognitive Development Reveal About Children's Ability to Appreciate and Cope with Advertising? *Journal of Public Policy & Marketing,* 24 (2), 186–201.

73 Callahan, D. (2001) Op. cit.

74 Allmark, P. (2006) Choosing Health and the Inner Citadel. *Journal of Medical Ethics,* 32, 3–6.

75 Lang, T. and Rayner, G. (2007) Overcoming Policy Cacophony on Obesity: An Ecological Public Health Framework for Policymakers. *Obesity Reviews,* 8 (Supp. 1), 165–81.

76 Verplanken, B. and Wood, W. (2006) Interventions to Break and Create Consumer Habits. *Journal of Public Policy & Marketing,* 25 (1), 90–103.

Chapter 2

The core principles of social marketing

Chapter objectives

On completing this chapter, you should be able to:

- understand some of the core principles of social marketing, and the debates around them;
- critically evaluate the use of commercial marketing theory in a social marketing context, e.g. exchange;
- critically evaluate the strengths and weaknesses of specific tools and techniques of commercial marketing in a social marketing context, e.g. the 4Ps/marketing mix;
- consider the value of alternative theories and tools for social marketing;
- debate whether social marketing should adopt a more service-driven approach versus the traditional product-driven approach.

The core principles

In this chapter we consider the core principles of social marketing, debating the theoretical and practical basis of the discipline. Since Wiebe asked, in 1951, 'Why can't you sell brotherhood and rational thinking like you sell soap?',[1] social marketing has been built upon the idea that behaviour change for social good can be achieved through the same means as selling commercial products and services. Here we consider the long-held assumption that social marketers should simply adopt the theory, tools and techniques of **commercial marketing**, and debate whether alternative options that *adapt* such approaches, or develop entirely new approaches, are needed.

While presenting the various arguments for and against the use of standard commercial marketing theory, tools and techniques, we give tentative conclusions about how social marketing might move forward as a discipline in its own right, stepping out from the shadow of commercial marketing.

Traditionalists versus convergents: the debate about commercial marketing technologies

When Kotler and Zaltman[2] first suggested the term 'social marketing', they called for 'the explicit use of marketing skills to help translate . . . social action efforts into more effectively designed and communicated programs that elicit desired audience response'. As shown in Box 2.1, commercial marketing has been central to definitions of social marketing for four decades, until very recently, when authors such as French and Blair-Stevens[3] included other 'concepts and techniques' besides those of marketing.

So should social marketing always play by the same rules as commercial marketing?

Commercial marketing is clearly successful, with big brands such as Mars, Tesco and Coca-Cola investing millions of dollars and pounds in their marketing strategies. However, marketers have long been frustrated with the negative connotations of their profession, and some desired to apply their skills to achieve more worthy goals. Social marketing sprang from this desire: it was a natural step to extend the proven efficacy of marketing beyond selling soap and chocolate bars, towards encouraging socially desirable behaviours such as recycling or stopping smoking. However, as Andreasen points out, 'the assumption that commercial marketing sector concepts and tools ought to migrate seamlessly to social marketing is . . . just an assumption'.[4]

Box 2.1 Evolving definitions of social marketing

Social marketing is:

'. . . the design, implementation, and control of programs calculated to influence the acceptability of social ideas and involving considerations of product planning, pricing, communication, distribution and marketing research'[5]

'. . . the *application of commercial marketing technologies* to the analysis, planning, execution, and evaluation of programmes designed to influence the voluntary behaviour of target audiences in order to improve their personal welfare and that of their society'[6]

'. . . the systematic *application of marketing concepts and techniques* to achieve specific behavioural goals relevant to a social good'[7]

'. . . the systematic *application of marketing,* **alongside** other concepts and techniques to achieve specific behavioural goals for a social good'[8]

'. . . a process that *applies marketing principles and techniques* to create, communicate, and deliver value in order to influence target audience behaviours that benefit society . . . as well as the target audience'[9]

This assumption has not gone unchallenged: soon after Kotler and Zaltman's seminal paper, others began to challenge the legitimacy of using the principles of marketing for wider social purposes.[10, 11] Rumblings of dissent have continued over the years, though they lost momentum in the 1980s as the focus moved to implementation.[12] More recent articles by Peattie and Peattie[13] and Wood[14] have rekindled the debate.

Two schools of thought have emerged: the **traditionalists** and the **convergents**. Traditionalists take a neoclassical approach to social marketing, using traditional marketing principles in this relatively new discipline. In contrast, convergents are more like magpies, taking tools and techniques from a variety of disciplines to supplement marketing techniques.[15] The traditionalists adopt a rational economic model of behaviour (exchange and transaction) to understand behaviour change, and advocate the direct transfer of commercial marketing tools to the social marketing context. The convergents, on the other hand, look beyond the domain of marketing to disciplines such as psychology and sociology and choose to use marketing theory *where it works*. They draw upon a wide range of theoretical sources, such as **stakeholder theory**, **diffusion theory** and **social network theory**. Convergents would argue that behaviour change is a far more complex phenomenon than 'selling', and that social marketers should not be bound by the limitations of the marketing discipline.

There are issues of **pragmatism**, i.e. whether the tools are practical for most social marketers, and **acceptability**, i.e. whether marketing tools are deemed appropriate by users like health professionals.[16] However, authors also disagree about the **validity** of transferring marketing theory to social marketing circumstances, and ultimately the **efficacy** of utilising marketing tools, without adaptation, for social marketing.[17] Some authors challenge certain commercial marketing assumptions (such as the marketing mix/4Ps and exchange) even in their original context, let alone when transferred to social marketing. Despite these disagreements, many social marketers would not consider an intervention to *be* social marketing unless it included specific aspects of marketing. For instance, both Andreasen[18] and the UK's National Social Marketing Centre use benchmark criteria which include use of the concept of exchange and implementation based upon the marketing mix. Interventions run the risk of being excluded as 'social marketing' if they do not use these controversial tools.

Traditionalists such as Andreasen[19] see social marketing as having passed through troubled times, akin to those of adolescence, when identity is questioned and rules established; however, he concludes that 'there ought to be few barriers to adopting virtually all concepts and tools from the commercial sector to social marketing.' In contrast, convergents such as Peattie and Peattie argue that 'social marketing needs the development of its own distinctive vocabulary, ideas and tools'.[20] A number of authors contend that it may be time for social marketing to step out from the shadow of its commercial big brother, and to establish its own rules for its own future.[21, 22, 23]

We will now review some of the key theories and tools, outlining arguments for and against the use of original marketing approaches, and offering alternatives where available. We will also consider which areas of marketing expertise can be easily transferred to social marketing. We hope you will be able to make up your own mind about where you think social marketing is heading.

The example of exchange: debating the use of commercial marketing theory

The concept of exchange is proposed as a 'grand theory of marketing' to defend its position as a discipline in its own right.[24] Defined as 'a transfer of something tangible or intangible, actual or symbolic, between two or more social actors',[25] the concept of exchange asserts that people are needs-directed with an innate tendency to improve their situation, i.e. always searching for a profitable exchange. This is based on principles of economics and psychology,[26] and is widely accepted as a defining characteristic of marketing (see Box 2.2 for examples). Such an approach assumes that people are ultimately rational creatures, who carefully balance the pros and cons of a situation so as always to achieve the best deal for themselves, acting as what John Stuart Mill called *Homo economicus*.[27] Thus marketing becomes a series of transactions between an organisation and its customers.

Box 2.2 Exchange as a defining characteristic of commercial marketing

Marketing is:

'. . . the exchange which takes place between consuming groups and supplying groups'[28]

'. . . the discipline of exchange behaviour, and it deals with problems related to this behaviour'[29]

'. . . a societal process by which individuals and groups obtain what they need and want through creating, offering and freely exchanging products and services of value with others'[30]

For the traditionalists who use this model as the underpinning theory of social marketing, the exchange is clear: the offer of intangible or tangible incentives in return for behaviour change. Intangible offers include improved self-esteem or confidence, while tangible offers may be financial or supportive, such as pedometers to record miles walked for exercise. Smith calls this the 'Let's make a deal' principle, where individuals volunteer to change behaviour because they perceive an 'exchange of value' that leaves them better off.[31] One advantage of this framework is that it allows the exchange to be mutually beneficial and achievable for both practitioners and target audiences. It also encourages practitioners to consider how to make a better offer to their target audience when asking for behaviour change.

Hastings and Haywood looked specifically at the concept of exchange for health promotion and proposed a model (see Figure 2.1) to identify exactly what is exchanged between the health promoter and the targeted: such a model is easily translated to social marketing to demonstrate potential exchanges.[32] Exchange encourages voluntary behaviour change by offering positive tangible and intangible benefits, rather than the threats often adopted by health promotion, which can be considered both disempowering and patronising.

So exchange has some useful ideas to offer social marketers, but can it really be used as the underpinning 'grand theory' of social marketing in the same way as suggested for commercial marketing?

There is much debate about how the concept of exchange dovetails with this broadened concept of marketing.[33, 34, 35] Peattie and Peattie suggest:

the idea that exchange . . . is central to social marketing has become widely accepted. This appears to have happened more on the basis of repetition, and a belief that exchange must be involved because social marketing is modelled on commercial marketing, rather than because anyone has created a compelling theoretical argument.[36]

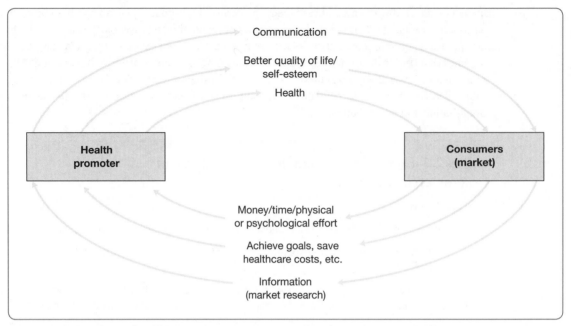

Figure 2.1 Exchange mechanisms between health promoters and consumers

Source: Adapted from Hastings, G. and Haywood, A. (1991) Social Marketing and Communication in Health Promotion. *Health Promotion International*, 6 (2).

Many of the questions about the application of exchange theory to social marketing concern the theoretical assumptions of transactional exchanges compared to the realities of behaviour change (see Box 2.3). Exchange is based on highly rational, economic models – yet people are not entirely rational. Many of the behaviours targeted by social marketing are subject to irrational influences, such as established habits, peer pressure, addiction or the effects of alcohol and drugs.[37]

Box 2.3 Five prerequisites for exchange

1 At least two parties are involved.

2 Each party has something that might be of value to the other – which may be tangible (money, products) or intangible (knowledge or skills).

3 Each party is capable of both communication and delivery.

4 Each party is free to accept or reject the other's offer, i.e. it is autonomous.

5 Each party believes it is appropriate and desirable to deal with the other party.[38]

The concept of exchange also assumes that both parties are knowingly involved in an exchange, negotiating and agreeing terms of a contract based upon perceived value of what is to be exchanged, and to be completed in a set time. Are these factors always clear in social marketing? For instance, if you want to give up smoking and attend a local public healthcare clinic, do you realise you are engaging in an exchange where they offer you both tangible (e.g. nicotine patches) and intangible (e.g. counselling) support in return for you giving up smoking? And what happens if you don't fulfil your part in this 'contract' and fail to give up smoking? In this case no exchange ultimately takes place, despite using these services. The equivalent in commercial marketing could be argued to be shoplifting.

Social marketers sometimes resort to stealth, perhaps offering free football coaching in the hope that young men will be distracted from binge drinking, or want to avoid hangovers to play better. But good social marketers also realise that revealing this subterfuge would undermine the strategy, so the young men have no idea that they are involved in an exchange. Or consider upstream social marketing, where reduced availability or increased cost of alcohol may change the same behaviour, but the target sees no value in the deal: both these scenarios flout the rules of exchange.

In commercial marketing, the timescales for exchanges are usually well defined. For instance, the exchange for a can of soft drink may last seconds as the consumer hands over the cash and then downs the drink. In social marketing the exchange may not happen for years, if ever, and possibly not with that individual. Consider the example where cycling (instead of driving a car) reduces CO_2 emissions in exchange for ultimately reducing climate change. However, cyclists may not see this benefit of their actions within their lifetime, never concluding the 'contract' of the exchange, while others benefit in the future. There is an argument that it would be better to use the principle of exchange with an offer that defines clearer benefits within a reasonable timescale, such as that in Figure 2.2.

Negotiating and agreeing the terms of such 'contracts' are also difficult where no financial exchange is made, and there are other problems in determining the value of what has been exchanged and whether this offers a 'good deal'. The principles of transactional exchange state that tangible or intangible items of discernible value are exchanged, which is difficult to apply to many social marketing processes where information, unsustained

Figure 2.2 Act on CO_2 advertisement from the UK government

Source: Advertising Archives.

behaviour change or even *not* doing something are 'exchanged'. Bagozzi counters this by arguing that exchange in social marketing is not *quid pro quo* and exchanges are more generalised or complex, though these violate some of the above prerequisites of exchange.[39]

The precise nature of the exchange offering can also be unclear. For instance, if you choose to do more exercise, perhaps prompted by seeing a character in a television show doing the same (which may be 'product placement' on behalf of insightful social marketers), are you really involved in an exchange? Have you received anything *from social marketers* in exchange for your efforts? The only person making a sacrifice is you, as you exchange sitting on your comfortable sofa for paying for a gym membership, investing in a new pair of trainers, and perhaps being embarrassed going to the gym, but ultimately feeling the benefits of exercise.

From an ethical perspective, using exchange also raises questions of what are acceptable exchanges for social marketing, and what could be considered mere bribery or coercion. Box 2.4 describes some scenarios that you might like to consider in this light, and link with the ethical issues raised in Chapter 5.

Box 2.4 Ethical implications of exchanges for behaviour change

Here are a number of scenarios where an exchange is offered in return for voluntary behaviour change. Which do you consider *unethical* and why?

1 One of the earliest examples of social marketing: the offer of radios or cash in return for sterilisation for Indian men and women who were already parents

2 Improving self-efficacy and confidence through taking up regular physical activity

3 Offering vouchers towards money off vegetables at the local supermarket when encouraging eating five fruit and vegetables a day

4 Entering a prize draw for every week that a household recycles, to win a family trip to a forest lodge

5 Offering lifts home in a limo in return for not driving home under the influence of alcohol

---

These are some of the reasons why many authors question whether social marketing truly maps onto the economic models that exchange arises from. In commercial marketing the parallels are clear, as marketers exchange customer satisfaction for profit, neither of which is a common goal of social marketing.[40]

However, brands such as Tesco view the relationship with their customers as more than a series of one-off transactions. The Tesco Club Card scheme, powered by one of the largest databases in the world, issues useful vouchers, salient offers and tailored magazines to millions of people across the UK in return for their business and information. Tesco realise that they must earn customer loyalty through ongoing communication, developing, creating and maintaining long-term relationships with their publics through a concept called **relationship marketing**.[41, 42]

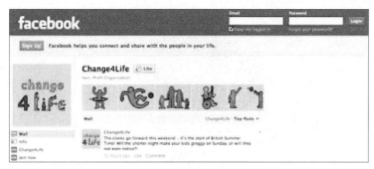

Figure 2.3 Change4Life Facebook page
Source: Facebook.

Figure 2.4 Change4Life Twitter page
Source: Twitter.

Hastings argues that relationship marketing is a better model for social marketing than transaction marketing (based upon exchange).[43] By building ongoing relationships with target groups, social marketers can earn their trust, develop better interventions and create truly supportive systems, focusing on long-term goals with no immediate expectation of success. For instance, the UK's Change4Life campaign is one of many social marketing interventions that now offer Facebook and Twitter sites to answer questions and offer advice (see Figure 2.3 and Figure 2.4), understanding that people get bored with one physical activity and will look for help and alternatives over many years.

Taking this a step further, **network marketing** not only engages in relational exchanges over time, but also encourages co-creation of interventions with participating target groups and other partners.[44] An increasingly popular concept for commercial marketers, it appears social marketers may be a step ahead in developing truly engaging marketing strategies.[45] For instance, the 'Lose the Fags' advertising campaign in Brinnington (UK) was created with and by local people trying to give up smoking, so the final campaign used local slang for cigarettes, local people as models, and mildly offensive imagery that symbolised how they truly felt about smoking (see Figure 2.5).

Figure 2.5 Brinnington local Andy Cheshire shows off one of the 'Lose the Fags' posters, featuring himself

These approaches show us that exchange, while useful in some cases, is not the only option. More recent marketing models may be more useful in some cases, and as marketing moves on, so can social marketing.

The example of the 4Ps: debating the use of commercial marketing tools

'The holy quadruple . . . of the marketing faith . . . written in tablets of stone'
Kent, 1986, cited in Grönroos, 1994[46]

The '4Ps' (**P**roduct, **P**romotion, **P**rice and **P**lace), often synonymous with the marketing mix, have been a guiding principle, a blueprint for marketing success and an aide-mémoire for generations of marketers since McCarthy suggested them in 1960.[47] The 4Ps have not remained static over the ensuing five decades, but the traditional understandings of each P is summarised below.

1 Product

In commercial marketing, the 'product' was originally a tangible entity, which expanded to include services. In social marketing, Kotler and Zaltman described the objective as something like safer driving, and sought to offer 'various tangible products and services which are "buy-able" to advance that social objective',[48] e.g. defensive driving courses or insurance policies for safer drivers, staying close to the familiar commercial marketing territory of 'selling' something. Rothschild later suggested that personal benefits, such as staying safe, be emphasised in the product offer, and over time social marketing has moved towards accepting that behaviour change itself may be the product, without the need for tangible aspects.[49]

2 Promotion

The concept of 'promotion' has remained largely unchanged over the years, incorporating accepted aspects of the promotional mix, i.e. advertising, personal selling, public relations and sales promotion.[50, 51, 52, 53] These activities have broadened, as in commercial marketing, to include direct marketing, the social media, and other new technologies.

3 Price

The concept of 'price' in social marketing has always included more than financial costs, for example 'money costs, opportunity costs, energy costs and psychic costs'.[54] Shapiro expanded this to time, effort, love, power, prestige, pride, friendship and abstinence costs.[55] Such ideas are important to the concept of exchange, as these are what we are truly bartering with when asking people to change behaviour.

4 Place

Kotler and Zaltman saw the intangibility of the product as a barrier, and called for 'clear action outlets for those motivated to acquire the product' to satisfy the 'place' element of the 4Ps.[56] At that time, the telephone was an innovative means of bringing the product to the people; nowadays the internet and mobile technology clearly have a role to play.

However, the 4Ps are not without their critics, and their value even for commercial marketing is debated.[57, 58] Many marketers argue that they fail to provide a complete guide to marketing implementation, and so have added more Ps, Cs and even Rs to provide better alternatives (see Table 2.1 for examples). Others argue that the 4Ps approach is fundamentally flawed because it is too product-oriented, with no focus on consumers.[59]

When it comes to services, the 4Ps fall short because of this focus on products. Services are characterised by the following qualities:

- Intangibility: using a service does not result in the ownership of a tangible product.
- Heterogeneity: services are often customised to the specific requirements of a customer, and vary in delivery quality, without a standardised product.
- Inseparability: production and consumption occur at the same time, with customers participating in both processes.
- Perishability: services often cannot be stockpiled in an inventory, such as airline seats or hotel rooms.[60, 61]

Booms and Bitner's 7Ps were developed for services, adding three more Ps:[62]

5 People

All the people directly or indirectly involved in the consumption of a service.

6 Process

The procedure, mechanisms and flow of activities by which services are consumed.

Table 2.1 Examples of where the four Ps fall short, and alternative suggestions

Author	Arguments	Alternative marketing mix
Kotler (1984)[1]	External factors should be included	Two extra Ps: • Political power • Public opinion formation
Brunner (1989)[2]	Each P needs to be extended to be truly useful	Expand each P to represent its own mix: • Concept mix • Cost mix • Channels mix • Communication mix
Robins (1991)[3]	The 4Ps Marketing Mix is too internally oriented	Four Cs replace the four Ps: • Customers • Competitors • Capabilities • Company
Booms and Bitner (1980)[4]	Services need additional elements compared to products	The Services Marketing Mix includes three extra Ps: • Participants • Physical evidence • Process
Lauterborn (1990)[5]	The 4Ps are too product oriented, need to place customer at the heart of the mix	Four Cs replace the four Ps: • Customer needs • Convenience • Cost (customer's) • Communication
English (2000)[6]	The 4Ps are not effective in health services marketing	Four Rs replace the four Ps: • Relevance • Response • Relationships • Results

[1]Kotler, P. (1984) *Marketing Management: Analysis, Planning and Control* (5th edn). New Jersey: Prentice-Hall.

[2]Brunner, G.C. (1989) The Marketing Mix: Time for Reconceptualisation. *Journal of Marketing Education*, 11: 72–7.

[3]Robins, F. (1991) *Four Ps or Four Cs of Four Ps and Four Cs.* Paper presented at MEG conference.

[4]Booms, B.H. and Bitner, B.J. (1980) Marketing Strategies and Organisation Structures for Service Firms. In Donnelly, J. and George, W.R (eds) *Marketing of Services.* American Marketing Association, pp. 47–51.

[5]Lauterborn, B. (1990) New Marketing Litany: Four Ps Passé: C-words Take Over. *Advertising Age,* 61(4): 26.

[6]English, J. (2000) The Four 'P's of Marketing are Dead. *Marketing Health Services,* 20(2): 20–3.

Source: Constantinides, E. (2006) The Marketing Mix Revisited: Towards the 21st Century Marketing. *Journal of Marketing Management,* 22: 407–38.

7 Physical evidence

The tangible evidence for the delivery and quality of the service, and intangible evidence of experiences of previous customers.

In the early days of social marketing, the 4Ps were used to demonstrate the transferability of existing marketing tools to new marketing challenges.[63, 64, 65] However, there are concerns about the use of the language of the 4Ps in socially sensitive contexts, and about how accurately those Ps reflect the realities of social marketing. In the context of social marketing, convergents see a potential trap in simply labelling social science concepts with marketing labels such as the 4Ps.[66] They also ask whether the 4Ps add anything truly unique to what health promoters had already considered or whether alternatives are required. Peattie and Peattie,[67] who critiqued the principle of exchange, also provided such alternative descriptions for the 4Ps framework:

Proposition (replacing 'Product')

Peattie and Peattie use the example of a campaign to encourage fostering in the UK. What is the product? Could it be 'children'? What would a 'mischievous newspaper' make of such terminology? Seeing children as a product is insensitive and inaccurate, as what we are really trying to do is encourage people to change their behaviour in a substantial fashion – offering time, care and a home to young people without a family of their own.

Other common social marketing goals include encouraging young people *never to start* smoking or using drugs. It can be difficult to define a clear product where not changing behaviour is the goal.[68] There are many circumstances in social marketing where we produce nothing that the consumer seeks to buy or offer an exchange for, or where the term 'product' seems inappropriate or even insensitive. Peattie and Peattie suggest redefining this concept as a *proposition,* sidestepping the issue of what the product is and defining it more closely as the overall behavioural goal, e.g. donating blood.

Social communication (replacing 'Promotion')

The concept of promotion was based upon the communications theory of the 1940s/1950s that described a message being encoded and transmitted by a sender, before being received, decoded and understood by the receiver.[69] Such one-way transmission has been supplanted by two-way processes of interaction and shared understanding that are particularly important in social marketing. Modern solutions create interventions with high levels of tailoring and feedback, enabled by technology such as databases and social media, and establishing dialogue with target audiences, so Peattie and Peattie suggest renaming this *'social communication'*. Another issue is that too much focus on promotion leads many to equate social *advertising* with social marketing, and it is essential that wider interventions are not neglected. In many cases overt promotion may not even be required (see Chapter 1 for more details).

Costs (replacing 'Price')

Despite the insights of early social marketers that the perceived price of behaviour change is often not financial but emotional, the model underpinning these calculations is based upon the costs plus profit method of determining financial prices in commercial marketing. Some modern social marketers think that this does not suit the non-profit-making area of social marketing. They acknowledge that audiences are more likely to think of their sacrifices of time, effort, emotion, etc. as *costs,* which we should acknowledge to assess the true cost of behaviour change more accurately in order to offer better-value alternatives.

Accessibility (replacing 'Place')

Place is an alliterative term that is used somewhat tentatively to describe both the location and practicalities of distribution in commercial marketing, and can be cumbersome when applied to social marketing. For many behaviours, such as smoking cessation, the actual behaviour change may occur on a daily basis in the home, at work, in the car or in the street, unlike that moment of one-off transaction that occurs in commercial marketing in a retail outlet, at a vending machine or over the internet. Modern means of social marketing creation, delivery and support are diverse and often not physically located anywhere but across the internet, mobile telephone, digital television and other 'cyber' alternatives. Social marketers are highly imaginative in their interpretation of 'place', offering clinics in social clubs, immunisation at carnivals or health checks in supermarket car parks, but the ultimate aim is to offer *accessibility,* which is why Peattie and Peattie suggest naming it as such.

These alternatives to the 4Ps are clearly based upon the original assumption of using this version of the marketing mix as a pillar of social marketing. They are indeed valuable tools to guide development and implementation of interventions, but the concerns that the 4Ps fall short of a truly comprehensive set of guidelines still hold for social marketing, as they do in commercial marketing. Peattie and Peattie's alternative suggestions go some way to defining behavioural goals, assessing how to access and convince target audiences and establishing what they truly sacrifice for behaviour change. This puts consumers closer to the heart of social marketing strategy than the traditional 4Ps, but have we gone far enough?

For instance, many social marketing interventions seem more like services than products.[70] Imagine taking up physical activity: every individual's experience is different, but while they may buy tangible products such as training shoes, the experience of exercise is intangible, variable and highly customised. Where one woman might enjoy zumba with her friends, another challenges herself to train for a marathon; where someone might knock a ball about with his mates for fun, someone else might cycle to work to avoid traffic. Each has a different solution to the same problem, tailored to their needs. In this case Booms and Bitner's 7Ps for services marketing may provide an even better starting point, adding concepts of people, process and physical evidence to consider. For instance, 'people' could mean using peers or role models to deliver interventions more effectively than authority figures. Providing feedback on progress, new ideas and ongoing support may satisfy the 'process' criterion, and diaries, photos or measures of health improvements can offer 'physical evidence' of success.

Finally, Bill Smith, a prominent US social marketer, suggests a more straightforward planning framework that could bypass these so-called 'essential components' of social marketing, and asks us to simply do whatever is 'fun, easy and popular' to encourage behaviour change. Perhaps opening our minds to using whatever tools are needed to make behaviour change attractive to our target groups is really the best route forward.

Why social marketing is different

So, social marketing challenges traditional marketing theories and tools, with some being more applicable than others, and better in some situations than others. Why is this?

The issues addressed through social marketing are diverse and sensitive. Some, like eating more healthily, have clear benefits for individuals, others, like recycling or reducing CO_2 emissions, may benefit future generations. Some, like physical activity, can be fun and offer an opportunity to meet new people, others, like getting tested for chlamydia, are embarrassing. Some may be one-off activities, like installing a smoke alarm, others may require months or years of hard work, like quitting smoking. So perhaps it is naive to think a one-size-fits-all approach would ever work. And that is the beauty of marketing.

With the focus upon putting consumers at the heart of everything we do, social marketers are at liberty to pick and choose from the array of marketing tools available, and to supplement these as we see fit – drawing from what we have learned from health promotion, psychology and economics.

Peattie and Peattie once again provide a useful tool to help distinguish where social marketing converges with commercial marketing, indicating that tools and theories can be directly applied, and where the two diverge, suggesting alternative approaches are required (Figure 2.6).

Essentially, the less likely we are to see personal benefits, the longer it takes to see these benefits, the less closely these can be attributed to our behaviour change, the more sensitive or controversial it is and the less customisable it is – the less like commercial marketing propositions the issue is. So, on this diagram, the further your goal is to the left of the chart, the more likely you are to be using traditional marketing tools such as the 4Ps and transaction marketing based upon exchange. If your goal is further to the right of the chart, these traditional tools are not so useful and you may consider adapting theories, learning from other disciplines such as psychology and developing new approaches. By testing such

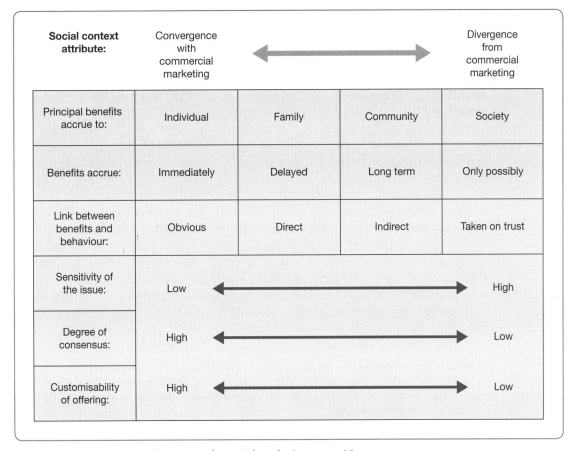

Figure 2.6 Key variations in the context for social marketing propositions

Source: Peattie, S. and Peattie, K. (2003) Ready to Fly Solo? Reducing Social Marketing's Dependence on Commercial Marketing Theory. *Marketing Theory,* 3 (3).

innovative new mixes, you can help others learn when they face similar circumstances and expand the field of social marketing. However, whatever you do, the target individuals will be at the heart of your strategy, and this is why it is called *social* marketing.

Other commercial marketing tools

The core idea in social marketing is consumer orientation, a concept often lacking in health promotion, and which engages target individuals with services, support, images, language and incentives tailored to their needs. But this is not the only useful concept from commercial marketing, which has a great deal more to offer social marketing, with processes, theories and tools that have been tried and tested around the globe in the commercial sphere, for instance:

- a proven planning process (Chapter 3)
- a consumer orientation based upon thorough market research (Chapter 7)
- deep understanding of the macro- and micro-environments (Chapter 7)
- competition analysis (Chapter 3)
- segmentation, targeting and positioning (Chapter 8)
- integrated intervention implementation and communication (Chapter 13)
- evaluation before, during and after implementation (Chapter 14).

These are all covered elsewhere in this textbook, and these fundamental links with commercial marketing provide an excellent starting point for the maturing discipline of social marketing.

Summary

Behaviours that benefit society do not always benefit the individual being asked to change their ways, and may not even benefit that social group, locality or generation; yet if such behaviours do not change, our future as a society is in jeopardy. Social marketing is a promising route forward precisely because its commercial cousin has been so successful. The focus upon target individuals is a genuine insight and advance upon health promotion, putting people at the heart of intervention development. However, the challenges facing social marketing go above and beyond those that commercial marketers have encountered, and therefore so should its theories and tools.

As Domegan points out, social marketing's unique position

> deepens the understanding of networks, of relationships, of complex economic and social exchanges, conflict, communication, and of the link between performance and practice. Social marketing delivers innovative insights into the communal, relational and economic exchange process that underlies marketing.[71]

Far from following in the footsteps of its commercial cousin, social marketing has the opportunity to be the vibrant young upstart of the marketing world. Dealing with issues beyond commercial marketing's traditional scope, social marketing takes these tools and addresses new challenges of long-term behaviour change with individuals who may be resistant to such change.

We conclude that, while social marketing is maturing, practitioners should be encouraged to experiment and to absorb successful strategies into the discipline, and not be confined to what has been done before in commercial marketing. In fact, this exciting discipline may blaze new trails that commercial marketers may learn from in their turn.

CHAPTER REVIEW QUESTIONS

1 Discuss the concept of 'exchange'. List likely positive and negative 'exchanges' for the following behaviours:
   - going to the gym regularly
   - reducing snacking
   - stopping smoking.

2 Use the 4P/marketing mix framework to discuss promoting accessing a sexual health clinic for a check-up/visiting a doctor for a vaccination. Do you find it easy to use the 4P framework? Are there aspects you think are not covered by the 4Ps? Which ones are these?

3 What makes social marketing different from 'commercial' marketing? Which aspects are similar?

4 What are the differences – and similarities – between health promotion and social marketing?

Recommended reading

Andreasen, A.R. (2003) The Life Trajectory of Social Marketing: Some Implications. *Marketing Theory,* 3 (3): 293–303.

Domegan, C.T. (2008) Social marketing: implications for CMP classification scheme. *Journal of Business & Industrial Marketing,* 23 (2): 135–41.

Glenane-Antoniadis, A., Whitwell, G., Bell, S.J. and Menguc, B. (2003) Extending the Vision of Social Marketing through Social Capital Theory: Marketing in the Context of Intricate Exchange and Market Failure. *Marketing Theory,* 3: 323–43.

Hastings, G. (2003) Relational Paradigms in Social Marketing. *Journal of Macromarketing,* 23 (1): 6–15.

Peattie, S. and Peattie, K. (2003) Ready to Fly Solo? Reducing Social Marketing's Dependence on Commercial Marketing Theory. *Marketing Theory,* 3 (3): 365–85.

Notes

1 Wiebe, G.D. (1951) Merchandising Commodities and Citizenship on Television. *Public Opinion Quarterly,* 15: 679–91.
2 Kotler, P. and Zaltman, G. (1971) Social Marketing: An Approach to Planned Social Change. *Journal of Marketing,* 35: 3–12.

3 French, J. and Blair-Stevens, C. (2006) Social Marketing National Benchmark Criteria. National Social Marketing Centre. Available from http://www.nsms.org.uk/images/CoreFiles/NSMC_Social_Marketing_BENCHMARK_CRITERIA_Sept2007.pdf (Accessed 4 March 2009).

4 Andreasen, A.R. (2003) The Life Trajectory of Social Marketing: Some Implications. *Marketing Theory,* 3 (3): 293–303.

5 Kotler, P. and Zaltman, G. (1971) Op. cit., p. 5.

6 Andreasen, A.R. (1995) *Marketing Social Change: Changing Behaviour to Promote Health, Social Development, and the Environment.* San Francisco: Jossey-Bass, p. 7.

7 Gordon, R., McDermott, L., Stead, M., Angus, K. and Hastings, G. (2006) A Review of the Effectiveness of Social Marketing: Physical Activity Interventions. London: National Social Marketing Centre, p. 6.

8 French, J. and Blair-Stevens, C. (2006) Op. cit.

9 Kotler, P. and Lee, N. (2008) *Social Marketing: Influencing Behaviors for Good.* Los Angeles: Sage.

10 Enis, B.M. (1973) Deepening the Concept of Marketing. *Journal of Marketing,* 37 (4): 57–62.

11 Luck, D.J. (1974) Social Marketing: Confusion Compounded. *Journal of Marketing,* 38 (4): 70–2.

12 Glenane-Antoniadis, A., Whitwell, G., Bell, S.J. and Menguc, B. (2003) Extending the Vision of Social Marketing through Social Capital Theory: Marketing in the Context of Intricate Exchange and Market Failure. *Marketing Theory,* 3: 323–43.

13 Peattie, S. and Peattie, K. (2003) Ready to Fly Solo? Reducing Social Marketing's Dependence on Commercial Marketing Theory. *Marketing Theory,* 3 (3): 365–85.

14 Wood, M. (2008) Applying Commercial Marketing Theory to Social Marketing: A Tale of 4Ps (and a B). *Social Marketing Quarterly,* 14 (1): 76–85.

15 Glenane-Antoniadis, A., Whitwell, G., Bell, S.J. and Menguc, B. (2003) Op. cit.

16 Wood, M. (2008) Op. cit.

17 Brownlie, D. and Saren, M. (1992) The 4Ps of Marketing Concept: Prescriptive, Polemical, Permanent, and Problematical. *European Journal of Marketing,* 26 (4): 34–47.

18 Andreasen, A.R. (2002) Marketing Social Marketing in the Social Change Marketplace. *Journal of Public Policy & Marketing,* 21 (1): 3–13.

19 Andreasen, A.R. (2003) Op. cit.

20 Peattie, S. and Peattie, K. (2003) Op. cit., p. 365.

21 Bloom, P.N. and Novelli, W.D. (1981) Problems and Challenges in Social Marketing. *Journal of Marketing,* 25 (Spring): 79–88.

22 Leather, D.S. and Hastings, G.B. (1987) Social Marketing and Health Education. *Journal of Services Marketing,* 1 (2): 49.

23 Hastings, G. (2003) Relational Paradigms in Social Marketing. *Journal of Macromarketing,* 23 (1): 6–15.

24 Bagozzi, R.P. (1975) Marketing as Exchange. *Journal of Marketing,* 39 (4): 32–9.

25 Bagozzi, R.P. (1979) Toward a Formal Theory of Marketing Exchanges. In Ferrell, O.C., Brown, S.W. and Lamb, C.W. Jr. (eds), *Conceptual and Theoretical Developments in Marketing*. Chicago: American Marketing Association, pp. 431–47.

26 Houston, F.S. and Gassenheimer, J.B. (1987) Marketing and Exchange. *Journal of Marketing,* 51 (4).

27 Mill, John Stuart (1836) 'On the Definition of Political Economy, and on the Method of Investigation Proper to It', *London and Westminster Review,* October.

28 Alderson, W. (1957) *Marketing Behavior and Executive Action: A Functionalist Approach to Marketing.* Homewood, NJ: Richard D. Irwin, p 151.

29 Bagozzi, R.P. (1975) Op. cit., p. 39.

30 Kotler, P. and Keller, K.L. (2009) *Marketing Management* (13th edn). Upper Saddle River, NJ: Pearson Education, p. 45.

31 Smith, W.A. (2006) Social Marketing: an Overview of Approach and Effects. *Injury Prevention,* 12 (Suppl I):i38–i43.

32 Hastings, G. and Haywood, A. (1991) Social Marketing and Communication in Health Promotion. *Health Promotion International,* 6 (2): 135–45.

33 Enis, B.M. (1973) Op. cit.

34 Luck, D.J. (1974) Op. cit.

35 Foxall, G. (1989) Marketing's Domain. *European Journal of Marketing,* 23 (8): 7–22.

36 Peattie and Peattie (2003) Op. cit., pp. 368–9.

37 Ferrell, O. and Perrachione, J. (1980) An Inquiry into Bagozzi's Formal Theory of Marketing Exchange. In Lamb, C. and Dunne, P. (eds) *Theoretical Developments in Marketing.* Chicago: American Marketing Association, pp.158–61.

38 Kotler, P. and Keller, K.L. (2009) Op. cit.

39 Bagozzi, R.P. (1975) Op. cit.

40 Peattie, S. and Peattie, K. (2003) Op. cit.

41 Grönroos, C. (1994) From Marketing Mix to Relationship Marketing: Towards a Paradigm Shift in Marketing. *Management Decision,* 32 (2): 4–20.

42 Gummesson, E. (1994) Making Relationship Marketing Operational. *International Journal of Service Management,* 5 (5): 5–20.

43 Hastings, G. (2003) Op. cit.

44 Coviello, N.E., Brodie, R.H., Danaher, P.J. and Johnston, W.J. (2002) How Firms relate to their Markets: an Empirical Examination of Contemporary Marketing Practices, *Journal of Marketing,* 66 (3): 33–47.

45 Domegan, C.T. (2008) Social marketing: implications for CMP classification scheme. *Journal of Business & Industrial Marketing,* 23 (2): 135–41.

46 Grönroos, C. (1994) Op. cit.

47 McCarthy, J.E. (1960) *Basic Marketing: A Managerial Approach.* Homewood, IL: Richard D. Irwin.

48 Kotler, P. and Zaltman, G. (1971) Op. cit., p. 7.

49 Rothschild, M.L. (1999) Carrots, Sticks, and Promises: A Conceptual Framework for the Management of Public Health and Social Issue Behaviors. *Journal of Marketing,* 563: 24–37.

50 Baker, M.J. (2000) *Marketing Strategy and Management* (3rd edn). Basingstoke: Palgrave Macmillan.

51 Zikmund, W.G. and d'Amico, M. (1993) *Marketing* (4th edn). St Paul, MN: John Wiley & Sons.

52 Kotler, P., Armstrong, G., Saunders, J. and Wong, V. (1999) *Principles of Marketing* (2nd European edn). London: Prentice Hall Europe.

53 Summers, J., Gardiner, M., Lamb, C.W., Hair, J.F. and McDaniel, C. (2005) *Essentials of Marketing* (2nd edn). Melbourne: Thomson.

54 Kotler, P. and Zaltman, G. (1971) Op. cit., p. 9.

55 Shapiro, B.P. (1973) Marketing For Nonprofit Organisations. *Harvard Business Review,* Sept/Oct: 123–32.

56 Kotler, P. and Zaltman, G. (1971) Op. cit.

57 Grönroos, C. (1994) Op. cit.

58 Peattie, S. and Peattie, K. (2003) Op. cit.

59 Dixon, D.F. and Blois, K.J. (1983) *Some Limitations of the 4Ps as a Paradigm for Marketing,* Marketing Education Group Annual Conference, Cranfield Institute of Technology, UK.

60 Payne, A. (1993) *The Essence of Services Marketing.* Hemel Hampstead: Prentice Hall.

61 Grönroos, C. (1990) *Service Management and Marketing.* Lexington, MA: Lexington Books.

62 Booms, B.H. and Bitner, B.J. (1981) Marketing strategies and organisation structures for service firms. In Donnelly, J. and George, W.R (eds) *Marketing of Services.* Chicago: American Marketing Association, pp. 47–51.

63 Kotler, P. and Zaltman, G. (1971) Op. cit.

64 Shapiro, B.P. (1973) Op. cit.

65 Rothschild, M.L. (1999) Op. cit.

66 Leather, D.S. and Hastings, G.B. (1987) Social Marketing and Health Education. *Journal of Services Marketing,* 1 (2): 49.

67 Peattie, S. and Peattie, K. (2003) Op. cit.

68 Andreasen, A.R. (1994) Social Marketing: Its Definition and Domain. *Journal of Public Policy & Marketing,* 13 (1): 108–14.

69 Berlo, D.K. (1960) *The Process of Communication.* New York: Rinehart & Winston.

70 Hastings, G. (2003) Op. cit.

71 Domegan, C.T. (2008) Op. cit., p. 140.

Chapter 3

The social marketing intervention planning process

Chapter objectives

On completing this chapter, you will:

- understand the stages involved in planning a social marketing intervention;
- be able to conduct a critical review of competitors to the target behaviour and other factors which may affect the planning process;
- be able to evaluate the potential of partnership development as part of the intervention planning process;
- be able to recognise the role of research in the planning process;
- be able to identify commercial marketing techniques which may be helpful in planning a social marketing intervention.

Introduction

Many social marketers would say that one of the most important criteria of the field is that it is based on the techniques and tools used in commercial marketing.[1] With that in mind, think how many marketing textbooks and academic papers have been dedicated to marketing planning in the past 50 years. Working through a careful planning process in social marketing is equally as important as in commercial marketing. There are differences, of course. In commercial marketing, there are often huge budgets involved and stakeholders are most concerned about planning effectively to maximise competitive advantage and profit. In social marketing, the budgets are often smaller, but the range of challenges often far more complex and intense. For example, social marketers have to maximise the chances of a short-term project being extended, by identifying potential commercial, not-for-profit and public partners, and by working with them to align goals, identify shared benefits and plan a longer-term, more sustainable project which has more chance of achieving the desired behaviour change.

Vignette 3.1 shows the complexity of the issues faced by social marketers. The reasons people behave in unhealthy ways are intricate and multifaceted, and social marketing planners need to grapple with complex issues when planning an intervention which tries to change behaviour. No simple one-size-fits-all approach will ever work.

VIGNETTE 3.1

ACTIVE for LIFE: Big budget, mass media, no behaviour change!

In 1995 the Department of Health commissioned a three-year social marketing campaign, *ACTIVE* for LIFE, to encourage uptake of physical activity in accordance with new policy.

The intervention included seminars with professionals and campaign resources targeted at priority groups, including posters, leaflets, websites, advertising in tabloids and women's magazines, PR, media advocacy, national press launches, national roadshows, competitions, workplace promotions and co-promotions with major retailers. A TV advertisement was also aired in two six-week blocks costing over £2 million.

A longitudinal, quantitative evaluation shows that awareness and prompted or unprompted recall of the campaign remained high over time. However, changes in participation were disappointing, with the proportion of active participants stable up until year 1 of the campaign but then reducing between years 2 and 3. Exposure to the campaign seemed to make little difference to long-term participation and the evaluation team concluded that 'there is no evidence that *ACTIVE* for LIFE improved physical activity, either overall or in any sub-group'.[2]

The *ACTIVE* for LIFE campaign aimed specifically to increase knowledge and acceptability of the new recommendation that adults should do five sessions of 30 minutes of moderate-intensity physical activity per week and presumed that achieving this aim would increase participation. With the campaign's main aim being 'awareness raising', it could be argued that the intervention was a success. However, could it then be called social marketing, given that measurable behaviour change is a key benchmark criterion? Would the huge budget be justified now?

Questions to consider

1 *What do you think went wrong in the* ACTIVE *for LIFE intervention?*

2 *What would you have done differently, in terms of planning, implementation and evaluation?*

This chapter will introduce you to a range of issues faced in social marketing planning, and introduce you to some key frameworks which help social marketers plan their work. As a starting point, Table 3.1 summarises many of the steps you might work through in social marketing planning. Many of these areas, such as gathering primary research (Chapter 7), developing partnerships (Chapter 4), ethics (Chapter 5) and evaluation (Chapter 14), are covered in more detail in other chapters, and these are signposted throughout. The table suggests activities which might be undertaken at each stage of the planning process.

Discussion question

Looking back at Vignette 3.1, which stages of the planning process do you think may have been missed out? What else do you think could have led to the lack of intervention effectiveness?

Table 3.1 Stages in a social marketing planning framework

	Planning stage	Suggested activities
1	Scope the problem	Gather data on the behavioural problem from secondary research. Define the behavioural problem.
		Identify the segment(s) performing the problem behaviour.
		Review existing and past interventions targeting the specific segment(s) with similar behavioural goals.
		Analyse ethical considerations. What are the potential wider implications if social marketers intervene and try to change the audience's behaviour?
		Identify known antecedents to the problem behaviour. What does the academic research literature tell us about the reasons why the target audience might be behaving in an unhealthy way, for example? What is already known about this problem behaviour from other research? What theories could help?
	Plan and implement primary research	Identify gaps in existing knowledge. What is not known about the target audience? What motivates their behaviour? What is the context of their behaviour?
		Design a primary research plan, if required.
		Undertake the primary research.
		Analyse the research results and identify key insights which will drive the social marketing intervention.
2	Situation analysis	PEST analysis (see p. 52). What is happening in the wider macro environment which might be affecting the target audience, and might affect the intervention? This should include a national intervention review and a policy review.
		Micro environmental audit. Identify strengths and weaknesses affecting the social marketing management organisation, including resources, expertise. This should include a competition analysis to analyse which behaviours the target audience might be motivated to choose instead of the desired behaviour.
3	Asset map	Identify partners who could align their goals with the social marketing intervention. Work with audience members to identify key potential partner organisations.
	A SWOT analysis at this stage may be a useful way of summarising stages 1–3 (see p. 59)	
4	Plan the evaluation	Identify baseline data, SMART objectives (see p. 50), evaluation criteria and plan evaluation research schedule. (This may include a pre-intervention survey.)
5	Develop the intervention	Having decided which segment to target, work with the target audience, stakeholders and partners to set up processes and services required to achieve the desired behaviour change. Identify commercial marketing techniques and other approaches which may be useful in achieving the desired behaviour change.
6	Implement the intervention	Pilot test the intervention and then launch fully. Ensure ongoing management processes are in place to monitor its progress.
7	Evaluate	Conduct a full evaluation, including soft evaluation (see p. 60), after a pre-designated intervention period. Feed back to key stakeholders and partners for ongoing improvement.
	Follow up	Ensure learning from the intervention is fed back to management and to partner organisations to improve future social marketing. Wider dissemination may be desirable with national and global academic and practitioner audiences.

Existing intervention planning frameworks

There is no single right way to develop a social marketing intervention. You may work through all of the seven stages in Table 3.1, or you may skip some which are not relevant for you. However, the key generic 'commercial' 'marketing texts[3, 4, 5] all provide the same advice regarding planning, which is that the following questions should be answered during the planning phase:

1 Where are we now?

2 Where do we want to be?

3 How are we going to get there?

4 Which way is best?

Table 3.2,[6] below, compares some commonly used marketing planning frameworks, locating them around these four key areas.

In terms of the specific requirements of a social marketing programme, the National Social Marketing Centre[7] suggests the following expanded questions:

1 What is the problem?

2 Who is affected or involved (including what different segments exist)?

3 Why are they affected or involved (identifying behavioural influences and appropriate theories (see Chapter 6)?

4 What should we focus on (behavioural focus and goals)?

5 What can we do about it (intervention options)?

The National Social Marketing Centre summarises the approach to the planning, development and implementation of social marketing interventions into a simple linear 'Total Process Approach', shown in Figure 3.1.

Although similar to the process used in commercial marketing campaigns, there are a number of issues that make planning for social marketing interventions more complex. This is demonstrated when we explore the expanded social marketing planning process (as outlined in Figure 3.2) provided by the US Department of Health.[8] This expanded process

Table 3.2 Classic commercial marketing planning frameworks

	APIC	SOSTTMMMM	SOSTAC
Where are we now?	Analysis	Situation analysis	Situation analysis
Where do we want to be?	Planning	Objectives	Objectives
How might we get there?		Strategy Targets	Strategy
Which way is best?	Implementation	Tactics	Tactics
		Men Money Minutes	Action
How can we ensure arrival?	Control	—	Control

stresses the need to look at *what* is to be delivered – not just how – and also considers the role of partners in the process. These may be organisations who will aid in some aspect of the intervention delivery but who may not be directly controlled or controllable by the main organisation developing the intervention.

An even more detailed set of steps for planning social marketing, again in the context of health-specific planning, comes from Health Canada's online Social Marketing resource.[9] Figure 3.3 provides an overview of this detailed internet-based resource, which explores planning issues in considerable detail.

While these approaches have been developed primarily within the health sector, they have relevance to all areas of social marketing. Answering the questions that each framework poses in a way that enables strategic decision-making can be a complex and time-consuming process.

Building on Figure 3.1, Figure 3.4 (on p. 46), provides an overview of the major steps required in expanding on the key planning questions. Figure 3.4 seems

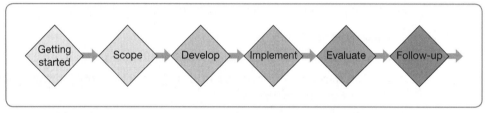

Figure 3.1 The National Social Marketing Centre's Total Process planning model
Source: National Social Marketing Centre (http://thensmc.com/). Reproduced with permission.

1 Assess the health issue or problem and identify all the components of a possible solution (e.g. communication as well as changes in policies, procedures or services).

2 Define communication objectives.

3 Define and learn about intended audiences.

4 Explore settings, channels, activities best suited to reach intended audiences.

5 Identify potential partners and develop partnering plans.

6 Develop a communication strategy for each intended audience, draft a communications plan.

Figure 3.2 US Department of Health planning process

1. Defining the role of social marketing in your overall health promotion

1.1 What are the overall goals in your area of health promotion?

1.2 Which factors have you identified to explain the current situation? Which factors need to change to improve the situation?

1.3 In your health promotion programme, which approaches (other than social marketing) are you currently using or planning to use to achieve your overall goals?

1.4 Which target audiences should you attempt to influence to meet your objectives and implement your advocacy or community development initiatives?

2. Audience analysis

2.1 Information gathering

2.2. Developing audience profiles

2.3 Summary and implications

3. Context for your social marketing plan

3.1 Organisational considerations

3.2 Environmental considerations

3.3. Implications

4. Defining measurable objectives

5. Strategies and tactics

5.1 Positioning

5.3 Delivering your message

5.4 Message development

5.5. Finding partners and sponsors

6. Monitoring and evaluation

6.1. Monitoring implementation

6.2 Progress in terms of measurable objectives

6.3. Progress in terms of health promotion programme goals

7. Working out operational details

7.1 Developing a schedule

7.2 Establishing a budget

Figure 3.3 Health Canada Social Marketing Planning resource

overwhelming at first glance, but it does demonstrate the wide range of factors that link with each other in the planning, development and implementation processes of social marketing.

Now we will explore key parts of the planning process in more detail.

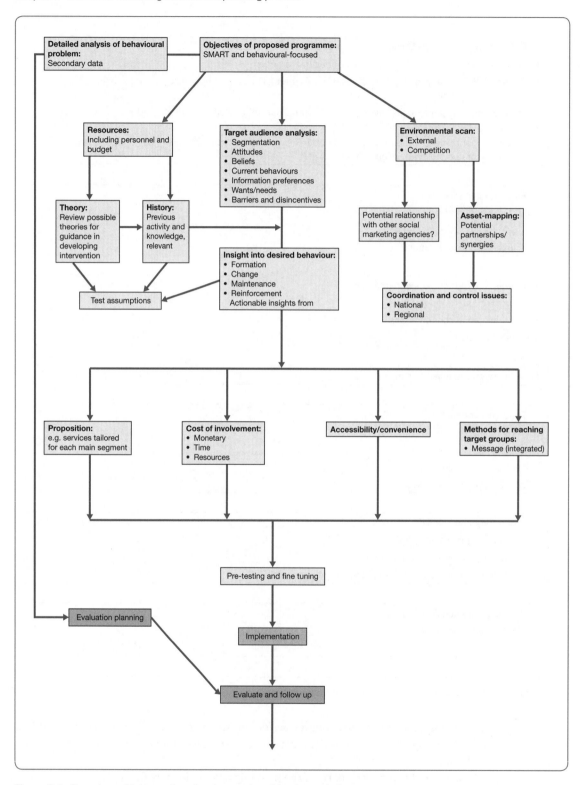

Figure 3.4 Overview of intervention development and implementation

Scoping the problem

The initial scoping phase is critical for guiding the rest of the planning process, and you can see from the number of boxes dedicated to it in Figure 3.4 that it can take some time. However, it is important to get scoping right. The behavioural problems faced by social marketing tend to be far more complex than the social and psychological drivers of commercial marketing problems. People's motivations for binge eating or drinking, for example, are far more complicated than motivations for choosing one type of washing powder over another. Behaviours such as binge drinking, practising unsafe sex or leading a sedentary life (i.e. not exercising) can be deeply ingrained and rooted in the socio-cultural structure of a community.[10, 11] They are not simple decisions. Therefore a deep understanding of the problem, and existing approaches to tackling it, is necessary as a starting point for new planning activities.

The following stages in the scoping process help planners gain a detailed understanding of the behavioural problem in question, and help them reach a point where they can set objectives for developing their intervention.

Understanding the behavioural problem

Getting to grips with the behavioural problem will initially involve considerable desk research. Various data might already have been gathered by other organisations which can be used to build a broad picture of the problem. There are dangers with using secondary research, however, which include the uncertainty about the **validity** and **reliability** of the research and the fact that it was collected for another purpose.[12] However, secondary data is a good place to start.

Secondary research may be published or unpublished (what is often called 'grey' material; i.e. reports published internally within organisations and public bodies). Some detective work may be required to hunt down relevant research reports, but often good-quality research is available from primary care trusts (which often have their own statistical or **epidemiology** departments), local government organisations, the Department of Health, public health observatories, charities, the King's Fund, the National Social Marketing Centre and many other places. Some key websites are listed below:

- Central Office of Information (http://coi.gov.uk/)
- King's Fund (http://www.kingsfund.org.uk/research/index.html)
- Cabinet Office (http://www.cabinetoffice.gov.uk/publications.aspx) and particularly their social exclusion pages (http://www.cabinetoffice.gov.uk/social_exclusion.aspx)
- Government white and green papers and research documents (http://www.publications.parliament.uk/pa/cm/cmpubns.htm)
- Local Government Association (http://www.lga.gov.uk/lga/core/page.do?pageId=1)
- NICE (http://www.nice.org.uk/)
- Government websites (http://www.direct.gov.uk/en/index.htm)

Published research will be available in the academic literature and, if not yet published in academic journals, then conference papers can be a good source.

Vignette 3.2 describes the secondary research materials gathered during the scoping phase of a social marketing intervention conducted to tackle binge drinking in the North of England.

VIGNETTE 3.2

Binge drinkers – who are they and how do we know?

Bristol Social Marketing Centre (BSMC) was commissioned to complete the scoping process for a PCT in the North of England which had a problem with binge drinking amongst local 16–21-year-olds. Young people were causing themselves harm by regularly drinking too much.[13] BSMC started by looking at the secondary data to see what was known about this group. Their purpose was to define the behavioural problem and recommend appropriate behavioural goals that the PCT could seek to achieve, as well as baselines which they could use in the evaluation process. The following reports formed part of the scoping:

Report title	Source	Useful data	Limitations
Young People, Alcohol and Unsafe Sex. Binge Drinking in Scotland	Scottish Health survey	Data on numbers of young people aged 18–25 who reported having unsafe sex whilst drunk.	Scotland, not the North of England. Limited behavioural insight into motivations for behaviour (just statistics). Self-reported behaviour. Age range not the same.
Binge Britain	Book by Martin Plant and Moira Plant	Insight into the scale of the problem and national policy responses. Useful references.	Nothing specific to the North of England. 5 years out of date.
Motivations for binge drinking	South West Public Health Observatory	Qualitative research into motivations to binge drink for a small group of purposively recruited teenagers (18–20).	South West, not North of England. Small sample. Not quite the same age range.
A&E admission data, North of England	Primary care trusts	Quantitative data relating to how many admissions (and at what time of day) were related to binge drinking. Age data also available.	No behavioural insight available.
Neighbourhood data	Neighbourhood renewal area household survey	Quantitative data by postcode in relevant part of the North of England on self-reported fear of crime, dislike of neighbourhood, general fear of neighbourhood, fear from antisocial behaviour in neighbourhood and general wanting to move.	No behavioural insight available. Small sample per postcode. No data on proportion of fear or other constructs which are directly related to the number of outdoor binge drinkers in the area.

Please note, this case study is based on a real case but the details are hypothetical.

Questions to consider

1 *What other secondary data could have been useful?*

2 *Which secondary data do you think were the hardest to locate?*

From Vignette 3.2, we can see that the range of secondary data available can help paint a picture of the behaviour and the problems it causes. This broad approach to scoping can help define the behavioural problem, find appropriate baseline data for evaluation and locate potential partners and stakeholders.

Another type of secondary research which can be a valuable resource in planning social marketing interventions is case studies of previous interventions targeting your audience. Case studies, which are often published in the academic literature, but can also be found on various social marketing case study databases,[14] help to paint a full picture of past interventions, whether or not they were successful, and which parts worked particularly well or poorly within their context. Unfortunately, published case studies often emphasise the positives and under-emphasise the negatives of an intervention, which can be unhelpful.

It is important to realise that there are limitations to the completeness of the picture you can paint through secondary research. Often a comprehensive primary research stage will be required to gather real insight into the behavioural problem and the motivations of those performing the behaviour, and even to help segment the audience and decide who to target. It is also common practice to undertake some preliminary interviews with experts 'on the ground' (such as health trainers, smoking cessation nurses, GPs and even police and youth workers) in the scoping stage to help build a picture of the target group from their perspective, and to help you understand the problem behaviour. Primary research is an important part of social marketing and Chapter 7 explores the topic more fully.

Finally, it is important to note that academic theories can be very practical ways of helping social marketers understand the motivations behind the problem behaviour, as well as ways the behaviour might be changed. Theories such as the Theory of Planned Behaviour, Transtheoretical Model and Health Locus of Control have been used in many social marketing interventions to guide both insight into the target audience and intervention design. They can be an important part of the scoping stage.

Defining the behavioural problem and intervention aims

From the insight gathered through secondary and primary data collection, it will be possible to carefully define the behavioural problem. However, defining the behavioural problem is not always as easy as it seems. Think about teenage pregnancy. Is the problem unsafe sex, lack of education or awareness, alcohol-related carelessness or a desire to get pregnant in order to become independent from parents?

Often, the causes of behavioural problems are multifaceted and social marketers must think carefully and realistically about what their intervention should aim to achieve. Within a short time frame of a few years, culture change will not be possible, so more modest intervention aims may have to be set in some cases.

Finally, it is important to align intervention aims with available **baseline** data. For example, a serious behavioural problem could result in a long-term (i.e. ten-year) effect, say teenage binge drinking resulting in early-onset liver cirrhosis,[15] but this will not be possible to evaluate within a one- or two-year funding and evaluation framework. Perhaps in this instance, although the overall project aims could be to reduce early-onset liver cirrhosis ten years down the line, more immediate behavioural goals could be to reduce self-reported weekly binge drinking sessions, evaluated using survey data.

Setting SMART objectives is an important part of the early planning process and these should have behaviour change as their primary goal. Although initially social marketing was defined as being 'calculated to influence the acceptability of social ideas',[16] it has now largely been accepted, after an interesting debate,[17] that behaviour change is the goal of social marketing. Authors now largely agree that social marketing should aim to achieve 'voluntary behaviour change to improve their personal welfare and that of the society of which they are a part'.[18] Therefore, intervention objectives should be SMART – a concept dating back to the mid-1950s and the start of the Management by Objectives movement spearheaded by the high-profile management guru Peter Drucker. The acronym has been adopted and modified by many authors in the following decades, as shown below:

Drucker (1954)[19]	*Tapp (2005)*[20]
Specific	**S**imple
Measurable	**M**easurable
Achievable	**A**spirational
Realistic	**R**ealistic
Time-bound	**T**ime-bound

Segmentation

The primary and secondary research data should provide enough insight about the customers, the problem behaviour and motivations for doing the problem behaviour, for target segments to be selected. You might know that 'teenage binge drinkers' are your target group and their binge drinking the problem behaviour, but this group may need to be segmented further. A recent social marketing intervention[21] in the North West of England segmented a group of young binge drinkers (18–25 years) into those who had 'settled down' with a steady job and partner, and those who were 'pre-responsibility'. Only the pre-responsibility group were the target segment for this intervention.

An intervention may target more than one segment. For example, if your intervention aim is to reduce chlamydia amongst 15–20-year-olds, you may choose to segment as in Table 3.3.

As Table 3.3 suggests, it is important to make sure you have a clear targeting strategy and a clear way of reaching your chosen segment.

There are no right or wrong ways to segment and it is often difficult, when resources are low and timescales tight, to decide which group to target. You might have various at-risk groups but only budget for one social marketing intervention. Segmentation is covered in more detail in Chapter 8, but here we discuss the concepts of **low-hanging fruit** and at-risk groups as key planning considerations.

Low-hanging fruit are those who are likely to make the most marked change the most quickly. These might be smokers who are ready to quit or overweight people who have already registered with a weight-loss club or exercise facility. These groups will be least resistant to change and therefore a likely target for achieving behavioural goals within a relatively short time frame. If the intervention has a short time frame, a limited budget

Table 3.3 Segmentation example

Segment	Segmentation technique	Objective	How to reach them
Target group – men	• By age (15–20yrs) • By gender (male) • By geographical area of residence • By behaviour (sexually active)	• Achieve increased regularity of testing • Achieve regular and correct condom usage	• School and college enrolment • Workplaces • Leisure facilities • GP surgeries
Target group – women	• By age (15–20yrs) • By gender (female) • By geographical area of residence • By behaviour (sexually active)	• Achieve increased regularity of testing • Achieve regular and correct condom usage	• School and college enrolment • Workplaces • Leisure facilities • GP surgeries
Health practitioners	• By area of practice	• Distribute chlamydia testing packs • Distribute condoms	• Workplaces
Youth leisure outlets	• By geographical area	• Distribute chlamydia testing packs • Distribute condoms	• Workplaces

and future funding relies on quick and positive results, then low-hanging fruit may well be selected. However, there are ethical considerations in this choice. Perhaps the low-hanging fruit are not those most in need of behaviour change, or perhaps encouraging them to change their behaviour will increase health inequality gaps and cause negative unintended consequences for other segments.

In contrast, people most at risk from a behavioural problem may be resistant to change, difficult to reach and may even be out of touch with society's normal mechanisms of support, like health services or community groups. Gathering primary research about them may be difficult, as will be gaining trust and achieving successful results. The group may have literacy challenges, for example.[22] Whatever the problems, however, those most at risk are also those who are most likely to be in need of behaviour change, for their own and society's benefit.

As has been suggested here, there may be ethical issues at stake with defining behavioural problems, setting 'desired' behavioural goals and targeting one segment over another. It is important in this early stage to consider that what may benefit society may not benefit the individual being asked to change their behaviour; or that what one organisation considers to be 'social good' may contravene another's moral code. Ethical dilemmas are rife in social marketing and are considered in detail in Chapter 5.

Situation analysis

The scoping stage is about finding out where you are now and where you want to be; a critical part of this is what commercial marketers call the 'marketing audit', but which we prefer to call the 'situation analysis'. This stage is the launch pad to planning,[23] because it encourages an organisation to analyse its ability to reach its goals. In other words, it encourages social marketers to assess what else is 'going on' in the **macro** and **micro environments** which might be affecting the audience's behaviour and might impact on the effectiveness of the intervention they are planning.

Macro environment (PEEST)

A commonly used framework in commercial marketing is the PEEST analysis,[24] which provides a framework for examining 'macro' influences within the wider environment that may affect a social marketing campaign. PEEST is an acronym for an evaluation of the following factors:[25]

Political

Economic

Environmental

Socio-cultural

Technological

Many of these factors are likely to be outside the control and influence of an organisation, but they may impact to varying degrees on the effectiveness of a campaign and the people the campaign is targeting, and therefore must be considered.

Political factors

These may include the attitudes and priorities of government, government policy and legislative and regulatory frameworks. Consider, for example, the impact of the smoking ban in England. This has reportedly reduced smoking, in combination with social marketing efforts.[26] Similarly, consider the plans to enforce the publication of nutritional information on fast-food packaging. Research is inconclusive as to whether nutritional labelling on takeaway food impacts healthy choices,[27] but a policy change forcing all fast-food restaurants to label their products may affect an intervention aiming to reduce obesity. These are important contexts for social marketing planning.

Other social marketing and policy-led interventions may also affect the social marketing intervention being planned, and will certainly affect the target audience. For example, Change4Life is a national social marketing intervention run by the Department of Health, aimed at reducing obesity. Local interventions targeting the same audience need to be aware of this background. Change4Life could be viewed by social marketing planners as a potential opportunity for intervention synergy and the sharing of resources, or as a source of competition for the target audience's attention. Competition analysis is considered later in this chapter.

Environmental factors

In the context of PEEST, environmental factors are elements of the world in which people live that impact their lives and can influence their behaviours, such as housing, transport or work environments. The climatic environment also has an impact on behaviours. Pressure from government and **lobbying activity** has affected how individuals in some sectors of society prioritise recycling, public transport use and cycling for short journeys.[28] This pressure is likely to increase and has affected the **social norms** in some communities, which may impact some social marketing initiatives.

Socio-cultural factors

These include lifestyle trends, changes to demographic profiles and evidence of major influences on the behaviour to be targeted. It is important to get a full picture of regional, national and global trends relating to your behavioural problem. For example, the national smoking rate is decreasing over time but is higher than average in lower socio-economic communities. Similarly, binge drinking occurs most often in the 18–24-year-old cohort and tends to tail off after that age. With this picture you can assess your own localised data more clearly. If you have a high number of 40–50-year-old binge drinkers, you know this is unusual and problematic.

Economic factors

Economic factors include trends in the economy such as employment levels, GDP trends, inflation and interest rates. Any or all of these factors may impact on decisions people make about how they allocate their time and financial resources, and this affects their lifestyle behaviours. With less disposable income (such as during a recession), people may spend less money on expensive healthy food and more on cheap energy-dense food. There is also evidence that people drink more alcohol in times of recession.[29]

Technological developments

Technological developments such as the use of the internet and mobile technology can significantly affect how an intervention is planned and executed. An intervention to increase registrations with local smoking cessation services in a specific area of Stockport, near Manchester, used a texting service as its call to action in the communications materials.[30] Some segments, such as teenagers, use a panoply of new technologies and often lead 'virtual' social lives on Facebook, and social marketers have commented on how powerful these interactive technologies will be in our attempt to build relationships with our audiences.[31] Another significant area of technological development occurs in the pharmaceutical field, with new medicines being made available all the time to help people in their fight against smoking and other kinds of addiction.

Micro environment

Understanding the micro environment of an organisation is all about getting to grips with factors in the organisation itself, those relating to the target audience and those pertaining to the competition which may impede the social marketing intervention from reaching its goals. There are three key areas to the micro environmental analysis in social marketing: customer insight, competition analysis and task environment. Issues relating to the importance of, and methods for, gaining customer insight have been discussed earlier in this chapter and will be discussed in Chapter 6. Competition analysis is discussed below, followed by task environment; this includes the importance of asset mapping, stakeholder analysis and partnership development in order to maximise the effectiveness of the social marketing intervention.

Competition analysis

Audiences are bombarded with competing messages from various sources, and also experience competing motivations to behave in different ways. For example, a key competitor to 'cycling for short journeys' is car use, because cars are comfortable and require little effort to use. In comparison, cycling is often seen as hard work and requiring skill and fitness. It is important to scope these competitions in advance so you can make plans to present a suitably appealing offer.

People are inundated with messages promoting 'social good', as Figure 3.5 shows.[32]

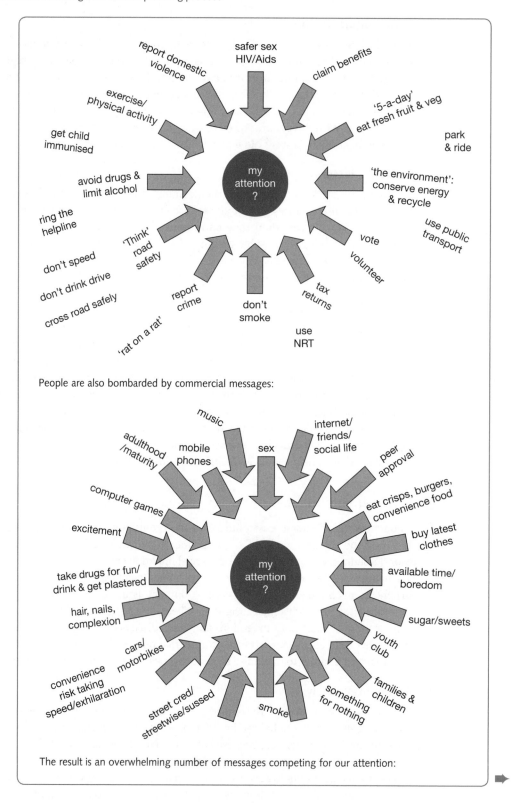

People are also bombarded by commercial messages:

The result is an overwhelming number of messages competing for our attention:

Courtesy of the National Social Marketing Centre for these images (http://thensmc.com).
Reproduced with permission

Figure 3.5 Competition

Source: National Social Marketing Centre (http://thensmc.com/). Reproduced with permission.

Competition may come in the form of commercial marketers, such as tobacco companies, supermarkets and fast food outlets. Cheap supermarket offers for alcohol will compete with interventions targeting binge drinkers, for example. However, competition may also come from other public health sources and from other social advertising. Your target audience will likely be bombarded by messages attempting to persuade them to change their behaviour. Key competitors should be mapped out to inform planning and possible lobbying activities and competition analysis should inform the communications strategy.

Peattie and Peattie refer to four different types of competing ideas in social marketing: 'counter marketing' (from directly competing commercial marketers such as the tobacco and alcohol industry or fast-food chains), 'social discouragement' (from social norms), 'apathy' and finally a person's 'involuntary disinclination to change their behaviour' (physical addictions, mental and physical ill-health, habitual behaviour or genetic predisposition).[33]

Vignette 3.3 illustrates how competition to the desired behaviour can come from within (i.e. lack of time to source alternative, healthy food) and from commercial organisations (Tesco sandwiches). The vignette also illustrates how difficult it can be to work with partners and at the same time how effective partnerships can be. Partnerships in social marketing are the topic of Chapter 4.

VIGNETTE 3.3

Competition: Experience Food at Work

Experience Food at Work is a pilot initiative aimed at improving eating behaviour within Breckland Council's offices. The offices are situated on an industrial estate with limited healthy food options available for staff for lunch. Breckland Council wanted to provide their workforce with healthy food opportunities within a limited budget and use social marketing to improve staff's healthy eating and, as a result, their sickness records, energy and well-being at work.

Sandwiches represent the main competition to a balanced, healthy lunch, and they are easily and conveniently available from the Tesco store, just near the Breckland Council office. Work was done to try to involve Tesco in the actual intervention. However, this did not lead to a working partnership.

Instead, to try to compete with their offer, the sandwich delivery van, which served the office, was supported to develop a more healthy lunchtime offer. One new product that was introduced was the 'Three of your 5-a-Day' lunch pack, which consisted of a main meal and two pieces of fruit for £3.75 – roughly the cost of a top-end deli sandwich from Tesco. This meal could be pre-ordered for convenience, and was delivered to the office.

The sandwich-delivery service was supported with other elements of the methods mix, such as

- health and nutrition;
- a personalised text service to remind and support;
- honesty fruit bowl system;
- re-vamp of the breakout zone;
- visiting chef event;
- publicity.

Questions to consider

1 *What were the problem behaviour, the target behaviour and the competing behaviours in this case?*

2 *What alternative approaches might the council have taken?*

Source: Thanks to the National Social Marketing Centre for this case study. Available from http://www.thensmc .com/sites/default/files/Experience%20Food%20at%20Work%20SUMMARY.pdf

Task environment analysis

Analysing the task environment is important for evaluating how well the social marketers will be able to perform the tasks required to manage the intervention. Activities may need to be undertaken to make changes to the organisation's structure, funding or knowledge to ensure the success of the intervention. For example, in the field of public health, social marketing is often undertaken by health experts who have little or no background in commercial marketing,[34] and so training in social marketing core principles may be required before social marketing is planned or commissioned.

Asset mapping

Turning now to resources outside the organisation, asset mapping is a way of mapping out existing resources on which the organisation could rely. Social marketing often takes a multi-agency approach to behaviour change, and assets may be other agencies with similar goals as well as individuals or organisations which are keen to work together to achieve joint aims.

It is often preferable to build an intervention around an existing infrastructure rather than try to set up a whole new system. This is particularly the case when the target segment is hard to reach and wary of 'outsiders'. Existing organisations may already have developed trusting relationships with the target audience, and it is often possible to base an intervention around existing organisations or services. For example, an intervention to increase the smoking quit rate in a specific community involved training the fitness instructors at a local gym and also nursery workers at the local children's centre to be smoking cessation advisers. These workers were already known and trusted by the target segment. The asset mapping process identified that the children's centre and leisure centre had goals that were already aligned with the organisation managing the intervention: improving health and decreasing smoking rates. Strong partnerships were developed as a result (see cases in other chapters which illustrate this point).

Potential assets may include:

- Existing services specialising in dealing with the behavioural problem (e.g. smoking cessation support services, alcohol counselling services or drug rehabilitation services). These services may be redesigned as part of the intervention.

- Existing services coming into contact with the target segment (e.g. probation services, social workers, midwives and health visitors, community workers and health trainers). These people may be able to support the intervention.

- Existing community institutions (e.g. coffee mornings, youth clubs, newsletters, leisure centres, residents' committees, etc.). These institutions may be vital for the communications strategy.

The asset mapping process can involve meeting representatives from relevant organisations face to face and growing knowledge through snowballing.

Stakeholder management

From its early days, any social marketing intervention will have various stakeholders who are interested and powerful to varying degrees. Managing these stakeholders can be challenging. The organisation managing the intervention and the target segment are two groups with an obvious interest in the social marketing intervention, but there are likely to be many others. Stakeholders will include upstream organisations (e.g. government departments, regional leads, chief executives) and downstream organisations (e.g. community organisations, service deliverers and end-users). Internal marketing is an important way of ensuring stakeholders are involved with the intervention, informed and that an appropriate relationship with them is developed over time. Internal marketing techniques may include:

- monthly newsletters with 'team news' and intervention updates;
- team meetings for the core intervention team;
- team newsletter specifically for the core intervention team;
- team incentive structure;

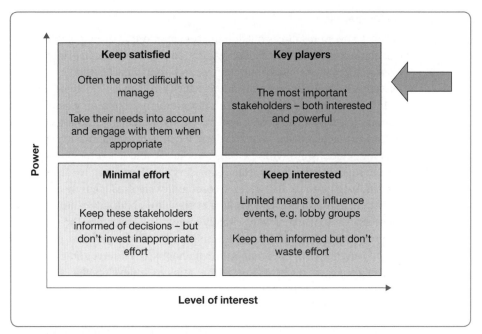

Figure 3.6 The stakeholder engagement matrix

Source: National Social Marketing Centre (http://thensmc.com/). Reproduced with permission.

- internally-focused intervention website;
- stakeholder meetings for updates;
- dissemination presentations for wider stakeholder audience on the social marketing process (e.g. invite the local MP).

The matrix in Figure 3.6 can be used to plot various stakeholders and then guide internal marketing activities.

Partnership development

From the asset mapping and stakeholder management processes, genuine partnerships may develop. Social marketing interventions can benefit greatly from going into partnership with organisations to achieve mutual aims (see also Chapter 4). For example, in the Fighting Back initiative, schools, police, courts and correctional facilities, healthcare organisations, the alcohol industry (excluding retailers), workplaces, faith-based organisations and neighbourhood associations all partnered together to combat alcohol-related problems across 11 US states.[35]

Commercial organisations may also make fitting partners. An intervention aimed at increasing consistent condom usage that is sponsored by Durex could find the funding to make it longer-lasting and have more impact. Clearly, there are potential ethical complexities at stake with commercial partnerships and some difficult questions have to be addressed. The controversy surrounding British Minister for Health Andrew Lansley's plan to involve the fast-food and alcohol industry in planning government public health initiatives is testament to the strength of feeling surrounding public–private partnerships in this arena.[36] It is important that partners can align their goals.

Discussion question

What are the possible ethical dilemmas when social marketers partner with commercial organisations, such as players in the alcohol industry, to try to achieve their goals?

SWOT (Strengths, Weaknesses, Opportunities and Threats) analysis

At this stage, it may be helpful to perform a SWOT analysis, to summarise key findings from the macro and micro elements of the scoping exercise. The SWOT analysis has proved to be a valuable aid to taking stock of macro and micro analyses. Completing a SWOT analysis will enable you to focus on making the most of opportunities you have with your strengths, and overcome weaknesses to minimise threats,[37] as shown in Figure 3.7.

	Internal factors	**External factors**
Favourable factors	**Strengths** • What experience does the organisation have of running similar interventions successfully? • Does it have the resources (financial, people, organisational) needed to develop and deliver the planned programme? • Does it have strong and effective systems and procedures, upstream and downstream relationships and support/awareness levels?	**Opportunities** • Has the preceding analysis identified new or more efficient ways of using resources that have not been used in the past? • Are there partner organisations who will add resources and expertise to the intervention? • Are there institutions in the community that can add invaluable insight and means of communication with the target group?
Unfavourable factors	**Weaknesses** • Are competitors able to outperform the organisation? • Are there weaknesses in internal systems or structures, including funding?	**Threats** • What are the major threats facing the organisation? • What would be the impact of a major competitor offering a new service? • What impact would negative publicity have on the organisation's credibility and ability to deliver its programmes? • What impact might external changes, such as worsening economic conditions, have on funding or the resources/attitudes of target groups?

Figure 3.7 SWOT analysis

Source: Valentin, E.K. (2001) SWOT analysis from a resource-based view. *Journal of Marketing Theory and Practice* (Spring).

Evaluation planning

While evaluation is often seen as a final research-based phase, planning for evaluation must start at the beginning of the planning process. Baseline data, for example, should form the cornerstone of your evaluation plan. Evaluation results should be quantifiable, at least in part, so finding suitable baseline data, which it is possible to gather again *after* the intervention has been running, is crucial. For example, if the aim of an intervention is to improve the number of non-smokers in a community, four-week quit data (which is routinely gathered by stop-smoking services) should be available before the intervention is launched so that it can be compared with data after the intervention has been running for a set period. This enables a quantifiable evaluation of the intervention's success.

Sometimes, evaluation research must be specially commissioned. A pre-post survey design with a control is a normal design for intervention evaluation. With this method, a statistically random sample is surveyed before the intervention goes live, then again afterwards. A **control group**, which is similar in demographic, size and incidence of problem behaviour, is also surveyed in the same way for comparison. There are many different ways of running a quantitative evaluation, and designing the questionnaire is often a highly complex process, needing considerable piloting and refinement. Often a qualified marketing research company is commissioned to take this on. Read more about evaluation in Chapter 14.

Often social marketers will choose to supplement their quantitative evaluations with qualitative research, to explore staff and client experiences of interventions and the social marketing process. A considerable amount of valuable feedback on success (or otherwise) can be gained through the qualitative opinions of stakeholders and partners. Qualitative, or 'soft' evaluation is important in social marketing because there are often important repercussions to behaviour change which may not be captured through a survey designed to measure the change in the incidence of the problem behaviour. An intervention in Bristol designed to decrease levels of dangerous driving amongst young males,[38] for example, had the positive repercussions of improving the men's social skills, social capital, perceived self-efficacy and confidence. These factors would not have been captured had the planners relied on the safe driving data alone.

Unintended consequences of social marketing interventions are not always positive, however, so it is important for social marketers to have a contingency plan for their intervention. Contingency planning enables planners to think through 'worst-case scenarios' and have a set of actions ready for implementation should the situation arise. Contingencies have been required in social marketing for some of the following reasons:

- Resource availability (personnel and funding) has changed, requiring a reduction in marketing output or dynamic changes to the intervention.

- Problems have arisen with partners and key stakeholders – for instance, they have withdrawn their support or created an ethically difficult scenario picked up by the media.

- The intervention has created unintended effects on the target audience; communications material can cause distress or anger.

- The policy basis for the intervention has changed, creating internal organisational conflict.

Rothschild's famous Road Crew intervention targeting drunk drivers in the USA[39] is a case in point (see the case study in Chapter 5 for more details). Although the intervention successfully reduced incidence of drink-driving, the unintended consequences (which were not measured) may have been an increase in binge drinking, in domestic violence and anti-social behaviour.

As in all project management, it is important to learn from the planning and implementation of your social marketing intervention. Key internal learning should be disseminated to relevant stakeholders and fed into the next project.

Developing the intervention

As in commercial marketing, social marketing interventions often combine a range of techniques, in recognition of the fact that the antecedents to behaviour change are also multi-faceted. For example, problem behaviours such as smoking may be in part automatic, and in part high-involvement and highly conscious, with cultural significance. Social marketers may decide, based on insight about the target audience from earlier planning stages, that upstream as well as downstream interventions are required to achieve the behaviour change.

Upstream activities are those which change the environment in which a decision is made as a way of influencing the decision. For example, changing the food that is available for purchase at the till in the supermarket from chocolate to fruit will influence the automatic behaviours of the 'point of purchase' shoppers, and change the amount of fruit they eat. Upstream interventions are often policy-related and can include legislation.

Social marketers have had an uncomfortable relationship with behavioural interventions through legislation (see Chapter 4), but are increasingly recognising that policy change is an integral part of effective behavioural intervention.

At the development stage of the planning process, the social marketer chooses the appropriate mix of techniques, largely based on techniques used in commercial marketing (or indeed in marketing 'alongside other concepts and techniques', according to French et al.).[40] Developing interventions is considered in more detail in Chapter 10, but as a taster, the following techniques are introduced as they have been used by social marketers to achieve their goals.

Co-creation

Relationship approaches and co-creation are important principles for working within a downstream intervention framework. Co-creation is the development of interventions alongside the target audience. It is an approach informed jointly by community development and relationship marketing thinking and based around the empowerment of a community to co-create the intervention they want. Co-creation is a complex and growing field and is discussed in more detail in Chapter 4.

Building relationships is at the heart of community-based interventions and relationship marketing techniques, such as regular and personalised communication, loyalty schemes and membership, can support branding activity by seeking to generate a loyal group of behavioural 'customers' who are emotionally attached to the 'brand' and for whom being disloyal would cause **dissonance**. This group may become valuable word-of-mouth promoters. New and digital media are underexplored tools in social marketing for building relationships with proactive, interconnected consumers.[41]

The 4Ps and the exchange

The 4Ps[42] (see Figure 3.8) form the cornerstone of much commercial marketing, and although there is a growing amount of criticism that the framework is difficult to transfer from commercial to social marketing[43] (a debate considered in more detail in Chapter 2), it can provide a useful way for social marketers to emphasise that an intervention is multi-faceted and not solely about communication.

Product

In social marketing, the 'product' is not necessarily physical. It could be an intangible service or an idea, like 'exercising regularly'. It is generally agreed that social marketing products are not products involved in social change, like condoms, pills or oral rehydration powders, but refer to the desired behaviour instead.[44] It might be useful to think of the social marketing product in terms of having two parts; the core product and the tangible product. For example, in the case of smoking cessation, the core product is freedom from cigarette addiction, but what is actually being offered might be a new smoking cessation club, membership pack, supporting website and monthly social meetings.

The exchange

The way the social marketing offer is marketed should present a new behaviour to the target group which is appealing enough for them to exchange it for their problem behaviour. This exchange is based on the economic principle of commercial marketing[45] and underpins much social marketing thinking. As Beverly Schwartz explains, social marketing is '. . . a programme planning process which promotes voluntary behaviour change based on building beneficial exchange relationships with a target audience for the benefit of society'.[46]

Essentially, what should be exchanged in marketing is 'value', which emphasises the importance of recognising what is important to the consumer now, and appreciating that just because people *know* how dangerous a behaviour is, unless they receive something of value in the short term this knowledge may not translate into action. Smith calls this the 'Let's make a deal' principle.[47]

Promotion

Social marketing communications strategies are often designed to support, rather than form the cornerstone of, the intervention. Communication alone is unlikely to promote sustained behaviour change. However, it is likely to form an important part of any intervention.

It is important to identify how best to communicate with the target segments. Early scoping and research work should have identified what information sources they use and

Product
Price
Place
Promotion

Figure 3.8 The 4Ps

value, what information type they prefer (e.g. verbal, pictorial or aural), and also the most appropriate message platform (e.g. medium). If the target group are used to communicating via sms, Facebook and YouTube, this media preference should be considered for the intervention. If the target group regularly read and contribute to online blogs, these should be an integrated part of the communications mix. It is also important to consider, for written material, whether it is comprehensible by the intended target. There is evidence that a considerable amount of material is written at a level higher than that of the average person's reading ability.[48, 49]

People draw information from a range of sources, including the news and entertainment media. (It is important to recognise that values portrayed in the media can conflict with social marketing messages.[50, 51]) Social marketing programmes are not dependent on traditional mass media to carry their messages. PR, for example, can be very effective. Press publicity can generate promotion for the intervention seen by the target audience, but also by upstream stakeholders including funders and policy makers.

There is more and more blurring between entertainment and persuasion.[52, 53] This is particularly evident in electronic media forms such as **advergames**, internet-based games containing embedded advertising,[54, 55] and product placements which involve the use of a recognisable branded product in a film or television programme.[56] These 'hybrid' promotional forms are not without their critics as their impact is not understood.[57]

A further consideration for social marketers is the promotion of a message within the storyline of a television programme itself. An example of this is the way in which specific health issues are featured on popular television shows such as *ER*[58] and supported further by links to specific websites. One website, 'Following ER' is part of a multimedia initiative by the prestigious Johns Hopkins University. Ninety-second 'programmettes' began to be produced in the late 1990s to follow the screening of each episode, backed by a web page and an interactive telephone facility. The aim of this initiative was to harness the 'power of television to deliver preventive health information'.[59]

An extension of this concept is the placement of social marketing messages, such as those aimed at influencing adolescent alcohol-related behaviours, in television programmes, rather than as advertisements, in order to control the context in which the messages appear.[60] There has been some criticism of this type of strategy. While viewers may not consciously watch fictional programmes to learn about health information, cultivation theory suggests that health information presented in entertainment media could affect their ideas about health-related issues.[61] As the effects, positive or negative, have not been studied, there is a danger that overly cautious regulatory measures could prohibit the use of potentially positive communications. More on branding and implementing the campaign can be found in Chapter 10, and we will discuss the various message platforms available more extensively in Chapter 13.

Summary

In this chapter you have been introduced to the complex field of social marketing planning. Planning is often not a linear process, but rather an iterative one, with various simultaneous activities occurring, each feeding into one another. Planning is the key to social marketing success and requires considerable expertise and resources.

Most commercial marketing texts include sections on planning and many of the concepts are transferable to the social marketing field, although there are often important differences. The antecedents to behaviours of concern to social marketers are often more complex, automated and culturally significant or ingrained – such as smoking, unprotected sex, teen-age pregnancy, drug use and poor dietary choices. Even with the best-quality research there are likely to be factors which have not been considered. Therefore, considering at every stage the possible repercussions to the social marketing intervention is crucial. This involves contingency planning and different types of evaluation as well as ethical considerations, like whether the target audience should be those most in need of the intervention, or those most likely to change.

Systematic and careful planning in social marketing has many benefits, including un-covering the potential to work with stakeholders who are already trusted by the target audience and who have aligned goals with the social marketer. Planning stages can also identify potential commercial or public partners who can inject funding and expertise into the intervention to ensure its longevity.

In summary, planning can increase the likelihood of the project's success by gaining insight into the behavioural problem through primary and secondary research; establish-ing internal resource and skills weaknesses within the managing organisation which need to be overcome; identifying opportunities for goal alignment with other organisations and potential commercial partners; setting objectives and goals; planning the techniques most appropriate to reaching the behavioural goals and setting up processes for evaluating and monitoring the intervention for future learning.

CHAPTER REVIEW QUESTIONS

1 What environmental factors are likely to impact on social marketing interventions for:
   ● Increasing physical activity?
   ● Reducing binge drinking?
   ● Increasing sun protection behaviours?
   ● Promoting sexual health?
   ● Decreasing domestic violence?
   ● Improving recycling rates?
   ● Reducing passive smoking?

2 Conduct an audit of competitors whose activity may impact on the effectiveness of interventions for the areas listed above.

3 What strategies do you recommend should be used to minimise the effects of the competition you identified in Question 2 above?

4 Using the set of segmentation characteristics in this chapter, describe the characteristics of at least three segments that are immediately apparent in relation to interventions in the areas listed in Question 1.

5 Develop and justify SMART behavioural objectives targeting one segment from each of these interventions.

6 Discuss potential problems regarding co-ordination and control of external partners at national, regional and local levels for interventions in each of the areas listed in Question 1. How do you recommend these issues should be resolved?

7 Consider possible promotional decisions and considerations for the following target groups and problem behaviours:

- teenage smokers;
- middle-aged binge drinkers;
- parents of obese children.

8 Do you think the 4Ps are an appropriate model for use in social marketing? You may like to consult Chapter 2 to formulate your answer.

Recommended reading

Drucker, P. F. (1971) *Drucker on Management*. London: Management Publications.

Fine, S.H. (2009) *Marketing the Public Sector. Promoting the Causes of Public and NonProfit Agencies*. New Brunswick, NJ: Transaction Publishers.

French, J., Blair-Stevens, C., McVey, D. and Merritt, R. (2010) *Social Marketing and Public Health: Theory and Practice*. London: Oxford University Press.

Friedman, A.L. and Miles, S. (2006) *Stakeholders. Theory and Practice*. New York: Oxford University Press.

McDonald, M. (2008) *Malcolm McDonald on Marketing Planning: Understanding Marketing Plans and Strategy*. London: Kogan Page.

Notes

1 Hastings, G. (2007) *Social Marketing. Why Should The Devil Have All The Best Tunes?* Oxford: Elsevier.

2 Hillsdon, M., Cavill, N., Nanchahal, K., Diamond, A. and White, I.R. (2001) National-level Promotion of Physical Activity: Results from England's *ACTIVE* for LIFE campaign. *Journal of Epidemiology and Community Health,* 55, 755–61.

3 McDonald, M. (2007) *Marketing Plans: How to Prepare Them, How to Use Them*. Oxford: Butterworth-Heinemann.

4 McGee, J., Thoms, H. and Wilson, D. (2005) *Strategy: Analysis and Practice*. Maidenhead: McGraw-Hill.

5 Sargent, A. (2005) *Marketing Management for Nonprofit Organisations* (2nd edn). Oxford: Oxford University Press.

6 The Chartered Institute of Marketing (2003) *Marketing Planning*. Maidenhead: CIM Publishing, p. 16–17.

7 http://www.socialmarketing-toolbox.com/.

8 US Department of Health and Human Services/National Institute of Health/National Cancer Institute (2001) *Making Health Communications Programs Work*. Washington: US Department of Health and Human Services/National Institute of Health/National Cancer Institute, p. 16.

9 Health Canada (2005) *Social Marketing*. Accessed from http:www.hc-sc.gc.ca

10 Spotswood, F. and Tapp, A. (2010) Socio Cultural Change – the Key to Social Marketing Success? A Case Study of Increasing Exercise in Working Class Communities. *International Journal of Health Promotion and Education,* 49 (2), 52–7.

11 Van Wersch, A. and Walker, W. (2009) Binge-drinking in Britain as a Social and Cultural Phenomenon: the Development of a Grounded Theoretical Model. *Journal of Health Psychology,* 14 (1), 124–34.

12 Bradley, N. (2007) *Marketing Research. Tools and Techniques,* Oxford: Oxford University Press.

13 Plant, M. and Plant, M. (2006) *Binge Britain. Alcohol and the National Response*. Oxford: Oxford University Press.

14 National Social Marketing Centre http://thensmc.com/resources/showcase

15 Heather, N. (2006) Britain's Alcohol Problem and what the UK Government is (and is not) Doing about it. *Addicciones,* 18 (3), pp. 225–36.

16 Kotler, P. and Zaltman, G. (1971) Social Marketing: an Approach to Planned Social Change. *Journal of Marketing,* 35, 3–12.

17 Donovan, R. (2011) Social Marketing's Mythunderstandings. *Journal of Social Marketing,* 1 (1), 8–16.

18 Andreasen, A. (1995) *Marketing Social Change: Changing Behaviour to Promote Health, Social Development and the Environment.* San Francisco: Jossey-Bass Publications.

19 Drucker, P. (1954) *The Practice of Management.* New York: Harper & Row.

20 Tapp, A. (2005) *Principles of Direct and Database Marketing* (3rd edn). Harlow: Prentice Hall.

21 Spotswood, F. and Tapp, A. (2011) Rethinking how to tackle Binge Drinking Using Social Marketing: a Neo-tribal Analysis. *Social Marketing Quarterly,* 17 (2), 76–91.

22 Kemp, G. and Eagle, L.C. (2008) Shared Meanings or Missed Opportunities? The Implications of Functional Health Literacy for Social Marketing Interventions. *International Review on Public and Nonprofit Marketing,* 5 (2), 117–28.

23 Brassington, F. and Pettitt, S. (2006) *Principles of Marketing* (4th edn). Harlow: Prentice Hall.

24 Sargent, A. (2005) Op. cit.

25 McGee, J., Thoms, H. and Wilson, D. (2005) Op. cit.

26 Department of Health (2008) *Smokefree England – one year on.* London: Department of Health.

27 O'Dougherty, M., Harnack, L.J., French, S.A., Story, M., Oakes, J.M. and Jeffery, R.W. (2006) Nutrition Labelling and Value Size Pricing at Fast-food Restaurants: a Consumer Perspective. *American Journal of Health Promotion,* 20 (4), 247–50.

28 Jones, P., Christodolou, G. and Whibley, D. (2006) Transport: Are Policymakers and the Public on the Same Track? in Park, A., Curtice, J., Thomson, K., Bromley, C., Philips, M. and Johnson, M. (eds) (2006) *British Social Attitudes 2005–2006. The 22nd Report.* London: Sage, p. 135.

29 Luoto, R., Poikolainen, K. and Uutela, A. (1998) Unemployment, Sociodemographic Background and Consumption of Alcohol Before and During the Economic Recession of the 1990s in Finland. *International Journal of Epidemiology,* 27 (4), 623–9.

30 Spotswood, F. and Clarke, S. (2011) Lose the Fags: Reducing Smoking Prevalence in a Deprived Community in North West England, in French, J. Merritt, R. and Reynolds, L. (eds) *Social Marketing Casebook,* London: Sage Publications.

31 Lefebvre, C. (2009) Integrating Cell Phones and Mobile Technologies Into Public Health Practice: A Social Marketing Perspective. *Health Promotion Practice,* 10 (4), 490–4.

32 Courtesy of the National Social Marketing Centre for these images (http://thensmc.com/). Reproduced with permission.

33 Peattie, S. and Peattie, K. (2003) Ready to Fly Solo? Reducing Social Marketing's Dependence on Commercial Marketing Theory. *Marketing Theory,* 3/3, 365–85.

34 Donovan, R. (2011) Op. cit.

35 Zakocs, R.C. and Guckenburg, S. (2007) What Coalition Factors Foster Community Capacity? Lessons Learned From the Fighting Back Initiative. *Health Education and Behavior,* 34 (2), 354–75.

36 Lawrence, F. (2010) McDonald's and PepsiCo to Help Write UK Health Policy. *The Guardian,* 12 November, (available online: http://www.guardian.co.uk/politics/2010/nov/12/mcdonalds-pepsico-help-health-policy), last accessed 7 April 2011.

37 Valentin, E.K. (2001) SWOT Analysis From a Resource-Based View. *Journal of Marketing Theory and Practice* (Spring), 54–68.

38 Collins, K., Tapp, A. and Pressley, A. (2010) Social Marketing and Social Influences: Using Social Ecology as a Theoretical Framework. *Journal of Marketing Management,* 26 (13/14), 1181–200.

39 Rothschild, M., Mastin, B. and Miller, T.W. (2006) Reducing Alcohol-impaired Driving Crashes through the Use of Social Marketing. *Accident Analysis and Prevention,* 38 (6), 1218–30.

40 French, J., Blair-Stevens, C., McVey, D. and Merritt, R. (2010) *Social Marketing and Public Health: Theory and Practice.* Oxford: Oxford University Press.

41 Lefebvre, C. (2009) Op. cit.

42 Borden, N.H. (1964) The Concept of Marketing Mix. *Journal of Advertising Research,* 4 (June), 2–7.

43 For example: Peattie, S. and Peattie, K. Op. cit. and Wood, M. Applying Commercial Marketing Theory to Social Marketing: A Tale of 4Ps (and a B). *Social Marketing Quarterly,* 14 (1), 76–85.

44 Andreasen, A. (2002) Marketing Social Marketing in the Social Change Marketplace. *Journal of Public Policy and Marketing,* 21 (1), 3–13.

45 Bagozzi, R. (1975) Marketing and Exchange. *Journal of Marketing,* 39, October, 32–9.

46 Beverly Schwartz cited in Hastings, G. (2007) Op. cit.

47 Smith, W.A. (2006) Social Marketing: An Overview of Approach and Effects. *Injury Prevention,* 12, i38–i43.

48 Raynor, D. (1998) The Influence of Written Information on Patient Knowledge and Adherence to Treatment. In Myers, L. and Midence, K. (eds), *Adherence to Treatment in Medical Conditions*. Amsterdam: Harwood Publishers.

49 Sluijs, E., Kerssens, J., van der Zee, J. and Myers, L. (1998) Adherence to Physiotherapy. In Myers, L. and Midence, K. (eds) Op. cit.

50 Kline, K. (2006) A Decade of Research on Health Content in the Media: The Focus on Health Challenges and Sociocultural Context and Attendant Informational and Ideological Problems. *Journal of Health Communication,* 11 (1), 43–59.

51 Larsson, A., Oxman, A.D., Carling, C. and Herrin, J. (2003) Medical messages in the media – Barriers and solutions to improving medical journalism. *Health Expectations,* 6 (4), 323–31.

52 Grigorovici, D.M. and Constantin, C.D. (2004) Experiencing Interactive Advertising Beyond Rich Media. Impacts of Ad Type and Presence on Brand Effectiveness in 3D Gaming Immersive Virtual Environments. *Journal of Interactive Advertising,* 4 (3), 1–26.

53 Shrum, L.J. (ed.) (2004) *The Psychology of Entertainment Media*. Mahwah, NJ: Lawrence Erlbaum.

54 Arnold, C. (2004) Just Press Play. *Marketing News,* 38 (9), 1–15.

55 Kretchmer, S.B. (2004) Advertainment: The Evolution of Product Placement as a Mass Media Marketing Strategy. In Galician, M. (ed.), *Handbook of Product Placement in the Mass Media: New Strategies in Marketing Theory, Practice, Trends and Ethics*. Binghamton, NY: Haworth Press, pp. 37–54.

56 Karrh, J.A. (1998) Brand Placement: A Review. *Journal of Current Issues and Research in Advertising,* 209 (2), 31–49.

57 Auty, S. and Lewis, C. (2004) Exploring Children's Choice: The Reminder Effect of Product Placement. *Psychology & Marketing,* 21 (9), 697–713.

58 Brodie, M., Foehr, U., Rideout, V., Baer, N., Miller, C., Flournoy, R., et al. (2001) Communicating Health Information Through the Entertainment Media. *Health Affairs,* 20 (1), 192–9.

59 Fillmore, R. (1997) SPH Reaches Out to Educate Following ER. *Johns Hopkins Gazette*, 21 January. Retrieved 16 February, 2003, from http://www.jhu.ed/~gazette/janmar97

60 Goldberg, M.E. (1995) Social Marketing: Are We Fiddling While Rome Burns? *Journal of Consumer Psychology,* 4 (4), 347–70.

61 Brodie et al. (2001) Op. cit., p. 192.

Chapter 4

Upstream, policy and partnerships

Chapter objectives

On completing this chapter, you should be able to:

- critically evaluate external, environmental and policy factors that may act as facilitators of, or barriers to, social marketing interventions;
- critically evaluate the complexities of developing collaborative partnerships within communities;
- critically discuss the specific challenges faced when establishing public–private partnerships;
- critically evaluate the current and potential role of the alcohol industry in social marketing partnerships.

Note: In this chapter, we use the example of the alcohol industry to discuss a range of very contentious issues. Other industry sectors, for example pharmaceutical marketers and marketers of foods and beverages deemed to be of low nutritional value, also present challenges. As you read through the chapter material, think about the specific challenges different industry sectors present for policy makers and for those seeking to enter into social marketing partnerships with them.

Upstream factors

Upstream versus downstream

The terms 'upstream' and 'downstream' are frequently used, often uncritically, in public health and social marketing.[1] Upstream influences on behaviour change are external factors such as legislation, policy or environmental factors that may facilitate, or act as barriers to, desired behaviour change. An example would be a law to stop cigarettes being sold in a particular town. The inhabitants' behaviour would be influenced by the law as an upstream factor. Another example might be the road layout of a new housing estate, which is designed with lots of corners and narrow areas to force drivers to slow down. The drivers' behaviour is being influenced through external, upstream factors and not their own independent cognitive decision-making.

The terms originate in a fable, which is said to have been popularised by the medical sociologist John McKinlay.[2] The fable relates to people falling off a cliff into a river and needing to be rescued downstream. It is used metaphorically to separate prevention and treatment strategies. Upstream prevention in the fable relates to warning signs or fencing to stop people falling into the river in the first place. Downstream interventions would focus on fishing people out before they drown! With complex behavioural problems like obesity, do you think an upstream or a downstream focus is best? Or both?

Upstream social marketing: the role of social marketing?

The use of upstream interventions in social marketing has been hotly debated. The literature has always stressed social marketers' emphasis on voluntary behaviour change, avoiding the use of legislation or coercion to press people into changing their behaviour, or situations where the target audience are not fully aware of and in agreement with the offer being made. To remind us, Bill Smith defines social marketing as '. . . a large-scale programme planning process designed to *influence the voluntary behaviour* of a specific audience . . .' (our emphasis).[3]

Despite this original emphasis on downstream voluntary behaviour change, many social marketers do now advocate that *other* institutions (such as schools and governments) should use their coercive influence in some circumstances to maximise behaviour change. Kotler and Lee write:

> We also join the voices of many who are advocating for an expanded role for social marketing and social marketers, challenging professionals to take this technology 'upstream' and influence other factors that affect positive social change, including laws, enforcement, public policy, built environments, business practices, and the media. We agree the time has come.[4]

Later they argue that 'many believe this heavy reliance on individual voluntary behaviour change is outdated and have moved on to applying social marketing technologies to influence other change factors in the environment as well (e.g. laws, policies, media)'.[5] They propose social marketing upstream activities which could be as effective as downstream motivation or persuasion activities, using the example of HIV/AIDS:

- Advocate to influence pharmaceutical companies to make testing more rapid and accessible.
- Work with GPs to create protocols to ask patients if they have had unprotected sex and to encourage testing.
- Advocate to add relevant material to curriculums in school.
- Support needle exchange programmes.
- Provide media with trends and personal stories.
- Pitch stories to the producers of soap operas and sitcoms.
- Testify before government to increase funding in research, condom availability or free testing facilities.

This argument has been echoed by other key authors (Hastings and Haywood (1991), McDivitt (2003), Donovan and Henley) who have argued that, where possible, social marketers should concentrate on changing the conditions in which people take decisions, to make it easier for them to make the right lifestyle choices for themselves and their society.[6]

Focus on upstream: some examples

Behaviour change interventions focusing on upstream factors to achieve population-wide behaviour change might involve actions such as adding iodine to table salt to counter goitre,[7] fortification of bread with trace elements and minerals,[8] and fluoridation of water supplies to reduce dental decay.[9] More recently, **legislation** introduced to prohibit smoking in public places[10] has had a significant impact on the number of people ceasing to smoke, or showing symptoms of being harmed by exposure to second-hand smoke. Many of these interventions were contested vigorously prior to their introduction, but they have generally shown significant health benefits.

While these examples are relatively straightforward, upstream interventions in other areas, such as obesity, have been less successful. The North Karelia Project in Finland deployed significant resources into healthier diets and increased exercise programmes over a 20-year period. High levels of awareness and good levels of participation in better nutrition and exercise were achieved, together with **body mass index** (BMI) reductions amongst the most unhealthy sectors, but, critically, at a population level, average BMIs were almost unchanged.[11]

Social marketers have used upstream factors as part of their interventions in areas such as sun protection and exercise. For example, schools in Australasia take an active role in promoting sensible sun protection behaviours as part of Australasian programmes such as SunSmart (http://www.sunsmart.com.au/sun_protection).

Some social marketers argue that the relationship between social marketing and upstream interventions should be one of support. They argue that social marketing can best be used to encourage people to comply with legislation, such as a smoking ban, or to gain public support for interventions such as the fluoridisation of water. Smith cites numerous social marketing programmes designed to support our compliance with laws. These include 'Click it or Ticket' (to increase seat-belt use), 'Zero tolerance means zero chances' (to raise awareness of the no tolerance law) and 'Friends don't let friends drive drunk'.[12] Although these are mostly examples of social advertising, Smith suggests that one of social marketing's roles is as a 'viable companion to control and education approaches to behaviour change'.[13]

Need for policy clarity

Upstream policy changes can be extremely effective in changing our behaviour, and can often change our social norms – making it normal, for example, to use a seat belt or not to smoke in pubs. These social norms are powerful behavioural influences.

In other areas, the policies that have evolved to address specific areas appear somewhat questionable. For example, addressing the long-standing problem of excessive alcohol consumption has resulted in several recent policy documents, such as the *Alcohol Harm Reduction Strategy*[14] and *Safe. Sensible. Social. The Next Steps in the National Alcohol Strategy*,[15] which have been strongly criticised, as the way in which such policy evolves is not clear. One critic notes that the Academy of Medical Sciences reviewed the evidence regarding factors leading to excess alcohol consumption and associated harm using the same data and evidence as was available to the Prime Minister's Strategy Unit, yet the former recommended increasing price and limiting availability as the strategies most likely to reduce consumption, whereas the latter declared these strategies would have 'unwanted side effects'.[16] The specific challenges of partnerships with the alcohol industry are discussed later in this chapter.

The terminology used in policy documents may be confusing. In the area of physical activity, terms such as 'exercise' and 'sport' should be used with caution as they may turn people off physical activity,[17] which can include walking and cycling as opposed to gym workouts or competitive sports. There is also confusion as to how much/what type of exercise is 'enough'.[18] Some evidence suggests even low-intensity exercise is beneficial.[19] However, cultural factors may dictate what type of activity is culturally acceptable, possibly preferring 'appropriate' activities such as dance or exercise classes offered within the specific community rather than being open to wider participation or encouraging community members to participate in activities aimed at the wider population.[20] Policies need to be carefully researched, carefully worded and actionable.

Upstream barriers

Smith and others have emphasised the importance of changing the conditions in which people make decisions because upstream factors can provide considerable barriers to making healthy choices. For example, social, economic and environmental factors may present barriers to physical activity, even where individuals intend to participate more.[21] More deprived communities face the barriers of unsafe streets and run-down (or a lack of) facilities,[22] which make it harder for people to take part in physical activity. These communities may also have problems accessing facilities such as safe recreational spaces, especially if walking is the primary mode of transport.[23] However, while access to supportive physical environments is necessary, it is not of itself sufficient to achieve a sustained increase in physical activity.[24] There may also be a lack of 'accessible' role models for children within these communities[25] to encourage trial of possible forms of physical activity. Social marketers tackling physical activity will often address downstream factors as well as upstream ones to try to achieve population-level behaviour change.

Policy change: a complex arena

While walking and cycling are both recognised as providing low-cost ways of increasing physical activity,[26, 27] neither is unproblematic. Separation of pedestrians and cyclists from traffic has already received considerable attention; traffic danger is a major barrier to both walking and cycling, particularly among children.[28] However, there is a strong case for separating cyclists from pedestrians as 'a cycle with a 80kg person aboard, and travelling at the relatively fast speed needed to counteract the cycle's efficiency yet raise the heart rate, is in fact a missile'.[29]

Consider the practical impact of upstream factors in a particularly problematic area, i.e. impact of smoking on non-smokers. While the smoking legislation prohibits smoking in public places, it does not (yet) cover private homes or cars, etc. Passive smoking, i.e. non-smokers inhaling tobacco smoke, is known to be a significant health risk, especially for children, and is linked to respiratory tract infections such as bronchitis and pneumonia, ear infections and increased severity of asthma,[30, 31] as well as contributing to heart disease.[32]

Even if legislation were to be introduced to address the problem of smoking in private homes and cars, how could it be enforced? This is yet another area in which individual freedoms, the impact of individual actions on the health or well-being of others and the limitations of effective or acceptable legislation can result in an uneasy stalemate, and present significant challenges to social marketers seeking to address the problem. In this instance, social marketers must develop strategies to encourage smokers to recognise the negative impact of their smoking on others and to modify their behaviour accordingly. Is there another role that social marketing might play?

The positive impact of local as opposed to national policy is shown in Case study 4.1.

CASE STUDY 4.1

Students Today Achieving Results for Tomorrow (START)[33]

Background

Policy makers are one of the possible target audiences for social marketers when considering where their resource can have the most impact. In the case of stemming the increase in obesity and diet-related chronic diseases, policy proposals can include imposing taxes on fatty and energy-dense foods and making fresh, unprocessed vegetables and fruit more available in schools and workplaces.

Overview

As a response to policy changes, the START programme (Students Today Achieving Results for Tomorrow) aimed to increase the fruit and vegetable servings during its after-school snack period.

START is an after-school club programme supported by the city of Sacramento's Parks and Recreation Department and mainly targets African American, Hispanic and Asian children at risk of nutrition-related illness. Since 1995, START has served reimbursable afternoon snacks for at-risk youths as part of the US Department of Agriculture's Child and Adult Care Food programme. The department's Afterschool Snacks programme provides funding to after-school centres like START to purchase afternoon snacks for children who are from low-income families and requires the snacks to meet specific nutritional measures.

Intervention

In 2001, START adopted the Children's 5 a Day-Power Play! curriculum, which teaches children to eat at least five daily servings of fruit and vegetables. Power Play! aims to motivate and empower California's 9- to 11-year-old children to eat three to five cups of fruits and vegetables and get at least 60 minutes of physical activity every day. These objectives are designed to improve children's short-term health and reduce their long-term risk of chronic diseases, especially cancer, heart disease, and obesity.

The following year, they changed their snack vendor and implemented a policy that increased the servings of fruit and vegetables on after-school programme snack menus to be more consistent with five-a-day guidelines. The snack menu was changed in 44 after-school START programmes serving 8000 low-income and ethnically diverse primary schoolchildren in Sacramento, California.

Results and evaluation

For two years, the menu cycles at START were monitored and software used to estimate selected nutrient values. SPSS was used to test the differences between the pre-policy and post-policy menus.

Results showed that, compared with pre-policy snack menus, the new menu provided more than half of the recommended servings of fruit, whereas the previous menu had provided less than one-third. The increase in fruit consumption came from fresh and juiced fruit. Overall fruit servings increased by 83%, although there was no improvement to vegetable consumption.

Other changes included a reduction in saturated fat, reduction in calcium and less vitamin A. Previously, the menu had provided 10% of the daily allowance of vitamin A and calcium whereas the new menu only provided 2–3%. There were no improvements in vegetable consumption from the new policy.

Conclusion

The evaluation team conclude that policy change can be an effective means to enabling children to meet nutritional guidelines, particularly in school settings. However, the decrease in other nutrients, particularly calcium, is of concern, although most children already receive two daily servings of milk at school through breakfast and lunch programmes.

Partnerships[34]

Partnership principles and benefits

Partnerships play an important role in social marketing, because they offer opportunities to use existing connections and relationships to target hard-to-reach groups and often rely on the expertise of others with similar goals. Partnerships are diverse[35] but have in common the following: they are voluntary and collaborative relationships in which the partners work together to achieve an agreed goal, sharing 'risks, responsibilities, resources, competencies and benefits'[36] and creating value for both partners and recipients of the partners' activity.[37]

Different types of partnership may be effective in different conditions[38] and there may be very different levels of input from different partners,[39] ranging from equal input, to information sharing, and provision of resources such as people to distribute material or simply the facility to provide space to display posters. Partnerships may operate at international, national, regional or local levels, and are particularly important at local community level where unique local conditions and needs may limit the effectiveness of nationally generated initiatives.[40] However, the United Nations and World Health Organization also place partnerships at the heart of their strategies on a global basis.

As we have discussed in the previous chapter, there are many advantages in establishing successful partnerships. For public partners, these include access to skills, expertise and resources lacking in the public sector.[41] Private partners may obtain credibility, access to market intelligence and a way of associating the organisation with ethical business practice.[42] Community partners gain insight into the decision-making processes and influence in the development of interventions. A key benefit for all partners is synergy – where the partnership can accomplish more than individual partners could on their own.[43, 44]

Partnerships are particularly important in health-related areas where community-based perspectives have been found to be more effective than national programmes in addressing issues of improving access and quality of care.[45] A social marketing initiative to tackle smoking in the North West of England, for example, was managed through a partnership between the National Social Marketing Centre and Stockport PCT.[46] These partnerships receive frequent exposure in international public health forums[47] and cover areas as diverse as waste management and care for the aged.[48]

Box 4.1 Some examples of the diversity of successful partnerships

Multiple community collaborations combating drug and alcohol-related problems – USA

The Fighting Back Initiative funded 15 communities across 11 US states to combat drug and alcohol-related problems. Partners included schools, police, courts and correctional facilities, healthcare organisations, the alcohol industry (including retailers), workplaces, faith-based organisations and neighbourhood associations.

The inclusion of faith-based organisations was seen as particularly important for reaching cultural minority groups, but also to build on existing local networks to reach into affiliated communities and involve families in the programme.

Activities included education in schools and assistance programmes for students and employees, together with the hosting of recovery groups by a range of community-based organisations.[49, 50]

Healthy food choices and physical activity – USA

Involvement of employers in combating problems associated with obesity and lack of physical activity via provision of healthier food offerings, providing discounted membership of fitness clubs and supporting physical activity programmes, has been shown to both reduce healthcare costs and increase productivity. Such programmes are not likely to achieve major changes in targeted behaviours, but the study authors observe that increasing the average level of physical activity and healthy eating by only 5–10% is predicted to 'dramatically reduce future cases of diabetes, heart disease and many other chronic diseases'.[51]

Non-conventional partnerships – USA

Thinking beyond conventional approaches to community partnerships can also be successful. In the USA, the use of hair salons and beauty salons to help disseminate information regarding smoking cessation, breast cancer screening and other health-related topics has proved effective in reaching low-income women from ethnic minority groups, particularly those unwilling or unable to access advice and support through mainstream medical channels.[52, 53, 54]

The UK Department of Health/NHS stance on partnering

Partnerships, including those between public and private organisations, have been seen as central to UK government policy since the mid-1990s. The Department of Health released several major strategy documents that are predicated on the development of partnerships;

for example, in 2004 *Choosing Health: Making Healthy Choices Easier* was released, setting out a health change agenda.[55] This was followed by two 2006 documents *Our Health, Our Care, Our Say*[56] and *Health Challenge England*.[57] The Department of Health then issued a document *Partnerships for Better Health*[58] in 2007, linking to these previous documents and providing examples of existing partnerships.

The importance of partnerships to health policy is evidenced by referral to partnerships 70 times[59] in the Department of Health's 2007 *Partnerships for Better Health* report. In the 2004 *Alcohol Harm Reduction Strategy for England* policy document, the alcohol reduction strategy relies on creating partnership at both national and local levels between government, the drinks industry, health service and policy makers, and individuals and communities to tackle alcohol misuse.[60] The following quotes from the Department of Health's (2008) *Ambitions for Health* report illustrate both the centrality of partnerships with the private sector in achieving health-related policies, and also the unproblematic way in which potential partnerships are viewed:

> The Department of Health (or even the whole of government) cannot change people's behaviour without the support of individuals themselves, or active help from the commercial and third sectors.[61]

> By establishing meaningful partnerships, we will make it easier for private sector companies, social enterprises and charities to play their part.[62]

> . . . partners play an essential role in influencing and shaping people's behaviour. Action by individuals and by the government must be aligned with that led by communities, third sector organisations and business.[63]

> Working with the private sector can add real value, as it can provide access to resources, expertise and key target groups.[64]

Partnerships are currently very fashionable. However, Richter asks whether they are the 'policy innovation of the new millennium – or unavoidable necessity'.[65] We go on to debate how to develop successful partnerships in social marketing.

Stakeholders as partners: selection and representation issues

All **stakeholders** should be identified at the start of the process, though not all stakeholders should become partners. This depends on who has a right or desire to be involved, and who has the right to speak on behalf of others. Issues relating to public participation are particularly important as there is a risk of being responsive to more affluent, assertive and organised communities' **'squeaking wheels'** at the expense of less vocal groups who may need or benefit more from an intervention;[66] and of deciding how best to identify and engage with communities to determine their priorities and preferences, which may differ from 'outside' views of what activity may be needed.[67]

Partners must agree on who has the right to set priorities for a community, and the process by which issue and priority selection will be decided if the community is divided.[68] Also, partners must agree as to who has the right to assess risks to communities and individuals,[69] who decides on norms, standards or goals, what incentives or rewards might be necessary to attract or enable under-represented groups to participate in a partnership[70] and what action should be taken if a group disagrees or decides to opt out after development of a partner-based intervention has commenced.[71] The sustainability of activity if/when contributions by either partner cease should also be considered.[72]

If an intervention is not supported or perceived as legitimate, those who have been excluded from its development and planning may undermine it.[73]

Box 4.2 Alcohol moderation: multi-sector collaboration – an Australian example[74]

Operation Drinksafe focused on providing a brief intervention based on offering personalised risk assessment to patrons in bars and taverns in New South Wales. This was a collaboration between health services, police and the hospitality industry and was successful in reducing overall alcohol consumption and frequency of binge drinking among those patrons who participated.

Features of successful partnerships[75]

Partnerships can clearly be valuable, but there is no one formula for putting a successful partnership together[76] and not all partnerships are equally desirable.[77] They take time to develop[78] and can be difficult to manage. In this section we bring together the research so far on developing successful partnerships.

Reviews of successful partnerships have identified several areas that need to be considered before embarking upon a partnership. Where partners have compatible and agreed goals that support their own organisational mission statement, they are more likely to be able to work together.[79, 80, 81] Long-term benefits for all stakeholders ensure ongoing engagement,[82, 83] and relevant complementary expertise helps to achieve this.[84]

One potential area of disagreement is the ethical standard to which policy or interventions are developed, so agreed ethical codes are essential, particularly for areas where the moral questions are unclear, for instance the control of alcohol or sexual health.[85] At a policy-making level, it is essential that all partners have the public interest at heart, making a positive contribution to community.[86, 87] Lipthrott calls for partners to accept personal responsibility and accountability for minimising any negative effects and for positive actions, as agreed with other partners.[88] She calls for respect for differences in the community being served and among partners, and consideration of how behaviours, policies and procedures impact on different sections of the community. Participants must be able to feel their contribution is valued and that their input results in real rather than illusory power to make a positive difference to the communities they represent.[89] Above all, partners should act with integrity towards other partners and the communities that they serve.

Once the partnership is in place, mutual respect and sensitivity to other partners' requirements will help it run smoothly.[90] Transparent arrangements ensure equity and help build trust between partners,[91] while equitable contribution of expertise and resources supports a fair partnership.[92] Loza then recommends that these processes and their outcomes be monitored, perhaps by an independent third party, to be sure that the arrangement is a genuine partnership.[93]

Ideally, the outcomes of such partnerships will continue to be viable long after the partnership itself ceases, building independent capacity and capabilities among partners and the community to encourage self-reliance in the future.[94]

The 'Seven Cs of Strategic Collaboration' are a simple mnemonic summarising the characteristics of successful partnerships:

- clarity of purpose;
- congruence of mission, strategy and values;
- creation of value;
- connection with purpose and people;
- communication between partners;
- continual learning;
- commitment to the partnership.[95]

Use of contracts

Partners in collaboration will be motivated by self-interest – but while this must be recognised, self-interest cannot be at the expense of others. Negotiation will be needed to agree and align goals and objectives across partners and to agree on what kind of governance will be needed to make it work;[96] given the voluntary nature of partnerships and the limited control any partner is likely to have over other partners, formal contracts may be developed for large, complex partnerships. Partnerships that involve financial reimbursement for service delivery will also be subject to formal contracts.

Box 4.3 Mental health: formal management structure – UK

Hertfordshire County Council and its 'NHS partners' (including eight PCTs) established a range of partnership activities in 2001 focusing on the integration of mental health services. Given the complexity of the activity, a Joint Commissioning Partnership board was established, with the Hertfordshire Partnership NHS Trust co-ordinating information provision.[97]

Other partnerships may represent formal arrangements between some partners, but informal contributions by others, as shown in the following example:

Box 4.4 'Midlands city': night time violence – UK

Formal partnership members for initiatives to deliver national policy in a form likely to be effective at a community level included police, the city council, town centre management and organisations focusing on reducing domestic violence. However, while factors such as increased police patrols were a key ingredient, building good working relationships with licensees and retailers was also essential to the effective delivery of the initiatives.[98]

At a local community level, formal contracts are not necessarily needed or likely to be welcomed, such as where local retailers provide display space or local organisations distribute material to their members. Reliance on goodwill may be effective, but such arrangements present problems if promised support is not provided.

Where formal contracts do not exist, interpersonal trust may be needed to resolve conflict. However, negotiating changes with one partner to points previously agreed by all partners may be seen as favouritism,[99] therefore issues such as co-ordination, control and conflict resolution need to be determined before a partnership begins to operate.

If the goals of partners are incompatible and there is no prospect of this changing, or a potential partner feels that they are likely to be hijacked by the interests of other partners, then the partnership should not proceed.[100]

Co-creation

When partnerships exist between the community and the social marketer to co-develop the social marketing intervention, this is known as **co-creation**. Co-creation involves the joint development of interventions, including the social and economic benefits of behaviour change, and the management of relationships by organisations and their clients.[101, 102]

Co-creation is a principle which comes from the relationship marketing literature. Whereas 'transaction marketing' emphasised the selling of goods through transactions – or exchanges – with customers, service marketers and business-to-business marketers recognised there was great potential to be realised by building longer-term relationships with customers and other stakeholders.[103, 104] In turn, commentators built on this new paradigm to develop the principles of relationship marketing, which emphasise the importance of trust and commitment[105] and the co-creation of value with customers as a way of gaining sustainable competitive advantage[106] and also of meeting customer needs.[107]

Although social marketers have, in practice, been borrowing from the principles of community organisation and community development for some time,[108] the stakeholder-relationship based principles of co-creation have more recently been adopted as a core principle in the social marketing literature.[109] Interest in co-creation and the relational paradigm is growing; particularly because trust and commitment are so important when working with the challenging behaviours of hard-to-reach groups and because the relationship between social marketer and customer is so often a long-term one, centred on high-involvement, entrenched behaviours.[110]

Most significantly, co-creation is gaining momentum in the social marketing literature now that customers are generally not considered to be passive 'target audiences' at a disadvantage in terms of information asymmetry, but rather proactive consumers wanting to be a part of the interventions designed for them.[111] Co-creation has been proved to enhance the perceived quality and value of offerings[112] in social marketing and enables the development of innovative ideas and, where online groups are involved, rapid dissemination of knowledge.[113, 114] The increased use of social media will continue to contribute to the application of co-creation and relationship marketing principles in social marketing.[115]

VIGNETTE 4.1

Healthy Communities Collaborative: working with partners in the community[116]

The Healthy Communities Collaborative approach is a social marketing approach which harnesses the collaborative methods of community development to effect behaviour change on a community level. This community action approach uses local 'change' teams, led by lay community members and supported by professionals, to deliver messages about and support behaviour change.

A key facet of the approach is the training of community members, who are encouraged to become 'health champions' and then use professionals and agencies as a resource for improving the health of the whole community.

The HCC has used this approach to target numerous behavioural problems, including falls by older people, widening access to a healthy diet, early detection of cancer and identification of those at risk of cardiovascular disease. The Collaborative plans to use its approach in the future to combat obesity and misuse of alcohol and to promote cervical screening in women aged 25–35.

The work is fully evaluated and behavioural changes measured. The 'falls' interventions, for example, which included projects such as 'How's your ferrule, Beryl?' (checking the iron or rubber base of walking sticks) and 'Sloppy Slippers' (checking for worn and potentially dangerous slippers) achieved over a 30% reduction in falls handled by the ambulance service, in care homes and sheltered accommodation.

Questions to consider

1 *The 'fall' intervention has a much higher behaviour change (fall reduction) rate than most other interventions. Why do you believe this has occurred and what lessons can be learned from this?*

2 *What is the benefit of using community members as health champions?*

3 *How would you evaluate the specific contribution made by health champions to the intervention success?*

4 *What contribution would you expect health professionals to make to this type of intervention and how would you measure it?*

Partnership challenges

As Widdus acknowledges, 'partnerships should be regarded as social experiments: they show promise but are not a panacea'.[117] Many partnerships do not last beyond one year.[118] Reasons may include the inability of partners to resolve differences in aims, procedures or autonomy, or the time and other resources required to manage logistics and the time taken to achieve goals, leading to frustration and partner de-motivation.[119] At its worst, antagonism, suspicion or distrust may fatally weaken a partnership[120] or it may be undermined by powerful private sector interests/conflicts of interest.[121]

The list below summarises the main drawbacks and frustrations evident in the literature regarding partnership operations.[122] In reading these, you should consider how each of the factors should be dealt with in order to make a partnership succeed:

- diversion of time and resources from other activity;
- reduced independence in decision-making;
- conflict between an organisation's own and partnership work;
- negative exposure due to association with other partners or the partnership;

- frustration and aggression with the collaborative process, including different relationship procedures from 'normal' activity;

- insufficient credit for contributions to the partnership.

Partnerships may dissolve in frustration when one partner does not perform as agreed. We have noted earlier the voluntary nature of partnerships and the lack of direct management control over individual parties. A key factor in developing effective management and evaluation systems is to consider in advance contingency measures in the event of unexpected outcomes, partner non-performance or the issues of possible 'tarnish' of a partnership or individual partners' image if one partner transgresses or does not deliver, compromising the ability of the partnership to deliver on its promises.

Public–private partnerships (PPPs)

Why public–private partnerships?

Pressure on funding and other resources, coupled with increasing healthcare costs have led to the reluctant recognition of what has been termed 'public health's inconvenient truth':[123] the need to develop partnerships with both commercial and non-commercial organisations. While joint activities with non-commercial organisations such as charities have existed for a considerable time, the more recent notion of joining forces with commercial organisations in health-related activity (**public–private partnerships**) creates some tension. Ethical issues arise in all areas of partnerships, but are particularly evident in partnerships between private (commercial) and public (non-commercial) organisations (PPPs). Should the alcohol industry be involved with advising on licensing laws, for example? This raises the question of the specific challenges of public–private partnerships, which are now discussed in more detail.

The term 'public–private partnership' is currently receiving frequent exposure in international public health.[124] The nature and effectiveness of these arrangements have not been widely studied; although it is noted that such activity is 'much copied but poorly researched',[125] while others suggest that the term is misleading and a more accurate term is 'strategic alliance' rather than 'partnership'.[126] Vignette 4.2 provides an example of a high-level PPP for alcohol moderation.

VIGNETTE 4.2

Public–private partnership at policy level: the Responsibility Deal on Alcohol

In the UK, three 'Responsibility Deals' were announced by the Coalition government in March 2011, resulting from public–private partnerships with representatives of the alcohol, food and fitness industries, and expert individuals and organisations from the related fields of health, alcohol moderation, nutrition and physical activity. The members of the Responsibility Deal on Alcohol Network are listed below.

Members of Responsibility Deal on Alcohol Network

(chaired by Jeremy Beadles, Wine and Spirit Trade Association)

ASDA	Department of Health
Alcohol Concern*	Diageo GB
Alcohol Health Alliance	Faculty of Public Health
Bacardi Brown-Forman Brands	Heineken UK
British Association for the Study of the Liver*	Institute of Alcohol Studies*
British Beer and Pub Association	Molson Coors
British Liver Trust*	Morrisons PLC
British Medical Association*	National Clinical Director for Liver Disease
British Retail Consortium	National Heart Forum
Cancer Research UK	Portman Group
Cardiff University	Royal College of Physicians*
The Co-operative	University of Southampton

*Members who rejected the deal when details were released in March 2011.

The deal resulted in seven pledges for alcohol producers and distributors to sign up to on a voluntary basis, including a pledge to achieve alcohol unit content and health warning labelling on 80% of packaging by December 2013. Other pledges commit to raising awareness of unit content at point of distribution, developing a new sponsorship code for alcohol promotion, continuing schemes to challenge under-age drinking and maintaining funding for Drinkaware and other alcohol moderation schemes.

However the six expert bodies indicated above rejected the deal, calling for stricter guidelines, more measurable goals, sanctions for those corporations who failed to live up to their pledges and far more stringent interventions. These partners considered that this PPP was their only option to make their voices heard in policy making, but felt that the private partners had more power. This is a good case for debating the role of partnership.

Source: Based on http://webarchive.nationalarchives.gov.uk/+/www.dh.gov.uk/en/Publichealth/Publichealth responsibilitydeal/Networks/DH_123038

Questions to consider

1 *Do all partners have equal power in this partnership?*

2 *How compatible are the goals of the alcohol industry and independent health bodies?*

3 *Of the three 'Responsibility Deals', on alcohol, nutrition and physical activity, are some better suited to PPPs than others? Why?*

4 *What are the ethical implications of these partnerships?*

Public–private partnership acceptability debates

Interest in the nature of these partnerships is tempered by questions regarding when, if at all, such partnerships are necessary or desirable.[127] There is a need to separate out commercial versus community or not-for-profit partnership involvement, with the former being the most controversial. There is philosophical opposition to any involvement of the commercial sector in social marketing, as evidenced by at least one recent title: *Social Marketing: Why Should the Devil Have All the Best Tunes?*[128]

This stance runs counter to current policy. For example, the Department for International Development (DFID) cautiously endorses direct and indirect private-sector involvement in activity such as health promotion through a range of rules, suggesting that the involvement can have a significant positive impact on intervention effectiveness. However, they add a caveat that the specific nature of private-sector involvement must be clarified before an intervention is implemented.[129]

It is easier for commercial organisations to engage in partnerships or alliances that support popular and media-attractive causes, such as breast cancer which has attracted over 70 commercial organisations.[130] Such causes may receive favourable publicity and are not associated with any controversial behaviour, though commercial associations are likely to be focused on 'glamorous' aspects such as research rather than mundane practicalities such as patient transport. The rationale for an organisation becoming involved in other areas of activity may be radically different.

Recent policy documents treat public–private partnerships aimed at addressing health-related problems as relatively unproblematic. However, some of the challenges inherent in partnership activity are recognised, as the following quotes from the UK Department of Health's 2008 *Ambitions for Health* report indicate:

> there was also some unease about working with the private sector: stakeholders don't know how to approach companies or feel nervous about being seen to condone certain products (such as alcohol, food and tobacco).[131]

> Partners from different sectors are inevitably going to have different strengths and different (sometimes opposite) goals – this is frequently the case with private organisations and those from the third sector. The challenge is to find common ground, maximise organisational strengths and avoiding any potential areas of conflict.[132]

There are differing levels of acceptability or perceived conflict of interest inherent across different industry sectors. For example, there is likely to be less controversy over insurance companies promoting the changing of fire alarm batteries than a pharmaceutical company promoting immunisation.[133] Tobacco industry partnerships with any aspect of health appear to be universally deemed unacceptable.[134] Alcohol marketers' involvement in responsible drinking promotion, while not universally condemned, has proved controversial,[135] being compared by some to 'fraternising with the enemy'.[136] We now look at the specific problems with this sector.

The challenge of health-related partnerships with the alcohol industry

(Before you read this section, please reread the note at the beginning of the chapter.)

Industry responsibility and credibility

Excess alcohol consumption causes significant problems to individuals and society at large. However, the magnitude of the problem is disputed and appears to vary considerably across countries. For example, it is claimed that in the USA, 'of those who drink, close to 90% consume an amount consistent with or less than the recommendations outlined in the US Dietary Guidelines on moderate drinking'.[137] This is a marked contrast to UK figures that suggest only 50% of men and 70% of women do so.[138]

In order to be perceived as a credible partner in alcohol misuse reduction strategies, the alcohol industry must be seen to be behaving in an exemplary manner. This is somewhat problematic, given reports that almost 1 in 12 UK alcohol advertisements were found to be in breach of advertising guidelines during 2006.[139] Further, there is concern over the growing popularity of alcohol websites containing games and other material known to have high appeal to young people, coupled with evidence that, in the USA at least, under-age people do use these sites.[140] Applying the voluntary advertising code for alcohol to Australian websites identified several sites that would be in breach of the code if it applied to the internet.[141] The practicality of restricting access to websites is, of course, problematic as warning messages that stipulate sites are intended for those over a specific age are not an effective deterrent and, in fact, may increase the desirability of those sites among young people.[142]

Issues relating to the credibility of partnerships with the alcohol industry are not addressed in the Department of Health's alcohol-related policy document and partnerships with industry are seen as both important and unproblematic.[143] For example, under 'Working with the alcohol industry', the focus is on 'improving the labelling on alcohol containers',[144] presumably to include alcohol moderation warnings. Later in the same document, under 'Actions to reduce harm', the statement is made that 'The Government believes that encouraging stronger local partnerships and greater industry participation will help drive real reductions in crime and disorder related to alcohol misuse and change people's perceptions of antisocial behaviour.'[145]

There is no discussion of how these partnerships will be formed and managed – or how their effectiveness will be evaluated.

Alcohol industry contributions towards alcohol moderation – warning labels

Considerable scepticism is evident about industry's social responsibility initiatives such as the insertion of drinking moderation messages, given that they require no substantive amendment to overall marketing strategies.[146] The use of warning labels was specifically condoned by Gordon Brown, then British prime minister: 'I would particularly welcome the industry exploring and piloting the idea of an end frame containing Department of Health and Home Office messages for drinks brands' TV and cinema ads. This has the potential to demonstrate partnership working between industry and government.'[147] There is no evidence of this stance having been evidence-led, nor of any formal objectives having been set, nor of any mechanism by which the impact of this activity might be assessed.

However, government strategy regarding warning labels on alcohol containers has been criticised as an analysis of prior research studies indicates that these strategies have not shown evidence of effectiveness.[148] Critics suggest that this is a largely symbolic strategy, requiring minimal change in marketing activity in return for positive public relations value in claiming responsiveness to societal concerns,[149, 150] particularly given long-standing positive public opinion regarding 'responsible drinking' promotion.[151] At best, it is suggested that warning messages raise awareness but have minimal effect on behaviour change,[152] reflecting a perception that activity, so long as it does no harm, represents a benefit.[153]

More seriously, warnings on labels and via mass media may in fact be counter-productive, producing 'boomerang' effects, i.e. the opposite of what was intended.[154, 155] This is explained by the theory of psychological **reactance**, which was originally developed in the 1960s and proposes that direct or potential perceived threats to personal freedom, such as limiting consumption of specific products or engaging in particular behaviours, may be resisted as a means to regain control of that freedom.[156, 157] Further, people may then become motivated by the perceived threat itself, rather than the actual consequences of the threat, to assert their freedom and regain control of their own decision-making and thereby of their threatened freedom.

It is suggested that the government is wasting expenditure on alcohol moderation communications as their policies in areas such as increasing the number of outlets selling alcohol and lengthening opening hours directly counter any possible moderation effects. Further, options such as the use of price increase, either directly or via higher taxation, have not been used as a strategy to reduce alcohol consumption,[158] and alcohol is now 40% more affordable than in the mid-1990s and alcohol strength has increased.[159] The *Safe. Sensible. Social* report of 2007 proposes an independent review of the link between pricing, promotional activity and adverse effects of excess consumption and the question could be asked as to why this was never carried out.

We must remember that the impact of commercial advertising is just one of many communication-related factors impacting on alcohol consumption – or on any other health-related behaviour. Persuasive messages such as advertisements containing moderation messages do not appear in isolation, but are seen in the wider context of news and programme content. In terms of news coverage, a widespread problem relates to the way in which news media discuss health threats and medical treatments. In particular, confusing and contradictory messages are often apparent. For example, 'news values can conflict with science, media and public health agendas'[160] and the information presented by mass media outlets is criticised for its lack of accuracy and tendency to 'hype' reports.[161]

Summary

Upstream factors must be considered for all social marketing interventions, particularly when considering potential barriers to behaviour change such as environmental factors, or the impact legislation, regulation or specific policies may have on hindering or enabling positive behaviour change. This can be complex when national, regional and local policies and practices conflict with each other.

Increasingly, partnerships are being used to implement interventions. There may be a very wide range of types and functions and in the nature of the organisations involved. Partnerships between public organisations such as government-funded agencies and the private (commercial) sector are increasing and are central to many national policies. There are numerous benefits from involving private partners, such as skills, expertise and resources. However, there is also considerable unease at the involvement of some industry sectors, such as alcohol and food marketers whose products are deemed to have low nutritional value. Partnerships must be seen as legitimate by the communities they serve in terms of priorities and views on intervention strategy and implementation options.

The success of partnerships cannot be guaranteed and considerable effort is needed to ensure effective operation. Where this is achieved, benefits can be substantial. Considerable success has been achieved in partnerships with the community being served, where interventions are 'co-created', often with innovative solutions and rapid dissemination across community groups. These types of interventions are often very successful with groups who may be hard to reach by conventional means.

CHAPTER REVIEW QUESTIONS

1 How do you think policy makers can most effectively be approached to consider changing upstream factors that may be barriers to behaviour change?

2 Make a list of industry sectors and rank them from potential appropriate social marketing partners through to totally inappropriate. Justify your rankings.

3 Use the partnership analysis form on pages 184 and 185 and consider a potential partnership-based intervention for one of the following:
   ● road safety
   ● smoke alarms
   ● energy reduction
   ● sustainable transport
   ● sexual health.
   List potential partners and decide on their suitability and possible types of involvement.

4 What do you believe the principal benefits of co-creation of interventions are?

Recommended reading

Department of Health (2004) *Healthy Lives, Healthy People: Our Strategy for Public Health in England*. London: Department of Health http://www.dh.gov.uk/en/Publicationsandstatistics/Publications/PublicationsPolicyAndGuidance/DH_121941

Department of Health (2004) *Choosing Health: Making Healthy Choices Easier* (White Paper). London: Department of Health www.dh.gov.uk/en/Publicationsandstatistics/Publications/PublicationsPolicyAndGuidance/DH_40945

Department of Health (2007) *Partnerships for Better Health. Small Change, Big Difference: Healthier Choices for Life*. London: Department of Health http://www.dh.gov.uk/en/Publicationsandstatistics/Publications/PublicationsPolicyAndGuidance/DH_075758

Department of Health (2007) *Safe. Sensible. Social. The Next Steps in the National Alcohol Strategy*. London: Department of Health.

Notes

1 Dorfman, L. and Wallack, L. (2007) Moving Nutrition Upstream: The Case for Reframing Obesity. *Journal of Nutrition Education and Behavior, 39* (2, Supplement 1), S45–S50.

2 Lytle, L.A. and Fulkerson, J.A. (2002) Assessing the Dietary Environment: Examples from School-based Nutrition Interventions. *Public Health Nutrition,* 5 (6A), 893–99.

3 Smith, cited in Hastings, G. (2007) *Social Marketing: Why should the Devil Have all the Best Tunes?* Oxford: Elsevier/Butterworth Heinemann.

4 Kotler, P. and Lee, N. (2008) *Social Marketing. Influencing Behaviors for Good* (3rd edn). Thousand Oaks, CA: Sage, p. 3.

5 Ibid. p 10.

6 Hastings, G.B. and Haywood, A.J. (1991) Social Marketing and Communication in Health Promotion *Health Promotion International,* 6(2), 135–45. McDivitt, J. (2003) Is there a Role for Branding in Social Marketing? *Social Marketing Quarterly,* 9(3), 11–17 (ISM Conference Proceedings). Donovan, R. and Henley, N. (2003) *Social Marketing: Principles and Practice*. Melbourne: IP Communications.

7 Vitti, P., Delange, F., Pinchera, A., Zimmermann, M. and Dunn, J.T. (2003) Europe is Iodine Deficient. *The Lancet,* 361 (9364), 1226.

8 Reilly, C. (1996) Too Much of a Good Thing? The Problem of Trace Element Fortification of Foods. *Trends in Food Science & Technology,* 7 (4), 139–42.

9 McDonagh, M.S., Whiting, P.F., Wilson, P.M., Sutton, A.J., Chestnutt, I., Cooper, J., et al. (2000) Systematic review of water fluoridation. *British Medical Journal (BMJ) (Clinical Research Edition),* 321 (7265), 855–9.

10 Adshead, F. and Thorpe, A. (2008) Creating Europe-wide Health Policies: A Case Study. *Public Health,* 122 (8), 767–70.

11 Vartiainen, E., Puska, P., Jousilahti, P., Korhonen, H., Tuomilehto, J. and Nissinen, A. (1994) Twenty-Year Trends in Coronary Risk Factors in North Karelia and in Other Areas of Finland, *International Journal of Epidemiology,* 23 (3), 495–504.

12 Smith, W.A. (2006) Social Marketing: An Overview of Approach and Effects. *Injury Prevention,* 12 (Suppl. 1), i38–i43.

13 Ibid.

14 Prime Minister's Strategy Unit (2004) *Alcohol Harm Reduction Strategy for England.* London: Cabinet Office.

15 Department of Health (2007) *Safe. Sensible. Social. The Next Steps in the National Alcohol Strategy.* London: Department of Health.

16 Marmot, M.G. (2004) Evidence Based Policy or Policy Based Evidence. *British Medical Journal (BMJ),* 328 (7445), 906–7.

17 Berkovitz, K. (2000) A Critical Analysis of Canada's 'Active Living': Science or Politics? *Critical Public Health,* 10 (1), 19–39.

18 Morgan, O.W. (2004) Increasing Physical Activity: An Exercise in Evidence Based Practice? *clinmed,* ref. 2004060001.

19 Andersen, L.B. (2007) Physical Activity and Health. *British Medical Journal (BMJ),* 334 (7605), 1173.

20 McKeever, C. and Koroloff, N. (2004) Wellness Within Reach: Mind, Body and Soul: A No-cost Physical Activity Program for African Americans in Portland, Oregon, to Combat Cardiovascular Disease. *Ethnicity & Disease,* 14 (3 (Supplement)), 93–101.

21 Lawlor, D.A., Ness, A.R., Cope, A.M., Davis, A., Insall, P. and Riddoch, C. (2003) The Challenges of Evaluating Environmental Interventions to Increase Population Levels of Physical Activity: the Case of the UK National Cycle Network. *Journal of Epidemiology and Community Health,* 57 (2), 96–101.

22 Kumanyika, S. and Grier, S. (2006) Targeting Interventions for Ethnic Minority and Low-Income Populations. *The Future of Children,* 16 (1), 187–207.

23 Bostock, L. (2001) Pathways of Disadvantage? Walking as a Mode of Transport Among Low-income Mothers. *Health & Social Care in the Community,* 9 (1), 11–18.

24 Giles-Corti, B. and Donovan, R.J. (2002) The Relative Influence of Individual, Social and Physical Environment Determinants of Physical Activity. *Social Science & Medicine,* 54 (12), 1793–812.

25 Leslie, J., Yancy, A., McCarthy, W., Albert, S., Wert, C., Miles, O., et al. (1999) Development and Implementation of a School-Based Nutrition and Fitness Promotion Program for Ethnically Diverse Middle-School Girls. *Journal of the American Dietetic Association,* 99 (8), 967–70.

26 Ogilvie, D., Foster, C.E., Rothnie, H., Cavill, N., Hamilton, V., Fitzsimons, C.F., et al. (2007) Interventions to Promote Walking: Systematic Review. *British Medical Journal (BMJ),* 334 (7605), 1204.

27 Ogilvie, D., Egan, M., Hamilton, V. and Petticrew, M. (2004) Promoting Walking and Cycling as an Alternative to Using Cars: Systematic Review. *British Medical Journal (BMJ),* 329 (7469), 763.

28 Desapriya, E. (2007) We Need to Promote Safe Walking Habits in Our Communities [electronic version]. *British Medical Journal (BMJ),* 334, Rapid response to Oglivie et al. Retrieved 13 February 2008.

29 Colquitt, P. (2007) Incompatibility of Cycling and Walking [electronic version]. *British Medical Journal (BMJ),* 334, Rapid response to Ogilvie et al. Retrieved 13 February 2008.

30 Arborelius, E. and Bremberg, S. (2001) Child Health-centre-based Promotion of a Tobacco-free Environment – A Swedish Case Study. *Health Promotion International,* 16 (3), 245.

31 Tyc, V.L. and Throckmorton-Belzer, L. (2006) Smoking Rates and the State of Smoking Interventions for Children and Adolescents With Chronic Illness. *Pediatrics,* 118 (2), e471–87.

32 Barnoya, J., Bialous, S.A. and Glantz, S.A. (2005) Effective Interventions to Reduce Smoking-Induced Heart Disease Around the World: Time to Act. *Circulation,* 112 (4), 456–8.

33 Cassady, D. Vogt, R. Oto-Kent, D, Mosley, R. and Lincoln, R. (2006) The Power of Policy: A Case Study of Healthy Eating Among Children. *American Journal of Public Health* 96 (9) 1570–71.

34 The material in this section draws on L.C. Eagle (2009) *Health Partnerships: Guide to the Ethics of Local Partnerships for Health: Report Prepared for the Department of Health via Oxford Strategic Marketing.* Project Report, London: Department of Health/Oxford Strategic Marketing.

35 Barr, D.A. (2007) A Research Protocol to Evaluate the Effectiveness of Public–Private Partnerships as a Means to Improve Health and Welfare Systems Worldwide. *American Journal of Public Health*, 97 (1), 19–25.

36 Richter, J. (2004) *Public–Private Partnershops and Health for All.* Helsinki: Ministry for Foreign Affairs of Finland, Development Policy Information Unit, p. 3.

37 Porter, M.E. and Kramer, M.R. (1999) Philanthropy's New Agenda: Creating Value. *Harvard Business Review,* 77 (6), 121–30.

38 Plamping, D., Gordon, P. and Pratt, J. (2000) Modernising the NHS: Practical Partnerships for Health and Local Authorities. *British Medical Journal (BMJ)*, 320 (7251), 1723–5.

39 Lasker, R.D., Weiss, E.S. and Miller, R. (2001) Partnership Synergy: A Practical Framework for Studying and Strengthening the Collaborative Advantage. *The Milbank Quarterly,* 79 (2), 179–205.

40 Lasker, R.D. and Weiss, E.S. (2003) Creating Partnership Synergy: The Critical Role of Community Stakeholders. *Journal of Health & Human Services Administration,* 26 (1), 119–39.

41 Widdus, R. (2001) Public–Private Partnerships for Health: Their Main Targets. Their Diversity, and Their Future Directions. *Bulletin of the World Health Organization,* 79 (8), 1–11.

42 Thomas, J. (2008) Happily Ever After . . .? Partnerships in Social Marketing. *Social Marketing Quarterly,* 14 (1), 72–5.

43 Lasker, R.D. and Weiss, E.S. (2003) Op. cit.

44 Weiss, E.S., Anderson, R.M. and Lasker, R.D. (2002) Making the Most of Collaboration: Exploring the Relationship Between Partnership Synergy and Partnership Functioning. *Health Education & Behavior,* 29 (6), 683–98.

45 Hasnain-Wynia, R. (2003) Overview of the Community Care Network Demonstration Program and Its Evaluation. *Medical Research Review,* 60 (4_suppl), 5S–16.

46 Spotswood, F. (2011) Lose the Fags: Community Social Marketing. In French, J., Reynolds, L. and Merritt, R. (eds) (2011) *Social Marketing Casebook.* London: Sage.

47 For an example, see Ridley, R.G. (2001) Putting the Partnership into Public–Private Partnerships. *Bulletin of the World Health Organization,* 79 (8), 694.

48 Jones, R. and Noble, G. (2008) Managing the Implementation of Public–Private Partnerships. *Public Money & Management,* 28 (2), 109–14.

49 Zakocs, R.C. and Guckenburg, S. (2007) What Coalition Factors Foster Community Capacity? Lessons Learned From the Fighting Back Initiative. *Health Education & Behavior,* 34 (2), 354–75.

50 Stevenson, J.E. and Mitchell, R.E. (2003) Community-Level Collaboration for Substance Abuse Prevention. *Journal of Primary Prevention,* 23 (3), 371.

51 Simon, P.A. and Fielding, J.E. (2006) Public Health and Business: A Partnership that Makes Cents. *Health Affairs,* 25 (4), 1029–39.

52 Wilson, T.E., Fraser-White, M., Feldman, J., Homel, P., Wright, S., King, G., et al. (2008) Hair Salon Stylists as Breast Cancer Prevention Lay Health Advisors for African-American and Afro-Caribbean Women. *Journal of Health Care for the Poor and Underserved,* 19 (1), 216–26.

53 Linnan, L.A. and Ferguson, Y.O. (2007) Beauty Salons: A Promising Health Promotion Setting for Reaching and Promoting Health Among African American Women. *Health Education & Behavior,* 34 (3), 517–30.

54 Linnan, L.A., Emmons, K.M. and Abrams, D.B. (2002) Beauty and the Beast: Results of the Rhode Island Smokefree Shop Initiative. *American Journal of Public Health,* 92 (1), 27–8.

55 Department of Health (2004) *Choosing Health: Making Healthy Choices Easier* (White Paper). London: Department of Health www.dh.gov.uk/en/Publicationsandstatistics/Publications/Publications PolicyAndGuidance/DH_40945

56 Department of Health (2006) *Our Health, our Care, our Say: a New Direction for Community Services.* London: Department of Health http://www.dh.gov.uk/en/Publicationsandstatistics/Publications/ PublicationsPolicyAndGuidance/DH_4122399

57 Department of Health (2006) *Health Challenge England – Next Steps for Choosing Health*. London: Department of Health http://www.dh.gov.uk/en/Publicationsandstatistics/Publications/Publications PolicyAndGuidance/DH_4139514

58 Department of Health (2007) *Partnerships for Better Health. Small Change, Big Difference: Healthier Choices for Life*. London: Department of Health http://www.dh.gov.uk/en/Publicationsandstatistics/ Publications/PublicationsPolicyAndGuidance/DH_075758

59 Mastache, C., Mistral, W., Velleman, R. and Templeton, L. (2008) Partnership Working in Community Alcohol Prevention Programmes. *Drugs: Education, Prevention & Policy,* 15, 4–14.

60 Prime Minister's Strategy Unit (2004) *Alcohol Harm Reduction Strategy for England*. London: Cabinet Office.

61 Department of Health (2008) *Ambitions for Health: A Strategic Framework for Maximising the Potential of Social Marketing and Health-related Behaviour* (No. 288118). London: Department of Health, p. 6. http://www.dh.gov.uk/en/Publicationsandstatistics/Publications/PublicationsPolicyAndGuidance/ DH_090348

62 Ibid. p. 10.

63 Ibid. p. 45.

64 Ibid. p. 48.

65 Richter, J. (2004) Public–private Partnerships for Health: A Trend with no Alternatives? *Development,* 47: 45

66 Thacher, D. (2001) Equity and Community Policing: A New View of Community Partnerships. *Criminal Justice Ethics,* 20 (Winter/ Spring), 3–16.

67 Lavery, J.V., Upshur, R.E.G., Sharp, R.R. and Hofman, K.J. (2003) Ethical Issues in International Environmental Health Research. *International Journal of Hygiene and Environmental Health,* 206 (4–5), 453–63.

68 Minkler, M., Fadem, P., Perry, M., Blum, K., Moore, L. and Rogers, J. (2002) Ethical Dilemmas in Participatory Action Research: A Case Study from the Disability Community. *Health Education & Behavior,* 29 (1), 14–29.

69 Minkler, M. (2004) Ethical Challenges for the 'Outside' Researcher in Community-Based Participatory Research. *Health Education & Behavior,* 31 (6), 684–97.

70 Himmelman, A.T. (1996) On the Theory and Practice of Transformational Collaboration, in Huxham, C. (ed.) *Creating Collaborative Advantage*. London: Sage Publications, pp. 19–43.

71 Roberts, M.J. and Reich, M.R. (2002) Ethical Analysis in Public Health. *The Lancet,* 359 (23 March), 1055–9.

72 Agha, S., Do, M. and Armand, F.O. (2006) When Donor Support Ends: The Fate of Social Marketing Products and the Markets They Help Create. *Social Marketing Quarterly,* 12 (2), 28–42.

73 Gray, B. (1996) Cross-sectorial Partners: Collaborative Alliances, in Huxham, C. (ed.) *Creating Collaborative Advantage*. London: Sage Publications.

74 Van Beurden, E., Reilly, D., Dight, R., Mitchell, E. and Beard, J. (2000) Alcohol brief intervention in bars and taverns: a 12-month follow-up study of Operation Drinksafe in Australia. *Health Promotion International,* 15 (4), 293–302.

75 Eagle, L.C. (2009) Op. cit.

76 Widdus, R. (2001) Op. cit.

77 Roberts, M.J., Breitenstein, A.G. and Roberts, C.S. (2002) The Ethics of Public–Private Partnerships, in Reich, M.R. (ed.). *Public–Private Partnerships for Public Health*. Cambridge, MA: Harvard Center for Population and Development Studies, pp. 67–86.

78 Barr, C. and Huxham, C. (1996) Involving the Community: Collaboration for Community Development, in Huxham, C. (ed.). *Creating Collaborative Advantage*. London: Sage Publications, pp. 126–40.

79 Lucas, A.O. (2002) Public–Private Partnerships: Illustrative Examples, in Reich, M.R. *Public–Private Partnerships for Public Health*. Cambridge, MA: Harvard Center for Population and Development Studies, pp. 19–40.

80 Loza, J. (2004) Business–Community Partnerships: The Case for Community Organization Capacity Building. *Journal of Business Ethics,* 53 (3), 297–311.

81 Ibid.

82 Ridley, R.G. (2001) Op. cit.

83 Widdus, R. (2001) Op. cit.

84 Ridley, R.G. (2001) Op. cit.

85 Widdus, R. (2001) Op. cit.

86 Lucas, A.O. (2002) Op. cit.

87 Loza, J. (2004) Op. cit.

88 Lipthrott, D.J. (2005) What IS Relationship? What is Ethical Partnership? *Ethical Health Partnerships*. Accessed 12 June 2009 from http://www.ethicalhealthpartnerships.org

89 Francisco, V.T. and Butterfoss, F.D. (2007) Social Validation of Goals, Procedures, and Effects in Public Health. *Health Promotion Practice,* 8 (2), 128–33.

90 Lucas, A.O. (2002) Op. cit.

91 Widdus, R. (2001) Op. cit.

92 Ibid.

93 Loza, J. (2004) Op. cit.

94 Ibid.

95 Austin, J. (2000) *The Collaboration Challenge: How Nonprofits and Businesses Succeed Through Strategic Alliances*. San Francisco: Jossey-Bass Publishers. Cited in Reich, M.R. (2002) *Public–Private Partnerships for Public Health*. Cambridge, MA: Harvard Center for Population and Development Studies, p. 10.

96 Buse, K. and Watt, G. (2002) The World Health Organization and Global Public–Private Partnerships: In Search of Good Global Governance, in Reich, M.R. (ed.). *Public–Private Partnerships for Public Health*. Cambridge, MA: Harvard Center for Population and Development Studies, pp. 67–86.

97 Freeman, T. and Peck, E. (2006) Evaluating partnerships: a case study of integrated specialist mental health services. *Health & Social Care in the Community,* 14 (5), 408–417.

98 Burrell, A. and Erol, R. (2009) Tackling violence in the night-time economy on the ground: Putting policy into practice in England and Wales. *Crime Prevention and Community Safety: An International Journal,* 11 (3), 189–203.

99 Weiner, B.J., Alexander, J.A. (1998) The Challenges of Governing Public–Private Partnerships. *Health Care Management Review,* 23 (2), 39–55.

100 Buse, K. and Watt, G. (2002) Op. cit.

101 Domegan, C.T. (2008) Social Marketing: Implications for Contemporary Marketing Practices Classification Scheme. *Journal of Business & Industrial Marketing,* 23 (2), 135–41.

102 Desai, D. (2009) Role of Relationship Management and Value Co-Creation in Social Marketing. *Social Marketing Quarterly,* 15 (4), 112–25.

103 Gummesson, E. (1994) Making Relationship Marketing Operational. *International Journal of Service Management,* 5 (5), 5–20.

104 Grönroos, C. (1994) From Marketing Mix to Relationship Marketing: Towards a Paradigm Shift in Marketing. *Management Decision,* 32 (2), 4–20.

105 Morgan, R.M. and Hunt, S.D (1994) The Commitment-Trust Theory of Relationship Marketing. *Journal of Marketing*: 58 (3), 20–38.

106 Prahalad, C.K. and Ramaswamy, V. (2004) *The Future of Competition: Co-creating Unique Value with Customers*. Cambridge, MA: Harvard Business School Press.

107 Ibid.

108 Glanz, K., Rimer, B.K. and Lewris, F.M. (2002) *Health Behavior and Health Education* (3rd edn). San Francisco: Jossey Bass. Minkler, M., Wallerstein N. and Wilson, N. (2008) Improving Health through Community Organization and Community Building, in Glanz, K., Rimes, B.K. and Viswanath, K.V., *Health Behavior and Health Education: Theory, Resource and Practice* (4th edn). San Francisco: Jossey Bass, pp. 287–312. Minkler, M. and Wallerstein, N.B. (2005) Improving Health through Community Orgnization and Community Building, in Minkler, M. (ed.) *Community Organizing and Community Building For Health*. New Brunswick, NJ: Rutgers University Press.

109 Lefebvre, R.C. (2011) An Integrative Model for Social Marketing. Journal of Social Marketing. 1 (1), 54–72.

110 Hastings, G. (2003) Relational Paradigms in Social Marketing. *Journal of Macromarketing,* 23 (1), 6–15.

111 Lefebvre, C. R. (2006) Partnerships for Social Marketing Programs: An Example from the National Bone Health Campaign. *Social Marketing Quarterly,* 12 (1), 41–54.

112 Ouschan, R., Sweeney, J.C. and Johnson, L. (2006) Customer Empowerment and Relationship Outcomes in Healthcare Consultations. *European Journal of Marketing,* 40 (9/10), 1068–86.

113 Nambisan, P. and Nambisan, S. (2009) Models of Consumer Value Cocreation in Health Care. *Health Care Management Review,* 34 (4), 344–54.

114 Brainard, L.A. (2003) Citizen Organizing in Cyberspace. *American Review of Public Administration,* 33 (4), 384–406.

115 Lefebvre, C.R. (2006) Op. cit.

116 Curry, N. (2006) *Preventive Social Care. Is it Cost Effective?* London: King's Fund www.kingsfund.org .uk/document.rm?id=8285

117 Widdus, R. (2001) Op. cit., 713.

118 Lasker, R.D. and Weiss, E.S. (2003) Op. cit.

119 Gray, B. (1996) Op. cit.

120 Reich, M.R. (2002) *Public–Private Partnerships for Public Health.* Cambridge, MA: Harvard Center for Population and Development Studies, pp. 1–18.

121 Buse, K. and Watt, G. (2002) Op. cit.

122 Lasker, R.D., Weiss, E.S. and Miller, R. (2001) Op. cit.

123 Majestic, E. (2009) Public Health's Inconvenient Truth: The Need to Create Partnerships with the Business Sector. *Preventing Chronic Disease,* 6 (2), A1.

124 Ridley, R.G. (2001) Op. cit.

125 Lefebvre, C.R. (2006) Op. cit., 41–54.

126 Sowers, W., Doner, L., Smith, W.A., Rothschild, M. and Morse, D. (2005) Synthesis Panel Presentation on Stretching the Limits of Partnerships, Upstream and Downstream. *Social Marketing Quarterly,* 11 (3/4), 61–6.

127 Ridley, R.G. (2001) A Role for Public–Private Partnerships in Controlling Neglected Diseases? *Bulletin of the World Health Organization,* 79 (8), 771.

128 Hastings, G. (2007) Op. cit.

129 Meadley, J., Pollard, R. and Wheeler, M. (2003) *Review of DFID Approach to Social Marketing.* London: Department for International Development: Health Systems Resource Centre.

130 Andreasen, A.R. and Drumwright, M.E. (2001) Alliances and Ethics in Social Marketing, in Andreasen, A.R. (ed.) (2001) *Ethics in Social Marketing.* Washington, DC: Georgetown University Press.

131 Department of Health (2008) Op. cit., p. 48.

132 Ibid., p. 51.

133 Kotler, P., Roberto, N. and Lee, N. (2002) *Social Marketing. Improving the Quality of Life.* Thousand Oaks, CA: Sage Publications.

134 Thomas, J. (2008) Happily Ever After . . .? Partnerships in Social Marketing. *Social Marketing Quarterly,* 14 (1), 72–5.

135 Bhattacharya, C.B. and Elsbach, K.D. (2002) Us Versus Them: The Roles of Organizational Identification and Disidentification in Social Marketing Initiatives. *Journal of Public Policy & Marketing,* 21 (1), 26–36.

136 Thomas, J. (2008) Op. cit., 72.

137 Ringold, D.J. (2002) Boomerang Effect: In Response to Public Health Interventions: Some Unintended Consequences in the Alcoholic Beverage Market. *Journal of Consumer Policy,* 25 (1), 27.

138 Alcohol Issues (2008) The U.K.'s Relationship with Alcohol. Accessed 15 September, http://www .alcoholissues.co.uk/uk-s-relationship-with-alcohol.html

139 Marketing Week (2007) One in 12 UK Alcohol Ads 'Non compliant' with EFRD Guidelines. *Marketing Week (01419285),* 30 (15), 4–4.

140 Centre on Alcohol Marketing & Youth (CAMY) (2004) *Clicking with Kids: Alcohol Marketing and Youth on the Internet.* Baltimore: Johns Hopkins University.

141 Carroll, T.E. and Donovan, R.A. (2002) Alcohol Marketing on the Internet: New Challenges for Harm Reduction. *Drug and Alcohol Review,* 21 (1), 83–91.

142 Ibid.

143 Department of Health (2007) *Safe. Sensible. Social.*

144 Ibid., p. 43.

145 Ibid., p. 49.

146 Baggott, R. (2008) *Alcohol and the Drinks Industry: A Partnership for Prevention?* London: Joseph Rowntree Foundation.

147 Campaign (2008) The Week: Advertising news – Brown Backs Ad Endframes. *PR Week,* 14 March, 5.

148 Barbor, T.F. (2004) Admirable Ends, Ineffective Means: Comments on the Alcohol Harm Reduction Strategy for England. *Drugs: Education, Prevention and Policy,* 11 (5), 361–5.

149 Wolburg, J.M. (2005) How Responsible are 'Responsible' Drinking Campaigns for Preventing Alcohol Abuse? *Journal of Consumer Marketing,* 22 (4), 176–7.

150 Ringold, D.J. (2002) Op. cit.

151 See, for example, Thamos, J. (2008) Op. cit.

152 Jamoulle, S. (2006) Do Health Warnings Prevent Alcohol Abuse? *Finweek*, 24 August, 60.

153 Greenfield, T.K., Graves, K.L. and Kaskutas, L.A. (1999) Long-Term Effects of Alcohol Warning Labels: Findings from a Comparison of the United States and Ontario, Canada. *Psychology & Marketing,* 16 (3), 261–82.

154 Stewart, D.W. and Martin, I.M. (1994) Intended and Unintended Consequences of Warning Messages: A Review and Synthesis of Empirical Research. *Journal of Public Policy & Marketing,* 13 (1), 1–19.

155 Ringold, D.J. (2002) Op. cit.

156 Bushman, B.J. (1998) Effects of Warning and Information Labels on Consumption of Full-Fat, Reduced-Fat, and No-Fat Products. *Journal of Applied Psychology,* 83 (1), 97–101.

157 Rummel, A., Howard, J., Swinton, J.M. and Seymour, D.B. (2000) You Can't Have That! A Study of Reactance Effects and Children's Consumer Behavior. *Journal of Marketing Theory and Practice,* 8 (1), 38–44.

158 Wall, A.P. (2007) Government 'Demarketing' as Viewed by its Target Audience. *Marketing Intelligence & Planning,* 25 (2), 123–35.

159 Anderson, P. (2007) A Safe, Sensible and Social AHRSE: New Labour and Alcohol Policy. *Addiction,* 102 (10), 1515–21.

160 Kline, K. (2006) A Decade of Research on Health Content in the Media: The Focus on Health Challenges and Sociocultural Context and Attendant Informational and Ideological Problems. *Journal of Health Communication,* 11 (1), 50.

161 Larsson, A., Oxman, A.D., Carling, C. and Herrin, J. (2003) Medical Messages in the Media – Barriers and Solutions to Improving Medical Journalism. *Health Expectations,* 6 (4), 323–31.

Chapter 5

Ethical issues in social marketing

Chapter objectives

On completing this chapter, you should be able to:

- compare, contrast and critically evaluate the strengths and weaknesses of the main ethical frameworks discussed in the business literature;
- critically evaluate the relevance of each of these frameworks to social marketing activity;
- evaluate ethical dilemmas that may occur in social marketing activity, drawing on these frameworks, and make reasoned recommendations as to how these dilemmas may be resolved;
- critically evaluate the role of codes of ethics in ensuring ethical behaviour from all participants in social marketing interventions and make reasoned recommendations as to how codes might be successfully implemented among social marketing practitioners.

Ethics defined

Ethics is a term which is debated vigorously within academic literature, with multiple definitions evident, depending on the perspective of the discipline within which the debate is occurring.

For example, within philosophy, the focus may be on moral choices – i.e. choices regarding what is right or just behaviour, as opposed to simply remaining within the provisions of the law – that a person may be faced with, and the nature of morals themselves. Within specific professions such as medicine or accountancy, the debate may be more focused on the rules or standards governing the conduct of members of that profession.

In terms of ethical choices that may be encountered in everyday life, the following quotation may help to illustrate the nature of the issues covered by ethical decision-making:

> Typically defined as the study of standards of conduct and moral judgement, [ethics] is particularly useful to us when it helps us to resolve conflicting standards or moral judgements.

It is not as simple as deciding what is right and what is wrong. The toughest ethical dilemmas arise when two seemingly right principles are in conflict.[1]

As with social marketing itself, there is no common agreement regarding a definition of ethics as it applies in the business/marketing context, although many definitions are similar to each other, as shown below:

Business ethics comprises moral principles and standards that guide behaviour in the world of business.[2]

Ethics is about norms and values of a certain seriousness, about standards and ideals, i.e., ones that people cannot easily neglect without harming others, or without being looked at disdainfully by significant others.[3]

Ethics should be viewed within the wider context of formal government structures. Every community has its own system of laws enacted by a central parliament. Member states of the European Union are also subject to endeavours to harmonise legislation and regulation across all members.[4] Beneath, and subordinate to, broad legislation is a series of regulations. These generally apply to a specific business sector or occupational category such as medicine. In the context of marketing, marketing communication is, in many countries, self-regulating.[5, 6]

The various marketing communication industry sectors, including advertisers, advertising agencies and the media, have co-operated in drawing up codes of practice. In the UK, this operates via the Committee of Advertising Practice. A major regulatory body, such as the Office of Communication (OFCOM) in the UK, oversees the processes by which advertising conforms to both the letter and the spirit of the relevant codes. Supporting this structure, joint industry bodies (in the UK, the Advertising Standards Authority) may exist to maintain and administer the codes and ensure consistent advertising standards across media. Additionally, they may provide an advisory service, interpreting relevant statutes and industry codes and applying them to scripts of proposed ads and vetting completed ads prior to their first screening. For an example of current codes, see http://www.asa.org.uk/asa/codes/.

These regulations do not explicitly state precise ethical principles. They provide only general guidelines regarding activity, such as decency, and circumstances under which fear and distress might be considered acceptable, yet the 'fishhook' ruling feature in Chapter 1 suggests that a de facto framework exists. This issue is discussed in more detail later in this chapter; however, the generation of fear is by no means the only dilemma facing social marketers, as the following section demonstrates.

Ethical dilemmas within social marketing

There is some evidence to suggest that some misgivings regarding the ethics of social marketing stem from a wider distrust of commercial marketing, particularly marketing communication/advertising.[7] The main criticisms of marketing communication overall include allegations that it is inherently untruthful, deceptive, unfair, manipulative, offensive and in bad taste. Other assertions relate to the creation and perpetuation of stereotypes, causing people to buy things they do not really need and playing on people's fears and insecurities.[8]

Doubts as to the ethicality of social marketing in particular mirror many of these concerns. For example, while concerns have been identified about the appropriateness of tactics used for social marketing and the use of fear appeals, issues have been identified relating to how competing wants might be judged and what information is reasonable to seek from people in order to develop social marketing campaigns.[9]

A surprisingly wide range of potential unintended effects of health communication campaigns have been reported in the academic literature; these have been summarised in Table 5.1.[10]

VIGNETTE 5.1

Give It Up For Baby: bribery or exchange?

Give It Up For Baby is a smoking cessation scheme, launched in 2007, aiming to reach areas of high social disadvantage. Focus groups revealed that using rewards gave mothers an excuse to opt out of the social norm of smoking within their peer group and did not isolate them from that group. So, Give It Up For Baby used financial incentives to reward sustained positive behaviour amongst its target audience. An incentive of £12.50 a week is paid for every week a woman demonstrates she is smoke-free. When mothers joined the scheme at the pharmacist (after a CO test) they received their National Entitlement Card (NEC) through which the payments have been monitored since.

By the end of year one, 55 mothers had quit in Dundee and a total of 140 had quit across Tayside. This was compared with the total of six pregnant women who made contact with smoking cessation services across Tayside in 2006, the previous year. None of the women in 2006 had remained on the smoking cessation programme for longer than four weeks.

Question to consider

Do you believe that paying people to cease unhealthy behaviour is an effective and ethical strategy? Justify your response.

Acknowledgements to Paul Ballard and Andrew Radley and NSMC Showcase. http://www.thensmc.com/resources/showcase/road-crew

---

Given the potential negative effects outlined in Table 5.1, there is a clear need for systems or structures to help prevent or resolve these issues.

Ethical frameworks

While there are a number of potential frameworks available which derive from the field of philosophy, there is no consistency in the literature as to which framework might apply in specific circumstances. The frameworks most commonly cited focus either on intentions (**deontology**, from the Greek word for 'duty') or consequences (**teleology**, from the Greek word for 'ends'; also referred to as **consequentialism**), with the latter being broken down further into utilitarianism and egoism.[11, 12, 13] Thus a social marketing intervention that was driven by good intentions without consideration of potential negative consequences would be acceptable under deontological reasoning but not under teleological reasoning.

Others suggest that there is no universal set of ethics that can apply across all sectors of society. In view of the increasing diversity of society and the different perspectives that

Table 5.1 Unintended effects of health communication campaigns

Effect	Definition
Obfuscation	Confusion and misunderstanding of health risk and risk prevention methods
Dissonance	Psychological discomfort and distress provoked by the incongruence between the recommended health states and the audience's actual states
Boomerang	Reaction by an audience that is the opposite of the intended response of the persuasion message
Epidemic of apprehension	Unnecessarily high consciousness and concern over health produced by the pervasiveness of risk messages over the long term
Desensitisation	Repeated exposure to messages about a health risk may over the long term render the public apathetic
Culpability	The phenomenon of locating the causes of public health problems in the individual rather than in social conditions
Opportunity cost	The choice of communication campaigns as the solution for a public health problem and the selection of certain health issues over others may diminish the probability of improving public health through other choices
Social reproduction	The phenomenon in which campaigns reinforce existing social distributions of knowledge, attitudes and behaviours
Social norming	Social cohesion and control accompanying marginalisation of unhealthy minorities brought about by campaigns
Enabling	Campaigns inadvertently improve the power of individuals and institutions and promote the images and finances of industry
System activation	Campaigns influence various unintended sectors of society, and their actions mediate or moderate the effect of campaigns on the intended audience

may be held within cultures or groups, each group's ethical perspective should be held to be equally valid. An additional perspective is suggested by **social contract theory**, which suggests that there is an implicit contract between the state/government and/or individuals within society.[14] This is reflected in documents such as the UN Charter, which makes reference to basic assumptions about the right of all citizens to health[15] and is consistent with the principle of exchange which is discussed in Chapter 2. Table 5.2[16] provides a brief overview of the main provisions of these frameworks.

A further problem is the lack of clear and unambiguous interpretation of the frameworks. For example, using the Ferrell and Fraedrich interpretation, the Department of Health (DoH) fear-based smoking cessation 'fishhook' intervention discussed earlier would be acceptable under deontological reasoning, given that its intention was to help smokers take steps to quit smoking. Others would argue that it is unacceptable to knowingly cause anxiety under deontological reasoning.[17, 18] Their argument is that, even though the intention was to help a specific segment of society, the methods used caused harm (anxiety) to others. This, they reason, violates the utilitarian principle of ensuring the greatest good for the greatest number.

Many social marketing texts provide, at best, only brief discussions of ethical challenges; much of the material promoting the potential benefits of social marketing is devoid of any significant consideration of ethical issues.[19, 20, 21] The one edited text that specifically focuses on ethics in social marketing[22] does not provide a consistent framework across the various contributions.

Table 5.2 Overview of common ethical frameworks

Ethical framework	Key provisions	Comments
Deontology (based on the work of 18th-century philosopher Immanuel Kant)	Holds that there are ethical 'absolutes' that are universally applicable, with the focus on means or intentions.	Accepts that actions intended to do good may have unintended negative consequences.
Teleology/ Consequentialism	Focuses on the outcomes or effects of actions. Usually divided into: (a) *Utilitarianism* in which behaviour is ethical if it results in the greatest good for the greatest number (b) *Egoism,* in which the benefits to the individual undertaking action are stressed and the impact on other people is de-emphasised.	Difficulties arise when comparing alternative courses of action with different levels of potential impact – for example, a programme that provides minor benefits to all, versus one that provides major benefits to many but no, or negative impact on others.
Relativism	There is no universal set of ethical principles; individual cultures, societies or social groups may have their own ethical frameworks. No set of principles is superior to others and no group should judge the ethical standards of other groups.	Ignores: (a) the possibility that a group's principles are based on incorrect information, and (b) the implications of a group's principles being repugnant to other groups (e.g. sexism or racism).
Social contract theory	Implicit contract exists between the state and/or organisations and individuals or groups regarding rights and responsibilities as a member of society.	Given that the contract is implied rather than stated explicitly, there is no shared understanding of what rights and responsibilities apply to the various parties.

Box 5.1 Ethical issues to consider

Considerable effort and expenditure are needed to treat health problems brought about by unwise lifestyle and behaviour choices made by individuals. For example, an unhealthy diet, unprotected sex, drug use, lack of physical exercise, smoking or excess alcohol consumption have all been shown to link to potentially serious health problems. Justify your responses to each of the following issues.

1 What role do commercial marketers play in reinforcing consumption decisions that might not be in the best interest of people's long-term health? Think specifically of the activities of marketers of food deemed to be of low nutritional value, and those of the alcohol industry.

2 What actions should commercial marketers take voluntarily or by legislation/regulation to minimise any harm that may result from their activity?

3 What role is there for legislation versus personal choice in reducing potentially harmful behaviours?

4 How would you respond to the suggestion that people whose health is affected by poor consumption or lifestyle decisions should pay for their own medical costs and not expect others to pay (via taxes, etc.) for their treatment?

5 How would you respond to the suggestion that there should be increased taxes on products such as alcohol or foods deemed to be of low nutritional value in order to treat those whose health has been affected, even if it was their personal choice that led to their subsequent health problems? Do you think such taxes would actually change people's behaviours?

Ethical issues in targeting

Some specific areas of communication activity that raise ethical issues relate to targeting. A fundamental strategy for marketers is to 'select target markets they can best affect and satisfy'.[23] This strategy, when applied to social marketing activity, may result in some segments of the target population being excluded because they are difficult, or comparatively costly to reach.[24]

Literacy issues tend to be largely ignored in the provision of health information material.[25] Varying definitions of literacy make cross-study comparisons difficult; however, there appears to be agreement that some 20% of the population of most developed countries have severe literacy problems and a further 20% have limited literacy.[26, 27] The specific needs of these groups must be taken into account, acknowledging their difficulties but avoiding the appearance of condescension in the design and delivery of appropriate interventions.[28]

Where social marketing campaigns are directed at children or adolescents, additional factors must be considered, starting with data collection. Depending on the age of the potential participant, **parental consent** may be required for the participation to commence and/or continue. An ethical dilemma may arise if the child or adolescent does not wish to participate; in such circumstances, they should not be made to feel that they are being coerced into participation in research, **treatment trials** or social marketing intervention trials simply to please 'parents or other authority figures'.[29]

A factor that appears to be overlooked are the needs of immigrant populations who may retain substantial influences, including cultural values and language preferences, from their country of origin for a considerable time and may be confused by messages such as those that recommend limiting intake of some foods when these are not restricted in their home countries.[30] Further, failure to take their (culturally-based) perceptions of health-related issues[31] into consideration may result in interventions not succeeding.

Is it ethical to target sectors of the population who are easiest to reach or likely to be the easiest to reach or the most receptive to an intervention (**low-hanging fruit**) rather than those who might benefit the most from changes to their behaviour? If the latter are targeted, but their intervention costs significantly more than interventions aimed at lower-priority groups, is it ethical to focus resources on one specific group at the expense of others? Is it ethical to target specific behaviours without considering the socio-economic or wider environmental factors that may drive the behaviours? These are not simple questions to answer and the solutions will be situation-specific.

An example of the type of challenge that needs to be considered relates to interventions aimed at improving medication compliance. Those who are least compliant with their medication regimen are also likely to miss hospital appointments or other forms of medical monitoring.[32] Thus, those who would benefit most from help may be difficult to reach or to persuade to participate in interventions aimed at improving their health and quality of life. Consider the arguments for and against allocating resources to trying to reach them, as compared to those who are easier to reach. The nature of proposed interventions also presents ethical challenges. For example, adolescents with epilepsy do not want to meet others with complications or problems as they perceive these patients' problems as both frightening and depressing, therefore interventions that could include peer support from others with the same medical condition are unlikely to be successful.[33]

Fear appeals

The nature of the campaigns used in social marketing communication may lead to increased levels of public concern and, for some, possibly increased **anxiety** or fear;[34] the Department of Health smoking cessation campaign described earlier is an example of this. Further, those who have responded to past **fear-based appeals** appear to be better educated and more affluent than average, and thus better able to respond to the persuasive message.[35] As well as signalling the need for caution in the use of fear appeals for which less well-educated sectors are a significant target group, there would appear to be a requirement for research into the attitudes, information needs and message framing preferences of these sectors.

There may be a more pragmatic reason for caution in the use of fear appeals. In spite of several laboratory studies in which short-term effectiveness was found, real-world effects do not show the same results.[36] Many of the unintended effects of health communication campaigns (see Table 5.1) are directly, but not exclusively, attributable to fear appeals – i.e. dissonance, discomfort and distress, boomerang effects, epidemics of apprehension and desensitisation.[37, 38] Additionally, strong fear appeals are more likely to be regarded as unethical if the target populations do not believe they can readily undertake the recommended behaviour or that the behaviour will be effective in minimising the perceived threat.[39]

Given the sample of ethical challenges reviewed so far, the next issue is how to provide guidance on identifying and resolving issues that may be faced by practitioners.

Role of culture in establishing ethical standards

Acceptable behaviour is determined in large part by **socialisation**, yet the role of culture in establishing ethical standards is largely ignored within the marketing literature.[40] For example, it is suggested that the use of fear appeals is contrary to Islamic beliefs.[41] Can social marketing interventions based on fear appeals therefore ever be acceptable? They are unlikely to be effective with this sector of the population. Further, issues such as **safe sex** may offend some cultural or religious groups who, while they may not be directly targeted, may still receive material relating to the topic.[42] However, when culture-based perceptions are at odds with prevailing perceptions of best practice, how should social marketers balance respect for minority cultural norms with the desire to challenge them in the interests of improving health and well-being?[43]

Culture may influence the acceptability of different ethical frameworks. For example, some cultures that emphasise collective responsibility – i.e. the greatest good for the greatest number – over individual self-interest may find utilitarian perspectives preferable, whereas a culture that emphasises individualism may display preferences for egoism-based frameworks.[44]

An additional factor is the effectiveness of different communication styles: it has been found that consumers in similar countries across Europe respond differently to positively or negatively framed advertisements.[45, 46] However, much of this work was conducted only with university students and needs to be repeated with a cross-section of the populations of the countries studied. If the original findings hold true for the wider population, there may be a conflict between the economies of scale possible if material is used across as wide a range of target groups as possible, versus the possibility that material may not be as effective across different cultural groups. This may also impact on the tone of message used, such as rational, information-based messages versus emotional appeals. This aspect of social marketing communication is addressed in more detail in Chapter 11.

There is, of course the issue of who defines desired behaviour and whether consideration of potential harm to others that may arise as a consequence of a social marketing intervention should be a requirement in the development of any intervention. Indeed, in developing interventions, 'who has the mandate to represent large and diverse populations for the purpose of informed consent, and how can this be implemented?'[47] How are individual freedoms of choice and individual rights balanced against benefits for society as a whole? In communicating risk, who decides whether levels of risk that may be acceptable to different segments of society are acceptable to society as a whole?[48]

Code of ethics

Codes of ethics are one mechanism that has been proposed for social marketing overall[49, 50] and for related areas such as health promotion.[51] Codes may be successful in educating inexperienced practitioners and in sensitising them to issues they may face in the future. However, codes are not a panacea as they are often broad statements of intent and cannot cover every situation that is likely to arise or provide guidance on how issues such as cultural differences should be resolved.[52]

There appears to be no question that consistently high levels of ethical behaviour should therefore be expected of social marketers, given the potential impact of interventions on individual and societal health and well-being. The potential negative consequences for ongoing social marketing activities of consumers feeling that they have based decisions on incomplete information or have yielded to coercive activities on the part of social marketers may be severe.[53]

While the discussion above suggests that there is an obvious willingness within the area to consider codes of ethics, social marketing activity occurs across a wide range of occupational sectors, including health, environmental planning and marketing. Developing codes that can be applied across all sectors, some of which may have existing codes, is problematic. Additionally, a mechanism for enforcement of the codes needs to be developed and debated.

Professions such as accountancy have mechanisms by which adherence to professional codes of ethics can be enforced.[54] For sectors such as marketing that lack enforcement mechanisms, can codes of ethics ever be more than statements of desired best practice?[55] While marketers use the term 'profession', marketing does not meet the characteristics of a true profession as outlined in Table 5.3.[56]

Many marketing organisations have codes of ethics for their members. For example, the American Marketing Association (AMA)[57] provides the following:

1 Marketers must do no harm.

2 Marketers must foster trust in the marketing system (not mislead), good faith and fair dealing.

3 Marketers must embrace, communicate and practise fundamental ethical values that will improve consumer confidence in the integrity of the marketing exchange system. These basic values are intentionally aspirational and include honesty, responsibility, fairness, respect, openness and citizenship.

Table 5.3 Characteristics of a profession

- A profession possesses a discrete body of knowledge and skills over which its members have exclusive control.
- The work based on this knowledge is controlled and organised by associations that are independent of both the state and capital.
- The mandate of these associations is formalised by a variety of written documents, which include laws covering licensure and regulations granting authority.
- Professional associations serve as the ultimate authorities on the personal, social, economic, cultural, and political affairs relating to their domains. They are expected to influence public policy and inform the public within their areas of expertise.
- Admission to professions requires a long period of education and training, and the professions are responsible for determining the qualifications and (usually) the numbers of those to be educated for practice, the substance of their training, and the requirements for its completion.
- Within the constraints of the law, the professions control admission to practise and the terms, conditions, and goals of the practice itself.
- The professions are responsible for the ethical and technical criteria by which their members are evaluated, and they have the exclusive right and duty to discipline unprofessional conduct.
- Individual members remain autonomous in their workplaces within the limits of rules and standards laid down by their associations and the legal structures within which they work.
- It is expected that professionals will gain their livelihood by providing service to the public in the area of their expertise.
- Members are expected to value performance above reward, and are held to higher standards of behaviour than are non-professionals.

The fragmentation of the marketing industry presents a barrier. While many sector organisations have codes,[58] there are no overarching industry mechanisms within individual countries, let alone cross-border initiatives, although there is evidence of some movement in this direction in sectors such as the European Association of Communication Agencies. Such codes are often little more than statements of good intent, for example, the latter organisation's Code of Ethics states only:

1 Society and citizens

We recognise our obligation to create advertising which is consistent with the social, economic and environmental principles of sustainable development. We further recognise that this obligation applies equally across the different societies that receive advertising that might not have been developed for them.

2 Consumers

We recognise that consumers are entitled to rely on our profession to operate not only within the law and within the letter and spirit of global, national and sectoral codes of practice but also within accepted ethical norms.

We accept that our understanding of the 'average consumer' might not always be the standard, acknowledging that there are groups who are vulnerable, for example, and that we should adopt a sensitive approach to judging how advertising will be understood and acted upon by society in general.[59]

A doctor, accountant, lawyer or member of an established, recognised, profession could potentially lose the right to practise in their profession if found guilty by their peers of a significant breach of professional ethics.[60] Marketers are not subject to the same level of peer control; there is no requirement that they be licensed and membership of sector organisations is voluntary. Marketers lack the ability to enforce such codes in the way that professional groups are able to do.[61]

If a marketer is found guilty of transgressing the implicit or explicit standard of behaviour for any sector organisation to which they may belong, they may be ejected from that organisation, but this does not, per se, prevent them from continuing in employment in the sector. There are, however, less direct sanctions available to organisations, and, indeed, to the industry overall in many countries. For example, in the UK, *The British Code of Advertising, Sales Promotion and Direct Marketing,* issued by the industry's self-regulatory body[62] and administered by the independent Advertising Standards Authority,[63] specifies provision for marketing communications in breach of the Codes to be withdrawn or amended. Adjudications are published on the ASA website (www.asa.org.uk) and often in the media, as occurred with the Department of Health smoking adjudication.[64]

In addition, the industry regulators may request the media to deny advertising space or time to non-compliant marketers. Further penalties may be incurred through the withdrawal of industry discounts such as those offered by the Royal Mail for bulk mailings. In the most serious cases, legal support can be obtained to enforce discontinuation of unacceptable material.[65]

Other implicit **sanctions** (penalties) appear to exist in areas such as undertaking social science research on behalf of the UK government, with specific expectations including, for example, obtaining 'valid, informed consent' from research participants, but also the requirement to take 'reasonable steps to identify and remove barriers to participation' and to avoid 'personal and social harm'.[66] While provisions for sanctions and redress are noted but not spelt out specifically, a logical conclusion is that consultants found to be in breach of the provisions would not obtain future commissions. This could readily be extended to include funding for social marketing intervention development and implementation as well as related research.

Four key principles from the medical sector are much more specific than the 'good intentions' of the AMA above and may be of relevance to social marketing, i.e.:

- Respect for autonomy of individuals or communities, requirement for consultation and agreement (i.e. effective two-way communication) and absence of deceit.
- Beneficence, i.e. provision of net benefit to target group or patient.
- Obligation to ensure no harm is caused by actions.
- Justice in terms of fairness in distributing resources, respecting of rights and for morally accepted law.[67]

We would add the necessity of recognising the extent – and boundaries – of our expertise as marketers. Few of us are formally qualified in medical or related health fields in which a considerable amount of social marketing activity occurs, such as smoking cessation and exercise promotion programmes. There is, however, a recognised role for communication expertise, as the following quote from leading behavioural theorists indicates:

> . . . communications can attempt to increase the strength of beliefs that will promote healthy behaviors, reduce the strength of beliefs that promote risky behaviors, or prime existent beliefs that support healthy behaviors (i.e. increase their accessibility) so that these beliefs will carry more weight as determinants of attitudes, norms, self . . . efficacy and intentions. Behavioral theories do not tell us how best to design messages so that they will be attended to, accepted and yielded to. We would argue that this is the role of theories of communication.

Although communication theory and research have advanced our understanding of factors influencing attention, it is just beginning to advance our understanding of what makes a message effective, that is of the factors that influence acceptance and yielding.[68]

Two possible resources have been proposed. The first is an ethical checklist for social marketing:[69]

- Ensure that the intervention will not cause physical or psychological harm.
- Does the intervention give assistance where it is needed?
- Does the intervention allow those who need help the freedom to exercise their entitlements?
- Are all parties treated equally and fairly?
- Will the choices made produce the greatest good for the greatest number of people?
- Is the autonomy of the target audience recognised?

The second is a code of ethics for social marketing:[70]

- Do more good than harm.
- Favour free choice.
- Evaluate marketing within a broad context of behaviour management (giving consideration to alternatives of education and law).
- Select tactics that are effective and efficient.
- Select marketing tactics that fit marketing philosophy (that is, meeting the needs of consumers rather than the self-interest of the organisation).
- Evaluate the ethicality of a policy before agreeing to develop a strategy.

While it is a positive step that these issues are being discussed, voluntary codes of ethics without buy-in and support from those the codes are intended to cover will be ineffective.[71, 72] One of the first priorities in developing and agreeing on a code will be to gain the input of all stakeholders so that there will be a sense of shared ownership. However, as discussed earlier, codes can never be exhaustive and there will need to be a mechanism by which those facing ethical dilemmas can gain advice and support. Coupled with this should be awareness raising and training to highlight the types of issues that should be considered at all stages of social marketing intervention development.

CASE STUDY 5.1

Road Crew: ethical or just effective?

Background[73, 74]

Alcohol-related crashes are a major cause of injuries and fatalities in the USA and in 2002 there were 17,219 alcohol-related deaths across the country. In 2001, the National Highway Traffic Safety Administration funded five traffic safety projects throughout the United States, and Road Crew was one, based in Wisconsin.

The counties where Road Crew ran were small, rural towns often several miles apart. The target audience typically drove between towns on a night out. At the end of the evening, their drive home involved driving drunk along poorly lit lanes full of curves and hills, which inevitably ended in significant numbers of crashes and fatalities.

The Road Crew programme sought to reduce the number of alcohol-related road crashes by 5% in the geographic area during the first year. It did not attempt to change the drinking culture, but sought to get the target audience to leave their vehicles at home so the temptation to drive would not arise. The target group was 21–34-year-old single male blue-collar workers in rural areas.

Started with insight

Road Crew began with a year-long research phase, including literature reviewing, focus groups (of expert observers and target audience members) and a pilot roll-out of the proposed intervention.

The research indicated that in fact it was unlikely to be possible to influence drinking behaviour, but might be possible to influence the target audience to change their current driving behaviour. The target occasionally *did* worry about drinking and driving, which spoilt their evening. The drink-drivers admitted making poor decisions at the end of an evening of drinking, so it was important to separate them from their vehicles early in the evening. If they were going to pay for an alternative round trip for their night out, this needed to happen early on, so they still had money available.

The alternative vehicle was important and had to be appealing because a significant 'cost' was the loss of social status by not driving themselves.

The intervention

Before drinkers go out for the evening, they arrange a ride with Road Crew. Vehicles pick up customers at their home, drive them around all evening from bar to bar, then deliver them home safely at the end of the night.

The intervention met the needs highlighted by the research because the men considered it to be high-status to ride in a limo; the ride becomes part of the party and enables them to socialise before and after the bar, free from worry about crashing or arrest.

In addition, monthly incentives for bartenders were promoted to encourage them to refer to Road Crew. Road Crew t-shirts, hats and fridge magnets were also distributed. There were free rides for volunteer drivers and free ride coupons for friends, girlfriends and employers. Finally, there was a free ride offered after 10 had been paid for.

The intervention was rolled out in more counties after its success in the pilot area. It was found to be an affordable and sociable way of travelling between home and various bars. The press and community events supported the project and the adoption was considerable; first by early adopters but soon across the full target audience.

The project cost US $850,000 of government funding from 2000 to 2007 ($250,000 spent on initial research and development, the remainder spent working with communities to get local programmes into place).

Evaluation and results

Road Crew has grown to provide service in six Wisconsin counties, serving 36 communities. As of February 2008, Road Crew had given over 97,000 rides, prevented an estimated 140 alcohol-related crashes and saved an estimated 6 lives.

Case study 5.1 (*continued*)

Conclusion

Road Crew had a behavioural goal of reducing alcohol-related car crashes and subsequent hospital admissions and fatalities. Undoubtedly, it achieved this aim. However, the drinking behaviour of the target males was unaffected by the intervention and the social marketer (Michael Rothschild) has been criticised by some for encouraging heavy drinking behaviour and for ignoring the other repercussions of drunkenness, such as domestic violence and ill health.

Questions

1 Do you think there are any ethical difficulties with Road Crew? Justify your response.

2 Does Road Crew highlight any responsibilities that social marketers have or should have? If so, what are these, and what action do you recommend be taken in the future?

3 Is there anything that you would have done differently if you had been in charge of this intervention? If so, what?

Summary

Ethical dimensions occur in social marketing – and in related activity such as health promotion. While there are many definitions of ethics, they all contain a central focus on norms, values, standards and the impact of activity on others. There are also several different frameworks within which ethics can be viewed. The principal frameworks are those focusing on either intentions (deontology) or consequences (teleology). Unfortunately, regulators, such as those controlling mass media, do not make clear the ethical frameworks they use.

Ethical issues in social marketing are evident in targeting – who to include as targets in interventions and who to exclude. Additional ethical issues concern the use of message appeals such as fear-based communications which may create anxiety in the groups targeted – and others who are not the focus of a specific intervention. Cultural factors may impact on the ethical framework used to determine what is acceptable, as both an intervention and a communications strategy.

While codes of ethics have been proposed for social marketing, the diverse nature of the industry and the lack of effective enforcement mechanisms make these impractical. A number of checklists are available to guide social marketers in the development and implementation of interventions. These, together with a growing body of case studies illustrating how specific ethical challenges have been dealt with, provide support for practitioners.

CHAPTER REVIEW QUESTIONS

1 Critically discuss under what circumstances fear appeals might be an acceptable tool.

2 Research consistently indicates that some segments of the population are unrealistically optimistic about their personal risk of illness as a result of lifestyle factors. What ethical issues must be considered in trying to reduce their optimism? Justify your answer, giving examples of specific social marketing interventions to illustrate your discussion.

3 Critically discuss the ethical issues that should be considered in researching the attitudes and beliefs underpinning the behaviours of children and adolescents in order to develop interventions that are aimed at changing their behaviours, such as binge drinking or use of illicit drugs.

4 Critically debate the ethicality of targeting 'low-hanging fruit'/easy-to-reach sectors rather than sectors that may be more difficult to reach or influence. How might decisions vary according to the different ethical frameworks? How should debates such as which framework is most applicable to a specific situation be resolved?

5 Critically discuss the ethics of targeting parents to change behaviours through the use of guilt imagery, such as that which suggests their behaviour may harm their children's health or well-being – for instance, by smoking near children or providing them with a diet deemed by nutritional experts to be unhealthy.

6 You have developed an intervention based on insights gained from the key target segments and their reactions to the material prepared are positive. However, there is a suggestion that the intervention may offend small groups within the population who are not the target of the intervention. Discuss how you can deal with this situation.

7 With regard to the Road Crew case, what ethical issues do you believe would have been considered during the development of the intervention? Given that there are known adverse health effects connected with excessive alcohol consumption and links between consumption and violence (including domestic violence), is it ethical to implement an intervention that targets an aspect of behaviour, such as driving after excess drinking, without addressing the issues that lead to that behaviour? Justify your answers.

Recommended reading

Andreasen, A.R. (ed.) (2001) *Ethics in Social Marketing*. Washington, DC: Georgetown University Press.

Bernheim, R.G. and Melnick, A. (2008) Principled Leadership in Public Health: Integrating Ethics Into Practice and Management. *Journal of Public Health Management & Practice,* 14 (4), 358–66.

Ferrell, O.C. and Fraedrich, J.B. (1994) *Business Ethics: Ethical Decision Making and Cases* (2nd edn). Boston: Houghton Miflin.

Hoffman, W.M., Frederick, R.E. and Schwartz, M.S. (2001) *Business Ethics: Readings and Cases in Corporate Morality* (4th edn). New York: McGraw-Hill.

Lere, J.C. and Gaumnitz, B.R. (2007) Changing Behavior by Improving Codes of Ethics. *American Journal of Business,* 22 (2), 7–17.

Rothschild, M.L., Mastin, B. and Miller, T.W. (2006) Reducing alcohol-impaired driving crashes through the use of social marketing. *Accident Analysis & Prevention,* 38 (6), 1218–30.

Notes

1 Andreasen, A.R. (ed.) (2001) *Ethics in Social Marketing*. Washington, DC: Georgetown University Press, p. x.

2 Ferrell, O.C. and Fraedrich, J.B. (1994) *Business Ethics: Ethical Decision Making and Cases* (2nd edn). Boston: Houghton Miflin, p. 6.

3 Harvey, B. (ed.) (1994) *Business Ethics: A European Approach*. Hemel Hempstead: Prentice Hall International (UK), p. 15.

4 Argandona, A. (1994) Business, Law and Regulation: Ethical Issues. In B. Harvey (ed.), *Business Ethics: A European Perspective*. Hemel Hempstead: Prentice Hall.

5 Boddewyn, J.J. (1989) Advertising Self-Regulation: True Purpose and Limits. *Journal of Advertising,* 18 (2), 19–27.

6 Le Guay, P. (2003) The Regulation of Advertising to Children in Australia. *International Journal of Advertising & Marketing to Children,* 4 (2), 63.

7 Calfee, J.E. and Ringold, D.J. (1994) The 70% Majority: Enduring Consumer Beliefs About Advertising. *Journal of Public Policy & Marketing,* 13 (2), 228–38.

8 Shimp, T.E. (2003) *Advertising, Promotion and Supplemental Aspects of IMC* (6th edn). Mason, OH: Thomson South-Western, p. 62.

9 Murphy, P.E. and Bloom, P.N. (1989) Ethical Issues in Social Marketing. In S. H. Fine (ed.) *Promoting the Causes of Public and Nonprofit Agencies: Social Marketing.* Boston: Allyn and Bacon, pp. 68–78.

10 Cho, H. and Salmon, C.T. (2007) Unintended Effects of Health Communication Campaigns. *Journal of Communication,* 57 (2), 300.

11 Andreasen, A.R. (ed.) (2001) Op. cit.

12 Hoffman, W.M., Frederick, R.E. and Schwartz, M.S. (2001) *Business Ethics: Readings and Cases in Corporate Morality* (4th edn). New York: McGraw-Hill.

13 Argandona, A. (1994) Op. cit.

14 Dunfee, T.W., Smith, N.C. and Ross Jr, W.T. (1999) Social Contracts and Marketing Ethics. *Journal of Marketing,* 63 (3), 14–32.

15 Easley, C.E., Marks, S.P., D'Etat, D. and Morgan Jr, R.B. (2001) The Challenge and Place of International Human Rights in Public Health. *American Journal of Public Health,* 91 (12), 1922–25.

16 Adapted from Ferrell, O.C. and Fraedrich, J.B. (1994) Op. cit.

17 Duke, C.R., Pickett, G.M., Carlson, L. and Grove, S.J. (1993) A Method for Evaluating the Ethics of Fear Appeals. *Journal of Public Policy & Marketing,* 12 (1), 120–9.

18 Hastings, G., Stead, M. and Webb, J. (2004) Fear Appeals in Social Marketing: Strategic and Ethical Reasons for Concern. *Psychology & Marketing,* 21 (11), 961–86.

19 Andreasen, A.R. (ed.) (2001) Op. cit.

20 Kotler, P. and Lee, N. (2007) *Marketing in the Public Sector.* Upper Saddle River, NJ: Pearson Education.

21 Weinreich, N.K. (1999) *Hands-On Social Marketing: A Step-by-Step Guide.* Thousand Oaks, CA: Sage.

22 Andreasen, A.R. (ed.) (2001) Op. cit.

23 Kotler, P., Roberto, N. and Lee, N. (2002) *Social Marketing. Improving the Quality of Life.* Thousand Oaks, CA: Sage Publications, p. 7.

24 Brenkert, G.G. (2002) Ethical Challenges of Social Marketing. *Journal of Public Policy & Marketing,* 21 (1), 14–36.

25 Eagle, L.C., Hawkins, J.C., Styles, E. and Reid, J. (2006) Breaking Through the Invisible Barrier of Low Functional Literacy: Implications for Health Communication. *Studies in Communication Sciences* 5 (2), 29–55.

26 Adkins, N.R. and Ozanne, J.L. (2005) The Low Literate Consumer. *Journal of Consumer Research,* 32 (1), 93–105.

27 Office for National Statistics (2000) International Adult Literacy Survey 2007, from http://www.statistics.gov.uk/ssd/surveys/european_adult_literacy_review_survey.asp

28 Guttman, N. and Salmon, C.T. (2004) Guilt, Fear, Stigma and Knowledge Gaps: Ethical Issues in Public Health Communication Interventions. *Bioethics,* 18 (6), 531–52.

29 Moolchan, E.T. and Mermelstein, R. (2002) Research on Tobacco Use Among Teenagers: Ethical Challenges. *Journal of Adolescent Health,* 30 (6), 409–17.

30 Moreno, C., Alvarado, M., Balcazar, H., Lane, C., Newman, E., Ortiz, G., et al. (1997) Heart Disease Education and Prevention Program Targeting Immigrant Latinos: Using Focus Group Responses to Develop Effective Interventions. *Journal of Community Health,* 22 (6), 435–50.

31 Kyngas, H., Duffy, M. and Kroll, T. (2000) Conceptual Analysis of Compliance. *Journal of Clinical Nursing,* 9 (1), 5–12.

32 Osterberg, L. and Blaschke, T. (2005) Adherence to Medication. *New England Journal of Medicine,* 353 (5), 487–97.

33 Kyngas, H. (2003) Patient Education: Perspective of Adolescents with a Chronic Disease. *Journal of Clinical Nursing,* 12 (5), 744–51.

34 Murphy, P.E. and Bloom, P.N. (1989) Op. cit.

35 Hastings, G., Stead, M. and Webb, J. (2004) Op. cit.

36 Ibid.

37 Cho, H. and Salmon, C.T. (2007) Op. cit.

38 Witte, K. and Allen, M. (2000) A Meta-Analysis of Fear Appeals: Implications for Efffective Public Health Campaigns. *Health Education & Behavior,* 27 (5), 591–615.

39 Snipes, R.L., LaTour, M.S. and Bliss, S.J. (1999) A Model of the Effects of Self-efficacy on the Perceived Ethicality and Performance of Fear Appeals in Advertising. *Journal of Business Ethics,* 19 (3), 273–85.

40 Pires, G. D. and Stanton, J. (2002) Ethnic Marketing Ethics. *Journal of Business Ethics,* 36 (1/2), 111–18.

41 Saeed, M., Ahmed, Z.U. and Mukhtar, S.-M. (2001) International Marketing Ethics from an Islamic Perspective: A Value-Maximization Approach. *Journal of Business Ethics,* 32 (2), 127–42.

42 Brenkert, G.G. (2002) Op. cit.

43 Guttman, N. and Salmon, C.T. (2004) Op. cit.

44 Vitell, S.J. and Paolillo, J.G.P. (2004) A Cross-cultural Study of the Antecedents of the Perceived Role of Ethics and Social Responsibility. *Business Ethics: A European Review,* 13 (2/3), 185–99.

45 Orth, U.R. (2005) Consumer Personality and other Factors in Situational Brand Choice Variation. *Journal of Brand Management,* 13 (2), 115–33.

46 Orth, U.R., Koenig, H.F. and Firbasova, Z. (2007) Cross-national Differences in Consumer Response to the Framing of Advertising Messages. *European Journal of Marketing,* 41 (3/4), 327–48.

47 Guttman, N. and Salmon, C.T. (2004) Op. cit.

48 Callahan, D. and Jennings, B. (2002) Ethics and Public Health: Forging a Strong Relationship. *American Journal of Public Health,* 92 (2), 169–76.

49 Rothschild, M.L. (2001) Ethical Considerations in the Use of Marketing for the Management of Public Health and Social Issues. In A. R. Andreasen (ed.) *Ethics in Social Marketing.* Washington, DC: Georgetown University Press, pp.17–38.

50 Donovan, R. and Henley, N. (2003) *Social Marketing Principles and Practice.* Melbourne, Australia: IP Communications.

51 Sindall, C. (2002) Does Health Promotion Need a Code of Ethics? *Health Promotion International,* 17 (3), 201–3.

52 Wright, D.K. (1993) Enforcement Dilemma: Voluntary Nature of Public Relations Codes. *Public Relations Review,* 19 (1), 13–20.

53 Murphy, P.E. and Bloom, P.N. (1989) Op. cit.

54 Hunt, S.D. and Vitell, S.J. (2006) The General Theory of Marketing Ethics: A Revision and Three Questions. *Journal of Macromarketing,* 26 (2), 143–53.

55 Lere, J.C. and Gaumnitz, B.R. (2007) Changing Behavior by Improving Codes of Ethics. *American Journal of Business,* 22 (2), 7–17.

56 Cruess, S. and Cruess, R.L. (1997) Professionalism Must Be Taught. *British Medical Journal (BMJ),* 7123 (315), 1676.

57 American Marketing Association (2007) American Marketing Association Code of Ethics: Ethical Norms and Values for Marketers (Publication. Retrieved January 2008: http://www.marketingpower.com/content21013.php#)

58 See, for example, Direct Marketing Association (2007) *Field Marketing Best Practice Guidelines.* Direct Marketing Association (DMA) and Market Research Society (undated) *Code of Conduct.* London: Market Research Society.

59 European Association of Communications Agencies (2007) Code of Ethics. Retrieved 7 January, 2008, from http://www.eaca.be/documentation/results.asp?type=1&open=4&#4

60 Cruess, S. and Cruess, R.L. (1997) Op. cit.

61 Hunt, S.D. and Vitell, S.J. (2006) Op. cit.

62 Committee of Advertising Practice (2005) *The British Code of Advertising, Sales Promotion and Direct Marketing.* London: Committee of Advertising Practice.

63 Advertising Standards Authority (2006) The Advertising Codes. Retrieved 14 November, 2006, from http://www.asa.org.uk/asa/codes/

64 Bale, J. (2007) Reprimand for Government Over Ads That Upset Children. *The Times,* online edition, from http://www.timesonline.co.uk/tol/news/uk/health/article1624180.ece

65 Committee of Advertising Practice (2005) Op. cit.

66 Government Social Research Unit (2005) *GSP Professional Guidance: Ethical Assurance for Social Research in Government,* p. 8. Retrieved from http://www.gsr.gov.uk/professional_guidance/ethics.asp.

67 Gillon, R. (1994) Medical Ethics: Four Principles Plus Attention to Scope. *British Medical Journal,* 309 (6948), 184.

68 Fishbein, M. and Cappella, J. (2006) The Role of Theory in Developing Effective Health Communications. *Journal of Communication,* 56 (August Supplement), S14.

69 Donovan, R. and Henley, N. (2003) Op. cit.

70 Rothschild, M.L. (2001) Op. cit.

71 Greene, W. E., Walls, G.D. and Schrest, L.J. (1994) Internal Marketing: The Key to External Marketing Success. *Journal of Services Marketing,* 8 (4), 5–13.

72 Rust, R.T. and Chung, T.S. (2006) Marketing Models of Service and Relationships. *Marketing Science,* 25 (6), 560–80.

73 National Social Marketing Centre Case Study Library (2011) http://www.thensmc.com/resources/showcase/road-crew

74 Rothschild, M., Mastin, B. and Miller, T. (2006) Reducing alcohol-impaired driving crashes through the use of social marketing. *Accident Analysis & Prevention,* 38 (6), 1218–30.

PART 2

Understanding the consumer

Understanding the consumer: the role of theory

Theory

As Kurt Lewin famously said, 'There is nothing so practical as a good theory', and the evidence points to this being as true for social marketing as for any other discipline. It is widely accepted by social marketers that the use of **theory** improves their chances of creating successful interventions,[1, 2, 3] but this assumption does not always translate into the use of theory in practice. Theories with titles such as the 'Theory of Planned Behaviour' can sound baffling to anyone who isn't immersed in the academic literature, and even simplified models such as the 'Transtheoretical Model' can appear daunting.

Yet theory has been shown to result in more effective interventions, helping to identify key factors that affect behaviour and guiding practitioners to trigger points for behaviour change. Theories can help pinpoint barriers before we encounter them, and help us learn from others who have trodden these paths before. Anyone who chooses to use theory in an intervention can offer invaluable feedback to the wider social marketing community by describing how well that theory worked and what should be improved upon in the future, driving forward the discipline of social marketing for ever more effective interventions.

This chapter aims to provide an easy introduction to theory in general, and to describe why theory is such an important tool in the social marketing toolbox. The evolution of key theories will be described, and some of the theories most commonly used in social marketing will be outlined and practical examples given to show how they can be applied in real-life interventions. The pros and cons of each theory will be discussed so you can decide how useful they are. By the end of this chapter, you should have the confidence to start applying these theories to your own interventions.

What is theory?

A theory describes a phenomenon, such as human behaviour, by breaking it down into its component **constructs** and **concepts**, and mapping the relationships between these. Each of these constructs consists of a combination of concepts, and it is these concepts that can be measured to determine the value of the construct, which may not be directly measurable itself. In the case of the Theory of Planned Behaviour, which we discuss in much more depth later in this chapter, an example of a core construct is '**perceived behavioural control**', which is a combination of the concepts 'control belief' and 'perceived power'. This provides a systematic way of *explaining* such a phenomenon[4] which, ultimately, allows us to also *predict* outcomes, by breaking down the variables into measurable elements and being able to calculate their impact. Through understanding these building blocks of behaviour, theories and models can contribute to the **planning**, implementation and **evaluation** of interventions[5] by pinpointing why people behave as they do, how programmes can impact upon people and what needs to be monitored to measure the success of the programme.[6]

Many call for theories to be **generalisable**,[7] but in the context of social marketing one could argue that segmentation calls for theories tuned to that particular segment or behaviour. There is also a need for testability,[8] to demonstrate the theory's aptness for the task.

There are a number of different types of theories. One type is explanatory theories, or theory of the problem, which describe the problem and seek to explain why it exists.[9] By breaking that problem down into the constructs that contribute to its existence, the factors that can be used to relieve or remove that problem can be identified. Change theories, or theories of action, are more orientated to problem-solving to help develop interventions.[10]

Theories are not blueprints to be followed without question – they do not provide concrete answers and may not suit complex questions. However, they do provide some guidance to potential trigger points or barriers that can be leveraged and can be of great value to the practising social marketer.[11]

Is theory really useful in practice?

In practice, theory is not used routinely. Even if it is used, theory often informs the groundwork of the strategy, but tends to be neglected during implementation.[12] When theory *is* used in developing an intervention, the results are rarely interpreted with the aim of seeing whether it really made a useful contribution. There are many reasons for this, but a key factor may be that clear explanations of theories are often confined to the world of academia. Many of the key papers are not easily accessible to practitioners without a university library at their disposal. It is also true that theories are not always easy to understand, being couched in technical language and using references and other academic conventions that may be intimidating and confusing for practitioners who lack the skills to use theory to full effect.[13]

More practically, many practitioners would contend that theory often bears little relation to the stark realities of human behaviour, and that such high-brow, academic thinking has little place in practice. The aim of theory – to offer a simplified description of complex phenomena – may seem *too* simplistic given the vagaries of human behaviour, and even impractical when it comes to implementing real-life interventions. Furthermore, many practitioners would argue that common sense and hard-earned experience are much more likely to result in the pragmatic approaches required to drive behaviour change 'on the ground', than the dry, bookish models that theories are often boiled down to.

Although common sense is a valuable quality that no social marketer should be without, we should beware the deeply held assumptions and ideologies that form the foundations of such pragmatism.[14] It may seem obvious to each of us what is 'good' or 'bad' behaviour in terms of health, the climate or social responsibility, and what factors are involved in determining how people actually behave under given circumstances, but different people may hold very different opinions and ours may not reflect the reality of the target audience.

We should therefore seek an objective view of other people and their behaviour – ideally, based upon numerous examples from across the world and across many different behaviours, in addition to our own, more limited experience. Good theories do precisely this, as long as we know how to use them.

The role of theory

The success of interventions often depends upon understanding the causal processes and mechanisms that determine behaviour – i.e. the psychological or structural changes that account for observed behavioural change. The most commonly used theories are the result of many decades' worth of **empirical** research and testing, across many thousands of participants and a variety of behaviours. Ultimately, theory breaks a complex phenomenon down into comprehensible and measurable chunks which can be analysed: a good theory then allows us to make predictions based upon what's happening with each of those chunks, and to then alter various chunks to affect the outcome. In the case of behaviour, these chunks tend to fall into three areas. The first is the factors that moderate the behaviour, such as knowledge, perceptions, and the impact of other people. The next is the relationships between the factors and their relative weights, to assess the strength of influence of each. Finally, there are the conditions that modulate those factors, including psychological traits such as self-esteem and external factors such as gender, socio-economic status and age.

Theory provides us with the language to share knowledge with other people doing similar things, whether in social marketing or beyond.[15] Every time a theory is used in an intervention, the outcome helps us to improve upon that theory. With the use of theory, even failed interventions can be analysed to identify where fault lies and to improve the theory for the next time, so no learning is ever wasted. This constant accumulation of knowledge, identifying successful factors, eliminating unsuccessful ones and building upon the experiences of other researchers, means that we are forever honing theories for future use: Sir Isaac Newton described us as dwarves standing on the shoulders of giants, adding our own small learnings to the mass of knowledge that already exists.

This accumulation of knowledge also helps us to justify choices as to how we spend that often hard-earned budget, based upon the evidence of previous interventions and the flexibility of theory to apply this to our own intervention. This should make it easier to plan effective interventions.

These many reasons are why theory should be a component of every social marketer's toolbox. The UK's National Social Marketing Centre has elaborated upon Andreasen's[16] original six benchmark criteria for recognising good social marketing to add two more criteria, one of which is the use of theory. They call for broad theoretical underpinnings from across disciplines such as biology, psychology, sociology and ecology. Trifiletti et al.[17] are amongst the many authors who call for the use of theory in planning, developing, implementing and evaluating interventions, seeing a clear role for theory not just for academics in the discipline of social marketing, but also practitioners.

VIGNETTE 6.1

A case to consider

A district nurse has secured a budget for a smoking cessation intervention in an area that suffers from high levels of deprivation, low quality of life and poor practical support.

She knows from her past experience that what individuals need is lots of support from fellow smokers who are giving up, friends and family and some extra help with medical interventions such as nicotine patches. However, she has noticed that people tend to stop and start quite a few times before they finally give up, even though they know smoking is bad for them, and is keen to cut this down to make the most of her budget.

Could theories such as the Health Belief Model and the Theory of Planned Behaviour help her? These theories could help show that, if friends and family are still smoking, social pressure may hinder the individual's attempt to give up. That, despite the knowledge of the negative consequences of smoking, if the costs of giving up (such as social and psychological costs) outweigh this then people are likely to take the habit up again.

The nurse might then consider how to help individuals resist such social pressures, and highlight other short-term and more tangible benefits of stopping smoking. This may include meeting new people who have given up smoking, providing role models and support, and encouraging people to spend the money they have saved on cigarettes on treats such as clothes or gadgets.

Question to consider

What do you think some of the advantages would be of this nurse using theory for the success of this and future interventions?

To make theory more accessible and 'user-friendly', models are often developed which distil out the core concepts and are often graphically presented as diagrams, a number of which are shown below. These may be used to represent an entire book of discussion on the theory, so must be treated with caution as they often represent far more than is apparent on the page.

The limitations of theory

Despite the many reasons listed for the use of theory, and these authors' firm belief in the value of theory, there are limitations to bear in mind. For instance, each of the theories detailed below was developed in a Western, first-world environment, often the USA, and therefore these theories will tend to reflect the dominant policy and cultures of these countries. Similarly, some theories have been developed through research into particular behaviours, and may not translate well across all behaviours. Every situation is different and some theories may work better than others, depending on the behaviour under scrutiny, the actors involved and their circumstances. Finally, the empirical evidence may support the use of these theories to help guide and predict behaviour change, but they do not account entirely for the variations observed in behaviour. Theory explains perhaps only 1% to 65% of variety in behaviour and 14% to 92% for behavioural intentions, i.e. we can only use theory to explain *some* of the observed behaviour or intent and other factors, not accounted for in our theories, must account for the other 8% to 99%.[18] Furthermore the operationalisation of the constructs involved (i.e. making them measurable) may vary dramatically between behaviours and researchers, offering a lack of consistent baseline from which to evaluate interventions.[19]

The behavioural theories that are described below are the key theories used in social marketing, and they tend to focus on the individual and their psychological predisposition to behaviour change given their social circumstances. Figure 6.1 shows concentric circles of influence on behaviour change by the individual: environmental, social and psychological, with psychological factors, such as self-esteem, being the most influential. Theories such as the Theory of Planned Behaviour, the Health Belief Model and the Transtheoretical Model tend to focus upon the psychological and social factors, as these impinge most strongly upon the individual and their motivation to change. However, in reality environmental barriers would play an important role in preventing action even if the individual was motivated to change. Therefore the social marketer should not be confined by theory, and needs to also think about the wider environment.

Theories provide frameworks for strategists, but cannot be considered to be comprehensive guides to developing interventions: they identify the broad areas that should be considered. The models discussed above are often shorthand representations of highly complex theories, and while useful for explaining how a theory works, it should be remembered that they represent far more than meets the eye. Theories do not provide hard and fast rules, and slapdash application of theory is unlikely to make a positive difference to interventions. It is worth using sources such as this book to gain some understanding of theory, and following this up by looking at specific academic articles relevant to your field, to be able to apply theories more effectively. Furthermore, theories are no substitute for up-to-date and targeted market research.

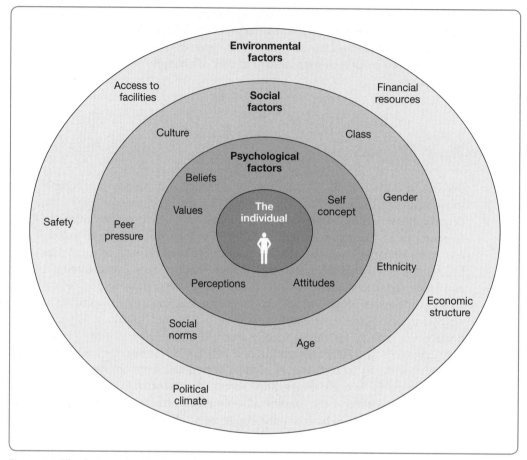

Figure 6.1 The factors affecting behaviour change

Specific limitations of each theory are briefly outlined below, and when using theories it is worth bearing these broad limitations in mind. Theories are one set of tools for social marketing, but are by no means the only useful options we have at our disposal.

Theories of behaviour change

Throughout this book you will encounter many theories: of communication, of mass population change and of the diffusion of ideas. This chapter looks specifically at theories of individual behaviour change. This is because behaviour change is at the core of successful social marketing strategies, and these theories are the ones you are most likely to encounter in developing, implementing and evaluating social marketing strategies. Theories of behaviour change tend to work at an individual level rather than a population level, explaining how individuals are motivated, choose a specific course of action and then finally 'behave' – i.e. do (or not do) something.

There are a vast number of behavioural theories, originating in fields such as sociology and psychology. The ones selected here are those that are most prominent in the existing literature and/or that have already been shown to have a useful role in developing real-life interventions. None of these theories is without its critics, as each generation seeks to identify flaws and improve these for future use, so we will discuss some of the criticisms.

For each theory, we briefly describe its origins and history, before presenting a simplified model and explaining the theory in more depth. We look at both the positive and negative aspects of each theory, and then give practical examples of where the theory has been successfully used in social marketing practice.

The theories that are discussed here are:

Psychosocial models

- Health Belief Model
- Protection Motivation

Social learning theories

- Social Cognitive Theory
- Theory of Reasoned Action
- Theory of Planned Behaviour
- Integrative Model of Behaviour Change

Stage-based theories

- Transtheoretical Model of Change
- Alternative Stage-based Models

Psychosocial models

Health Belief Model

One of the earliest theories proposed, and one of the most commonly used in social marketing, is the Health Belief Model (HBM). This is a value-expectancy type of theory, which explains behaviour choices as rational decision-making based upon expected outcomes.[20] In the case of the HBM, it is argued that individuals weigh up their perceived personal risk of negative health outcomes from continuing their current behaviour against the likelihood of alternative health outcomes though behaviour change. These perceptions are also modified through the impact of personal characteristics and knowledge, and cues to action in their environment.

The current behaviour is evaluated in terms of disease or disability risks, i.e. *perceived threat*, which consists of two components:

Perceived susceptibility

The individual's own perception of their chance of being affected by the condition: this takes into account not only the prevalence of the condition in the population, but also their assessment of their personal risk. This may take into account acknowledged genetic, behavioural or environmental risk factors.

PLUS

Perceived severity

The individual's perception of the likely severity of the condition in terms of morbidity and mortality, but also social, financial and other consequences.

The alternative behaviour, i.e. behaviour change, is evaluated by balancing the benefits of behaviour change against the barriers:

Benefits of behaviour change

The benefits that the individual perceives will realistically accrue from changing behaviour to reduce the risk of getting the condition or the severity of its consequences: these may include health, social, financial and other benefits in the short and long term.

MINUS

Barriers to behaviour change

The individual's perceived costs of behaviour change, which may be financial, environmental or other barriers to actually changing behaviour, or negative consequences of behaviour change, such as social, financial or other outcomes.

Modifying factors, which may be psychological, physical, social or environmental, affect the individual's perceptions of the perceived threat of disease and outcomes of behaviour change:

Demographic, psychological and knowledge factors

Characteristics of the individual that affect perceptions: these include demographic factors such as age, sex, ethnicity, psychological factors such as personality and self-efficacy, and knowledge about the condition and behaviours.

AND

Cues to action

These cues may be physical, such as symptoms of disease, or environmental, such as peer pressure, education, or social marketing, and prompt behavioural change.

These six components each contribute to a final outcome of the likelihood of taking a recommended action, which is a step away from actual behavioural change. The relationships between these factors are illustrated in Figure 6.2, and an example of the application of this theory is given in Box 6.1. For a chance to see how we've used this model to guide our own work, see Vignette 6.2.

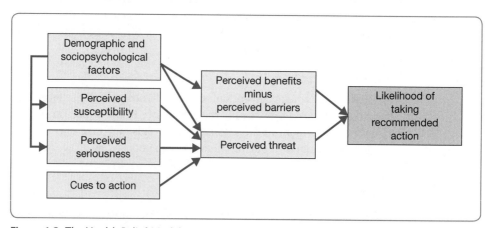

Figure 6.2 The Health Belief Model

Box 6.1 The Health Belief Model – an application

Perceived threat of disease

Perceived susceptibility

Awareness and evaluation of:

- genetic risk factors such as a history of heart disease in his family, his peers or his ethnic group as a whole, and the additional risk contributed by his gender;
- behavioural risk factors such as diet, smoking or lack of exercise;
- environmental risk factors such as passive smoking, pollution or an environment not conducive to physical activity.

PLUS

Perceived severity

Awareness and evaluation of:

- seriousness of disease in terms of magnitude of consequences, such as degree of disability or pain;
- health consequences such as long-term illness or disability, or death;
- social consequences, e.g. impact on family, isolation due to immobility;
- financial consequences, e.g. loss of earnings or cost of care;
- other consequences that impact on quality of life, such as loss of confidence.

VERSUS

Perceived benefits minus perceived threats of behaviour change, i.e. smoking

Perceived benefits

Awareness and evaluation of:

- short-term health benefits such as improving shortness of breath, reducing coughing and feeling healthier;
- long-term health benefits such as reduced risk of heart disease, and also lung cancer, other cancers and emphysema;
- social benefits such as fresher-smelling clothes and breath;
- financial benefits such as money saved on tobacco products, and money saved on healthcare;
- other benefits such as not being excluded from pubs while smoking.

MINUS

Perceived barriers:

- social barriers such as potential exclusion from, or discomfort among, groups of friends who smoke;
- barriers associated with addiction and the physical and mental symptoms of nicotine withdrawal.

Modifying factors

Demographic, psychological and knowledge factors:

- impact of culture, age, gender on perceptions, e.g. regarding perceived health risks of smoking and social role of smoking;
- impact of personality, such as level of self-efficacy in believing that he can successfully instigate and sustain smoking cessation.

The theory was based upon the work of Lewin[21] but first suggested by Hochbaum et al.,[22, 23, 24] who was part of a group of social psychologists seeking to explain what they considered to be the surprisingly low uptake of free X-rays to screen for tuberculosis in the USA. The theory was then developed by Rosenstock[25, 26] into the form shown above, and later Rosenstock, Strecher and Becker[27] suggested adding Bandura's[28] concept of self-efficacy.

The long history and extensive use of the HBM provide considerable evidence for its efficacy across different kinds of health behaviours. Janz and Becker[29] reviewed studies using the HBM and concluded that there was substantial empirical support for the use of the theory. They also found that the construct of perceived barriers was the strongest predictor across a variety of behaviours. Burns[30] reviewed studies using the HBM, and concluded that it is most successful in explaining one-off preventive measures such as immunisation, and less successful for long-term preventive strategies, such as maintained physical activity.

The HBM model is not without its critics. As with a number of other models, the focus upon intention rather than actual behaviour change may reduce the real-life validity of the model.[31] Burns also highlighted the narrow scope of the model, which fails to take into account environmental factors such as lack of facilities, or non-health factors such as hypochondria. Burns also questioned whether the HBM accounts for habitual behaviour such as smoking or exercise, which reflects its lower levels of efficacy for long-term behaviour change. Glanz et al.[32] highlight the lack of consistent measurement of the constructs of the theory, making it difficult to evaluate its true efficacy.

In conclusion, the HBM has been a mainstay of social marketing and health promotion for many decades, and its usefulness proved both empirically and through experience. There are, as with all theories, flaws, as described above; however, these can be mitigated if understood.

VIGNETTE 6.2

An example of use of the Health Belief Model

In 2010, we worked with Avon Fire and Rescue Service in the UK to encourage older people to install smoke alarms and engage in behaviours to reduce the chances of fires starting in their homes, or at least improve chances of escape should a fire occur.

Considering the benefits versus the barriers of behaviour change helped us to identify the importance of habit and routine to older people as a barrier to behaviour change. This led to more one-off approaches, such as firefighters installing smoke alarms and safer appliances in one simple visit.

We then used the HBM as a guide to developing questions for our preliminary research, to

1 Discover whether older people perceived themselves to be *susceptible* to fire

2 Learn what the perceived *severity* of a fire would be for this group

3 Determine what the perceived *threat* of fire was for this group.

We found that older people did not think they were susceptible to fire: they thought it unlikely that a fire would ever occur and that they could do little to prevent it. However, the consequences of a fire were perceived to be severe: the loss of home, relatives or friends, pets, independence and a lifetime's worth of possessions and memories would be devastating.

At the time of writing this book we are now testing whether we need to work on the susceptibility component or the severity component of the model. Focus on susceptibility would lead us to increase the perceived likelihood of a fire occurring by communicating statistics and recalling local incidents. However, focus on perceived severity may be a sufficient trigger, so our focus could be more emotive communications about preventing the loss of independence, loved ones and possessions.

Question to consider

*What would **you** suggest to improve perceptions of personal susceptibility to fire amongst this target group?*

Protection Motivation Theory

The Protection Motivation Theory (PMT)[33] was developed from the HBM specifically to understand the effect of fear appeals. This theory bridges the gap between pure behavioural theories and communications theories, which are expanded upon in Chapter 11.

PMT seeks to describe the response to fear appeals through adaptive and maladaptive behavioural responses, and that these are the results of the constructs described for the HBM i.e. perceived threat, benefits versus the barriers of the desired behaviour and the individual's perceived self-efficacy.

Social learning theories

Social Cognitive Theory

Social Cognitive Theory (SCT)[34, 35] proposes that behavioural, personal and environmental factors are reciprocal, interacting determinants of each other (reciprocal determinism), so changing one element has implications for the others (Figure 6.3). In contrast to the other models described in this chapter, SCT includes the element of environment, stretching into the outer circle of Figure 6.1 above.

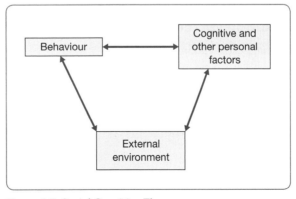

Figure 6.3 Social Cognitive Theory

Environment includes perceived facilitators and impediments in the social environment, such as friends, family or peers, or the structural environment, such as safety and access (Bandura, 2004).[36] One element of this environmental construct is *observational learning*. SCT draws heavily on the Skinnerian tradition by acknowledging that observation of others in the social environment affects *behaviour*, as observing the outcomes of the actions of others provides a model for the individual. This is thought to increase the observer's behavioural capability and boost self-efficacy. Positive reinforcement, such as feeling better, money saved or the feedback of others, also supports behaviour change. This modelling of behaviour and its positive outcomes has been successfully used in social marketing interventions. *Personal factors* refer to the innermost circle of Figure 6.1, and how an individual's characteristics affect their ability to perform a behaviour, interact with the environment and interpret others' actions.

Perceived self-efficacy (PSE) is a central mechanism of SCT not shown on the model. According to Wood and Bandura,[37] PSE is governed by:

- mastery experiences – past performance, failure or success leading to self-doubt or strengthening self-belief, such as previous success at maintaining the behaviour;

- modelling – observation of successful models, comparing own capabilities with others and seeing how similar others compare (vicarious experience);

- social persuasion – receiving realistic encouragement, but if raised to unrealistic levels may undermine self-perceptions with failure.

Levels of PSE affect motivation, effort expended and duration of perseverance before settling for mediocre solutions. Those with low PSE tend to dwell on their deficiencies and perceive more threat from their environment than those with high PSE, who suffer less apprehension.

SCT is one of the most extensive and comprehensive theories that attempt to explain human behaviour,[38] though this makes it one of the most difficult to grasp and to use in the implementation of social marketing programmes. Box 6.2 summarises some of the other concepts used in this theory. Many other theories have adopted the aspect of PSE, but reciprocal determinism is also a valuable concept. It is useful to remember that changing one factor, such as environment, can have impacts on other factors such as cognitive factors. However, it is the combination of environment, personal/cognitive factors and behaviour that may result in long-term change and a multifaceted intervention which targets all of these may have more chance of being successful.

Box 6.2 Other core concepts in Social Cognitive Theory

Outcome expectations

Beliefs about whether behaviours lead to certain outcomes, for example:

- personal anticipation of gains and losses, tangible and intangible;
- social responses – social approval/disapproval;
- how changing behaviour fits with wider personal values, e.g. self-satisfaction and self-worth.

Outcome expectancies

The *value* placed on the consequences of the behaviour.

Emotional coping responses

Responses used to cope with emotional stimuli, such as psychological defences (e.g. denial or repression), cognitive techniques (e.g. problem restructuring) and stress management.

Enactive learning

Learning from the consequences of one's own actions.

Rule learning

Generating and regulating behavioural patterns, often vicariously.

Self-regulatory capability

Internal standards and self-evaluation to generate and regulate behaviour.

Knowledge of health risks and benefits of different practices

The knowledge of potential outcomes to allow weighing up of alternative behaviour options.

Health goals

Long-term goals for health.

Behavioural capability

Knowledge and skills necessary to perform the desired behaviour.

Theory of Reasoned Action, Theory of Planned Behaviour

The Theory of Reasoned Action (TRA)[39, 40] and its successor, the Theory of Planned Behaviour (TPB)[41] explain behaviour change as the outcome of behavioural intention, and behavioural intention as the outcomes of social norms and an individual's attitude to the behaviour. Social norms represent an individual's beliefs about what is normal or acceptable in their social environment of significant others, while personal attitude towards the behaviour consists of beliefs about that behaviour. If both are positive, the person is more likely to perform the behaviour; however, negative beliefs, low motivation or negative social norms can undermine perceived norms and attitude, and hence intentions. Social environment consists of significant others such as spouse, peers, family or role models.

The TPB goes a step further as it includes the element of perceived behavioural control (PBC) to account for variance in behaviours with incomplete volitional control, i.e. where individuals lack complete control of the behaviour. Figure 6.4 shows both theories with the additional elements of the TPB highlighted in a darker colour.

PBC is compatible with Bandura's[42, 43] concept of perceived self-efficacy (PSE) of 'how well one can execute courses of action required to deal with prospective situations', which arose from Social Cognitive Theory, explained below. PBC can influence:

- choice of activity, i.e. choosing an activity that one can expect to succeed at;
- preparation for an activity to maximise chance of success, e.g. having the correct equipment, finding social support, mental preparation;
- effort expended during performance;
- thought patterns and emotional reactions.[44]

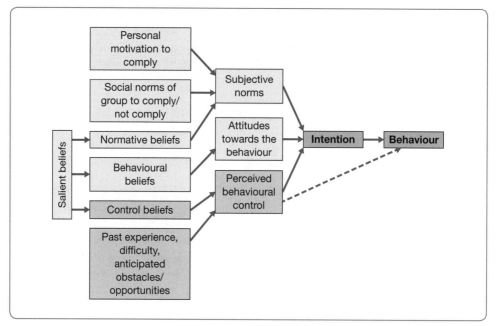

Figure 6.4 Theory of Planned Behaviour

However, high PBC may be less achievable if the individual does not have enough information about the behaviour, if there are not sufficient resources, the requirements are too high, or if there are new and unfamiliar considerations. Many of these are potential roles for social marketing.

Originally developed by Fishbein and Ajzen in 1975, the Theory of Reasoned Action was updated to include constructs of PBC by Ajzen in 1991 and was renamed the Theory of Planned Behaviour. The theories are some of the most extensively quantitatively tested theories in social marketing, with a large number of researchers applying them to a wide variety of behaviours. What distinguishes the TRA and TPB from many other behavioural theories is their focus on the actual behaviour, rather than upon the problematic outcome such as a disease or environmental issues.

Like the HBM, the TRA and TPB are value-expectancy types of theory, where an individual judges the value of the outcome of behaviour change by weighing up the expected pros and cons in an act of rational decision-making. These theories focus on the psychological and social levels shown in Figure 6.1, broken into the constructs shown in Figure 6.4. Each element is described in more detail below.

The *subjective norm* is the belief about whether the behaviour is acceptable amongst significant others, and is determined by:

Personal motivation to comply

Motivation to change to desired behaviour

PLUS

Normative beliefs

Beliefs about how significant others judge the behaviour

PLUS

Social norms of group to comply/not comply

The beliefs amongst one's peers about whether the behaviour is socially acceptable

The *attitude towards the behaviour* is the individual's overall cognitive and emotional evaluation of the behaviour, which is based upon:

Behavioural beliefs

Beliefs about the consequences of a behaviour, and its likelihood of producing desired outcomes

Perceived Behavioural Control (PBC) is akin to perceived self-efficacy and rates an individual's own perception of their ability to actually perform a behaviour. Factors that contribute to this are:

Control beliefs

Beliefs about the influence of factors that may facilitate or impede performance of the behaviour

PLUS

Past experience

Previous experiences related to the behaviour, such as previous attempts, observational learning of others and anticipated opportunities and barriers

There is a well-defined process for identifying the factors that contribute to each of these constructs through preliminary interviews, as demonstrated in Box 6.3. These factors are then developed into scales to quantitatively measure each of these constructs.

Box 6.3 Applying the Theory of Planned Behaviour

Young white women who currently do not engage in adequate levels of physical activity may suggest the following as aspects of their belief set during elicitation interviews:

Sources of influence
These may include:

- friends
- family
- partners
- physicians
- role models

Behavioural beliefs
Engaging in regular physical activity will . . .

- help me to lose weight
- pive me more energy
- make me too muscular to be attractive
- improve my mental health
- lead me to meet new people
- be boring
- be fun

Normative beliefs
- Friends and family's perceived support may depend on their own activity levels or attitudes to physical activity.

Control beliefs
Barriers to physical activity include:

- lack of local facilities
- cost of organised activities

➡

Box 6.3 (*continued*)

- Partners are often considered unsupportive, but this depends on the individual.
- Doctors are likely to be thought to be supportive but may not be as influential.
- Role models such as famous actresses or singers may be considered supportive because of their own lifestyle choices.

- embarrassment of wearing sports clothing
- embarrassment of being bad at the activity
- lack of transport
- lack of childcare (if applicable)

Facilitators of physical activity include:

- having a friend to go with
- personal instruction
- beginners' groups with similar people
- enjoyable activities
- free try-out sessions

One of the key flaws of these theories is the considerable gap between intention and behaviour: many studies have shown that intention is not a reliable indicator of actual behaviour change.[45] The introduction of the concept of PBC helped to account for some of this variation; however, environmental or circumstantial factors can also discourage behaviour change, despite strong intention. Criticisms of both the HBM and TPB have been based on their omission of personality and individual differences as factors.[46] It has also been found that different behaviours and target audiences place emphasis on different parts of the model, so the influence of each construct is not uniform.

Other criticisms of the theories include the lack of universal applicability of the constructs of the TRA and TPB,[47] so some studies have shown that social norms had little or no effect in predicting outcomes,[48, 49, 50] while others showed the same for PBC[51, 52] and attitudes.[53] This does not mean that the models are wholly defunct, though, as elements of them *are* useful for a variety of different behaviours.

In reality, many practitioners are not equipped to use the quantitative aspects of the TRA or TPB. However, methods such elicitation interviews can be crucial in identifying some of the key barriers and motivations towards behaviour change, and the significant others who have influence upon the target audience. Each theory provides a map of influencing constructs for practitioners to consider in developing, influencing and evaluating interventions. Furthermore, these theories account for the influence of social norms to a degree unparalleled by other behavioural theories.

The TRA and TPB have been some of the most extensively researched models, though they may appear complicated to use in everyday interventions. We have found the TPB to be one of the most useful models for guiding early scoping of projects and developing interventions, working through each of the factors and considering how it can be applied to maximise the effectiveness of programmes of action.

VIGNETTE 6.3

Stakeholder engagement in the VERB campaign[54, 55]

VERB was a multicultural campaign in the USA aimed to increase and maintain physical activity among children aged 9–13. It was based on the Theory of Planned Behaviour and Social Cognitive Theory (interplay of intrapersonal factors, environment and behaviour), described above.

There were two main targets: 'tweens' aged 9–13 years – between childhood and adolescence, beginning to make their own lifestyle decisions, and a secondary group of targets, including parents (especially mothers aged 29–46), teachers and youth programme leaders. Children from ethnic minority groups and those with physical disabilities were specifically targeted.

The intervention objectives were to:

- Increase knowledge and improve attitudes and beliefs about tweens' regular participation in physical activity.
- Increase parental and influencer support and encouragement of tweens' participation in physical activity.
- Heighten awareness of options and opportunities for tween participation in physical activity.
- Facilitate opportunities for tweens to participate in regular physical activity.
- Increase and maintain the number of tweens who regularly participate in physical activity.

Exploratory research showed that, for mothers, activity for kids was not at the forefront of their minds; they were focused on the present – getting through the day was a significant challenge and they found it difficult to juggle all calls on their time. This made them vulnerable to feelings of guilt because they were not spending more time doing activities with their children – but they also had safety concerns if children were unsupervised. Hence their personal motivations to engage kids in physical activity were low.

Research with the tweens found that they responded to having a sense of purpose/ accomplishment/self-esteem (self-efficacy) and responded positively to encouragement and support from family and peers, adjusting their perceptions of social norms around physical activity. Competitive sport turned many off, but tweens dream of finding their 'thing'. For all of them, action and adventure are important.

Branding was important, with the aim being to build a relationship with the brand, which was intended to lead to affinity, attitude change and, in the longer term, to loyalty to VERB activities and events. VERB was developed as the brand on the basis of the research with the tween groups who saw it as an 'active' word and also suggested the line – now part of the logo – 'It's what you do'. The intervention has been able to achieve significant improvements in physical activity rates among this group and to sustain the activity over a long period of time.

So, while theories may appear abstract and distanced from implementation, they can be used to identify underlying reasons for uptake of the desired behaviour – or resistance to it. Then, using marketing tools, we can address these aspects and develop successful interventions.

For more information see: http://www.cdc.gov/youthcampaign/

An integrative model

In 2000, Fishbein reviewed the above theories, and many more, and concluded that certain variables were common to many.[56] He went on, with Capella, to combine these theoretical perspectives into the integrative model shown in Figure 6.5.

This model indicates that intention is a predictor of behaviour, as suggested in the TPB, but must be supported by the skills and abilities to perform the behaviour, and an environment that is conducive to the behaviour, for behaviour change to occur. This effectively combines the three levels demonstrated in Figure 6.1, embracing perceived self-efficacy, attitudes to the behaviour and perceived norms about that behaviour with external factors, uniting psychological, social and environmental factors in developing interventions.

Fishbein and Capella describe this theory in some depth in their 2006 paper,[57] and highlight how different behaviours use different elements of the model. For instance, for adults aged over 40, intentions to get a colonoscopy would be under normative control (i.e. what is normal for that culture), while intention to exercise is related both to attitude to exercise and self-efficacy, so interventions for either would use different approaches to engage the target group in the desired behaviour. Therefore this model is useful in guiding early exploratory research to identify which factors are at work for a

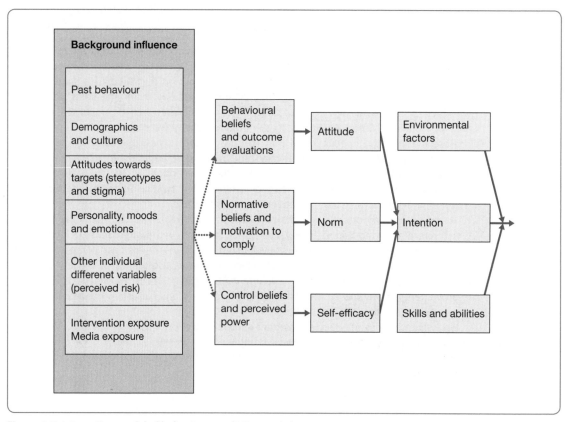

Figure 6.5 Integrative model of behaviour prediction and change

Source: Fishbein, M. and Capella, J. (2006) The Role of Theory in Developing Effective Health Communications. *Journal of Communication, 56.*

particular behaviour, and to then determine how to develop interventions that work at the right level, with the right characteristics, and promoted by the right messages and media, if appropriate.

Stage-based models

Stage-based models depict behaviour change as a step-wise process, as people progress in well-defined stages between not performing a behaviour and maintaining that behaviour over the long-term.

Transtheoretical Model of Change

The Transtheoretical Model of Change (TTM), also known as the Multi-component Stage Model or **Stages of Change Model**, is a stage-based model that seeks to explain behaviour change as a step-wise process. The theory proposes that individuals do not jump from their current behaviour to maintaining the desired behaviour, but progress slowly through stages between not even knowing the risks of their current behaviour to maintaining the desired behaviour change, as illustrated in Figure 6.6.[58, 59] Furthermore, individuals may relapse and regress down the stages. Each of these stages is characterised by different decision-making processes and the TTM uses 'stages of change to integrate processes and

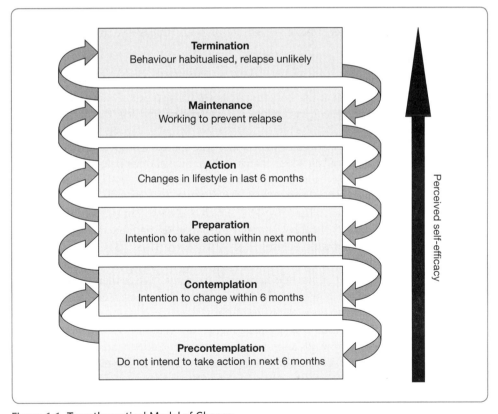

Figure 6.6 Transtheoretical Model of Change

Source: Cancer Prevention Research Center, The University of Rhode Island, 2006.

principles of change from across major theories of intervention, hence the name is *transtheoretical*.[60] The six stages outlined in Figure 6.6 can be further elaborated on as below.

Precontemplation

No intention to take action in the next six months. The most 'hard to reach' group, these individuals cannot see the advantages of behaviour change, whether through lack of awareness or lack of interest. They may actively avoid educational materials.

Contemplation

Intend to take action within the next six months. Pros beginning to outweigh cons, but individuals may be stuck in a stage of 'chronic contemplation' for long periods of time.

Preparation

Intend to take action within the next month, and have planned *how* they will take action, such as joining a class or group. Immediate prompts to take action are useful at this stage.

Action

Have made 'specific overt modification to their lifestyle within the past six months', which is sufficient to reduce their risk of negative consequences such as disease.

Maintenance

Working to maintain the behaviour change, usually over twelve months, and prevent relapse. For instance, smokers are not termed 'non-smokers' until twelve smoke-free months have elapsed.

Termination

When the desired behaviour has become habitualised and relapse is unlikely, even under circumstances such as boredom or stress. This stage may never be reached by most people for behaviours such as condom use, exercise or a healthy diet.[61]

The TTM is also a value-expectancy type of theory, proposing that individuals weigh up the pros and cons of behaviour change in a rational manner before progressing to the next stage. The decisional balance sheet, which identifies pros and cons, is often used to measure this.

Perceived self-efficacy (PSE) also features in this theory, as precontemplators and contemplators tend to have low PSE, which is observed to rise as the stages progress towards maintenance.[62] Notably, failure at the action or maintenance stages may cause erosion of PSE, associated with relapse.

Prochaska and DiClemente developed the model through studies of smoking cessation. However, other researchers have applied the model since then to a variety of health and other behaviours, such as alcohol and substance abuse, sunscreen use, condom use, compliance with medication and weight control.[63]

The TTM is useful for planning interventions because it can help segment a target group by their progress towards adopting a new behaviour, and to tailor interventions using the appropriate theories for that stage. Such theories can guide implementation, and then progression (or regression) along the stages can be measured to evaluate the effectiveness of the intervention. For instance, individuals at earlier stages may benefit from information about the costs and benefits of behaviour change, while later stages warrant more prompts to immediate action.

Despite the logical and empirical support for the TTM, it is not without its critics. One common criticism is the assumption that behaviour change is a step-by-step process along qualitatively different stages, rather than a smooth continuum, or even a circular process.[64] Some reviewers question the 'arbitrary' time spans allotted to each stage,[65] while others call for more standardised and reliable methods for assessing stage of change[66] and better understanding of the mediators and moderators of stage change.[67] The variety of versions of the TTM used across different behaviours and researchers makes it difficult to make comparisons and assess its effectiveness,[68, 69, 70] while goals such as physical activity, which consists of many single behaviours, may be too complex to assess using the TTM.[71]

The predictive ability of the TTM has been questioned[72] as Herzog et al. (1999) found that the TTM failed to predict progressive stage movements at one or two year follow-ups, so the TTM may be more valuable as a measure than a predictive tool. A substantial review of the TTM across all health behaviours showed that roughly equal proportions demonstrated a positive effect for TTM as showed no significant difference versus alternative interventions.[73] The authors of the review also questioned whether a model developed for cessation of addictive behaviours would suit other behaviours, such as uptake of physical activity or condom use.

Despite these criticisms, the TTM is in wide use across social marketing applications and has a substantial body of evidence for its usefulness. Its use for short-term behaviour change has been proved and more research may help to identify important factors in stage-change.[74] The comparatively simple approach provides a useful framework for practitioners, who can use it to define an adoption process with interventions designed to match the appropriate stages for their target markets.

Alternative stage models

While none of the following models has the breadth of empirical support of the TTM, a number of alternative stage models have been proposed, for instance:

- Precaution Adoption Model – Weinstein 1988,[75] 1998[76]
- Health Action Process Approach – Schwarzer, 1992[77]
- Goal Achievement Theory – Bagozzi, 1992[78]
- Model of Action Phases – Gollwitzer, 1990; Heckhausen, 1991[79, 80]

Armitage and Conner[81] review these in more detail, but all emphasise that different stages exist in behaviour change, and that these stages warrant different approaches for interventions, based upon the different characteristics of people at these stages. Many attempt to define the time taken to move between stages.[82] However, none of these is used to the extent of the transtheoretical model.

Reactance Theory

All of the theories described above are very rational, and tend to consider behaviour change in a vacuum, separate from the emotional influences that we all know affect our judgement on a daily basis. An example of a theory which attempts to tackle these more tricky circumstances is Reactance Theory.

Reactance Theory was developed to explain the way in which many of us react against attempts to restrict our behavioural freedom by acting in the opposite fashion to the attempted restriction.[83, 84, 85] For example, if a smoker sees a poster exhorting them to give up smoking it may simply strengthen their resolve to fight for their right to choose how to live their own life, so they carry on smoking anyway.

The assumption of Reactance Theory is that threats to personal freedom result in a state of motivational arousal, which can drive individuals to defend this state of freedom by acting in the opposite way to that requested. This counterforce to reduction of freedom is termed 'psychological reactance'.

Freedom to behave as one wishes can refer not only to *what* the behaviour is, but *when* it can be performed and *where* and *how*. So even attempting to modify behaviour by restricting it to certain times, places or styles can spark a reaction to protect one's right to perform that behaviour how and when one wishes. Again, smoking is a good example of this, as has been observed when steps have been taken to change the design of cigarettes, the places one can smoke and the availability of cigarettes – all of which have frequently been flouted by sticking with roll-ups or smoking in non-smoking areas. The ultimate reaction came with the brand 'Death' cigarettes, heavily embossed with skulls and cross bones and health warnings, and considered the coolest of cigarette brands at the time. Vignette 6.4 provides an example of an intervention that risked reactance from the group it wished to target, and how social marketers overcame this risk.

VIGNETTE 6.4

'Preaching to the converted' – EcoTeams rethink their offering in order to reach their target 'low-income' group

EcoTeams was an intervention attempting to improve the environmental impact of lower-income communities by supporting groups of neighbours to improve and measure changes they made to their recycling efforts. Groups met once a month for five months to map out the practical actions they could take to reduce their environmental impact. Waste was then weighed and monitored.

Within the trial communities, waste reduction rates were higher than average. However, evaluation showed that the type of households which had been attracted to the programme were actually 'middle-income', even though the geographical area was 'low-income'. EcoTeams was accused of preaching to the converted.

EcoTeams faced the risk of being branded 'middle-class' and alienating the target group, who reacted against the middle-class image, were not attracted by the self-managed intervention design and struggled to weigh their household waste and energy usage because of their communal facilities and council-run properties.

The organisers responded to this failure by developing the Evergreen process, which involved a project officer working with the community, developing trust and creating pro-environmental participatory activities (e.g. allotment schemes, scrap workshops), and support installations (e.g. recycling facilities, energy-efficient lighting). As a result, the Evergreen project achieves similarly impressive results, albeit in a more intensive and higher-cost way.

For more information visit http://www.globalactionplan.org.uk/communityhousehold.aspx and for a full case study visit http://www.nsmcentre.org.uk/public/CSHome.aspx.

Question to consider

Think of occasions when you have reacted against what someone else wanted you to do, even if it was for your own good. What made you react in this way? What can this teach you about how to be an effective social marketer?

CASE STUDY 6.1

Foolsspeed

Background

Speeding on the UK's roads is a major contributor to accidents involving pedestrians, cyclists and other vehicle users. While speed cameras and police vehicles are used to enforce speed limits, educating and convincing drivers to slow down, especially in urban areas, are common social marketing goals. The Foolsspeed campaign was created by Road Safety Scotland, working with the Centre for Social Marketing in Stirling, Scotland, and is one of few that explicitly incorporates behaviour change *theory* to design, implement and evaluate a campaign. In this case, the Theory of Planned Behaviour (TPB) was used because, as the researchers point out, there have been 'surprisingly few attempts to use the TPB to design actual interventions'.[86]

This case study describes the Foolsspeed promotional campaign which ran in Scotland from 1998 until 2005, and aimed to reduce the use of excessive and inappropriate speeds on Scottish roads. This was the first attempt in the UK to use TPB to develop a large-scale intervention for driving behaviour. It was targeted at drivers in Scotland, but focused upon the sub-group of those most likely to speed – i.e. males aged 25–44, social classes ABC1 (professional, white-collar and clerical workers).

Role of theory

Previous studies about speeding indicated that TPB could account for significant variances in intentions to speed, with attitudes, subjective norms and perceived behavioural control (PBC) being particularly indicated as contributing to an intention to drive over the speed limit.[87, 88, 89, 90] See Figure 6.4 to identify these on the model of the TPB.

In terms of attitudes, those who speed rate the chances of a crash or other negative event as a result of driving as less likely than non-speeders do, and they think the consequences would be less serious.[91] Speeders also see more rational benefits to speeding, such as getting to their destination more quickly, and also get more of an emotional buzz from speeding.[92, 93]

Meanwhile, speeding is generally considered more acceptable than drink-driving, and is somewhat legitimised as a behaviour, so driving above the speed limit becomes the subjective norm.[94]

Finally, people tend to believe they are better drivers than they actually are. They feel pressurised into undesirable behaviours in certain driving situations, which contributes to their driving faster, and indicates that they have high PBC in terms of maintaining control while having low PBC in terms of resisting external and internal pressures over driving.[95, 96]

Researchers therefore used these three main predictors from the TPB to start developing messages for television commercials. This was supported by local focus groups (with male and female drivers aged 18–44) to explore beliefs and norms about speeding and feelings about road safety advertising.

The intervention

Though initial ideas were generated from the TPB, the early focus groups also indicated that road safety campaigns needed to be more credible, featuring realistic, non-extreme driving behaviours and events that drivers encounter regularly. Drivers wanted empathy for the pressures of driving: congestion, time pressures and 'hassle', rather than to be patronised or told off. As a result, well-known streets in Glasgow were featured to emphasise the relative localness of the advertisements, using a softer, more empathetic approach than the usual fear campaigns. Ten short ads were used to establish brand awareness of the

133

Case study 6.1 (*continued*)

campaign, while three television/cinema ads were developed: one each to target attitudes, subjective norms and PBC.

The attitude ad was the first to be aired and ran the longest. It features a male driver in his 30s driving through residential streets while his alter-ego/conscience appears in the rear-view mirror, commenting upon the foolishness of speeding when the car he overtook only catches him up at the next lights. The driver responds that he's 'a better driver than most' moments before he needs to brake suddenly and noisily to avoid ploughing into a car stopped at a school crossing. The strapline reads: 'Take a good look at yourself when you're driving.' See the ad for yourself at http://www.road-safety.org.uk/resources/video/foolsspeed-advert-1—take-a-look-at-yourself-whilst-driving/.

The second ad, about subjective norms, shows the passenger's view on a man's driving, as first the female partner and then his male best mate comment to camera on his driving style. His partner describes how he becomes 'totally unrecognisable' behind the wheel, and protests as their young son is jolted along on the back seat. His friend accuses him of becoming a 'boy racer' as he spills juice as the driver races away at traffic lights. The strapline reads: 'Put yourself in the passenger seat. If you don't, others won't.' See the ad at http://www.road-safety.org.uk/resources/video/foolsspeed-advert-2—put-yourself-in-the-passenger-seat/.

The final ad focuses on perceived behavioural control, using a child's voice-over of the nursery game 'Simon says' as three different drivers are pressured by normal driving circumstances: being in traffic at 40mph in a 30mph zone, being late for work and a 'white van man' driving close behind. This final driver almost hits a cyclist as a result. It encourages drivers to 'be your own man' rather than give in to these common external and internal pressures. See the ad at http://www.road-safety.org.uk/resources/video/foolsspeed-advert-3—be-your-own-man/.

The Foolsspeed campaign developed from these three initial television/cinema commercials to a five-year mass media campaign through a process of careful development, testing and feedback to improve the campaign. In addition to advertising, public relations in the local press and corporate sponsorship were used. The more recent 'Doppelganger' version of the attitudes ad can be seen here http://www.road-safety.org.uk/resources/video/foolsspeed-advert-doppleganger/.

Evaluation

While it is difficult to link actual driving behaviour to watching and recalling these advertisements, the campaign was evaluated for its success in achieving communication goals and changes in the targeted constructs of the TPB (attitude, subjective norms and PBC). This was assessed both qualitatively and quantitatively, and both as a means of providing baseline data, feeding back into, and improving, the campaign, and to summatively assess it.

Qualitatively, six target audience focus groups were conducted each year for three years. Quantitatively, a 20–40-minute face-to-face questionnaire was used to assess response to the campaign from baseline and over the next three years. This was a longitudinal survey with a cohort of 550 drivers aged 17–54 who were recruited door-to-door in an area where the local population was typical of the wider Scottish population.

The baseline survey established respondents' demographic and driving characteristics before the intervention began. It also measured aspects of the respondents' attitudes, norms and PBC (i.e. the TPB constructs) at baseline. Three more surveys over the next three years asked the same questions and assessed response to the advertising. They measured awareness, recall, comprehension, identification, involvement and perceptions of key messages to assess success against communication goals.

Results

The attitude ad performed particularly well: people liked it, found it easy to understand and did not find it patronising, though it prompted them to think about their own driving behaviours. Frequent speeders felt the ad was targeted at them – and tended to agree it made them feel like they 'drove too fast'.

Significant changes were seen in desired communications outcomes, e.g. recall (74% recalled the attitude ad in year 1 and 86% in years 3 and 4). Attitudes also shifted towards anti-speeding, on items such as 'finding it difficult to stop in an emergency' and 'driving at what you feel is a comfortable speed'. Similar responses were recorded for the other two ads but were less pronounced.

The TPB could be used to predict 47–53% of the variance in intentions to speed and 33–40% of variance in actual reported speeding behaviour (speeding on a 30mph road).

The elements of the TPB that contribute to the psychological underpinnings of driving behaviour were also observed to change, as changes in attitude to speeding were significantly associated with awareness of the attitude ad. Beliefs about the rational consequences of speeding, and the emotional benefits and drawbacks, changed over the course of the campaign. The evidence for changes in subjective norms and PBC was less clear, which may be attributable to the fact that the attitude ad was screened earlier and for longer, or perhaps was more creatively compelling, all aspects that are difficult to measure.

Reported speeding decreased significantly from baseline by the third and fourth surveys, but it is difficult to establish a link to seeing the ads, and intentions showed no change.

Conclusion

As one of the few interventions to rigorously attempt to measure theoretical constructs, and their links to behaviour, this is a promising start to the use of theory in developing, implementing and evaluating interventions. This campaign showed that it is possible to design advertising and other interventions based upon theory, though clearly the ads need to be creative and stand out to be noticed (see Chapter 12).

There was an additional finding that low-key, credible and empathetic advertising can be as effective as the emotionally charged, fear-based advertising that typifies road safety campaigns. But, most promising of all, this ad seemed to cut through to those who we most want to influence: frequent speeders were amongst those that identified most strongly with the campaign's messages, and were most challenged to reassess their own behaviour.

Questions

1 Name three advantages of using theory in the development of the Foolsspeed campaign.

2 Why do you think it is so unusual for social marketing practitioners to use theory in this way?

3 Imagine you had tried to apply the Health Belief Model to the same problem of speeding in urban areas. In that case you might want to increase the perceived *likelihood* of an accident occurring under normal driving circumstances, and the perceived *seriousness* of such an accident happening, while showing how slower driving can be rewarding. Suggest an advertisement for one or more of these constructs, keeping in mind the need to be credible and address everyday scenarios.

4 Identify attitudes (subjective) norms and perceived behavioural control (self-efficacy) on Fishbein and Capella's integrative model of behavioural prediction and change. Note how these form intention, but actual behaviour is also determined by environmental factors and skills/abilities. What *other* social marketing interventions could you develop to support the existing promotional campaign?

Summary

A number of theories have been outlined in this chapter, all of which have been used in social marketing interventions around the globe. Pros and cons of each theory have been discussed, but it is clear that none can account for behaviour change in its entirety. No theory can be complex enough to describe any behaviour change in complete detail, without being too complex to use, so we accept theories as useful tools to help guide us in developing interventions.

What theories do offer is a more objective understanding of behaviour than we could gather through experience alone. Theories such as the HBM, SCT, TPB and TTM have been tested empirically for decades, and their flaws and strengths debated amongst practitioners and researchers. None is perfect, but each time a theory is used and evaluated, we learn a little more. With few direct comparisons of the theories and their explanatory ability or predictive power,[97, 98, 99] practitioners have an important role to play in using, evaluating and developing such theories.

You will have noted that many of these theories are based upon similar ideas, or constructs, with different names, like those listed below:

- 'Perceived susceptibility to the issues' *or* 'perceived seriousness of the issues';
- 'Weighing up of perceived risks versus perceived benefits' or 'pros and cons' or 'costs and benefits';
- 'Influence of social norms' or 'influence of the people around the individual';
- 'Self-efficacy' or 'perceived behavioural control' or 'locus of control'.

Using these theoretical constructs as the framework for developing research, interventions and communications ensures that the factors that motivate, facilitate or inhibit behaviour are considered throughout the development process.

Theoretical constructs are used to design research questions and interpret research data, creating strong behavioural insights. A practitioner can use these insights in many ways, for example, to inform the construction of service level agreements for intervention providers, or to develop creative briefs for marketing and communications agencies. By using insight based on behavioural theory, practitioners are able to deliver programmes that align with the needs of the target group and are more likely to achieve behaviour change goals.

After reading this chapter, you should feel ready to explore the use of theory while developing your own social marketing interventions. If you want to read in more detail about how to do this, some recommendations for comprehensive texts are made below.

CHAPTER REVIEW QUESTIONS

1 A quote used in this text and frequently cited elsewhere is Kurt Lewin's assertion that 'there is nothing so practical as a good theory'. Critique this quote, giving examples to illustrate your answer.

2 Review each of the theories described in this chapter and identify the factors that would need to be reviewed for each if you were developing an intervention for condom use for young people aged 16–24 to prevent sexually transmitted infections such as chlamydia.

3 Review the evidence for and against the Transtheoretical Model, using some of the recommended references. What recommendations would you make for its use across a range of social marketing interventions?

4 We have noted in this chapter that models such as the Theory of Reasoned Action and the Theory of Planned Behaviour do not account for all the variance in behaviour seen. What else would you guess would be important?

5 Review the interventions undertaken to address a social marketing issue of your choice. How do these reflect the behaviour change theories outlined in this chapter?

Recommended reading

For a comprehensive guide to health behaviour theories (many of which also cover general behavioural theories):

Glanz, K., Rimer, B.K. and Lewis, F.M. (2002) *Health Behavior and Health Education* (3rd edn). San Francisco: Jossey-Bass.

Lefebvre, R.C. Theories and Models in Social Marketing. In Bloom, P.N. and Gundlach, G.T. (eds) (2000) *Handbook of Marketing and Society*. London: Sage, pp. 516–18.

Notes

1 Kirby, D.B., Laris, B.A. and Rolleri, LA. (2007) Sex and HIV Education Programs: Their Impact on Sexual Behaviors of Young People throughout the World. *Journal of Adolescent Health,* 40, 206–17.

2 Trifiletti, L.B, Gielen, A.C., Sleet, D.A. and Hopkins, K. (2005) Behavioral and Social Sciences Theories and Models: are they used in Unintentional Injury Prevention Research? *Health Education Research,* 20 (3), 298–307.

3 Andreasen, A.R. (2002) Marketing Social Marketing in the Social Change Marketplace. *Journal of Public Policy and Marketing,* 21 (1), 3–13.

4 Kerlinger, F.N. and Lee, H.B. (2000) *Foundations of Behavioral Research* (4th edn). New York: Harcourt College Publishers.

5 Trifiletti, L.B, Gielen, A.C., Sleet, D.A. and Hopkins, K. (2005) Op. cit.

6 Glanz, K., Rimer, B.K. and Lewis, F.M. (2002) *Health Behavior and Health Education* (3rd edn). San Francisco: Jossey-Bass.

7 Van Ryn, M. and Heaney, C.A. (1992) What's the Use of Theory? *Health Education Quarterly,* 19 (3), 315–30.

8 Ibid.

9 Glanz, K., Rimer, B.K. and Lewis, F.M. (2002) Op. cit.

10 Ibid.

11 Parker, E.A., Baldwin, G.T. and Salinas, M. (2004) Application of Health Promotion Theories and Models for Environmental Health. *Health Education and Behavior,* 31 (4), 491–509.

12 Kobetz, E., Vatalaro, K., Moore, A. and Earp, J.A. (2005) Taking the Theoretical Model into the Field: A Curriculum for Lay Health Advisors. *Health Promotion Practice,* 6 (3), 329–37.

13 Jones, S. and Donovan, R.J. (2004) Does Theory Inform Practice in Health Promotion in Australia? *Health Education Research,* 19 (1), 1–14.

14 Naidoo, J. and Wills, J. (2005) *Public Health and Health Promotion: Developing Practice.* Edinburgh: Baillière Tindall.

15 Caplan, R. (1993) The Importance of Social Theory for Health Promotion: from Description to Reflexivity. *Health Promotion International,* 8 (2), 147–57.

16 Andreasen, A.R. (2002) Op. cit.

17 Trifiletti, L.B, Gielen, A.C., Sleet, D.A. and Hopkins, K. (2005) Op. cit.

18 Ogden, J. (2003) Some Problems with Social Cognition Models: A Pragmatic and Conceptual Analysis. *Health Psychology,* 22 (4), 424–28.

19 Ibid.

20 Scheeran, P. and Abraham, C. (1996) The Health Belief Model, in M. Conner and P. Norman (eds), *Predicting Health Behaviour*. Buckingham: Open University Press.

21 Lewin, R.W. (1951) *Field Theory in Social Science*. New York: Harper.

22 Cited in Weissfeld, J.L., Brock, B.M., Kirscht, J.P. and Hawthorne, V.M. (1987) Reliability of Health Belief Indexes: Confirmatory Factor Analysis in Sex, Race, and Age Subgroups. *Health Services Research,* 21 (6), 777–93.

23 Cited in Becker, M.H. (1974) The Health Belief Model and Personal Health Behavior. *Health Education Monographs,* 2 (4), 324–508.

24 Hochbaum, G.M. (1958) *Public Participation in Medical Screening Programmes: A Socio-psychological Study*. Washington, DC: Public Health Service Publication No. 572, US Government Printing Office.

25 Rosenstock, L.M. (1966) Why People Use Health Services, *Millbank Memorial Fund Quarterly,* 44, 94–124.

26 Rosenstock, L.M. (1974) Historical Origins of the Health Belief Model. *Health Education Monographs,* 2, 1–8.

27 Rosenstock, L.M., Strecher, V.J. and Becker, M.H. (1988) Social Learning Theory and the Health Belief Model. *Health Education Quarterly,* 15 (2), 175–83.

28 Bandura, A. (1977) Self-Efficacy: Toward a Unifying Theory of Behavioural Change. *Psychological Review,* 84, 191–215.

29 Janz, N.K., and Becker, M.H. (1984) The Health Belief Model: A Decade Later. *Health Education Quarterly,* 11, 1–47.

30 Burns, A.C. (1992) The Expanded Health Belief Model as a Basis for Enlightened Preventive Health Care Practice and Research. *Journal of Health Care Marketing,* 12 (3), 32–45.

31 Janz, N.K. and Becker, M.H. (1984) Op. cit.

32 Glanz, K., Rimer, B.K. and Lewis, F.M. (2002) *Health Behavior and Health Education* (3rd edn). San Francisco: Jossey-Bass.

33 Rogers, R.W. (1975) A Protection Motivation Theory of Fear Appeals and Attitude Change. *Journal of Psychology,* 91, 93–114.

34 Bandura, A. (1986) *Social Foundations of Thought and Action: A Social Cognitive Theory*. Englewood Cliffs, NJ: Prentice Hall.

35 Wood, R. and Bandura, A. (1989) Social Cognitive Theory of Organizational Management. *Academy of Management Review,* 14 (3), 361–84.

36 Bandura, A. (2004) Health Promotion by Social Cognitive Means. *Health Education and Behavior,* 31, 143–64.

37 Wood, R. and Bandura, A. (1989) Op. cit.

38 Baranowski, T., Perry, C.L. and Parcel, G. (1997) How Individuals, Environments and Health Behaviors Interact: A Social Cognitive Theory. In K. Glanz, B.K. Rimer and F.M. Lewis (2002). *Health Behavior and Health Education* (3rd edn). San Francisco: Jossey-Bass.

39 Fishbein, M. and Ajzen, I. (1975) *Belief, Attitude, and Behavior: An Introduction to Theory and Research*. Reading, MA: Addison-Wesley.

40 Ajzen, I. and Fishbein, M. (1980) *Understanding Attitudes and Predicting Social Behavior*. Englewood Cliffs, NJ: Prentice-Hall.

41 Ajzen, I. (1991) The Theory of Planned Behaviour. *Organizational Behavior and Human Decision Processes,* 50, 179–211.

42 Bandura, A. (1977) Op. cit.

43 Bandura, A. (1982) Self-Efficacy Mechanism in Human Agency. *American Psychologist,* 37 (2), 122–47.

44 Ibid.

45 McCaul, K.D., Sandgren, A.K., O'Neill, H.K. and Hinsz, V.B. (1993) The Value of the Theory of Planned Behavior, Perceived Control, and Self-Efficacy Expectations for Predicting Health-Protective Behaviours. *Basic & Applied Social Psychology,* 14 (2), 231–52.

46 Sultan, S., Bungener, C. and Andronikof, A. (2002) Individual Psychology of Risk-taking Behaviors in Non-adherence. *Journal of Risk Research,* 5 (2), 137–45.

47 Ogden, J. (2003) Op. cit.

48 Bozionelos, G. and Bennett, P. (1999) The Theory of Planned Behaviour as a Predictor of Exercise. *Journal of Health Psychology*, 4, 517–29.

49 Jamner, M.S., Wolitski, R.J., Corby, N.H. and Fishbein., M. (1998) Using the Theory of Planned Behaviour to Predict Intention to Use Condoms among Female Sex Workers. *Psychology and Health*, 13: 187–205.

50 De Wit, J.B.F., Stroebe, W., De Vroome, E.M.M., Sandfort, T.G.M. and Van Griensven, G.J.P. (2000) Understanding AIDS Preventive Behaviour with Casual and Primary Partners in Homosexual Men: The Theory of Planned Behaviour and the Information-Motivation-Behavioural-Skills Model. *Psychology & Health*, 15, 325–40.

51 Flynn, B.S., Dana, G.S., Goldstein, A.O., Bauman, K.E., Cohen, J.E., Gotlieb, N.H. and Solomon, L.J. (1997) State Legislators' Intentions to Vote and Subsequent Votes on Tobacco Control Legislation. *Health Psychology*, 16, 401–4.

52 Sutton, S., McVey, D. and Glanz, A. (1999) A Comparative Test of the Theory of Reasoned Action and the Theory of Planned Behaviour in the Prediction of Condom Use Intention in a National Sample of English Young People. *Health Psychology*, 18, 72–81.

53 Yzer, M.C., Siero, F.W. and Buunk, B.P. (2001) Bringing up Condom Use and Using Condoms with New Sexual Partners: Intentional or Habit? *Psychology and Health*, 16, 409–21.

54 Huhman, M.E., Potter, L.D., Duke, J.C., Judkins, D.R., Heitzler, C.D. and Wong, F.L. (2007) Evaluation of a National Physical Activity Intervention for Children: VERB(TM) Campaign, 2002–2004. *American Journal of Preventive Medicine*, 32 (1), 38–43.

55 Price, S.M., Potter, L.D., Das, B., Wang, Y.-C.L. and Huhman, M. (2009) Exploring the Influence of the VERB Brand Using a Brand Equity Framework. *Social Marketing Quarterly*, 15 (4), 66–82.

56 Fishbein, M. (2000) The role of theory in HIV prevention. *AIDS Care*, 12, 273–8.

57 Fishbein, M. and Cappella, J. (2006) The Role of Theory in Developing Effective Health Communications. *Journal of Communication*, 56 (August Supplement), S1–S17.

58 Prochaska, J.O. and DiClemente, C.C. (1983) Stages and Processes of Self-Change in Smoking: Toward an Integrative Model of Change. *Health Education Research*, 14, 641–51.

59 Prochaska, J.O., Velicer, W.F., Guadagnoli, E., Rossi, J.S., DiClemente, C.C. (1991) Patterns of Change: Dynamic Topology Applied to Smoking Cessation. *Multivariate Behavioral Research*, 26 (1), 83–107.

60 Prochaska, J. and Velicer, W. (1997) The Transtheoretical Model of Behavior Change. *American Journal of Health Promotion*, 12 (1): 60.

61 Snow, M.G., Prochaska, J.O. and Rossi, J.S. (1992) Stages of Change for Smoking Cessation among Former Problem Drinkers: A Cross-Sectional Analysis. *Journal of Substances Abuse*, 4, 107–16.

62 Marcus, B.H., Pinto, B.M., Simkin, L.R. and Taylor, E.R. (1994) Application of Theoretical Models to Exercise Behavior among Employed Women. *American Journal of Health Promotion*, 9 (1), 49–55.

63 Bunton, R., Baldwin, S., Flynn, D. and Whitelaw, S. (2000) The 'Stages of Change' Model in Health Promotion: Science and Ideology. *Critical Public Health*, 10 (1), 55–70.

64 Bandura, A. (1997) Editorial: The Anatomy of Stages of Change. *American Journal of Health Promotion*, 12 (1), 8–10.

65 Sutton, S. (2001) Back to the Drawing Board? A Review of Applications of the Transtheoretical Model to Substance Use. *Addiction*, 96, 175–86.

66 Adams, J. and White, M. (2003) Are Activity Promotion Interventions based on the Transtheoretical Model Effective? A Critical Review. *British Journal of Sports Medicine*, 37, 106–14

67 Marshall, S.J. and Biddle, S.J.H. (2001) The Transtheoretical Model of Behavior Change: A Meta-Analysis of Application to Physical Activity and Exercise. *Annals of Behavioral Medicine*, 23 (4), 229–46.

68 Bridle, C., Riemsa, R.P., Pattenden, J., Sowden, A.J., Mather, L., Watt, I.S. and Walker, A. (2005) Systematic Review of the Effectiveness of Health Behaviour Interventions Based on the Transtheoretical Model. *Psychology & Health*, 20 (3): 283–301.

69 Sutton, S. (2001) Op. cit.

70 Adams, J. and White, M. (2003) Op. cit.

71 Ibid.

72 Herzog, T.A., Abrams, D.B., Emmons, K.M., Linnan, L.A. and Shadel, W.G. (1999) Do Processes of Change Predict Smoking Stage Movements? A Prospective Analysis of the Transtheoretical Model. *Health Psychology*, 18 (4), 369–75.

73 Bridle, C., Riemsa, R.P., Pattenden, J., Sowden, A.J., Mather, L., Watt, I.S. and Walker, A. (2005) Op. cit.

74 Brug, J., Conner, M., Harré, N., Kremers, S., McKellar, S. and Whitelaw, S. (2005) The Transtheoretical Model and Stages of Change: A Critique. *Health Education Research*, 20 (2): 244–58.

75 Weinstein, N.D. (1988) The Precaution Adoption Process. *Health Psychology,* 7 (4), 355–86.

76 Weinstein, N.D., Rothman, A.J. and Sutton, S.R. (1998) Stage Theories of Health Behaviour: Conceptual and Methodological Issues. *Health Psychology,* 17 (3), 290–99.

77 Schwarzer, R. (1992) Self-efficacy in the Adoption and Maintenance of Health Behaviors: Theoretical Approaches and a New Model. In: *Self-efficacy: Thought control of Action* by Schwarzer, R. (ed.). Washington, DC: Hemisphere Publishing Corp.

78 Bagozzi, R.P. (1992) The Self-Regulation of Attitudes, Intentions and Behavior. *Social Psychology Quarterly,* 55 (2), 178–204.

79 Gollwitzer, P.M. (1990) Action Phases and Mind-Sets. In E.T. Higgins and R.M. Sorrentino (eds) *Handbook of Motivation and Cognition: Foundations of Social Behaviour.* New York: Guilford Press.

80 Heckhausen, H. (1991) *Motivation and Action.* New York: Springer.

81 Armitage, C.J. and Conner, M. (2000) Social Cognition Models and Health Behaviour: A Structured Review. *Psychology & Health,* 15 (2), 173–89.

82 Brug, J., Conner, M., Harré, N., Kremers, S., McKellar, S. and Whitelaw, S. (2005) Op. cit.

83 Brehm, J.W. (1966) *A Theory of Psychological Reactance.* New York: Academic Press.

84 Brehm, J.W. and Brehm S.S. (1981) *Psychological Reactance: A Theory of Freedom and Control.* New York: Academic Press.

85 Brehm, J.W. (1989) Psychological Reactance: Theory and Applications. *Advances in Consumer Research,* 16, 72–5.

86 Stead, M., Tagg, S., MacKintosh, A.M. and Eadie, D. (2005) Development and Evaluation of a Mass Media Theory of Planned Behaviour Intervention to Reduce Speeding. *Health Education Research,* 20 (1), 36–50.

87 Manstead, A.S.R. (1991) Social Psychological Aspects of Driver Behaviour. Invited paper presented at the meeting *New Insights into Driver Behaviour,* organized by the *Parliamentary Advisory Council for Transport Safety,* London. Manchester: University of Manchester.

88 Stradling, S.G. and Parker, D. (1996) Extending the Theory of Planned Behaviour: The Role of Personal Norm, Instrumental Beliefs and Affective Beliefs in Predicting Driving Violations. Presented at *International Conference on Traffic and Transport Psychology,* Valencia.

89 Parker, D., Stradling, S.G. and Manstead, A.S.R. (1996) Modifying Beliefs and Attitudes to Exceeding the Speed Limit: An Intervention Study Based on the Theory of Planned Behaviour. *Journal of Applied Social Psychology,* 26, 1–19.

90 Lawton, R., Parker, D., Manstead, A.S.R. and Stradling, S.G. (1997) The Role of Affect in Predicting Social Behaviours: The Case of Road Traffic Violations. *Journal of Applied Social Psychology,* 27, 1258–76.

91 Stradling, S.G. (1999) Changing Driver Attitude and Behaviour. Presented at *DETR Speed Review Seminar,* London.

92 Vogel, R. and Rothengatter, J.A. (1984) *Motieven voor Snelheidsgedrag op Autosnelwegen: Een Attitude-onderzoek* [Motives for Speeding on Motorways: A Survey on Attitudes]. Groningen: Rijksuniversiteit.

93 Corbett, C. (1991) Drivers' Attitudes Towards Offending. In *Proceedings of the PACTS Conference on New Insights into Driver Behaviour,* London.

94 Stradling, S.G. (1999) Op. cit.

95 McKenna, F. (1991) Drivers' Perceptions of Risk. In *Proceedings of the PACTS Conference on New Insights into Driver Behaviour,* London.

96 Simon, F. and Corbett, C. (1991) A Small Roadside Study of Drivers Caught Breaking Speed Limits. Paper given at the *Seminar on Behavioural Research in Road Safety,* Manchester University, Manchester.

97 Garcia, K. and Mann, T. (2003) From 'I Wish' to 'I will': Social Cognitive Predictors of Behavioral Intentions. *Journal of Health Psychology,* 8 (3), 347–60.

98 Nigg, C.R., Allegrante, J.P. and Ory, M. (2002) Theory-Comparison and Multiple-Behavior Research: Common Themes Advancing Health Behavior Research. *Health Education Research,* 17 (5), 670–79.

99 Noar, S.M. and Zimmerman, R.S. (2004) Health Behavior Theory and Cumulative Knowledge Regarding Health Behaviors: Are We Moving in the Right Direction? *Health Education Research,* 20 (3), 275–90.

Chapter 7

Conducting research in social marketing

Chapter objectives

On completion of this chapter you should be able to:

- critically describe the principles and practice of research within a social marketing context;
- critically evaluate ethical challenges that may apply to research on a range of topics and across a range of population segments;
- design and justify research projects for specific interventions;
- critically evaluate the design and outputs of research projects;
- design and justify research programmes to evaluate the effects and effectiveness of an intervention.

Overview of research

Role of research

The role of research in social marketing is simply to provide a foundation for decision-making at all stages of intervention: scoping, development, implementation and evaluation. There is insufficient space to cover all possible research strategies and techniques in depth. A number of excellent research methods texts are available and we have provided a list of recommended resources at the end of the chapter. The focus here is, first, on providing a guide to help you think about the possible sources of existing research that may aid in the development of social marketing interventions. Secondly, we provide an overview of the process for deciding on appropriate research strategies.

Choice of methodology

Research takes many forms and the choice of methodologies will be determined by the task at hand – and constrained by the resources available. The flowcharts in Figure 7.2a and b provide an indication of the steps that are normally followed. (The types of research that may be appropriate when evaluating the impact of an intervention are discussed in detail in Chapter 14. It is worth noting that the evaluation phase should not be done in isolation – it should also be a foundation for the development of the next cycle of the intervention.)

If you are going to do a lot of statistical analysis and feel you need help and support – particularly if you have not formally studied market research and/or statistics – we suggest you equip yourself with one of the many easy-to-read (as opposed to highly technical) data analysis guides such as those listed at the end of the chapter.

Primary versus secondary research

Before deciding to conduct original research (**primary research**), you should investigate what is already known from existing data sources (**secondary research**), both within your own organisation and from external sources, including government agencies and commercial sources. You should be able to identify the significance of the problem or issue you are trying to address, the sectors of the population most affected and trends over time – is the problem becoming more or less severe in different segments of the population? The advantage of using secondary data sources is that the data already exists, therefore there may be considerable time and resource savings if you are able to obtain the information you need. However, secondary data may be out of date and not reflect changes in the environment. It may have been collected for purposes other than your area of activity and therefore may not give you all the information you need.

Problem definition

In deciding on what questions to ask and how to obtain the desired data, it is important to ensure that you have identified the specific problem for which you are seeking a solution. Simply identifying the symptoms of a problem will not provide a solution to the underlying cause. So although historical data is frequently used to map trends, such as road accidents, rates of sexually transmitted diseases or cancer rates, it is important to look beyond this data to understand the problem. For example, Figure 7.1 shows the trends in hospital admissions for self-harm-related injuries. The upward trend is of obvious concern, but it is essential to investigate the possible causes of the increase before action is taken to try to reduce the admission rates.

When investigating data and behaviours, be wary of assuming, because two factors vary together, that one causes the other – **correlation** does not imply **causation**. For example, consumption of ice cream and incidents of drowning may appear to be correlated, but in no way is there any cause-and-effect relationship![1]

When causation appears to be evident, be careful in deciding in which direction the cause and effect runs. Take, for example, the presumed link between children's television and obesity. Do children become overweight because they watch television instead of being involved in more active pursuits, or do children who are overweight feel uncomfortable or self-conscious about participating in activities such as sport and games and therefore seek out other, less active pursuits? There is, in fact, mixed evidence on this issue, including some evidence that television viewing is not always a substitute for physical activity.[2, 3]

You should have reviewed relevant behavioural theories, such as those described in Chapter 6, which might provide guidance in developing both research questions and ultimately the intervention itself [4] by providing 'a framework to help identify the determinants of any given behaviour'.[5] It may also be useful to review case studies of other interventions to

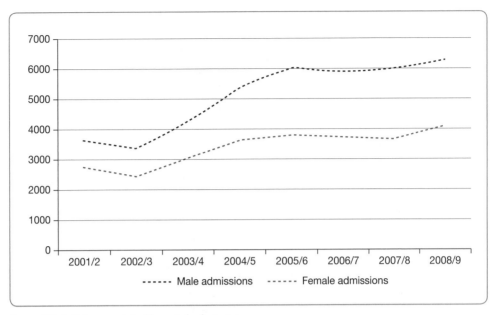

Figure 7.1 Self-harm-related hospital admissions

Source: South West Health Observatory (2011): Local Authority Suicide and Self Harm Audit 2010, Bristol.

identify which theories have proved particularly effective and useful. Bear in mind, however, that interventions can rarely be transferred without modification from one setting to another!

Figure 7.2(a) and (b) show flowcharts of the processes commonly used in research decisions. The techniques shown are by no means exhaustive.

Research ethics

Information, consent and confidentiality

Before we go any further, we need to provide some caveats. The first relates to research ethics and the need to consider the following:[6, 7]

- **Informed consent:** all participants should be fully informed about the nature and purpose of the research and the use to which any data collected will be put. This may involve providing access to a summary of the overall study findings upon completion of the research component. Potential respondents have the right to refuse to participate in a study – or to withdraw their consent before completion of the research.

- **Right to privacy and confidentiality:** all participants have the right to remain anonymous – no individual should be identifiable from their responses.

- **Right not to be deceived or harmed:** this includes psychological harm as well as physical harm.

In all research activity, you should provide potential participants with a simple information sheet outlining the purpose of the project, the type of research to be conducted, the use to which findings will be put and guarantees about confidentiality. You should also ask each participant to sign a consent form confirming that they understand the nature of the project and are prepared to participate.

143

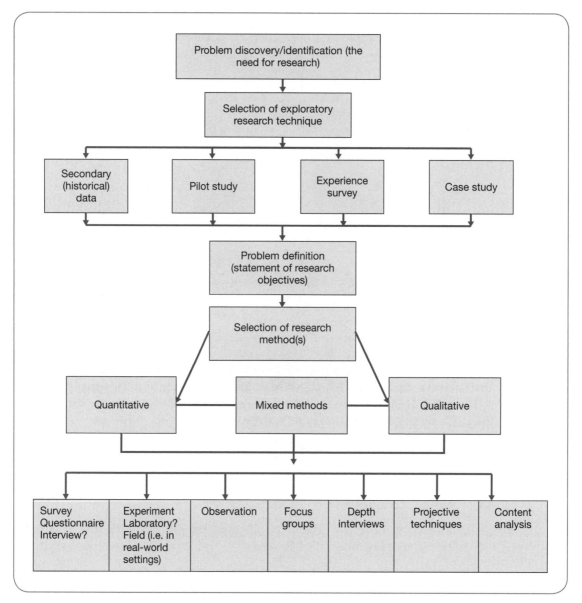

Figure 7.2a Flowchart of the marketing research process: Part A – Problem discovery and definition and research design

Source: Adapted from Zikmund, W.G. (2000) *Exploring Marketing Research* (7th edn) Orlando, FL: The Dryden Press.

Each project will be different; however, social marketing research frequently involves topics where potential research participants may have concerns about the nature of the research and the uses to which it will be put. The following are examples of information sheets and consent forms drawn from recent projects. These include:

● Attitudes towards breastfeeding among teenage mothers – some of whom were still at school;

● Attitudes towards nutrition among ethnic minorities;

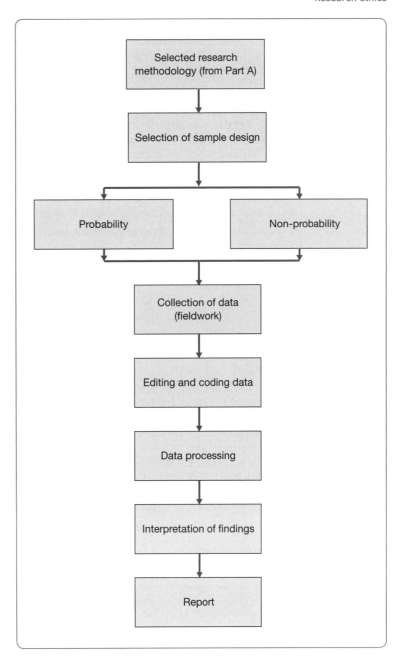

Figure 7.2b Flowchart of the marketing research process: Part B – sampling, data gathering, data processing and analysis

Source: Adapted from Zikmund, W.G. (2000) *Exploring Marketing Research* (7th edn) Orlando, FL: The Dryden Press.

- Knowledge about aspects of ageing and preferred information/information sources among elderly people;
- Factors influencing fitness centre participation.

Note – this latter project was an online study, therefore the information provided was comprehensive – there was no mechanism whereby participants could ask for clarification. For online research, consent forms are not used, as completing the questionnaire is taken as a de facto form of consent.

Research project to explore attitudes to breastfeeding
Parental consent form

Dear Parent,

As part of this research project, we are looking to hold some discussions with children of different ages to learn from their experiences of breastfeeding. Would you be prepared to allow your child to take part please? The discussion will last no longer than 60 minutes and as a thank-you for time given, a donation will be made to the [School] towards nursery equipment. The discussions will be conducted by a professional researcher adhering strictly to the code of conduct relating to the interviewing of children.

Please initial each box.

1 I confirm that I have read and understand the information sheet for the above study

2 I understand that my child's participation is voluntary and that he/she is free to withdraw at any time

3 I agree to my child taking part in the above study.

Name of Parent/guardian   Date   Parent/guardian's signature

....

Name of participant

....

Researcher   Date   Signature

....

Data Protection Act

I understand that data collected about my child during his/her participation in this study will be stored on computer, and that any files containing information about him/her will be made anonymous. I agree to the [University] recording and processing this information about my child's views on breastfeeding. I understand that this information will be used only for the purpose of this study and my consent is conditional upon the University complying with its duties and obligations under the Data Protection Act.

Signature ....   Date ....

Interviewer declaration:

I have recruited this person to the criteria specified by this questionnaire and other briefing provided. Please explain that respondents may be called by telephone, to check that recruitment and booking procedure meet quality standards. Thank you.

Name ....   **Signed** ....   **Date** ....

Pupil consent form

Name ....

Year ....

Tutor group ....

Date ....

I am happy to take part in the research project looking at attitudes to breastfeeding. I have had the project explained to me. I understand that if I am unhappy about anything that I am being asked to do, I can say so and if I want to I can stop taking part. If I am not sure about anything then I can ask the researcher, [Name], and she will explain it to me.

Signed ………………………….…………..

Date ………………………………………

Investigator …………………………………

Healthy eating initiatives consent form

About this focus group/interview

This focus group/interview is part of a research project about attitudes to healthy eating, food and diet. The focus group/interview will involve a discussion about what people think about healthy eating, and their experiences with shopping for food, cooking food, planning meals and diet etc.

This sheet is for you to keep and tells you more about the project and what it involves.

- This research project is carried out on behalf of the [Name] NHS who want to find out what people think about healthy eating, food and diet in the community

- The researcher who is coordinating this project is [Name] who is based at the [University] in [City].

- The focus groups and interviews are being held with members of the Somali, South Asian and African Caribbean communities in [City].

- A focus group is a small-group discussion between 6-8 people with a researcher or moderator present to steer the discussion. The aim of the group is to get a range of opinions and understandings about healthy eating from a range of different people.

- The focus group/interview will last about 60 minutes.

- The focus group/interview will be digitally-recorded, and then written up so that we have a record of what people have said in the discussion.

- When the focus groups/interviews are written up people's names and any references that they make to other people, places and events will be changed in order to protect the identities of everyone who has taken part. In other words participants will remain unidentifiable.

- Extracts from the focus groups/interviews will be used in a report given to [Name] Primary Care Trust. Extracts may also be used in other research reports and publications related to this project.

- If you agree to take part in this focus group/interview, but feel at any stage that you would like to stop, you are free to do so at any time.

For any queries or for more information on the project please contact:

[Name, address, telephone number, email address]

Healthy Eating Initiatives Consent Form

(researcher keeps this section)

I agree to take part in the focus group under the conditions described on the attached sheet:

Signed: .... Date: ....

Are you: Male .... Age: ....

(Please tick one) Female ....

*Employment/education status (Please state)

----

*How would you describe your ethnic identity? (Please state)

----

*Area that you currently reside in

Would you be happy for us to interview you about healthy eating again? ☐ Yes ☐ No

If you stated yes to the above question, could you please write your contact details below:

Name _____

Mobile _____

Email_____

*Questions about employment/education status, ethnic identity and residential area are for the purposes of keeping an accurate record of the numbers of participants from each community group, and to identify whether issues impacting on healthy eating might be affected by locations and employment status. **The information on this sheet will in no way be used to render participants identifiable.**

Thank you for participating in this project!

An Investigation into the maintenance or cancellation of memberships at the [Name of organisation] (online questionnaire)

Introduction

The following informed consent is required for any person invited to participate in a research study conducted by the [University]. This study has been approved by the University's Ethics Committee.

Purpose of the study

This is a study in social marketing that is being conducted by [Name], a Senior Lecturer in Marketing at the [University] (as part of a doctoral thesis) on behalf of [Name of sponsoring body]. The purpose of this study is to examine the perceptions and attitudes of the [organisation's] members, and how this relates to the cancellation or maintenance of their memberships.

What will be done

You will complete a survey, which will take approximately 10 minutes to complete. For this study, you will be responding to questions about your attitudes towards exercising at the [organisation's] gymnasium, such as: exercise enjoyment, barriers to exercising, health benefits, intensity levels of exercise and motivation.

We also will ask for some demographic information (e.g., age, marital status, number of children, education level, and travel time to the gymnasium) so that we can accurately describe the general traits of the groups and individuals who participate in the study.

Benefits of this study

You will be contributing to knowledge about gymnasium members' attitude and behaviours when exercising at the [organisation's] gymnasium to inform academic knowledge and improve the service provided. In addition, you will be entered in a draw for an annual membership package. After we have finished data collection, we will conduct the draw for the prizes. Winners will receive the notification via email.

Risks or discomforts

No risks or discomforts are anticipated from taking part in this study. If you feel uncomfortable at any point, you can withdraw from the study altogether. If you decide to quit at any time before you have finished the questionnaire, your answers will NOT be recorded.

Confidentiality: *Your responses will be kept completely confidential.*

We will NOT know your IP address when you respond to the internet survey. If you wish to be entered into the prize draw, we will ask you to include your email address when you complete the internet survey so that we can connect your survey answers to the data we collect. You will be assigned a participant number, and only the participant number will appear with your survey responses. Only the researchers will see your individual survey responses. The list of email addresses of our participants will be stored electronically in a password protected folder; a hard copy will be stored in a locked filing cabinet. After we have finished the data collection, we will destroy the list of participants' email addresses.

Decision to quit at any time

Your participation is voluntary; you are free to withdraw your participation from this study at any time. If you do not want to continue, you can simply leave this website. If you do not click on the 'submit' button at the end of the survey, your answers and participation will not be recorded. If you click on the 'submit' button at the end of the survey, and provide your email address you will be entered in the draw for the prizes.

How the findings will be used

The results of the study will be used for scholarly purposes and to inform the management of the [Name of organisation] facility only. The results from the study will be presented in educational settings and at professional conferences, and the results might be published in a professional journal in the field of Social Marketing as well as being used by the management of [Name of organisation] to improve the service provided to you. All survey responses you provide for this study will be completely confidential. When the results of the study are reported, you will not be identified by name or any other information that could be used to infer your identity.

Contact information

If you have any questions before you complete this survey, please email me, [Name] at [email address]. You can also view my profile on the University's website [website address]. By clicking 'Yes' below you acknowledge that you have read and understand that: By beginning the survey, you acknowledge that you have read this information and agree to participate in this research, with the knowledge that you are free to withdraw your participation at any time.

☐ Yes, I want to participate

☐ No, I do not want to participate

This is the introductory email message to be used to invite people to take your survey

Subject: Your chance to win an annual membership package at the [Name of organisation] Gymnasium. Doctoral Thesis Survey – An Investigation into the maintenance or cancellation of memberships at the [organisation's] Gymnasium.

Dear Member,

My name is [Name] and I am a Senior Lecturer in Marketing at the [University]. Below is a link to a survey that is part of my research for my doctoral thesis. This research is being undertaken in collaboration with [Name of sponsoring body] and the management of [the organisation's] gymnasium.

It is a 10-minute survey about members' attitudes towards exercise and its impact upon the decision to cancel or maintain a membership. By completing this survey you will be entered into a prize draw. Winners will be randomly selected to receive a prize of an annual membership. Your participation is greatly appreciated.

If you have any questions before you decide to complete this survey, please email me, [Name] at [email address]. You can also view my profile on the University's website. To complete the survey please click on the URL below

[URL]

This link is unique to you. Please do not forward it.

Thanks for your time,

Regards

[Name]

If you wish to opt out of receiving any emails about this research please click on the link below
I no longer wish to receive future emails

Physical activity in elderly people project consent form

I am writing to you as a Principal Investigator for the [Name] Project. You have been asked to participate in a one-hour focus group, and the focus group is scheduled for **10am** on **Tuesday, 29 March**. A focus group is an informal discussion group, where you will be encouraged to share your views with other participants. Please read this letter prior to attending the group. Please sign the letter and bring it with you when attending the group as a sign of informed consent.

This is to certify that I, **«Firstname» «Lastname»,** have been given the following information with respect to my participation as a volunteer in a research programme under the supervision of [Name].

1 **Purpose of the study:** This project seeks to provide background data on motivational factors for and perceived barriers to engaging in physical activity. Approximately 20 people are participating in focus groups for this aspect of the research project.

2 **Procedures to be followed:** You will be asked some questions and can answer and discuss these questions with others in the focus group. The session will last one hour and will be tape-recorded. We will transcribe the tape recordings, removing any identifying information such as individual names and then will destroy the tapes. These are standard procedures for focus groups.

3 **Participation is voluntary:** Your participation in this focus group is voluntary. ***You may decline to answer any or all questions, and you are free to leave at any time.***

4 **Discomforts and risks:** There are no known discomforts or risks. However, some physical activity issues can be sensitive. We will be making every effort to ensure the confidentiality of any information provided; however, there is a slight possibility that you could be identified if you provide very specific information on your circumstances.

5 **Benefits to me:** There is no directly attributable clinical benefit to you from participating in this study. However, you may find it beneficial to discuss your views on physical activity with other people in a structured way.

6 **Benefits to society**: We are hoping to identify ways to improve physical activity in elderly people.

7 **Time duration of the procedures and study:** The focus group lasts approximately one hour. If people wish to continue the discussion longer than one hour, we will continue but also provide the opportunity for participants to leave after one hour.

8 **Statement of confidentiality:** Every attempt will be made to ensure confidentiality. There will be a short period of time during which the researchers could identify individuals, but all data will be stripped of identifying information before anything is reported from the project. Once identifiers have been removed, the only individuals who could identify your information are those who participated in this focus group with you.

If you have any questions about the project, please do not hesitate to contact me. My contact details are: [Name and address]. My telephone number is [tel. no.] or you can reach me via email: [email address].

The contact details of the secretary to the [Name] Research Ethics Committee are [Name], [Address]. Email: [email address], tel. [tel. no.].

Signature _____   Date _____

Children as a special case

It is not just situations such as the breastfeeding example discussed above that may require careful thought about ethical issues. All research involving children will be subject to careful scrutiny due to children's perceived vulnerability and limited cognitive development[8] and researchers working with children will need to undergo a police check.

If projects involve collection of data from schoolchildren, mechanisms need to be set in place to ensure that ethical considerations regarding informed consent and privacy are taken into account, with the same strategy for all schools that agree to participate in a study. Generally, formal approval for the project will be required from the head teacher and, via them, from the board of governors after careful consideration of ethical issues for parents/ caregivers and their children.

This means that a letter outlining the objectives of the study and guaranteeing confidentiality for all respondents will be sent to parents. This would be similar in structure to the information sheets and consent forms discussed in the previous section. A covering letter from the head teacher endorsing the study and asking for parental co-operation would be requested. Formal written parental/caregiver consent would be required before the research could proceed.

In the information letter, researchers should stress that there will be no ramifications should parents elect not to permit their children to participate. Alternative classroom activities may need to be organised by the relevant class teachers to ensure that no child will be placed in a situation of feeling inferior or 'left out' of activities if they do not participate in the study or their parents elect to withdraw their permission for participation.

The information letter should also stress that only the aggregate results will be used and that no individual child or their parent/caregiver will be able to be identified. Advice will need to be taken from participating schools regarding any need to translate the material for parents into the relevant country languages.

The participating school should be asked to nominate a specific teacher to liaise with the researcher on all aspects of the research and regular liaison will need to be maintained by the supervisory team. There is a considerable input required from the schools; we therefore recommend that you consider making a donation to each participating school (rather than to individual participating children) after the study has been completed. This should not be used as an incentive or as a coercive device to gain parental co-operation. At all stages of the research programme, the school management team and parents should be kept fully informed, including debriefing upon completion of the fieldwork and provision of the draft report before final dissemination of findings.

The way that data is to be captured for research involving children also needs to be considered. Videotaping sessions, while appealing in terms of the richness of data obtained, would present privacy concerns for both parents and caregivers and the children's teachers. It would also be a distraction for the participating children and would add to the complications associated with finding equivalent activities for the non-participating children. Audio-taping is usually acceptable as a primary aid for later analysis and coding.

Specific health ethics approvals

The second caveat relates to potential obligations under the Research Governance Framework of the Department of Health[9] which extends considerably beyond clinical trials for medicine, covering all research and intervention activity involving existing or prospective patients and service users. If there is any doubt as to whether the NHS provisions apply to a particular project, advice should be sought from the relevant organisation such as the NHS Regional Ethics Committee (REC) or PCT in whose catchment area the project is to be conducted. The process of applying for, and obtaining, REC approval can extend project timelines considerably.

It is important to consider this in the planning of research or intervention projects in NHS environments.

However, it should be noted that not all research activity requires full National Research Ethics Service approval. The NRES provides a useful checklist as to whether advice is needed regarding the requirement for NHS approval.

As this checklist is updated regularly, we recommend you check the NRES website (http://www.nres.npsa.nhs.uk/) before you commence any research that may require NRES consideration. Table 7.1 shows different definitions of research, requiring full approval, and clinical audits or service evaluations, possibly not requiring full REC review.

Guidance on research ethics issues and sample ethics application forms for our two universities can be found at: http://rbi.uwe.ac.uk/internet/Research/ethics/default.asp and http://www.hull.ac.uk/php/sbsad2/HUBS%20Ethical_Procedures_for_Research_and_Teaching.pdf.

Table 7.1 Differentiating audit, service evaluation and research (NRES)

Research	Clinical audit	Service evaluation
The attempt to derive generalisable new knowledge, including studies that aim to generate hypotheses, as well as studies that aim to test them.	Designed and conducted to produce information to inform delivery of best care.	Designed and conducted solely to define or judge current care.
• Quantitative research – designed to test a hypothesis. • Qualitative research – identifies/ explores themes following established methodology.	Designed to answer the question: 'Does this service reach a predetermined standard?'	Designed to answer the question: 'What standard does this service achieve?'
Addresses clearly defined questions, aims and objectives	Measures against a standard.	Measures current service without reference to a standard.
• Quantitative research – may involve evaluating or comparing interventions, particularly new ones. • Qualitative research – usually involves studying how interventions and relationships are experienced.	Involves an intervention in use ONLY (the choice of treatment is that of the clinician and patient according to guidance, professional standards and/ or patient preference).	Involves an intervention in use ONLY (the choice of treatment is that of the clinician and patient according to guidance, professional standards and/ or patient preference).
Usually involves collecting data that are additional to those for routine care, but may include data collected routinely. May involve treatments, samples or investigations additional to routine care.	Usually involves analysis of existing data, but may include administration of simple interview or questionnaire.	Usually involves analysis of existing data, but may include administration of simple interview or questionnaire.
• Quantitative research – study design may involve allocating patients to intervention groups. • Qualitative research – uses a clearly defined sampling framework underpinned by conceptual or theoretical justifications.	No allocation to intervention groups: the healthcare professional and patient have chosen intervention before clinical audit.	No allocation to intervention groups: the healthcare professional and patient have chosen intervention before clinical audit.
May involve randomisation.	No randomisation.	No randomisation.
Although any of these three may raise ethical issues, under current guidance: Research requires REC review	Audit does not require REC review	Service evaluation does not require REC review

Qualitative, quantitative and mixed methods techniques

Selection of methods

Research may be **exploratory**, **descriptive** or **causal**. The research techniques to be selected will be determined by decisions as to which of these types of research is appropriate. Exploratory research is needed in situations when you are starting from scratch (no suitable/ relevant research exists), or specific segments have not been the focus of activity previously – how do they differ from other segments? Descriptive research focuses on determining the size/characteristics of a target population, what the profile of each segment is or how members of each segment behave in relation to your area of focus. Causal research is usually the most complex as the focus is on issues such as:

'Does A impact on B?'

In commercial marketing, this type of research would be used to determine whether raising the price means fewer sales. In social marketing, it would be used to identify which types of interventions are most likely to be effective for different segments. It would also be used to determine which elements of the theories discussed in Chapter 6 have the most influence on intentions and actual behaviours. Space prevents us from giving a detailed description of the various techniques; we have provided an overview of some of the main techniques and recommend you consult appropriate research texts should you want more detailed information.

We do not advocate either **qualitative** or **quantitative** methods – the selection of either or both should be determined by the specific objectives of the research and the resources/ expertise you have available with which to conduct the research. Each technique brings its own challenges, strengths and weaknesses.[10] In deciding which techniques to use, bear in mind the sort of data that funding bodies are likely to require – or value in determining ongoing funding.

Quantitative data provides measures of the extent and strength of attitudes, and the frequency of particular behaviours of interest. Data from comparatively large numbers of respondents can be gathered quickly and cheaply. However, questionnaires and other quantitative instruments are unlikely to provide the depth of data required to determine 'Why?', i.e. what underpins attitudes and behaviours and what might motivate people to change their behaviours.

Questionnaire-based data does not usually permit investigation of the often complex reasons behind specific attitudes, beliefs or behaviours, whereas qualitative techniques can provide this – but are limited in terms of being able to provide population-wide profiles of the extent of the attitudes or behaviours that may be perceived as problematic. We frequently advocate using mixed methods, whereby both qualitative and quantitative methods are used in tandem. This enables different techniques to compensate for weaknesses in other techniques.[11]

In addition, the means by which you recruit participants is crucial to the success of the data gathering process. Some population segments may be difficult to recruit.[12] We have noted the challenges presented by those who may have limited functional literacy. Consider how these groups may react to being asked to participate in a research project that involves complex wording in the information sheets and consent forms, let alone the survey instruments themselves. You may need to modify wording and formats to meet the needs of these groups.[13]

Consider also cultural dimensions. Reluctance to participate may be due to cultural issues such as a gender mismatch between interviewer and interviewee. Some sections of communities may believe that previous research has caused harm or stigmatised their community and thus be reluctant to participate in any further studies.[14] Also, even when consent is given, do not assume that participants understand the exact processes involved if participation is in forms not commonly used in their culture.[15]

Consider, too, the timing of the research. It is known that self-reports of past behaviour may be affected by recall bias[16] and therefore that the ideal time to conduct research is immediately after that behaviour has occurred. For the sun protection study given as an example in the following sections, ideally this would have been immediately after the last summer season.

Validity and reliability

Issues of validity and reliability tend to be overlooked in qualitative research, yet they are just as important as in quantitative research activity.

- **Validity**: are we really measuring the construct we intend?[17]
- **Reliability**: would we obtain similar results if the questionnaire (or other research instrument) was independently administered?[18, 19]

Socially desirable responding

Socially desirable responding[20] is a term encompassing a range of biases or distortions in responses to research questions. Generally, undesirable behaviours tend to be under-reported and desirable behaviours may be over-reported. There are two main types of socially desirable responding: impression management and self-deception.

Impression management involves deliberate endeavours to give a positive or favourable description of one's own attributes or behaviours.[21, 22] Self-deception may reflect an honest attempt at self-description that is biased because it may reflect what people aspire to rather than what they actually achieve, even if the respondent honestly believes the response to be true.[23]

Quantitative techniques

Overview

We now briefly review some of the main types of quantitative research activity that may be used. This is not an exhaustive description and it is common for different methods to be combined.

Surveys/questionnaires

Surveys and questionnaires enable 'counts' – how many hold specific beliefs/strength of support for statements (but not why). Surveys are recommended for benchmark data against which effects and effectiveness of interventions can be measured – having quantitative data thus also helps to justify requests for future funding as they enable changes in attitudes, beliefs, intentions or actual behaviour to be tracked over time. They should be used with caution in predicting future behaviours (wording is crucial) as the gap between reported intentions and subsequent actual behaviours is often substantial. Survey and questionnaire data may be collected in several ways.

Mail surveys

Mail surveys can provide better quality data for sensitive/potentially embarrassing questions than face-to-face data collection methods. Additionally, respondents can work through questions at their own pace. The disadvantages of this type of data collection include the fact that respondents cannot seek clarification about any item which may be confusing. There is also no way of checking who actually completes the questionnaire. Additionally, the quality of the mailing list itself is paramount in ensuring that the primary target segments are reached. This technique also generates low response rates due to the amount of competition for attention and time experienced by the recipients.

Telephone

The quality of the contact list is again paramount in achieving success in **telephone surveys**. If calls are made individually, this can be a time-consuming and expensive process. Many of the commercial market research organisations have computer-based automated systems that streamline the process. Generally, telephone surveys, if targeted specifically at those who may find the topic of personal interest, achieve higher response rates than mail surveys.

Face-to-face/'mall intercepts'

The **face-to-face** or 'mall intercept' technique uses central locations such as shopping malls or other central locations (beaches, concerts, shows, etc.) where the target population is likely to gather. However, the sample may not match the overall target and the weather may or may not be a problem, depending on the venue. This technique is generally more expensive than mail questionnaires and is most successful when the questions do not take more than a few minutes to answer and do not include sensitive or potentially embarrassing topics.

Web-based questionnaires

Several of the caveats listed for other forms of quantitative techniques apply to this type of activity. Questionnaires need to be easy to find/complete, therefore ways of contacting potential respondents to invite them to participate need to be explored. With this type of technique, you cannot be sure who is actually responding – but this potential problem is not restricted to web-based activity alone. It has been suggested that web-based surveys may result in lower levels of socially desirable responding, but recent research indicates that this does not appear to be the case.[24]

Attitude measurement

One of the major tasks of social marketing research is the measurement of attitudes towards particular issues or behaviours. The measurement of attitudes is not simple and the academic literature has featured a wide range of perceptions as to whether attitudes can be measured at all and, if so, what techniques are best to do so.[25] The main challenges relate to the intangible nature of attitudes; they are abstract concepts that relate to people's feelings or predispositions and, as such, they cannot be measured directly.[26]

Attitudes usually have three components: affective (feelings, emotions), cognitive (awareness/knowledge) and behavioural (intentions/expectations).[27] It is therefore important to define exactly what is meant by a specific attitude and what measurement will link the attitude as construed to the real-world situation under study.[28] Space does not permit more than a brief discussion of the techniques involved; however, any good market research textbook will provide examples of the use of attitude measurement techniques.

Scale techniques

Scale techniques, often referred to as Likert scales or Likert-type scales after their developer, are frequently used to measure attitudes, for example:

5 Extremely favourable	4 Quite favourable	3 Neither favourable nor unfavourable	2 Quite unfavourable	1 Extremely unfavourable

Scales are also used to capture a wide range of other types of data. The wording will obviously vary, depending on exactly what you are trying to measure. Consider the wording you would use for scales to measure the following:

- perceived quality
- importance
- interest
- satisfaction
- frequency
- truth/credibility.

The following provides guidance on the use of Likert scales: 'Usually, a Likert Scale will have 20–30 statements. An even number of favourable and unfavourable statements should be used so that the scale is balanced. A balance of unfavourable and favourable statements reduces the likelihood of acquiescence bias (the tendency to agree or disagree with a set of questions) which is more likely if all the statements are in the same direction.'[29] If you are in doubt as to which types of scales might be most appropriate for a specific task, consult specific resource material in this area[30] (see also the end of chapter recommended reading).

Caveats re Likert scales

Children and those with limited literacy

If you are planning to get children to answer questionnaires, consider their cognitive development and what they can understand. Whether they can 'cope' with Likert scales is a matter of debate. There is general agreement that those over the age of 8 can provide reliable reports via Likert scales, but those with limited reading skills may find difficulties responding to negative items.[31]

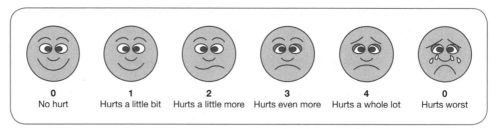

Figure 7.3 Example of a 'Smiley Likert Scale' which can be used for children

Modified versions of scales to use more pictorial content may be more appropriate for younger children, as shown in Figure 7.3.[32]

Cultural issues

Care is also needed when using Likert scales in situations where responses relate to attitudes, beliefs, values or behaviour that may reflect comparisons against perceived norms. Cultures where collective views and behaviours are more valued may provide very different responses to those from cultures where personal achievements and goals are regarded more highly.[33]

Qualitative techniques

Overview

As for the quantitative section, our objective here is to give an overview and a selection of illustrative examples that show how these techniques can be used.

Focus groups

Focus groups can provide more detail/complexity than a questionnaire (especially in relation to attitudes and beliefs underpinning behaviours) and are particularly useful for exploring factors underpinning actual behaviours, idea generation, critique of existing/alternative material, sparking new thoughts/suggestions.

Before you start, decide whether a focus group is the most appropriate method for discussing sensitive issues such as sexual behaviour, alcohol consumption or domestic violence. Even if participants are willing to discuss topics, think about the possibility of socially desirable responding noted earlier.

Each focus group is generally made up of 6–10 participants who should have common characteristics, such as mothers with young children, outdoor workers, etc. It is not an informal chat; it is a planned and guided discussion on a defined area of interest and usually lasts between 90 minutes and 2 hours.

Focus groups are led by a moderator who guides the discussion using a discussion guide (also called a moderator's guide) which is a plan of topics to be covered. The moderator's role is not to express their own views but rather to listen to individuals who belong to target segments, ensure everyone is able to speak, and keep the discussion focused on topics of interest. The key to successful focus groups is to listen to views, encourage discussion and to try to move beyond 'what' happens by probing for 'why' it happens and what might change behaviours. The discussions are usually audio-recorded then transcribed for analysis/identification of key themes. It is important to ensure that all participants understand the objectives and structure of the focus group before it commences, as the process may be completely new, and potentially threatening, to some participants.[34] An example of a moderator's guide is shown below.

Teenage mums and breastfeeding
Focus group topic overview

At the start of the session the participants will be welcomed and told the purpose of the study.

The confidentiality procedures will be explained as follows:

'Before we start I just want to explain how focus groups like this usually work. If everyone is happy for us to do so, we will be tape-recording our conversation. This is so that we have an accurate record of what is said. The tapes will only be used by the small team of researchers on this project. We will store them without your names on so that no one else would be able to connect you to the comments on the tape. It is also important that you, as participants, respect the confidential nature of anything that is said by people in the group – so we would ask you not to talk to anyone outside of this group about what has been said here.'

We will then go over the process of the focus group and ask the participants to speak clearly and to let everyone speak.

The focus group will then start and will cover the following topics:

- Opening views about breastfeeding
- Barriers and triggers to participation
- Prompted ideas about the use of various social marketing approaches to encourage breastfeeding – and the views about these. Some stimulus material might be used.
- The use of simple projective techniques such as cartoon bubbles, the use of 'How do you think other people will react?'-based questions and so on.

Practical exercise

(a) Develop your own moderator's guide for an issue that interests you, then test it with a colleague. Practise asking questions as they can sound different than when read. Keep questions short and open-ended to avoid getting just 'yes' or' no' answers.

(b) Critique the following questions:

How useful and practical was the programme for you?

In this, there are two related but distinct concepts – usefulness and practicality. It would also be very difficult for someone who felt the programme was weak on one or the other to voice criticism if they felt that the expectation was for positive comments.

Which of the following is the most important for you?

This limits the discussion. By constraining a group with a finite number of options, you may miss the things that are the most important to them if the items are not on your list.

Depth interviews

These can be time-consuming and expensive, but are useful when input from those with specific expertise is valued, when social norms may lead to 'conforming'/socially desirable responses in group discussions, or the subject matter is so sensitive that respondents are unlikely to speak openly, or when a step-by-step description of procedures is needed.

Projective techniques

These are useful when respondents cannot or will not communicate feelings directly – but will project their own feelings and beliefs into interpretation of the behaviour of others. This allows attitudes and beliefs that underlie actual behaviours to be identified in a way that is non-threatening to the participants. Examples of common projective techniques are:

(a) *Word association*, where respondents are asked to give the first word that comes to mind when a stimulus word is given, as shown in the examples below.

Stimulus word	*Response*
Summer	....
Outdoor activity	....
Suntan	....
Beach	....

(b) *Sentence completion*, where respondents are asked to complete a sentence with the first thought that comes to mind, as shown in the examples below.

People who are suntanned are ....
People who use sunbeds are ....
People who let their children get sunburnt are ....

(c) *Unfinished scenario*: respondents complete a story.

Bill was going to meet his friends at the local beach. His mother had recently bought some sunscreen lotion. Bill decided to _____ because _____. He believed his friends would _____ if they saw him putting sunscreen on.

(d) *Cartoon or caption completion*: here subjects are asked to fill in the dialogue between characters in a cartoon or photo.[35]

Practical exercise

For each of the projective techniques, draw up suitable stimulus words, partial sentences and unfinished scenarios for:

- sexual health
- binge drinking
- driving safety
- recycling
- energy consumption reduction.

Observation

As the name implies, this involves observation of behaviour directly or indirectly, for example:

- What percentage of children at a beach are wearing sunhats?
- What percentage of people at a beach reapply sunscreen after swimming?

We would add caveats that this technique is costly in terms of the time required to conduct the observations – and people may react badly to being observed!

Ethnography/netnography

Ethnography is a research technique related to observational techniques in which the researcher gains first-hand experience of the social, cultural or working environment in which the population of interest operates. Data is collected unobtrusively via field notes and journal entries which may focus on behaviours, attitudes and possibly also sample dialogue between those being studied.[36] For example, a social marketing intervention designed to reduce workplace accidents among miners was based primarily on ethnographic research, supplemented by other techniques, that was designed to:

Collect data in the natural setting of the culture.
Give researchers intensive participation in workplace cultures.
Allow researchers to interpret behaviours in a way that the culture finds credible.
Use multiple methods to gather data in order to generate a range of perspectives on the behaviours under observation.[37]

Netnography adapts the principles of ethnography to the study of online communities.

Content analysis

Content analysis is a set of techniques most commonly used to analyse the content of specific types of communication or behaviour portrayals in the media – for example, analysis of smoking portrayal and editorial coverage of smoking and health in a range of media. A content analysis of the MySpace media site found that 54% of the online profiles of 18-year-olds contained health-risk behaviour such as references to substance abuse, unwise sexual behaviour or violence.[38] A study that evaluated the portrayal of foods deemed of low nutritional value in advergames against the advertising codes that applied to more conventional media found that, if these codes had applied to internet-based persuasive communication, the majority of the sites evaluated would have been in breach of the codes.[39]

Two newer forms of content analysis are infodemiology and infoveillance, which combine the principles of content analysis with those of epidemiology. **Epidemiology** is the science of the distribution and determinants of disease in a population. **Infodemiology** is the study of the distribution and determinants of information and communication patterns regarding health, illness and health-related public policy.[40] It can identify changes in information and communication patterns via social media that can be symptoms of changes in population health. For example, it can provide early detection of disease outbreaks such as influenza.[41, 42, 43]

Infoveillance uses infodemiology data for surveillance purposes, such as identifying a surge of misinformation[44] or epidemics of fear[45] to enable communications to be targeted at countering possible negative effects.

Pre-testing

Whatever method is selected, **pre-test** it before using it in the wider community. Trial it with internal colleagues first, then with small groups of the target segments. Check for understanding, points of confusion, ease of completion – and completion time. This applies equally to research conducted at the scoping stage, the testing of specific propositions and intervention components with specific target segments, and the final evaluation and review stage.

Qualitative data analysis

You may opt to rely on memory or notes taken during your research, but generally for focus groups, detailed interviews and content analyses, you will be faced with a large amount of data, possibly 40–50 pages or more. This is particularly true of interviews which are audio-recorded and transcribed. Go back to your original questions and remind yourself of what you set out to find – then go looking for it.

You may do your analysis manually, crossing out irrelevant material, highlighting common themes, grouping material by themes – either mark them in different colours or cut them out/copy them to different documents, selecting illustrative quotes. If you have large amounts of data, it is worth investing in a computer package such as NVivo, Atlas or eximancer that is specifically designed to help make sense of non-numeric data. Samples of the use of one of these packages are shown below.

Box 7.1 NVivo© software package

This package assists in the organisation and analysis of complex non-numerical data such as transcripts, videos, audio and still images. The software allows researchers to categorise, sort and arrange numerous pieces of information; examine complex relationships in the data and combine the analysis with linking, developing, searching and graphical modelling techniques.

The software provides a much deeper level of analysis than is possible through non-computerised methods. It can test theories, identify trends, and answer questions in a variety of ways, using the search engine and query functions. The results from the analysis can assist in the production of a body of evidence either to answer research questions or to support a business case or project.

Figure 7.4 includes the transcript files of the study (focus groups, in-depth interviews) that have been loaded into the software. The bottom window provides the detail of the transcript. This is where the coding takes place, with the coded content placed in nodes.

Figure 7.5 highlights the transcript from the female parent sun study focus groups. Text from the transcript (bottom window) has been 'coded' and placed in 'nodes' (top window) that assist in the organisation and categorisation of the data.

The coding of the data allows for questions to be posed, such as: 'Do female parents, male parents and outdoor workers differ in their views about spray tans and sun bathing behaviour at home and on holiday'? (See Figure 7.6.)

The NVivo software also allows for graphical representations of the coding to explore relationships within the data and emerging ideas and concepts, as shown in Figure 7.7.

There are a growing number of sophisticated analytical packages available that can be used for both qualitative and quantitative analysis, such as IBM SPSS Modeler which is compatible with the widely used Statistical Package for Social Sciences data analysis package. Modeler, and other similar packages, enable not just analysis of current communications but also the ability to predict future communications activity and therefore provide valuable insights for the development of future communications.

This software package enables both qualitative and quantitative analysis of data from a range of sources, including databases and standard text document formats, such as Microsoft's Word, Excel, PowerPoint, as well as Adobe PDF, XML, HTML. In addition, this package can import and support analysis of web feeds, such as blogs or news feeds in RSS or HTML formats. Predictive models can be developed from this material. An example of application to social marketing is the use of this type of software to analyse scratch-pad notes from inbound or outbound telephone or email callers which can be conducted in real time, with the subsequent analysis being used to guide changes to communication messages and to improve the accuracy of predictive data models.

The package's text mining analysis facility enables the analysis of diverse collections of textual materials in order to capture key concepts and themes and uncover hidden relationships and trends without requiring knowledge of the precise words or terms that original authors have used to express those concepts. Connections and relationships can then be analysed, either alone or in combination with other types of data, both qualitative and

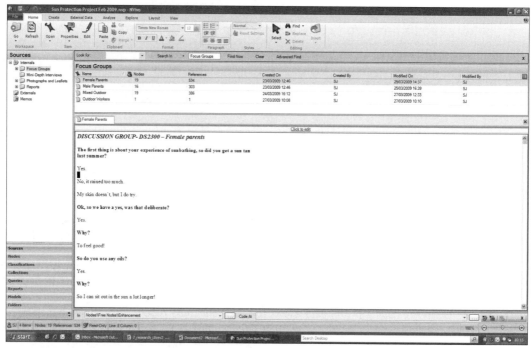

Figure 7.4 Example of an NVivo screen

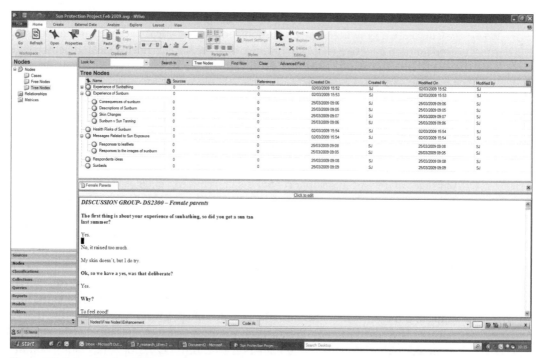

Figure 7.5 Example of an NVivo screen

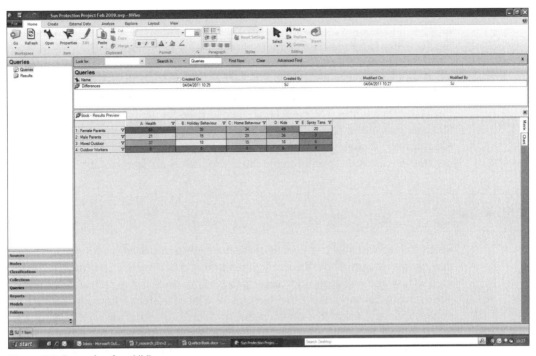

Figure 7.6 Example of an NVivo screen

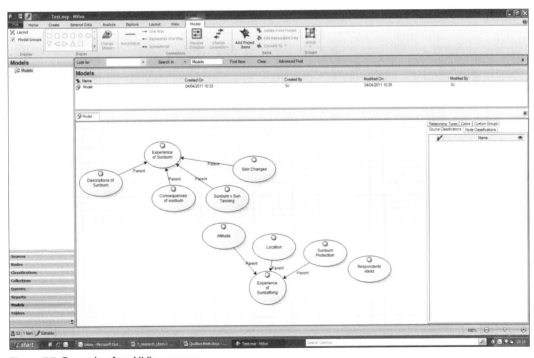

Figure 7.7 Example of an NVivo screen

quantitative, such as survey data. It is thus far more powerful than standard information retrieval and analysis. A specific value of this type of analysis is that it provides insight into the nuances of attitudes and opinions that influence behaviour.

Algorithms are developed to describe clusters of concepts, or associations between concepts or named entities. Results can be incorporated in models using classification techniques such as network analysis, decision trees and regression, association and segmentation techniques. The models can then be used for predictive analytics to aid decision-making. Specialised reports can be created, based on specific objectives or people's roles. Alternatively, models can be integrated with systems to highlight extremely positive or negative feedback on specific communications or suggest patterns of behaviour.

Summary

Research is an essential component of interventions as it provides a foundation for decision-making at all stages. There are many different forms of research; choices will depend on the specific task and resources such as budget available and staff expertise.

Existing (secondary) data can often provide a lot of useful background material; however, original (primary) research is often necessary. All participants in research have the right to be fully informed about the objectives of research, and have the right to privacy, confidentiality and not to be deceived or harmed. Specific ethics approval processes exist for vulnerable groups such as children and for some aspects of health research.

You should consult a dedicated research text if you are unsure about processes and analytical options. There are also a number of excellent analytical packages available to support both qualitative and quantitative analysis.

CHAPTER REVIEW QUESTIONS

1 Discuss the relative benefits of primary versus secondary data sources. Under what circumstances might secondary data only be used? Discuss the strengths and weaknesses of relying only on secondary data.

2 Develop and justify specific research objectives or interventions in the following areas:
- increasing physical activity
- reducing binge drinking
- increasing sun protection behaviours
- promoting sexual health
- decreasing domestic violence
- improving recycling rates
- reducing passive smoking.

3 Develop a moderator's guide for a series of focus groups for each of the above areas.

4 Develop a short (two-page maximum) questionnaire to gain initial benchmark data on attitudes and beliefs underlying behaviours for each of the areas above. Recommend and

justify the method you would use to collect the data. What ethical issues are likely to be encountered and how would you recommend these be resolved?

5 It has been suggested that observational data should be collected in relation to physical activity, binge drinking and sun protection. Discuss possible ways in which data could be collected and any ethical issues that may arise.

6 Design and justify research-based programmes to evaluate the effects and effectiveness of interventions in each of the above areas.

7 Design and justify ways of evaluating the contribution made by partners in the above interventions. Use examples to illustrate your answer.

Recommended reading

Research methods texts

Bearden, W.O. and Netemeyer, R.G. (1999) *Handbook of Marketing Scales: Multi-Item Measures for Marketing and Consumer Behavior Research*. Thousand Oaks, CA: Sage Publications.

Coates, S.J. and Steed, L.G. (2001) *SPSS Without Anguish*. Milton, Queensland: John Wiley & Son.

Dillon, W.R., Madden, T.J. and Firtle, N.H. (1994) *Market Research in a Marketing Environment*. Burr Ridge, IL: Irwin.

Gaiser, E.J. and Schreiner, A.E. (2009) *A Guide to Conducting Online Research*. London: Sage Publications.

Krueger, R.A. and Casey, M.A. (2009) *Focus Groups: A Practical Guide for Applied Research*. Thousand Oaks, CA: Sage Publications.

Lipsey, M.W. and Wilson, D.B. (2001) *Practical Meta-analysis*. Newbury Park, CA: Sage Publications.

Malhotra, N. and Birks, D. (2006) *Marketing Research: An Applied Approach* (3rd edn). Harlow: Pearson Education.

Pallant, J. (2010) *SPSS Survivial Guide*. Maidenhead: Open University Press/McGraw Hill.

Wilson, A. (2006) *Marketing Research: An Integrated Approach* (2nd edn). Harlow: Pearson Education.

Zikmund, W.G., Babin, B. (2010) *Exploring Marketing Research* (10th edn). Orlando, FL: The Dryden Press.

See also online reference sources via the American Marketing Association, e.g. Bruner, G.C., James, K. and Hensel, P.J. (2001) *Marketing Scales Handbook: A Compilation of Multi-Item Measures*. Chicago: AMA (online link www.marketingpower.com – also includes link to other online public domain research resources).

Journal articles

Bellows, L., Anderson, J., Gould, S. and Auld, G. (2008) Formative Research and Strategic Development of a Physical Activity Component to a Social Marketing Campaign for Obesity Prevention in Preschoolers. *Journal of Community Health*, 33 (3), 169–78.

Fishbein, M. and Yzer, M.C. (2003) Using Theory to Design Effective Health Behavior Interventions. *Communication Theory*, 13 (2), 164–83.

Fishbein, M. and Cappella, J. (2006) The Role of Theory in Developing Effective Health Communications. *Journal of Communication*, 56 (August Supplement), S1–S17.

Gravdal, L. and Sandal, G.M. (2006) The Two-factor Model of Social Desirability: Relation to Coping and Defense, and Implications for Health. *Personality and Individual Differences*, 40 (5), 1051–61.

Notes

1 Zikmund, W.G. (2000) *Exploring Marketing Research* (7th edn). Orlando, FL: The Dryden Press.

2 Anderson, R.E., Crespo, C.J., Barlett, S.J., Cheskin, L.J. and Pratt, M. (1998) Relationship of Physical Activity and Television Watching with Body Weight and Level of Fatness among Children: Results for the Third National Health and Nutrition Examination Survey. *Journal of the American Medical Association*, 279 (12), 938–42.

3 Lowry, R., Wechsler, H., Galuska, D.A., Fulton, J.E. and Kann, L. (2002) Television Viewing and its Association with Overweight, Sedentary Lifestyle and Insufficient Consumption of Fruits and Vegetables Among US High School Students: Differences by Race, Ethnicity, and Gender. *Journal of School Health*, 72 (1), 413–21.

4 Fishbein, M. and Yzer, M.C. (2003) Using Theory to Design Effective Health Behavior Interventions. *Communication Theory*, 13 (2), 164–83.

5 Fishbein, M. and Cappella, J. (2006) The Role of Theory in Developing Effective Health Communications. *Journal of Communication*, 56 (August Supplement), S1–S17.

6 Alsmadi, S. (2008) Marketing Research Ethics: Researcher's Obligations toward Human Subjects. *Journal of Academic Ethics*, 6 (2), 153–60.

7 MacQueen, K.M. and Buehler, J.W. (2004) Ethics, Practice, and Research in Public Health. *American Journal of Public Health*, 94 (6), 928–31.

8 Eagle, L.C. (2007) Commercial Media Literacy: What Does it Do, to Whom – and Does it Matter? *Journal of Advertising*, 36 (2), 101–10.

9 Department of Health (2005) *Research Governance Framework for Health and Social Care*. London: Department of Health.

10 Koelen, M.A., Vaandrager, L. and Colomer, C. (2001) Health Promotion Research: Dilemmas and Challenges. *Journal of Epidemiology and Community Health*, 55 (4), 257–62.

11 Berry, T.R., Spence, J.C., Plotnikoff, R.C., Bauman, A., McCargar, L., Witcher, C., et al. (2009) A Mixed Methods Evaluation of Televised Health Promotion Advertisements Targeted at Older Adults. *Evaluation and Program Planning*, 32 (3), 278–88.

12 Yancey, A.K., Ortega, A.N. and Kumanyika, S.K. (2006) Effective Recruitment and Retention of Minority Research Participants. *Annual Review of Public Health*, 27 (1), 1–28.

13 Dormandy, E., Tsui, E.Y.L. and Marteau, T.M. (2007) Development of a Measure of Informed Choice Suitable for Use in Low Literacy Populations. *Patient Education and Counseling*, 66 (3), 278–95.

14 Vastine, A., Gittelsohn, J., Ethelbah, B., Anliker, J. and Caballero, B. (2005) Formative Research and Stakeholder Participation in Intervention Development. *American Journal of Health Behavior*, 29 (1), 57–69.

15 Curtis, K., Roberts, H., Copperman, J., Downie, A. and Liabo, K. (2004) 'How Come I Don't Get Asked No Questions?' Researching 'hard to reach' Children and Teenagers. *Child & Family Social Work*, 9 (2), 167–75.

16 Adams, M.A., Mayer, J.A., Bowen, D.J. and Ji, M. (2009) Season of Interview and Self-report of Summer Sun Protection Behaviors. *Cancer Causes & Control: CCC*, 20 (2), 153–62.

17 Van Ittersum, K., Pennings, J.M.E., Wansink, B. and van Trijp, H.C.M. (2007) The Validity of Attribute-importance Measurement: A review. *Journal of Business Research*, 60 (11), 1177–90.

18 Crossley, T.F. and Kennedy, S. (2002) The Reliability of Self-Assessed Health Status. *Journal of Health Economics*, 21 (4), 643–58.

19 Tripp, M.K., Carvajal, S.C., McCormick, L.K., Mueller, N.H., Hu, S.H., Parcel, G.S., et al. (2003) Validity and Reliability of the Parental Sun Protection Scales. *Health Education Research*, 18 (1), 58–73.

20 Sullman, M.J.M. and Taylor, J.E. (2010) Social Desirability and Self-reported Driving Behaviours: Should we be Worried? *Transportation Research Part F: Traffic Psychology and Behaviour*, 13 (3), 215–21.

21 Lajunen, T. and Summala, H. (2003) Can we Trust Self-reports of Driving? Effects of Impression Management on Driver Behaviour Questionnaire Responses. *Transportation Research Part F: Traffic Psychology and Behaviour*, 6 (2), 97–107.

22 Ginis, K.A.M. and Leary, M. (2004) Self-Presentational Processes in Health-Damaging Behavior. *Journal of Applied Sport Psychology*, 16 (1), 59–74.

23 Risko, E.F., Quilty, L.C. and Oakman, J.M. (2006) Socially Desirable Responding on the Web: Investigating the Candor Hypothesis. *Journal of Personality Assessment*, 87 (3), 269–76.

24 Ibid.

25 Churchill, G.A. and Iacobucci, D. (2005) *Marketing Research: Methodological Foundations* (9th edn). Mason, OH: Thomson South-Western.

26 Dillon, W.R., Madden, T.J. and Firtle, N.H. (1994) *Marketing Research in a Marketing Environment* (3rd edn). Burr Ridge, IL: Irwin.

27 French, D.P., Sutton, S., Henning, S.J., Mitchell, J., Wareham, N.J., Griffin, S., et al. (2005) The Importance of Affective Beliefs and Attitudes in the Theory of Planned Behavior: Predicting Intention of Increased Physical Activity. *Journal of Applied Social Psychology*, 35 (9), 1824–48.

28 Ajzen, I. and Madden, T.J. (1986) Predictions of Goal-Directed Behavior: Attitudes, Intentions and Perceived Behavioral Control. *Journal of Experimental Social Psychology*, 22 (5), 453–74.

29 Dillon, W.R., Madden, T.J. and Firtle, N.H. (1994) Op. cit., p. 318.

30 Dean, D.L., Hender, J.M., Rodgers, T.L. and Santanen, E.L. (2006) Identifying Quality, Novel, and Creative Ideas: Constructs and Scales for Idea Evaluation. *Journal of the Association for Information Systems*, 7 (10), 646–98.

31 Van Laerhoven, H., van der Zaag-Loonen, H.J. and Derkx, B.H.F. (2004) A Comparison of Likert Scale and Visual Analogue Scales as Response Options in Children's Questionnaires. *ACTA PAEDIATRICA*, 93, 830–5.

32 Tomlinson, D. (2010) A Systematic Review of Faces Scales for the Self-report of Pain Intensity in Children. *Pediatrics*, 126 (5), e1168–98.

33 Heine, S.J., Lehman, D.R., Kaiping, P. and Greenholtz, J. (2002) What's Wrong With Cross-Cultural Comparisons of Subjective Likert Scales? The Reference-Group Effect. *Journal of Personality and Social Psychology*, 82 (6), 903–18.

34 Curtis, K., Roberts, H., Copperman, J., Downie, A. and Liabo, K. (2004) Op. cit.

35 Ackerman, J. (2007) The Great Sunlight Standoff. *Psychology Today*, 40 (6), 97.

36 Cook, K.E. (2005) Using Critical Ethnography to Explore Issues in Health Promotion. *Qualitative Health Research*, 15 (1), 129–38.

37 Cullen, E.T., Matthews, L.N.H. and Teske, T.D. (2008) Use of Occupational Ethnography and Social Marketing Strategies to Develop a Safety Awareness Campaign for Coal Miners. *Social Marketing Quarterly*, 14 (4), 2–21.

38 Dewhirst, T. (2009) New Directions in Tobacco Promotion and Brand Communication. *Tobacco Control*, 18 (3), 161–2.

39 Dahl, S. and Eagle, L.C. (2009) Analyzing Advergames for Children: Active Diversions or Actually Deception? *Young Consumers*, 10 (1), 46–58.

40 Eysenbach, G. (2009) Infodemiology and Infoveillance: Framework for an Emerging Set of Public Health Informatics Methods to Analyze Search, Communication and Publication Behavior on the Internet. *Journal of Medical Internet Research*, 11 (1), 1–8.

41 Wilson, K. and Brownstein, J.S. (2009) Early Detection of Disease Outbreaks Using the Internet. *CMAJ*, 180 (8), 829–31.

42 Polgreen, P.M., Yiling, C., David, M.P. and Nelson, F.D. (2008) Using Internet Searches for Influenza Surveillance. *Clinical Infectious Diseases*, (47), 1443–8.

43 Ginsberg, J., Mohebbi, M.H., Patel, R.S., Brammer, L., Smolinski, M.S. and Brilliant, L. (2009) Detecting Influenza Epidemics Using Search Engine Query Data. *Nature*, 457 (7232), 1012–14.

44 Eysenbach, G. (2002) Infodemiology: the Epidemiology of (Mis)information. *American Journal of Medicine*, 113 (9), 763–5.

45 Eysenbach, G. (2003) SARS and Population Health Technology. *Journal of Medical Internet Research*, 5 (2), e14.

Chapter 8

Segmentation

Chapter objectives

On completing this chapter, you should be able to:

- compare, contrast and critically evaluate the strengths and weaknesses of different forms of segmentation used in social marketing activity;

- evaluate possible segmentation frameworks and make reasoned recommendations as to which frameworks should be used for different types of social marketing interventions and make reasoned recommendations as to how codes might be successfully implemented among social marketing practitioners;

- analyse the reasoning behind the segmentation strategies used in past interventions and make recommendations for future improvements.

Segmentation defined

Segmentation originates from market research and is based on the analysis of survey data using cluster analysis techniques,[1] i.e. sorting into sub-groups on the basis of similar characteristics, dividing the target population into clearly defined, and mutually exclusive, sub-groups with particular emphasis on factors that influence behaviours.[2] For a detailed description of cluster analysis techniques, see any good market research text.

In social marketing, segmentation is an important and often neglected aspect of campaign development. Within each segment, members will have common characteristics – which will also differentiate them from other segments. Identifying specific segments allows strategies to be developed that meet the specific needs of each. This may involve separate interventions for specific segments or different ways of delivering services. Totally different ways of communicating with each segment, including different media selection, may also be identified.

Segmentation involves a trade-off between likely greater effectiveness in terms of customisation of material and the costs involved in developing products, services or delivery options specifically for each segment to best meet their needs. By identifying the needs of members of individual segments, interventions can be tightly targeted, with a more effective allocation of resources/less wastage than if one standard intervention is used to cover all segments.

Segmentation methods

There are many ways in which a target population may be segmented, including:

- **Cultures** or subcultures, including aspects of ethnicity and factors such as religious beliefs[3] (for example, some religious groups oppose immunisation);[4]
- **Demographics** such as gender, age, marital status, occupation, income, socio-economic status (for example, areas of low socio-economic status may be over-represented in some health behaviours, such as exposure of children to passive cigarette smoke);[5]
- **Attitudes** towards a specific behaviour (for example, in some communities, teenage pregnancy is regarded as totally acceptable, rather than as a problem);[6]
- Behavioural activity (e.g. heavy smokers, or young people deemed to be at high risk of starting smoking).[7] Another example would be that inexperience, coupled with peer influence and the desire for excitement, means that young drivers are much more at risk of road traffic accidents from following too closely than older drivers;[8]
- Decision processes – for example, in sun protection, outdoor workers may feel their job prevents them from even trying to protect against sunburn,[9] while adolescents may feel that acquiring a suntan is so important to their attractiveness and sense of self-esteem that they are prepared to ignore the health risks associated with regular use of sunbeds;[10]
- **Psychological**: motivations; personality; perceptions, interests and opinions; **attitudes, interests and opinions (AOI)**; motives; beliefs; values;
- **Psychographics**, including lifestyles, knowledge, activities, family life cycles;
- Usage/behaviour – usage statistics, or benefits sought;
- **Geodemographics**: based on the assumption that people who live close to one another are likely to have similar financial means, lifestyles and consumption habits;
- **Epidemiology** (identifying parts of a country where the highest concentration of a specific illness occurs).

Effective segments – characteristics

Issues relating to segment identification and selection are particularly important as there is a risk of being responsive to more affluent, vocal, assertive and organised groups or communities' 'squeaking wheels' (see Chapter 4) at the expense of less vocal groups who may need or benefit more from an intervention.[11] Careful consideration needs to be given to how best to identify and engage with communities to determine their priorities and preferences, which may differ from 'outside' views of what activity may be needed.[12]

Increasingly, partnerships may be involved in delivering interventions, particularly in health-related areas, where community-based perspectives have been found to be more effective than national programmes in addressing issues of improving access and quality of care.[13] Partners may vary across segments and their relative credibility may vary. Pressure on funding and other resources, coupled with increasing healthcare costs, has led to the reluctant recognition of what has been termed 'public health's inconvenient truth'[14] – the need to develop partnerships with both commercial and non-commercial organisations (as we noted in Chapter 4). While joint activities with non-commercial organisations such as charities have existed for a considerable time, the more recent notion of joining forces with commercial organisations in health-related activity (public–private partnerships) creates some tension. However, partners may be able to reach specific segments more effectively or more economically than one organisation trying to reach a diverse range of segments. For segments to be viable, they must be:

- **Identifiable** (have specific characteristics that differentiate one segment from another);
- **Measurable** (the attitudes, behaviours or other characteristics must be able to be evaluated);
- **Accessible** by traditional ways of contact and communication, via new electronic media forms or by non-standard methods, such as the use of hair salons to distribute health advice to Afro-American women.[15] Decisions may need to be made if some segments are extremely difficult to reach or the cost of reaching them is far higher than other segments;
- **Substantial** (the segments must be of sufficient size to warrant the development of material specifically aimed at them);
- **Stable** in terms of size, location and other key characteristics;
- **Appropriate** (defined according to characteristics that are important in relation to the behaviour being targeted).[16, 17]

Many of these factors are identified using **Likert scales** (see Chapter 7) to identify strength of agreement or disagreement with a range of relevant statements. For small samples, this data can then be analysed using simple cross-tabulations to identify broad common characteristics such as demographics. For larger samples, the use of more sophisticated data analysis using software such as SPSS (Statistical Package for Social Sciences) enables a much more detailed analysis to be undertaken, particularly in relation to common factors that may underpin segments based on attitudinal, behavioural or psychographic features.

The characteristics of each segment will also influence the intervention development. Consider the differences between an intervention targeting a segment that perceives significant barriers to performing a behaviour (for example, reducing children's exposure to passive smoke within groups where smoking is seen as 'normal' behaviour) versus an intervention aimed at helping those who really want to quit smoking.

Be honest with yourself in assessing how responsive a segment is likely to be. With scarce resources, decisions will need to be made about where they should be concentrated. Consider the ethics of deciding not to target a specific segment that may have high levels of health problems but that has been extremely resistant to behaviour change and that has not responded to previous interventions.

The key beliefs to be targeted should be identified as these will underpin the specific interventions. They become the basis of an initial proposition, i.e. how to move the target segments from their current behaviour to the behaviour change sought.

It can also be valuable to also look at segmentation within the competition and ask yourself the following questions:

- What competition exists in each segment?
- What impact does this have on our activity?
- How does it differ across segments?
- What are the implications for our ability to reach the target segments?
- How can we minimise the impact of competitive activity?

Potential partners may vary across segments in terms of their ability to access target segments and their credibility with members of each segment. Care must be taken to ensure there is agreement with partners as to how segments are defined, targeted and ultimately served by an intervention.

Commercial segmentation packages

There are a number of commercial segmentation packages available – we have listed some of the major ones below. You will need to assess whether/how well these packages give you insights into the specific attitudes, beliefs and behaviours that are the focus of any specific intervention.

Box 8.1 ACORN

ACORN is the leading geo-demographic tool used to identify and understand the UK population and the demand for products and services. Businesses use this information to improve their understanding of customers and target markets and to determine where to locate operations.

Informed decisions can be made on where direct marketing and advertising campaigns will be most effective; where branches should be opened or closed; or where sites are located, including retail outlets, leisure facilities and public services.

ACORN categorises all 1.9 million UK postcodes, which have been described using over 125 demographic statistics within England, Scotland, Wales and Northern Ireland, and 287 lifestyle variables, making it the most powerful discriminator, giving a clearer understanding of clients and prospects.

Source: http://www.caci.co.uk/acorn/whatis.asp

Box 8.2 Mosaic™

Mosaic is a classification system, devised by Experian, which was originally designed to profile consumers for market research purposes. Consumers were classified into 61 *types*. Each type is a member of one of 11 *groups*. Both demographic and socio-economic data is available for each type and comparisons can be made between types over a wide range of indicators. Indeed, Mosaic provides a detailed 12-page report on each of the 61 types,

---

Box 8.2 (*continued*)

examining factors such as education, health, economic well-being, demography, cultural activities and so on.

Each postcode is assigned a Mosaic type to provide insights into the *likely* characteristics of the residents living at the postcode. Clearly, not every resident will conform to these characteristics, but as a broad-brush approach to the socio-demographic features one might expect, Mosaic appears to perform extremely well, based on what we know from other sources. Moreover, because types are assigned to postcodes and groups are comprised of distinct types, we can map the geographical distribution of both types and groups.

Mosaic typology uses 400 input variables to arrive at a classification. Fifty-four per cent of the data used to construct Mosaic is sourced from the 2001 Census and the other 46% comes from the Experian Lifestyle Survey, consumer credit databases, the electoral roll, shareholder registers, Land Registry data, Council Tax information, the British Crime Survey, Expenditure and Food Survey, the Health Survey for England, and other sources. Postcode classifications are updated annually. In addition, the classification methodology includes validation fieldwork and observational research.

Source: http://opinions.discussit.co.uk/downloads/assets/Mosaic_and_its_uses.pdf

Box 8.3 Values and Lifestyles Survey (VALS)

This originated in the USA (Stanford University). The latest version uses eight major groups:

Innovators: High resources, motivated by ideals, achievement and self-expression

Thinkers: High resources, motivated by ideals

Believers: Low resources, motivated by ideals

Achievers: High resources, motivated by achievement

Strivers: Low resources, motivated by achievement

Experiencers: High resources, motivated by self-expression

Makers: Low resources, motivated by self-expression

Survivors: Low resources, no primary motivation, often feel powerless

Source: Della et al., 2009[18]

Box 8.4 Department of Health

A specific UK Department of Health segmentation system is evolving: 'Healthy Foundations – a segmentation model'. This combines age/life-stage data with family/individual circumstances/environments plus attitudes/beliefs towards health and health issues.

The philosophy is as follows:

The research used epidemiology, social and consumer research and the public health targets to produce a model to target audiences. The model is intended as a building block for a customer-focused approach to the development of health behaviour change interventions. It should *not* be viewed solely as a segmentation for informing communications.

The use of segmentation is not new to DH. However, at present there is no single consistent approach to segmentation across different public health target areas.

One of the objectives of this project was to develop a segmentation framework or model that can be applied across issues, thereby giving a '360 degree' picture of the population rather than a series of overlapping views of people from the perspective of each issue.

Pulling the three dimensions together, we are able to create a rich picture and model and a consistent approach for DH. It should be acknowledged that working with three dimensions rather than two is relatively unusual in health segmentation models, although the approach is frequently used in commercial applications. It is clear from the research that the task of looking at the entire population in terms of a range of motivations, environment and life stage requires this extra level of sophistication.

Insight is built from demographic, behavioural, psychographic and epidemiological data, prior evidence and intelligence about what has worked elsewhere, together with data about what motivates people, what they say will help them and perceived barriers. There is rarely a 'one size fits all' solution that can be appropriately applied across the population.

Our future health promotion and social marketing programmes will be built on shared insight into audiences, clearly defined through segmentation analysis, to bring about specific behaviour. The approach should lead to a more cost-effective and integrated approach to future research and targeted health interventions within DH.

For details, see: http://www.dh.gov.uk/prod_consum_dh/groups/dh_digitalassets/documents/digitalasset/dh_086291.pdf

About now, you may be saying: 'But what if I don't have the budget to buy segmentation data from commercial sources? My organisation is small and it has a very limited budget – I simply can't consider commercial segmentation data!' This is a common problem. You may be able to do an effective segmentation analysis using data you already hold, such as light, medium or heavy users of a service. Weigh up the benefits of segmentation against providing totally uniform services for everyone. Think about what data you already have within your organisation and how it can be used – or how you can obtain additional data using your existing staff and facilities. Also read the literature and talk to other organisations with experience in the area, including local community groups.

An example of 'segmentation on a shoestring' is provided by the following American case.[19] Three different reasons were identified from existing service provision for parents not agreeing to their children being immunised.

1 lack of knowledge about healthcare risks of not immunising;

2 fear of side effects;

3 religious beliefs.

The strategy used was to treat the parents as three different segments with strategies as outlined in Table 8.1.

If you have staff with statistical expertise to analyse sets of data, complex segmentation analysis can be done using widely available analysis packages such as SPSS. Segmentation is usually done in one of two ways:

You may decide in advance on the basis for segments, such as regular recyclers, occasional recyclers and those who do not recycle, and then identify the characteristics of the people falling into each group. You may use statistical analyses such as **cluster analysis** to 'group' or 'cluster' people (such as those completing a survey, those taking part in qualitative research

Table 8.1 Segmentation strategy: immunisation

Segment	Relevant characteristics	Message	Channels	Evaluation
Unaware	Fatalism Do not know benefits Perceived lack of access High respect for doctors Low knowledge Low education Recent immigrants Low incomes	Effectiveness of vaccines Free vaccinations at clinics Use testimonials from others like them Use doctors as spokespeople	Posters and flyers with map to clinic – in grocery stores, convenience stores, churches, schools	Pre- and post-number of first-time vaccinations at clinic
Afraid and untrusting	Afraid of side effects Believe extreme claims about the risk of immunisation Very health-oriented Community-minded Educated Alternative-oriented Income varies	Risk of not doing (to others as well as own kids) Thimerosal-free (i.e. mercury-free) vaccine	Posters and brochures in stores, schools. Try to get article or advertisement in health-food shopper monthly paper re Thimerosal-free availability	Pre-and post-intercept survey outside health food stores measure perceptions and intentions
Religious opponents	Sect forbids vaccination	None currently acceptable given policy limits	None	None

such as interviews, those using specific services) on the basis of similar behaviour or commonly held attitudes towards an aspect of behaviour. Each cluster can then be described or profiled according to its distinctive features, such as attitudes towards behaviour change, frequency of potentially harmful behaviours, etc.

If you want to know more about the techniques used, any good market research text (see, for example, those listed at the end of Chapter 7) will provide an overview of the processes involved. If statistics are not your thing, you can still come up with perfectly usable segments by using programmes such as Excel.

Case studies for discussion

We have included a number of short case studies using a range of segmentation strategies, from very simple to more complex, for discussion. We recommend that you read the full papers from which the material has been taken to get a full understanding of the way interventions have been developed using segmentation data.

VIGNETTE 8.1

American firefighters

Firefighters were identified as being at risk of coronary heart disease.[20] A North Carolina (USA) social marketing intervention used a segmentation strategy based on observations and informal discussions with 100 firefighters. Older firefighters (40–55 years) viewed themselves as less fit and more at risk of health problems than their younger colleagues. The older group also valued workplace fitness interventions more highly. The research also identified an overarching competitive spirit which could also be used to increase participation in activity-based interventions across different crews.

Questions to consider

1 *What challenges do you believe targeting older firefighters rather than all firefighters may have presented in gaining acceptance of the intervention?*

2 *Given the information above, what type of interventions might be considered? Justify your selection.*

3 *How would you evaluate the potential acceptability of the interventions and how would you plan to monitor their implementation and impact?*

4 *How might younger firefighters help to support the interventions? What other groups might support the activity?*

VIGNETTE 8.2

UK recycling

As part of a Waste and Resources Action Programme (WRAP), an intervention to encourage more household recycling commenced with a review of the recent recycling literature which identified potential motivators for, and barriers to, recycling.[21] Seventy-two semi-structured interviews were conducted to explore the actual barriers within the regions taking part in the programme. A survey of 1,512 households across seven local authority areas was used to gain data across different recycling collection regimes. This data was analysed by ACORN category and by the four main identified categories of recycling barrier:

- *Situational:* not having adequate containers; lack of space for storage; unreliable collections and lack of means to get to recycling drop-off points.

- *Behavioural:* disorganised households; getting organised and getting into regular recycling routines not seen as a priority.

- *Knowledge:* lack of knowledge as to what material can be put into which container; lack of understanding of how the scheme works; confused about when to put different containers out for collection.

- *Attitudes and motivation:* do not accept there is an environmental benefit; resistant to having to sort – believe it is council or industry problem; object to being told what to do.

The research has provided the foundation for customised programmes linked to the different barriers to recycling evident in different population segments.

Questions to consider

1 *Evaluate the UK recycling case above. How do you recommend interventions be developed and delivered to each identified segment?*

2 *Consider a segment whose attitudes and motivation lead to resistance to the concept of recycling. What type of intervention can you recommend particularly to deal with the resistance?*

3 *What help can be given to households whose current lack of organisation prevents them from recycling?*

4 *What potential partners might be encouraged to assist in this type of intervention?*

VIGNETTE 8.3

High-risk drinkers

A US intervention targeted at high-risk drinkers[22] used socio-demographic segmentation to identify ten lifestyle clusters most likely to engage in excess alcohol consumption.

Due to limited funding which would have prevented effective interventions being developed for each of the segments, clusters were then aggregated to provide five clusters.

These were defined on the basis of ethnicity, age, family type, education, employment, urban/suburban residence and region as:

Cyber Millenials

Avante-Garde Mix

City Producer

Metro Newbies

Mobile Ladder

This data was then combined with commercial data on media usage to identify the principal media usage (television programmes regularly watched, main radio stations listened to, print media read and digital communications) of each segment.

The main alcoholic beverage preferences for members of each cluster were then added to the profile, along with sports and leisure activities.

Questions to consider

1 *How should the data now be used to develop specific interventions for each segment?*

2 *What problems might be encountered in targeting high-risk drinkers?*

3 *What ethical issues may arise in developing an intervention of this nature?*

4 *Revisit the Road Crew case in Chapter 5. What problems associated with heavy drinking were not addressed in this intervention?*

5 *What should the role of the alcohol industry be for an intervention of this type?*

VIGNETTE 8.4

Fruit and vegetable intake

Lifestyle analysis using VALS was adopted for a US analysis of fruit and vegetable intake as part of the international *5 A Day* initiative.[23] This case is noteworthy as the Transtheoretical/Stages of Change Model was originally used for interventions but criticisms of its effectiveness led to its replacement by the Theory of Planned Behaviour (TPB).

The TPB was used as the foundation of the analysis, with the aim of investigating how the relative impact and importance of constructs varied across segments.

For example, attitudinal questions included evaluation of how eating five servings of fruit and vegetables was seen by the respondents; subjective norms were evaluated by exploring how people important to the respondents, including family and friends, would see this behaviour; behavioural control was evaluated by assessing how easy respondents saw the behaviour would be that would result in them being able to eat five servings a day. Behavioural intentions included self-reported intentions, personal desire to change behaviour, and expectations of this behaviour being carried out.

Interesting differences were found in some groups. Perceived behavioural control was more strongly mediated by behavioural intentions in some groups than in others and differences between groups were evident regarding the relationship between attitudes and intentions. For example, attitudes had a significant effect on behaviours within the 'Makers' group; ideals were a strong influence on 'Thinkers' and 'Believers'.

The knowledge gained from this study has the potential to help refine interventions and tailor programmes for specific segments.

Questions to consider

1 *How might interventions vary according to whether subjective norms or behavioural control factors were the more important for specific segments?*

2 *Refer back to the description of VALS earlier in the chapter. What types of interventions would you recommend for 'Thinkers' and 'Believers' versus 'Makers'?*

3 *Refer back to Chapter 6 – why do you believe that the TPB might have been more useful in planning interventions than the Stages of Change Model?*

In relation to this fruit and vegetable example, consider the following instances of media coverage criticising official advice.

Two recent media articles state that the recommendation of consuming five portions of fruit/vegetables a day is not only ineffective for health and nutrition, but that experts have known this and concealed evidence. For examples of media coverage of this issue, see:

- *Daily Mail* 'This cynical five-a-day myth: Nutrition expert claims we've all been duped' by Zoe Harcombe (http://www.dailymail.co.uk/femail/food/article-1349960/5-day-fruit-vegetables-myth-claims-nutrition-expert.html?ito=feeds-newsxml)

- '5-a-day 'Not enough' fruits and vegetables: New research finds 8-a-day may be needed to cut the risk of dying from heart disease' by Tim Locke, WebMD Health News (http://www.webmd.com/heart-disease/news/20110118/5-a-day-not-enough-fruits-vegetables)

Question to consider

How might each of the VALS segments respond to this media coverage and how might you counter its effect?

CASE STUDY 8.1

Segmentation strategies for strengthening sun protection behaviours within the UK

(Note: Do not be too concerned about the technical description of the clustering in this case study – just follow the principles and concentrate on the description of the clusters that were identified.)

Overview

Skin cancer rates in the UK have risen steadily, doubling in the past decade, resulting in significant public and personal costs. Cancer Research UK has run the national SunSmart awareness programme since 2003, but budget restrictions have prohibited the use of large-scale mass media interventions. A behavioural segmentation approach based on situations and locations where sunburn has occurred may offer the foundations for specifically targeted interventions. A large-scale national telephone survey of the general population was conducted regarding the circumstances and sun protective behaviours where sun exposure had led to sunburn. The data indicates a range of attitudinal, behavioural and knowledge factors that should be addressed in developing future interventions. A cluster analysis shows clear behavioural differences across different population segments.

Introduction

Skin cancer is the most common cancer in the United Kingdom, with estimates of nearly 82,000 cases of non-melanoma and 10,400 cases of melanoma registered in 2006.[24] Skin cancer rates have risen steadily in the United Kingdom, doubling in the past decade, and continue to increase at some 8% per year, faster than any other cancer.[25] More Britons die of melanoma each year than in Australia, which has four times the UK rate of skin cancer diagnosis. The difference in mortality rates can be attributed to earlier detection and higher levels of effective sun protection strategies in Australia.[26]

Mass media campaigns, coupled with interventions targeted at specific population segments, have significantly reduced sunburn rates in Australia.[27] Activity in the UK has been limited, due to budgetary constraints, and centres primarily on website and school-based activity. A recent study showed that prompted awareness of SunSmart increased from 6.5% in 2003 to 17.5% in 2009.[28] This indicates growing awareness of SunSmart, though key messages are not reaching the population as quickly as mass media-supported interventions would permit. Information about sun protection and skin cancer is largely passively acquired,[29] therefore, in the absence of mass media initiatives, consideration should be given to taking sun protective messages to specific segments of the population where behaviour that has resulted in sunburn in the past is occurring.

Research methodology

A Cancer Research UK-sponsored telephone survey of 5,034 people aged 16+ years, 46% male and 54% female, was conducted in August and early September 2009. As most skin cancers are related to sun exposure,[30, 31] questions centred on the incidence of self-reported sunburn, the situations in which the sunburn occurred and sun protective behaviours at the time.

Potential interventions based on segmentation

Segmenting the population on the basis of key behaviours would enable interventions to be targeted at specific segments, drawing on the collaboration and resources of potential partners. A segmentation strategy based on four clusters is presented. Before you read on, reread the note at the start of this case. A two-step cluster analysis was undertaken on responses from survey respondents who had indicated that they had been sunburnt within the current year. The filtering of the data file for the respondents that had reported burning resulted in a sample size of 1,606 (31.9%), selected from the main data file of 5,034 records. The clustering process was exploratory and automatically determined with a maximum of 15 clusters allowed within the calculations. The clustering criterion used was Schwarz's Bayesian Criteria (BIC), BIC ratio of change and ratio of distance measures[32] using a combination of categorical and continuous variables. Cluster memberships were created, added to the file and group membership to these clusters was allocated to the individual respondents. A total of four clusters (segments) were identified during the two-step analysis. The clusters were reported at the 95% confidence level, with non-significant variables being automatically omitted from the model. Within Table 8.2, the significant variables from the cluster analysis are detailed for the segments. Cross-tabulations with non-significant descriptor variables have been used to further analyse the segments.

Segment 1 – Outdoor gamers

The smallest of the four segments (17.5%) is divided between male (47%) and female (52%) members. Over 75% of this segment reported being sunburnt while within the United Kingdom and 50% of those reported that it had occurred within the four weeks preceding the survey. All respondents obtained their sunburn by participating in sporting activities, with 80% reporting that exposure was over two hours. Although a sunscreen factor-15 was used by more than 50% of the segment members, over 60% reapplied the sunscreen less than once in every two hours.

Interventions appropriate for this segment should focus on addressing self-efficacy and social norms. Integration of activity with recreational facility providers (e.g. parks and recreation centres) should be investigated, regarding signage and other ways of raising awareness. Sports governing bodies or associations, and sports coaches could be key role models to educate sports participants regarding effective sun protection, to model effective sun protection behaviours and to address the social acceptability of behaviour change.[33]

Segment 2 – Aqua-'bathers'

The second-largest of the four segments (23.6%) is divided between male (47%) and female (52%) members. Over 80% reported being sunburnt while abroad, with 50% of those reporting that it had occurred within the four weeks preceding the survey. Respondents obtained their sunburn by participating in water activities, with 70% reporting that their exposure was over two hours. Although a sunscreen factor-15 was used by more than 60% of the segment members, approximately 40% reapplied the sunscreen less than once in every two hours. A key challenge with this segment is that the majority of sunburn occurs outside the UK. Strategies that could be considered would be to integrate activity with travel agents, airlines, hotel chains, etc., placing information on websites and possibly providing practical tips and information with airline tickets and hotel reservations.

Case study 8.2 (*continued*)

Table 8.2 Sub-sample – Respondents who indicated that they had burnt within the current year – Segment stereotypes

Variable	Sig.	Segment 1 Outdoor gamers	Segment 2 Aqua 'bathers'	Segment 3 Out and about	Segment 4 Sun seekers
Segment size		17.5%	23.6%	36.2%	22.6%
Demographic variables					
Gender	Sig.	Male: 47% Female: 52%	Male: 47% Female: 52%	Male: 27% Female: 72%	Male: 32% Female: 68%
Geographic					
UK/abroad sunburnt	Sig.	Over 75% in the UK	Over 80% abroad	Over 60% in the UK	Over 80% abroad
Behavioural/knowledge					
Recency of sunburn	Sig.	Approximately 50% within last 4 weeks	Over 50% within last 4 weeks	Over 60% within last 4 weeks	Less than 50% within last 4 weeks
Activity participating in when sunburnt	Sig.	100% sporting activities, running, playing football, etc.	100% in and out of the water such as sea, pool and rivers	100% walking around shopping, in the park, in the garden	100% sunbathing
Factor sunscreen worn	Sig.	Over 50% higher than factor 15	Over 60% higher than factor 15	Approximately 60% higher than factor 15	40% higher than factor 15
Physical					
Sunburnt on head (face, neck, ears)	Sig.	Approximately 50% burnt: face (29%), top of head (10%), neck (19%), ears (less than 1%)	Approximately 25% burnt: face (20%), top of head (4%), neck (4%), ears (less than 1%)	Approximately 40% burnt: face (29%), top of head (7%), neck (17%), ears (less than 1%)	Approximately 25% burnt: face (18%), top of head (3%), neck (7%), ears (less than 1%)

Sig. = Significant variable used in cluster development

Segment 3 – Out and about

The largest of the four segments (36.2%) is dominated by female members (72%). It has a higher proportion of members aged 55–64 (20%) and 65+ (11%) than the other segments, possibly due to the more sedentary type of activities involved. Over 60% reported being sunburnt while within the UK. All respondents obtained their sunburn by 'walking around shopping', or being in the park and in the garden, with 60% reporting that their duration of exposure was over two hours. Although a sunscreen factor-15 was used by more than 60%, approximately 60% of these reapplied the sunscreen less than once in every two hours. This segment has a clear educational need as regards the strength of the UK sun.[34] Strategies could include signage in retail premises, such as pharmacy windows and tourist information centres, and collaborative promotional activity with both retailers and commercial sunscreen manufacturers.

Segment 4 – Sun seekers

The third-largest of the four segments (22.6%) is dominated by female members (68%). This segment has the highest proportion of 16–24 year olds (20%), and the smallest proportion of 25–34 year olds (13%), when compared to the other segments. Over 80% of this segment reported being sunburnt while abroad, with fewer than 50% of those reporting that it had occurred within the four weeks preceding the survey.

All respondents obtained their sunburn by participating in sunbathing, with approximately 70% reporting that their exposure was over two hours. Although a sunscreen factor-15 was used by more than 40% of the segment members, fewer than 40% reapplied the sunscreen more than once in every two hours. To change behaviours will be a challenge as it will involve influencing social norms, a known significant influence on behaviour.[35] Competition comes from messages counter to recommended sun protection strategies which are regularly shown in consumer media, including glamorising suntans and showing celebrities with poor sun-protective behaviours.[36]

Recommendations for future research

The segmentation analysis identifies four key behaviourally based segments and raises the possibility of intervention strategies that could usefully supplement those currently in use. The segmentation analysis also illustrates the possibility for greater partnership collaboration in order to effectively reach the members of each segment where sub-optimum sun-protective behaviours actually occur.

Questions

1 Previous interventions have centred on activity within schools and on the Cancer Research UK website. Visit the website and discuss how the content could be modified to meet the specific needs of each segment.

2 Select one of the segments and use the partnership analysis form on page 184 to identify possible partners in your intervention and clearly spell out the role of each partner and how you would manage the partnership.

3 Analyse the in-store displays and communication activity for commercial sunscreen manufacturers and discuss how their activity might hinder or reinforce your proposed activity from the previous question. What action do you recommend taking?

4 Identify competitors for your selected segment and, using the competitive analysis form on page 185, provide recommendations as to how the effects of this activity could be minimised.

Source: This case study is based on Jones, S., Eagle, L., Kemp, G., Scammell, K., Naumann, L. and Hiom, S. (2011) *Segmentation Strategies for Strengthening Sun Protection Behaviours within the UK*. Presented at World Social Marketing Conference, Dublin, April 2011.

Partnership analysis

Partnership evaluation factor	Evaluation comments
How well do their aims and objectives overlap with the partnership and with other partners?	
What specific involvement do they have or do you want them to have?	
Level of responsibility within organisation	
Support of senior management within organisation	
What data/information are they able to provide?	
What resources are they able to provide?	
Are there any potential ethical issues? If so, how should they be evaluated/resolved?	
How successful has previous activity with the partner been?	
What problems have been encountered? Are these likely to recur? If so, how significant is this to the future success of the partnership?	
How is co-ordination/control to be decided and agreed?	
How are problems to be resolved?	
How is success to be measured and by whom?	
How flexible and adaptable are they likely to be if unexpected issues arise?	
What contingency plans are needed in case of problems?	

Competitive analysis

Organisation	Activity	Potential impact on our intervention	Potential strategies for minimising their impact

Summary

Segmentation means dividing the target population into clearly defined, and mutually exclusive, sub-groups on the basis of similar characteristics – for example, on the basis of culture, demographic or geo-demographic variables, attitudes, behavioural, physiological or psychological features. Segments must be identifiable, accessible, substantial, stable, measurable and appropriate to be useful to marketers. Often marketers can rely on commercial segmentation tools, such as ACORN, VALS or Mosaic, to guide segmentation. However, these tools are often more effective for social marketers when used in conjunction with other, more behaviour-specific segmentation tools. Different behavioural outcomes are likely to require very different segmentation strategies; thus, a good social marketer is likely to spend considerable time on selecting appropriate strategies; for each social marketing intervention.

CHAPTER REVIEW QUESTIONS

1 Discuss the ethics of not addressing segments of target groups who cite religious beliefs as a reason for not changing behaviours or trying to reduce health risks within their families (such as immunisation of children).

2 Discuss the ethics of deciding that a segment of the population that has high levels of a particular health problem but that is difficult to reach and to motivate will not be made a specific target for an intervention as the resources that would be needed would mean that other, larger and more accessible segments would not be provided with adequate services.

3 Discuss the types of segmentation analysis that could be considered for:
- road safety;
- smoke alarms;
- energy reduction;
- sustainable transport;
- sexual health.

4 (a) Discuss the implications of an ACORN segmentation report that identifies the areas in which people with the highest need for a social marketing intervention live but which are well away from any of your current service provision facilities.

   (b) Select an intervention type from question 3 above and discuss possible alternative service delivery venues for it. Justify your recommendation and discuss how you would research the acceptability of the alternative venue to the target groups and those who might be tasked with delivering the intervention at the venue.

5 A potential social marketing intervention area that does not have as high a profile as many health-related topics is disaster preparedness (floods, severe storms, unusually heavy snow falls, earthquakes,* etc.). Develop recommendations for research to identify what specific segments may exist and outline the type of intervention that could be developed to raise awareness and to improve people's disaster preparedness strategies.

   *If you do not think that the UK and western parts of Europe are at risk for earthquakes, consider the following:

A suspected tsunami in the Bristol Channel which killed 2,000 people happened 400 years ago. Experts believe severe flooding on 30 January 1607 in south west England and south Wales was caused by a tsunami - and not a storm surge or high tides. It is estimated 200 square miles (520 sq km) of land were covered by water. Professor Simon Haslett from Bath Spa University said there was currently no tsunami warning system in place.

http://news.bbc.co.uk/1/hi/england/6311527.stm

An earthquake in 1755 that devastated Lisbon and coastal parts of Portugal resulted in a 3-metre tsunami hitting the southern coast of England and also Ireland, the west coast of Europe – up to Scandinavia.

For more details, visit: http://socyberty.com/history/lisbon-city-portugal-earthquake-and-tsunami/

In terms of other potential natural disasters, consider the following extract from the *Financial Times*:

Air travellers have always recognised that a range of natural and man-made factors can lead to flight delay or cancellation. These include technical failures of aircraft and air traffic control equipment, strikes and political upheaval, fog and blizzards.

Over the past year the emphasis has fallen more heavily on the forces of nature. Exceptional snowstorms in North America and Europe caused more weather-related chaos than usual during the winter, but the big event, which caught European aviation almost completely unprepared, was the shutdown caused by ash clouds from Iceland's Eyjafjallajökull volcano. For more than a month after a sustained eruption started in mid-April, sending ash up to 11km into the atmosphere, European airspace was periodically closed to prevent possible damage to aircraft and their engines from fine volcanic particles – at huge cost to travellers and the industry.

Cookson, C. (2011) Science briefing: Poor planning and preparation worsened the effects of volcano's fallout; http://www.ft.com/cms/s/0/c05941bc-5682-11e0-84e9-00144feab49a.html#axzz1I4j7nNyw

Recommended reading

Farr, M., Wardlaw, J. and Jones, C. (2008) Tackling Health Inequalities Using Geodemographics: A Social Marketing Approach. *International Journal of Market Research,* 50 (4), 449–67.

Fraze, J.L., Uhrig, J.D., Davis, K.C., Taylor, M.K., Lee, N.R., Spoeth, S., et al. (2009) Applying Core Principles to the Design and Evaluation of the 'Take Charge. Take the Test' Campaign: What Worked and Lessons Learned. *Public Health,* 123 Supplement 1, e23–e30.

Jones, S.C., Waters, L., Holland, O., Bevins, J. and Iverson, D. (2010) Developing Pandemic Communication Strategies: Preparation without Panic. *Journal of Business Research,* 63 (2), 126–32.

Kolodinsky, J. and Reynolds, T. (2009) Segmentation of Overweight Americans and Opportunities for Social Marketing. *International Journal of Behavioral Nutrition and Physical Activity,* 6 (1), 13.

Lee, N.R., and Kotler, P. (2009) Ending Poverty: 'What's Social Marketing Got to Do With It?' *Social Marketing Quarterly,* 15 (4), 134–40.

Lee, N.R., Spoeth, S., Smith, K., McElroy, L., Fraze, J.L., Robinson, A., et al. (2006) Encouraging African-American Women to 'Take Charge. Take the Test': The Audience Segmentation Process for CDC'S HIV Testing Social Marketing Campaign. *Social Marketing Quarterly,* 12 (3), 16–28.

Madill, J. and Abele, F. (2007) From Public Education to Social Marketing: The Evolution of the Canadian Heritage Anti-Racism Social Marketing Program. *Journal of Nonprofit & Public Sector Marketing,* 17 (1/2), 27–53.

McCausland, K.L., Allen, J.A., Duke, J.C., Xiao, H., Asche, E.T., Costantino, J.C., et al. (2009) Piloting EX, a Social Marketing Campaign to Prompt Smoking Cessation. *Social Marketing Quarterly,* 15, 80–101.

Plant, A., Montoya, J.A., Rotblatt, H., Kerndt, P.R., Mall, K.L., Pappas, L.G., et al. (2010) Stop the Sores: The Making and Evaluation of a Successful Social Marketing Campaign. *Health Promotion Practice,* 11 (1), 22–33.

Rimal, R.N., Brown, J., Mkandawire, G., Folda, L., Bose, K. and Creel, A.H. (2009) Audience Segmentation as a Social-Marketing Tool in Health Promotion: Use of the Risk Perception Attitude Framework in HIV Prevention in Malawi. *American Journal of Public Health,* 99 (12), 2224–9.

Also recommended:

Segmentation chapters of the research texts recommended in Chapter 7. These will give you greater insights into some of the more commonly used statistical techniques used to develop segments.

Notes

1 Churchill, G.A. (1995) *Marketing Research: Methodological Foundations* (6th edn). Fort Worth: The Dryden Press.

2 Moss, H.B., Kirby, S.D. and Donodeo, F. (2009) Characterizing and reaching high-risk drinkers using audience segmentation. *Alcoholism, Clinical and Experimental Research,* 33 (8), 1336–45.

3 Huhman, M., Berkowitz, J.M., Wong, F.L., Prosper, E., Gray, M., Prince, D., et al. (2008) The VERB Campaign's Strategy for Reaching African-American, Hispanic, Asian, and American Indian Children and Parents. *American Journal of Preventive Medicine,* 34 (6 suppl.), S194–S209.

4 Slater, M.D., Kelly, K.J. and Thackeray, R. (2006) Segmentation on a Shoestring: Health Audience Segmentation in Limited-Budget and Local Social Marketing Interventions. *Health Promotion Practice,* 7 (2), 170–3.

5 Moffatt, J. and Stanton, W.R. (2005) Smoking and Parenting Among Males in Low Socio-economic Occupations. *International Journal of Health Promotion & Education,* 43 (3), 81–6.

6 Cassell, C., Santelli, J., Gilbert, B.C., Dalmat, M., Mezoff, J. and Schauer, M. (2005) Mobilizing communities: an overview of the Community Coalition Partnership Programs for the Prevention of Teen Pregnancy. *Journal of Adolescent Health,* 37 (3S), S3–10.

7 McKenna, J., Gutierrez, K. and McCall, K. (2000) Strategies for an Effective Youth Counter-marketing Program: Recommendations from Commercial Marketing Experts. *Journal of Public Health Management & Practice,* 6 (3), 7–13.

8 Williams, A.F. (2006) Young Driver Risk Factors: Successful and Unsuccessful Approaches for Dealing with them and an Agenda for the Future. *Injury Prevention,* 12, i4–i8.

9 Oh, S.S., Mayer, J.A., Lewis, E.C., Slymen, D.J., Sallis, J.F., Elder, J.P., et al. (2004) Validating Outdoor Workers' Self-report of Sun Protection. *Preventive Medicine,* 39 (4), 798–803.

10 Cokkinides, V., Weinstock, M., Lazovich, D., Ward, E. and Thun, M. (2009) Indoor Tanning Use among Adolescents in the US, 1998 to 2004. *Cancer,* 115 (1), 190–8.

11 Thacher, D. (2001) Equity and Community Policing: A New View of Community Partnerships. *Criminal Justice Ethics,* 20 (Winter/Spring), 3–16.

12 Lavery, J.V., Upshur, R.E.G., Sharp, R.R. and Hofman, K.J. (2003) Ethical Issues in International Environmental Health Research. *International Journal of Hygiene and Environmental Health,* 206 (4–5), 453–63.

13 Hasnain-Wynia, R. (2003) Overview of the Community Care Network Demonstration Program and Its Evaluation. *Medical Care Research and Review,* 60 (4_suppl), 5S–16.

14 Majestic, E. (2009) Public Health's Inconvenient Truth: the Need to Create Partnerships with the Business Sector. *Preventing Chronic Disease,* 6 (2), A39.

15 Linnan, L.A. and Ferguson, Y.O. (2007) Beauty Salons: A Promising Health Promotion Setting for Reaching and Promoting Health Among African American Women. *Health Education & Behavior,* 34 (3), 517–30.

16 Dawson, C. (2005) How Customers are Segmented and Organised. In I. Doole, P. Lancaster and R. Lowe (eds), *Understanding and Managing Customers.* Harlow: Prentice Hall.

17 Hawkins, D.I., Best, R.J. and Conet, K.A. (2001) *Consumer Behavior: Building Marketing Strategy*. Boston: McGraw Hill.

18 Della, L.J., DeJoy, D.M. and Lance, C.E. (2009) Explaining Fruit and Vegetable Intake Using a Consumer Marketing Tool. *Health Education & Behavior,* 36 (5), 895–914.

19 Slater, M.D., Kelly, K.J. and Thackeray, R. (2006) Op. cit.

20 Staley, J.A. (2009) 'Get Firefighters Moving': Marketing a Physical Fitness Intervention to Reduce Sudden Cardiac Death Risk in Full-Time Firefighters. *Social Marketing Quarterly,* 15 (3), 85–99.

21 Jesson, J. (2009) Household Waste Recycling Behavior: A Market Segmentation Model. *Social Marketing Quarterly,* 15 (2), 25–38.

22 Moss, H.B., Kirby, S.D. and Donodeo, F. (2009) Characterizing and Reaching High-risk Drinkers Using Audience Segmentation. *Alcoholism, Clinical and Experimental Research,* 33 (8), 1336–45.

23 Della, L.J., DeJoy, D.M. and Lance, C.E. (2009) Op. cit.

24 Garside, R., Pearson, M. and Moxham, T. (2010) What Influences the Uptake of Information to Prevent Skin Cancer? A Systematic Review and Synthesis of Qualitative Research. *Health Education Research,* 25 (1), 162–82.

25 National Institute for Health and Clinical Excellence (2006) Press Release: NICE Issues Guidance to Improve Healthcare Services for Skin Cancers, 21 February.

26 Miranda, C. (2008) Poms Topple Aussies in Melanoma Deaths, *Herald Sun,* online edition, 20 December. Accessed 12 January 2009 from http://www.news.com.au/heraldsun/story/0,21985,24824277-663,00.html

27 Sinclair, C., and Foley, P. (2009) Skin cancer prevention in Australia. *British Journal of Dermatology,* 161 (0 suppl.), 116–23.

28 Jones, S., Eagle, L., Scammell, K., Naumann, L., Hiom, S., (2010) 'Trends in Skin Cancer Awareness – Implications for Intervention Development'. Report compiled for Cancer Research UK.

29 Eadie, D. and MacAskill, S. (2007) Consumer Attitudes Towards Self-referral with Early Signs of Cancer: Implications for Symptom Awareness Campaigns. *International Journal of Nonprofit & Voluntary Sector Marketing,* 12 (4), 338–49.

30 Falk, M. and Anderson, C. (2008) Prevention of Skin Cancer in Primary Healthcare: an Evaluation of Three Different Prevention Effort Levels and the Applicability of a Phototest. *European Journal of General Practice,* 14 (2), 68–75.

31 Murphy, G.M. (2002) Photoprotection: Public Campaigns in Ireland and the U.K. *The British Journal of Dermatology,* 146 Suppl 61, 31–3.

32 Fraley, C. and. Raftery, A.E. (1998) How Many Clusters? Which Clustering Method? Answers Via Model-Based Cluster Analysis. *Computer Journal,* 41(8), 578–88.

33 Dadlani, C. and Orlow, S.J. (2008) Planning for a Brighter Future: a Review of Sun Protection and Barriers to Behavioral Change in Children and Adolescents. *Dermatology Online Journal,* 14 (9).

34 Hedges, T. and Scriven, A. (2008) Sun Safety: What are the Health Messages? *Journal of The Royal Society for the Promotion of Health,* 128 (4), 164–9.

35 Fishbein, M. and Cappella, J. (2006) The Role of Theory in Developing Effective Health Communications. *Journal of Communication,* 56 (August Supplement), S1–S17.

36 Dixon, H., Dobbinson, S., Wakefield, M., Jamsen, K. and McLeod, K. (2007) Portrayal of Tanning, Clothing Fashion and Shade Use in Australian Women's Magazines, 1987–2005. *Health Education Research,* 23 (5), 791–802.

Chapter 9

Social forces and population-level effects

Chapter objectives

On completing this chapter, you should be able to:

- critically discuss the influence of social groups on individual and collective behaviours;
- critically evaluate the impact of conformity on social marketing activity;
- critically discuss the concept of tipping points for a range of behaviours;
- critically evaluate the impact of social norms on indivdual and group behaviours;
- make reasoned recommendations as to how these factors should be evaluated and appropriate action incorporated into social marketing interventions.

Social forces

To what extent are we influenced by the people around us? Thinking about your own life for a moment, how much would you say the people you come into contact with influence the decisions you make? Perhaps you can think of specific instances here and there, where someone you respected helped you decide. Perhaps you would robustly refute the idea of social influence. In truth, delineating the effect of how much we conform to the social norms around us in everyday life is really quite difficult – but there is solid evidence for the existence of social influence.

This chapter explains the origins of **social forces**, and offers ways in which social marketers can deal with them to best advantage. Social norms, influences and group effects are of vital importance for social marketers. If there were no social norms, the economic model of social marketing would always apply – that is, to create change, social marketers would provide cognitively driven reasons to change, maximising incentives, and minimising costs. But, effective though such approaches are, they are far from being the whole story.

Between the first and second world wars (1920s–1930s), the prevailing view in **social psychology** was that a group of people added up to the sum of their parts but no more – i.e. that they were a group of individuals and should be treated as such. The seminal work of Sherif in 1935 helped to change this view and to establish the idea of group influences.[1] Sherif demonstrated through experiment that, when individuals subjected to an eye test on their estimates of light movements were placed together in a group, they always adjusted their individual answers such that a single, agreed estimate was created. This agreed estimate became known as the *social norm*.

This pressure to socially agree can be quite startling in its power. In 1951 experimenter Soloman Asch asked students to 'visually discriminate' by identifying which line on the right of the diagram (Figure 9.1) was the same length as line X on the left. This was done individually, but within earshot of other respondents (who were secretly part of the experiment). Each of the others responded with line C – and as each one responded in this consistent way, the pressure built: Do you say line B, as your eyes are telling you, in contradiction of the group? The pressure is too much: 'Line C', you find yourself saying, hardly believing you are saying it. In Asch's experiment, respondents overwhelmingly (over 75% of the time) gave line C as the answer. Left on their own, 99% gave the correct answer of line B.[2]

Asch also found that at least three accomplices were needed for the group effect, but that only one (planted) dissenter amongst many (for example, one dissenter amongst 15) largely dissolved the group influence, leading to much more accurate answers.

Soloman Asch's experiments illustrated what may be termed 'conscious' social pressure. You consciously 'feel' the pressure to conform. But social influence may work at a lower level of involvement. In a subconscious, everyday way we may go along with all sorts of inconsequential socially driven behaviours. We routinely accept what is around us without particularly thinking about it.

There are three levels at which we behave according to influence from others.[3] The most 'direct' and obvious is **obedience**. This is the performance of a behaviour in response to a direct *order,* usually from someone in a position of power or authority. Typically, obedience arises in work, or where the law of the land is being evoked – paying taxes, for example. If we take the example of speeding, we can see that, if a police car is visible or known to be in the vicinity, drivers tend to be obedient. This is not social marketing, and is better placed within legal frameworks of behaviour change.

The second level of influence is **compliance**. When we comply, we are behaving in accord with a *direct request.* People can exhibit external compliance in which they have complied

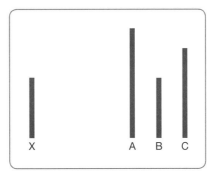

Figure 9.1 Asch's famous social influence experiment

with a request that they privately don't agree with – in order to keep the social peace. Or they can exhibit internal compliance in which they respond to a request to do something that accords with their values and beliefs. One can envisage young male drivers exhibiting both types of compliance. Perhaps with a group of peers in the car with them they might speed, even though privately they would drive more slowly. A group of females in the car may encourage slowing down – something that the young man might be content to comply with.

The most subtle level of influence is **conformity**. Conformity is yielding to perceived group pressure by copying others, often based on visible demonstrations of behaviour. We see people around us driving slowly – so we do too. A lot of conformity is unconscious in nature, acting below the level of cognition. It takes on an automatic nature, neither noticed by the actor, nor remarked upon or subsequently analysed.

The mechanisms of influence for each of these influence systems are quite different. Apart from the level or strength of influence, we should think about its directness, and the fact that conformity comes from groups of people, whereas compliance and obedience come through individuals.

For much of this chapter we will deal with social conformity and its importance for social marketing. Later in the chapter we will take a closer look at compliance. See Figure 9.2 for how conformity links with compliance and obedience.

Conformity

If we stop and consider our own lives for a second, we may agree that conformity is something we all exhibit in hundreds of small ways on a regular basis. Little things like shaking hands in business meetings; how we dress for work versus social gatherings; how we behave when extended family are present as compared to a group of peers; laughing at jokes socially that we privately see as puerile; keeping our front gardens tidy when we don't care about tidiness. All these may be acts of conformity. McKenzie Mohr and Smith describe how 'front garden' (public) activities are prone to conformity (recycling), while 'back garden' (private) activities may be prone to private more selfish behaviours (outdoor heaters).[4]

Social marketers can and should use compliance and conformity systems for voluntary change. A social marketer could create a community development project in which local people were recruited as players in a scheme to influence young men to drive more sedately. If a strong leader were to be found then a compliance model could be adopted. More likely, a group of role models could be recruited to encourage copycat behaviour – conformity.

Our mention of the experiments of Sherif and Asch earlier highlighted two ways in which conformity to social norms can act. The first is when people are in an unusual situation and are *unsure how to behave*. This is called informational influence. Cialdini has observed and demonstrated this in a number of different ways.[5] In his view, this effect explains why people will pass by someone needing help in a public place. When faced with, say, someone apparently staggering about after a car accident, passers by tend to look at *other passers by* for guidance in what to do. If everyone is passing by, they tend to do the same. Cialdini does not see this as a callous act of calculation, but rather an automatic copycatting response in an uncertain situation. The second situation is the one so graphically illustrated by Asch's visual judgement experiments with the line lengths, in which people *avoided what they perceived as social embarrassment* by copying everyone else's answer. This is called normative influence.

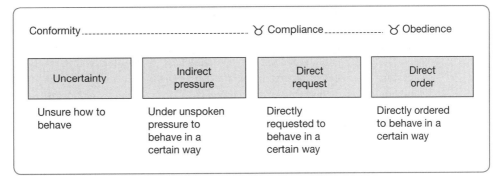

Figure 9.2 Linking conformity with compliance and obedience

VIGNETTE 9.1

Ha ha ha ha ha ha ha . . .

What do you think of the use of canned laughter on TV shows? Most people dislike it and cannot understand its widespread use. Great shows don't need to cue up their audience – right? Well, wrong, it seems. Rather surprisingly, tests consistently show that TV execs knew what they were doing. The audience does tend to laugh more, have warmer feelings towards and appreciate a show more when canned laughter is on in the background. Cialdini attributes this to 'social proof' – another term to explain the type of conformity people exhibit when unsure how to behave.

In theory, either social uncertainty or social pressure could be capitalised upon in social marketing, by communicating a positive social norm in a clear way. But, often, such a scenario would depend on there being a social norm already established, and highly visible, such that the *natural expectation* is that people would behave in the desired manner. It may be the case that a desired behaviour is such a strong cultural norm that the undesirable behaviour is kept at low levels just through social norming. Dropping litter in Switzerland is – more or less – simply not done. Here the cultural norm is so strong that to drop litter would be a *gross act* of anti-social behaviour. Binge drinking so as to appear publicly drunk is very unusual in many Southern European countries. Again, such behaviour would be shocking, and again, social norms reinforce positive behaviours. The exact opposite takes place in Northern Europe, with weekend public drinking to excess a long-standing 'norm' that goes back hundreds of years.

The key issue, then, is not to deny that social norms exist, or that they act powerfully to influence desired and undesirable behaviours, but to ask how social marketers can help generate the conditions through which positive social norms can work. They have two broad options. They can convert one individual at a time to the desired behaviour, and keep going until the sheer weight of converted numbers makes the desired behaviour 'normal', and therefore puts pressure on the remainder to copy. Or, social marketers can attempt to work at an aggregated level, ether with groups or at a population level, to create a new set of behavioural norms that people sign up to en masse. Neither route is easy.

A classic example is the case of everyday (commuter and other trips) cycling in the UK. At present the 'mode share' of cycling trips compared to other forms of transport in the UK languishes at about 2%. Getting people out of cars and onto bikes is highly desirable, ticking boxes for good health, lowered congestion, lower pollution, improved well-being, and lowered carbon footprint. It is hard to think of another behavioural shift that has so many benefits. But of course, cycling takes effort, confidence, time, and, crucially, a perceived safe environment.

The Dutch and Danish experience (they have commuter cycling levels of 30+ %) is that cycling is subject to powerful social norms. This impacts on a number of levels. First, it is normal to be seen with a bike. Teenagers in Holland meet and socialise on bikes. So, first, there is a cultural norm which leads to congruence between self-image and cycling. Second, the more cyclists there are, the fewer cars there will be, and the safer cyclists feel. There is safety in numbers.

Meanwhile, back in the UK, cycling has a different feel to it. Cyclists feel exposed and 'different' from the UK norm, which is to drive. The infrastructure for cycling in the UK is little better than woeful, so cyclists are forced onto busy roads. Cycling England had the task of creating a shift in the travel habits of UK adults such that cycling levels had at least doubled by 2011. Social marketing was very much part of their armoury. Amongst the social marketing mix, Cycling England deployed tactics that have some basis in social influence. Promotion events in which roads are closed to traffic may encourage one-off leisure cycling that gives a 'feel' for riding as part of a group. Workplace champions organise cycling 'buddies' who will accompany new cyclists on a journey. Workplace competitions encourage social interactions.

The bigger picture for social marketers faced with negative social norms, as with UK cycling, is to create a critical mass of role models who can, in turn, create a 'tipping point'. These concepts were made famous by Gladwell,[6] whose book *The Tipping Point* became a best seller.

The idea of the tipping point is that an idea or behaviour can spread slowly initially through society but can reach a point where the spread, or diffusion, suddenly accelerates (see Figure 9.3). This is a point of critical mass in which the power of the viral effect of the social spread becomes suddenly increased.

Gladwell's thesis was that tipping points can be encouraged through the social mechanisms created through 'salesmen', 'mavens', and 'connectors'. Each of these roles is explained in Figure 9.4.

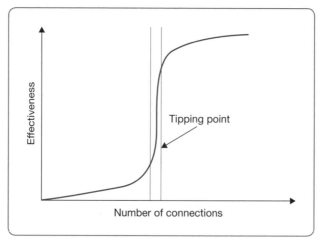

Figure 9.3 How tipping points can suddenly change mass behaviours

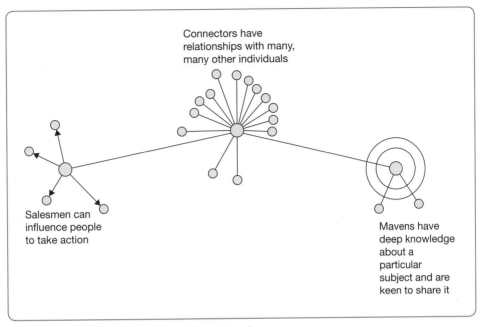

Figure 9.4 The roles of connectors, salesmen and mavens

The possibilities for marketers are, in theory, quite straightforward. Social marketers could profile salesmen, mavens and connectors, identify likely candidates, and incentivise these individuals to do what they do in support of the cause at hand. A prominent figure could help spread the word for self-checking for cancer symptoms. A 'connector' could be incentivised to allow his network to be used to promote the cause. And so on. Connectors may be well-educated people with extensive networks that are geographically spread out, and these networks are maintained through email, online media, social networking sites, or web. Traditional neighbourhoods, on the other hand may also have connectors who act as social glue in a face-to-face, local way. These individuals are often crucial for social marketers faced with problems entrenched in deprived communities. As yet, however, the use of salesmen, connectors and mavens to create 'tipping points' remains new to marketing in general and social marketing in particular. We have a long way to go to understand better how to intervene to make best use of these social forces.

The debate to here has dealt with instances in which desirable behaviours are yet to be established and hence desirable social norms have still to be created. However, what happens when the desired behaviour is *already prevalent,* and merely needs to be communicated to specific targets? This presents an easier job for social marketers. They can deploy what are known as 'social norm campaigns'.

Social norm campaigns

Berkowitz wrote a lengthy report on the use of social norms campaigns.[7] His focus was primarily on preventive campaigns that look to correct misplaced social norms, and his research is overwhelmingly US-based. For example, many US college students upon first arrival are under the impression that most of their fellow students will drink to excess regularly – many times each week. In fact, in the USA, the levels of average drinking are much lower than this perception, hence the opportunities for *correcting misplaced* social norms. For this particular situation, corrective social norm campaigns appear to have worked well, at least according to the US National Institute on Alcoholism and Alcohol Abuse.[8] Apparently, 'persistently communicated accurate norms have resulted in alcohol intake reductions of about 20%'.

Social norms campaigns have also been effective in reducing cigarette smoking and sexual assault. The opportunity, one senses, comes from arenas in which false perceptions exist that 'habit X must be OK because everyone else is doing it', when, in fact, activity X is much less common than supposed. Perhaps the presumptions of some people in relation to domestic violence may fall into this category. Of course, an opposite set of circumstances may also arise, where the extent of a healthy behaviour may be *underestimated*: 'No one eats vegetables any more, all my peers eat fast food', and so on. Either way, communicating the correct social norm is, in theory, a valid strategy.

The core principle is that peers will often exert more influence over people than other groups – even close ties such as family, or authority figures. Note that there is a subtlety here: what exerts the influence is the *perceived* norm – what people think their peers value, rather than the *actual* norm – what they value in reality. Close friends exert the most influence, while more distant groups exert less.

As we can see then, the key currency of social norms campaigns is **misperception**. The most common misperception is when a majority of people who engage in healthy behaviour incorrectly believe they are in a minority. This is called pluralistic ignorance. This misperception may arise from the lack of visibility of different types of *behaviours* (the majority behavioural norm is known as the descriptive norm, while the majority attitudinal norm is known as the injunctive norm), with the most visible being the unhealthy behaviour (e.g. binge drinking), and the healthy behaviour being less visible. An extremely common variant of this is that people may publicly behave unhealthily – binge drinking being a classic example – while not enjoying it, in the belief they are the only one who privately doesn't enjoy the episode. However, in fact, the majority of people they are with may feel the same way. Here, social norms marketing works by informing people that their feelings are more common than they thought.

The opposite, **false consensus**, occurs when, say, heavy drinkers falsely believe that most others are similar to themselves. Heavy smokers falsely believe that smoking is common, and heavy gamblers falsely believe the same is true of gambling. This is sometimes called **self-serving bias**, to justify one's own behaviour. Interestingly, the strongest and most vocal views in a community are held by those who engage in false consensus. They see themselves as the 'guardians of truth' about their reference group. Behaviours such as consistent speeding or climate change denial may be the subject of very vocal carriers of false consensus. This aggressive vocalisation can lead to an increasing passivity amongst the majority, who themselves may not be aware they constitute the majority. This leads to a '**spiral of silence**' effect which can be very damaging. Social norms campaigns have been shown to be effective in combating these vicious circle effects created by false consensus and pluralistic ignorance.

There may well be false consensus, pluralistic ignorance, and spirals of silence about a number of issues linked to social marketing in the UK. How much false consensus exists about speed cameras for example? 'No one wants them.' Is this true? Or drug use amongst young people: 'Everyone else is taking them', and so on.

Social marketers can create communication-based norm campaigns with messages such as '96% of college students want to give up smoking before graduation'. More targeted one-to-one feedback may be offered to vulnerable individuals. Norms campaigns will often be linked to multiple interventions, perhaps as part of things such as weight reduction, smoking cessation trials, and so on. Keys to marketing success include:

- Present any survey data in detail, and with access to open data.

- Present the messages in a clear manner, using sources that are trusted and seen as reliable.

- Ensure the imagery and messages are in close congruence. One alcohol norms campaign that failed had an image of a student throwing up, which both overpowered, and seemed at odds with, the message.

So far in this chapter we've established that people are influenced by other people, and we've noted that this looks to be important for social marketers. There seem to be various mechanisms through which such influence will spread, and clearly it's important for social marketers to understand these mechanics. We can now turn to some recent studies on *viral effects* that really bring this home. Have a look at Vignette 9.2.

VIGNETTE 9.2

Quitting smoking is contagious, study of former smokers shows

Rob Waters

21 May 2008 (Bloomberg) – The same peer pressure that leads people to try their first cigarette can work in reverse, pushing members of social circles to quit smoking together, a study says.

The analysis published today in the *New England Journal of Medicine* says groups of friends, relatives and co-workers often stop smoking in clusters.

The percentage of Americans who smoke *dropped* to 20.8% from 41.9% between 1965 and 2006, according to the US Centers for Disease Control and Prevention. Many quit at the same time as other people they knew, the study found.

'People quit in droves,' said Nicholas Christakis, a Harvard University researcher and co-author of the study. 'In a very fundamental way, decisions to quit smoking in humans are like decisions to fly to the left or right in birds in a flock. The individual bird doesn't decide alone.'

The researchers at Harvard in Cambridge, Massachusetts, and the University of California, San Diego, tracked people who were involved in a *long-running health study* and recorded the smoking status of their friends, spouses, neighbors and colleagues. The researchers found that people linked in social networks tended to quit around the same time.

According to the study, a smoker was 67 percent more likely to quit if a spouse did so, 36 percent more likely if a friend did so, and 25 percent more likely if a sibling did so.

It takes a village

Christakis said in a telephone interview today that he wasn't surprised at the influence of spouses or close friends. What impressed him, he said, was the effect of less direct relationships.

> **Vignette 9.2** (*continued*)
>
> 'We showed that people are more likely to quit not only when their friends quit, but also when their friends' friends and their friends' friends' friends quit,' Christakis said. 'Decisions to quit are made not only by isolated individuals but also reflect collective decisions.'
>
> Though groups often seemed to stop smoking in concert, Christakis said the process appears largely unplanned.
>
> 'It's spontaneous organization. There's no head fish,' he said. 'We think what's happening is a change in norms within the networks. We think for the norm to be transmitted, people have to be connected. You don't affect the habits of people to whom you have no connection.'
>
> The study shows that social networks can be an important tool in public health campaigns aimed at ending smoking or other unhealthy habits, said Richard Suzman, director of the US National Institute on Aging's division of behavioral and social research.
>
> 'The culture of individualism is so strong that we sometimes forget how powerfully and silently social networks and those around us influence our health,' Suzman said in an e-mailed statement.
>
> *Source*: Waters, R. (2008) *Quitting Smoking is Contagious*. Available from: http://www.bloomberg.com/apps/news?pid=20601124&sid=aG5hXLHTYmcM&refer=home

The particularly interesting item in this story is the way in which the behavioural influence seems to be travelling through the friendship network as a cultural norm – spread without any particularly calculative or cognitive element to it. People seem to be observing what friends of friends are doing, absorbing it, and being 'unconsciously' influenced by it. Once again, this is quite new material for our field: social marketers could look for ways to facilitate and accelerate this 'natural' effect.

Group types

Much of our discussion so far has concentrated on peer or, in the example above, viral groups. Let's now have a closer look at the many different group types.

There are a number of different types of groups:

Close-knit

- Neighbourhood driven by local geography, income, social class
- Professional
- Friendship and family
- Activity/interest – sometimes known as *tribes*

Diffused

- Second/third/fourth-hand effects spread virally through loose social networks
- The influence of remote communication with similar people that we don't personally know – possibly through new media

- General community, e.g. the social identity of one's local town
- National groups create cultural effects such as British culture

This is good territory for marketers. Commercial marketing is heavily infused with the principles of targeting, in particular, and also with segmentation of a market into its different sectors. Commercial players may be experts at identifying a niche segment who may fit the concept of a 'tribe', for example. A tribe is a group of people who share a common interest that, in turn, creates a shared history, shared narratives, customs and practices. *Max Power* magazine identifies young males who are car enthusiasts, and are keen to modify their cars with accessories. If a Ford Escort with an oversized exhaust and massive speakers thumps by, its owner may be part of a 'tribe' of 'Modders' – young lads who enjoy modifying their own cars. The less socially attractive side to this group may, however, be their tendency to drive in what other could regard as an aggressive or even dangerous manner. Can social marketers be part of the solution in reducing aggressive driving? If so, taking advantage of the tribal nature of the group may be crucial.

VIGNETTE 9.3

Max Driver: tribe-inspired social marketing?

Young male drivers are notorious for their aggressive driving. This is particularly true of 'Modders', a group of young men, car enthusiasts, who modify their cars with accessories. (See http://www.manolith.com/2009/08/31/15-most-ridiculous-car-mods/ for some outlandish examples.)

Sometimes dubbed 'boy racers', these lads overestimate their own driving ability, have poor risk perception and relatively low empathy for other road users – a toxic combination.

Criticisms of this group from mainstream society are understandably frequent. This criticism extended to *Max Power* magazine, which, for example, often ran stories that celebrated 'cruising', a form of tribal behaviour in which many Modders would gather at specific places to spend time. *Max Power* was also criticised for its campaigns against speed cameras and older drivers, who were dubbed 'coffin dodgers'.

Perhaps to counter such criticism, in 2006, *Max Power* magazine launched an advanced driving scheme called Max Driver. This was launched in conjunction with the Institute of Advanced Motorists (IAM), Adrian Flux Insurance Services, Honda and Ripspeed. It was designed to offer drivers professional tuition in handling their cars responsibly. Those who pass were guaranteed a 25% discount on insurance. Max Driver was given a strong promotional push by the magazine, and branded so as to counter the rather old-fashioned image portrayed by the IAM. As one press article put it, 'the IAM have got about as sexy an image as Cliff Richard, they have got together with *Max Power* and designed a course that will appeal to 17 to 25 year olds. The IAM have got 50 years of experience and Max Power has got the cool factor. On paper, it seemed like a good idea.' This branding was used on the manual 'Drive like a God' created for the scheme. 'C'mon big boy, max your driving' was one of the picture captions describing an attractive, if skimpily clad, young woman behind the wheel of a car. There was significant interest in the scheme, though unfortunately the scheme fizzled out quite early on due to operational difficulties.

Max Driver was, in theory, a good example of the use of 'tribal branding' to promote a social good. Although results from this scheme were inconclusive, future projects in the area could use the design as a good starting point.

In 2009–11 the Bristol Social Marketing Centre (BSMC) was asked by the UK's Department for Transport to help run a social marketing pilot scheme to promote safer driving amongst young men from deprived communities. For the young men in our test area, values included a relatively low regard for their own and others' safety and placing a high value on visceral, spontaneous thrill-seeking. These lads had a social 'hierarchy' that resulted partly from the ability to drive aggressively and to tell entertaining stories about their exploits. Sociologists inspired by Bourdieu would have explained these stories as part of the young men's cultural capital – that is, their driving, and subsequent storytelling are social assets that they use to attain positions of hierarchy in their social arenas. Whatever the description, these culturally driven behaviours militated against careful driving.

Working with the local Road Safety Partnership, the BSMC found that a strong neighbourhood effect was in play, with the boys acting as a group. It also found that best results in other spheres had come from partnership working, and so a community development approach was taken.

One problem was the hostility to the idea of 'road safety'. The value set of the audience did not align with road safety, and attempts to shift this in the past through campaigns such as the national Think! campaign had been resisted. This led to a design which hid the safety theme and rebranded the intended outcome around skilful driving. This rebranding is very important: it allowed the recipients to fit together their participation in the trial with their social fabric and personal values. The rebranding also offers the best chance of spreading the social norm of more skilful, alert driving (see Figure 9.5).

Participants were recruited to the campaign through an incentive of free monthly karting events. A data recorder fitted into the boys' cars would enable specific skills-based feedback on their driving to be given. The project is designed to change individual habits, and to spread a new social norm. In the longer term, spreading the social norming effect beyond the participants is vital for the ultimate success of the trial.

The intention is that the new behaviours of the triallists will be observed by others with whom they are in direct contact, and that this direct observation will encourage a diffusion effect that spreads the new behaviour. The engine room of this diffusion will be the desire to conform to a new norm of 'skilful driving'. This must be internalised as being 'cool' – in other words, as being consistent with a socially approved 'basket' of behaviours.

The interface between social marketing and community development is equally vital for the success of this design. The early adopters of the trial have themselves been integrally involved in the design of the project, and will be involved as leaders of the post-trial dissemination to others in the community. Much of this work will be voluntary.

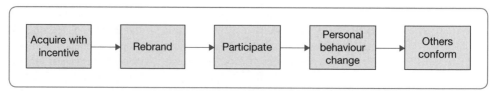

Figure 9.5 Social effects as part of the road safety marketing project

Group effects

We have just discussed a number of different group types, and so far in this chapter we've also mentioned some group effects. Perhaps it's time to pull these effects together, and ensure we have listed out those that are key for social marketers (see Table 9.1).

Group effects raise a set of questions that need to be understood to design effectively a social marketing intervention.

- Are the different groups discussed earlier resistant to change, compliant, or actively seeking change?
- Are they hierarchical in nature, or consensual? Are there prominent people or leaders within the group, or is the group a 'flat' democracy?
- Are decisions to change made in an 'active', highly communicated way, or emergent?
- Linked to this, is the type of interaction anarchic in nature (climbing fraternities, for example, are notoriously so), or strongly organised, clubby and rule-bound (a typical golf club)?
- Is the interaction between individuals conscious/cognitive (groups that have lots of explicit rules), emotional in nature (groups that form as social movements based on a perceived social mission or cause) or automatic/subconscious (groups that do not acknowledge their group status)?
- Is there a role for different media – we discussed *Max Power* magazine above – in defining, organising, influencing, leading the group? What is the effect on change of the physical nature of the interactions that go on, for example, social media such as Facebook as compared to chat sites, as compared to, say, radio phone-ins.

Table 9.1 Types of social or group effect

Conforming	Copying behaviour around you either cognitively, emotionally or automatically
Norming	When people are new to a group or placed together for the first time, they are keen to adjust their behaviour to each other as they develop social habits that make social interactions or teamwork seem more natural and fluid. Group members often work through this stage by agreeing on rules, values, behaviour, shared methods, working tools and even taboos. During this phase, group members begin to trust each other.
Groupthink	First coined by William Whyte in 1952, Groupthink is a type of thought exhibited by group members who try to minimise conflict and reach consensus without critically testing, analysing, and evaluating ideas. Groupthink arises from group cohesion – for example, young men living in the same working-class neighbourhood exhibit high group cohesion. The closer group members are in outlook, the less likely they are to raise questions that might break their cohesion. This is both a strength, in that it creates strong social bonds, but also a weakness, preventing new ideas coming in.
Diffusion of innovations	Dating back to the 1890s and the work of a French sociologist, diffusion of innovations is a theory of how, why, and at what rate new ideas and technology spread through cultures. Everett Rogers's extensive work on this concept led to the well-known bell-shaped curve of diffusion that spreads ideas through innovators, early adopters, early and late majorities, and laggards. Clearly, some individuals are more influential than others and adopt leadership roles through their actions and communications. Gladwell's tipping point work builds upon this theory. The diffusion of innovations also implies a 'viral' style of effects, in which more remote, larger-scale effects can flow between people who may have people in common but not know each other directly.

- Is there a role for commercial marketing in the group? A well-known example is the Harley Owners Group of motorcycle enthusiasts.

- Ultimately, to what extent do the members of the group act as part of the group, and to what extent are individuals influenced by the group? Put another way, what percentage of the behavioural variance for people in the group is explained by group effects? We may expect young men in the same deprived neighbourhood to have a higher percentage of group-explained behaviour than young men sharing a 'web-based' interest.

Let's have a go at answering some of these questions through a discussion of some of the underlying mechanisms of group effects.

The mechanisms of influence

One of the fascinating things about group effects is how unconscious so much of the influence is. If we are asked, 'OK – do you think you're influenced by friends and family?' all too often we say – 'No, not me, mate. I make my own mind up.' This may be our instant reaction to the idea of us being influenced to change our minds in ways that we may see as a bit weak-minded or flabby, or implying that we are not in control of our own decisions. Admitting that our actions are socially derived goes against the grain of modern, Western life – the principles of individuals being responsible for their own decisions, and having the freedom to exercise these. Of course, there is much truth in the idea of individual decision-making, so that it is often very hard for a researcher to unravel the exact scope of social versus personal factors that have combined to make up a behaviour. Researching this is often extremely difficult: the Theory of Psychological Reactance[9] describes the effect of people's resistance to being, as they may see it, socially coerced into changing their ways. In the UK this reactance takes on a cultural hue – 'I don't like the government telling me how to live my life'; 'It's the nanny state', and so on. (All too often these apparent government dictats are imaginary, but still the media driven campaigns to stop the 'nanny state' persist.) Thus, social marketers need to be aware of the importance of self-presentation, the need for individuation, and people's desire for personal control.

Self-presentation is about ensuring people are seen as intelligent, or cool, or attractive if they conform. Individuation is about ensuring that individual identities are preserved throughout any change – perhaps by emphasising to a potential smoking quitter *other ways* in which they can express their rebel image. Personal control will be felt by people who are not being lectured at, but co-opted as partners, involved in the process, and part of the decision-making. Here, social marketing is a partnership process – and the social marketing design may be **co-created** with the audience.

The important thing is to keep a clear head by assessing the evidence that both social and personal effects do exist, identifying the size and scope of such social effects, and understanding how best to deploy them for good effect in social marketing. In order to do this we need a model of how such effects work.

The three routes for social influence

Cognitive

A cognitive route for social influence may be one that 'rationally' calculates the gains or losses of behaving according to group norms. 'All my friends have given up smoking so I'd better do the same in order to be part of the gang.'

In cognitive-based conformity, social marketers may be best undertaking their own behaviour changes through a cognitive route by offering people calculative reasons to change. McKenzie Mohr and Smith cite the case of farmers moving through a line of reasoning to copy 'first-mover' farmers who have undertaken a new technique. One conclusion from this work was that the copycat behaviour moved through a cognitive function, rather than an unthinking, automatic or emotion-driven route.[10]

Emotive

An emotive-driven route may hang on emotions such as social self-image. 'My image of myself is as a socially edgy, radical person. Therefore I'm going to hang out with other people on the edge of society – and if that means using drugs then so be it.' Another form of emotional conformity may be the perceived social embarrassment of publicly behaving in a contrary way to those around us. Asch's experiments that we examined at the start of the chapter illustrated the power of social embarrassment.

In emotion-based conformity, social marketers could follow an emotion-based route to change, perhaps making emotional appeals such as fear appeals, or self-image-based appeals.

Automatic-habitual

An automatic route would include the kind of subconscious visual copying of behaviour that we have discussed elsewhere in this chapter. Throwing litter 'automatically' – because 'Everyone does it, so why think about it?' – may be a classic example. A lot of cultural norms would be habitual, or 'normal', and hence automatic.

With automatic conformity, social marketers could try to cognitively interrupt the automatic behaviour and encourage thought-driven change. Or they may try to trigger automatic (subconscious) change. Ensuring streets are kept litter-free introduces a barrier to the cultural norm of littering – it may make a litter-bug hesitate.

One technique in fairly common practice in, say, new product development in the drinks industry is to pay for actors to order the new drinks in clubs, looking for copycat behaviour. Of course this is ethically questionable but, of course, the commercial sector will only not do it if it is illegal.

A social marketer could recruit actors/influential people to behave in healthy, environmentally sound or other advantageous ways.

Is this a good idea? Is it ethical, or is it unacceptably manipulative or deceitful?

Conformity at a group level

Franzoi pointed out that, under certain conditions, the minority can influence the majority.[11] Think of the minority cycling lobby working on motorists, or environmentalists trying to influence mainstream holidaymakers. Minorities can sometimes work successfully to change things, but must be consistent and clear in making their points. At the same time, extensive research suggests they must not appear dogmatic or rigid. The cycling lobby in the UK often seems mistaken in making demands that motorists find confusing or unreasonable. Cycling purist groups are not experts at dealing with the general public, and have difficulty setting a tone that works over time to influence change. Part of this problem lies with the competing cultures at play: the value set of some cyclists (who become spokespeople) is that cycling is a good thing, that car drivers are selfish and lazy, and so on. In turn, the car culture is deeply embedded in the UK. Attempts to curb driving through, say, cutbacks in road building usually lead to hysterical charges of 'penalising the motorists'. Not surprisingly, this creates difficulties in generating dialogue such that the minority can influence the majority in mainstream society.

The minority need to be flexible, and their best chance of achieving change will be to take advantage of 'evolving norms' or, put more simply, going with the flow of emerging new ways of thinking. For instance, there is growing consensus that motoring is contributing to global warming and we should look for ways to curb car use. However, such battles are tough to fight. Changing majority views is difficult, but a vital part of social marketing. One problem is that people's social identities usually consist of majority-held values and beliefs, which may need time to work on. On the other hand, behaviour like car use may be largely a socially contagious habit that has been taken on without much thought, and here the task may be to work on habit change.

In summary, most of this chapter has examined conformity – copying – of one sort or another. Compliance contrasts with conformity in that it is a more direct type of social influence involving asking for a behaviour in response to a direct request. To finish, we discuss some of the techniques deployed and their significance for social marketing.

Compliance

The multi-layered subtleties of conformity and influence can get tiring. Why not simply ask our audience directly to change their ways? Perhaps social marketers sometimes overcomplicate and forget this most direct of all routes to behaviour change. Direct compliance techniques are often best deployed in one-to-one situations between the influencer and the citizen. This work has led to well-known commercial selling techniques of which two of the best known are:

- *Foot in the door* – Here the influencer will ask for some small concession such as asking if someone will display a window sticker supporting lower car use. The next step is to ask for a substantive behaviour change – for example, to walk to the shops for small errands rather than driving. Tests have shown that people's desire for internal consistency makes compliance much higher for those who had displayed the sticker.

- *Door in the face* – In this influence-sequence, a person is asked upfront to comply with a large request – say, to cease all car use. This is likely to be refused, something anticipated by the influencer, who then apparently compromises by asking for the smaller concession they had wanted from the start. Again, tests show this strategy can be very effective.

But of course these are 'tricks', rooted in human psychology. This presents a problem for social marketers. Ethically, where do we stand with such techniques? Do the socially good ends justify the (arguably manipulative) means? This question is addressed, in depth, in Chapter 5.

> **CASE STUDY 9.1**
>
> ## Ideas for the future: Fixed action patterns and breastfeeding
>
> In 2008, the Bristol Social Marketing Centre was asked to help with ideas for encouraging teenage breastfeeding using social marketing. Some ideas based on Cialdini's work are relevant here.[12]
>
> Fixed action patterns are semi-automatic behavioural sequences in animals triggered by outside influence. The idea of fixed action patterns was used as a metaphor by Cialdini to describe some human behaviours. Such sequences are imprinted on our behavioural memories, and are used by us as shortcuts to save on thinking effort and time. An example might be *reciprocation*: our learned human instinct to return a favour with a favour.
>
> Let us have a closer look at a number of techniques based on Cialdini's work that could be applied to encouraging breastfeeding in teenage mothers – a group with low levels of breastfeeding. The techniques described below have the potential to be powerful if breastfeeding is a semi-automatic process based on things like social copying (wanting to be liked and to fit in), rather than a cognitive choice, rationally based on a calculation of benefit pros and cons. However, some of these approaches are likely to be more successful than others when implemented with a target segment of teenage mothers. Read through them, thinking about the the pros and cons of each.
>
> ### Create a sense of obligation
>
> Here, for example, patients' consciences could be alerted to the good care they have received at the hospital, and they could be asked to do their best for their baby by breastfeeding: 'We've done our best for you – in return can you do your best for your infant?'
>
> ### Use the power of consistency
>
> Here the technique described by Cialdini often involves pledges. The health professional could discuss breastfeeding with the mother, and ask for a pledge to breastfeed – maybe for a specific time period. Evidence from other fields suggests that, having given this pledge, the mother is more likely to breastfeed. Follow-up may be possible – effectively looking to see of the pledge has been honoured.
>
> ### Making use of social proof
>
> Social norms are strongly influential when we are unsure how to behave. This is presumably often the case for new, young mothers faced with the issue of how to feed their child. These mothers look around to see if they can see people similar to themselves, and copy their behaviour. There is considerable evidence to illustrate this behavioural trait. The breastfeeding problem, however, is precisely that there is a lack of such social evidence: breastfeeding is not seen around the place as a normal, everyday activity. We could, therefore, consider devices such as peer-led discussions or demonstrations, or communications that simply show breastfeeding as normal and everyday amongst teenage mums. One misunderstanding may be that teenagers are immune to such social norming because they are rebellious and independent. However, their rebellious tendencies extend to their parents, but rarely to each other – with peers, conformity is very strong.

Case study 9.1 (*continued*)

Leverage liking

In commercial settings people buy from people they like; they buy from friends; they buy from physically attractive people; and they buy from people they see as similar to themselves.

How do we translate these principles to breastfeeding? Perhaps start by involving friends who already may be mums in the influence process as much as possible. We could use attractive-looking people in communications – without resorting to impossibly good-looking models, with whom ordinary people cannot identify. The principle of 'similarity' may be evoked in communications by using similar looks, speech and everyday living that our target audience exhibit.

If we combine social proofing and liking, we could powerfully influence new mums by making use of a peer-led face-to-face endorsement of breastfeeding from a good-looking, likeable friend who is similar to the new mum.

Use the power of contact, co-operation and teamwork

Engendering contact and co-operation with others means that we are more likely to co-operate on other things. This often is codified by creating a sense of us against them – by creating an opponent against whom everyone pulls together to fight. This could be illustrated for breastfeeding as follows: 'Look – those suppliers of formula milk are the bad guys – we need to team up against them, and the way we do that is by everyone breastfeeding.'

Authority

Experiments demonstrate clearly that figures of authority are powerful influencers. The reaction to authority is often obedience. The implication is that a white-coated doctor/medical expert having a personal word about breastfeeding should in theory be a powerful influence on the new mum. This does, however, resemble traditional health patronage, which has not had a good track record in successful health outcomes. There is presumably a thin line between obedience and (so says reactance theory) defiance – Don't tell me how to live my life – something particularly prevalent in British culture.

Source: Bristol Social Marketing Centre, 2009, 'Using social marketing to encourage breastfeeding'; for Bristol PCT.

Question

Ask yourself about the pros and cons of each of these techniques. When do you think they are appropriate? When not?

The following case study shows how two of the techniques identified in Cialdini's work outlined above have been used in a breastfeeding campaign targeting young mothers. The campaign leverages *liking* by showing young mums breastfeeding in a series of posters and online resources. The women fronting the campaign are all young mums who endorse breastfeeding. This endorsement provides *social proof* for the target audience that breastfeeding is something that people like themselves do. But this campaign goes further; by positioning young women who breastfeed as role models who are 'stars', it aims to change perceptions that breastfeeding is something that young mums *should do,* into something they *want to do*; a highly aspirational behaviour.

CASE STUDY 9.2

'Be a star' – Breastfeeding initiation campaign

Brief

To increase breastfeeding initiation amongst 18–24-year-old white women, in the 'hard-pressed' ACORN segment group.

Research

Discussion groups and interviews with service providers yielded insight into the socio-cultural factors influencing the audience's views on breastfeeding. The opinions of partners, parents, friends and the community emerged as key factors in the decision to breastfeed. Some specific insights included:

- Young women do not believe breastfeeding is for people like them – It is for 'yummy mummies'.
- They are interested in and influenced by glamour, brands, image and celebrity, but are fickle about celebrity – stars are here today, gone tomorrow. They cannot identify their 'issues' with those of celebrity mums.
- They cannot identify with national campaigns.
- They do not wish to expose themselves in front of their parents.
- Mothers and their immediate network see breastfeeding as 'weird', incestuous, embarrassing – something that is uncomfortable to see.
- Breastfeeding in public is not accepted within their community. Trust networks are incredibly strong and many girls do not travel far outside of their community.
- The babies' fathers, mums' friends and mums' own parents are key influencers.
- Support from each other helps them continue breastfeeding.
- There is confusion about what is best. The target audience does seek advice and is receptive.
- Mothers can feel isolated and seek refuge online where support is not available at home.
- Self-esteem is an issue.

Approach

To completely redefine the perception of breastfeeding by leveraging the cult of celebrity to engage and persuade, empower, motivate and inspire. Using real members of the audience to gain authenticity and stimulate peer-to-peer information transfer. Behavioural goal mapping along infant-feeding decision journey allowed for effective targeting of resources and focused interventions.

Tactics

Campaign resources include: a 24-hour support helpline and motivational SMS; outdoor, posters and printed material; a blog site; radio advertising; online social networking; a YouTube viral; peer-to-peer support groups.

The campaign has been rolled out in 18 Primary Care Trusts (PCTs) in the UK and has been refined to fit the needs of young women in each PCT. Some PCTs have launched aligned services as part of the campaign to support behaviour change, For example,

---

Case study 9.2 (*continued*)

in Lancashire a breastfeeding peer support service 'Little Angels' was introduced to provide women with practical advice and support from young mums like themselves.

Results

- 13% increase in initiation of breastfeeding in the target group over the first 6 months of the campaign. And a 9% increase sustained over 12 months against a 2% target (Central Lancashire).

- Increased efficiencies and cohesion in delivery of breastfeeding services.

- Mobilisation of internal staff through increased morale and aspiration.

- Over 85,000 hits on blog site within first year.

- Positive feedback from mums who used the peer support services and the blog.

- Empowerment: five 'Stars' have become peer-to-peer supporters and one enrolled on a midwifery course.

- Extensive media coverage – regionally, nationally and internationally.

For further information on this campaign see:

http://thensmc.com/resources/showcase/be-star.

The campaign viral: http://www.youtube.com/watch?v=DPwyqEXBDPI

For an insight video on the design, development and roll-out of the campaign from the National Social Marketing Centre see: http://www.youtube.com/watch?v=1sM18W0h-AE

Source: Collaborative Change/Steven Johnson.

Figure 9.6 Examples of 'She's a star' campaign posters

Question

What alternative ways of using Cialdini's work could have employed? Compare your answers with your discussion related to Case study 9.1.

CASE STUDY 9.3

Pssst! Be Alcohol Aware – reaching binge drinkers

Background

In 2007, binge drinking in Liverpool was estimated as the highest in England and crime attributed to alcohol was amongst the highest in the North West. On some weekends, 70% of Accident and Emergency admissions were alcohol-related.

'Pssst! Be Alcohol Aware' aims to encourage students to behave responsibly towards alcohol consumption and subsequently reduce the level of alcohol-related incidents in Liverpool. The project aims to raise awareness of alcohol-related health and safety messages, provide a non-alcoholic alternative to students on a night out and enable students to adopt healthy drinking behaviours.

The specific behavioural goal was for students to adopt healthy drinking behaviours and safety whilst drinking, including:

- eating a substantial meal in advance of drinking;
- alternating alcoholic drinks with non-alcoholic ones;
- drinking less;
- planning how to get home in advance;
- travelling home in groups.

The project targeted 18–35-year-olds, of whom 40% are students. This group are not low-hanging fruit and are generally considered to be in a liminal phase where they are free from feelings and burdens of responsibility, free from the curtailments of living with parents and willing to try new behaviours and search out new identities.

Started with insight

Research was used at all stages to develop an innovative and targeted programme. Students were involved in the development of the campaign and all concepts were extensively pre-tested to ensure that they were relevant to the target audience and that communication channels/tone of voice were appropriate.

The scoping stage consisted of a mix of secondary and primary research. This was supplemented by focus groups with students aged 18–21. They were held to find out attitudes and behaviour surrounding alcohol and drinking.

Research at the scoping stage revealed that students acknowledge the negative consequences of excessive drinking (e.g. hangovers, vomiting, crime, embarrassing behaviour) but they ignore these factors because drinking is seen as an integral part of the university experience. Students feel university is their last opportunity to get really drunk frequently

> **Case study 9.3** (*continued*)
>
> before the responsibility of a career. They also perceive that 'everyone does it', that drinking to excess is normative behaviour and that there is no alternative.
>
> ### The intervention
>
> There are approximately 50,000 students in Liverpool and drinking is part of their social scenery. Most social situations targeting students encourage binge drinking, and new students are 'initiated' by activities that involve alcohol consumption. To mitigate this culture, Pssst! negotiated support from the universities and had a strong presence at the freshers' fairs, handing out promotional materials. Students were encouraged to show how 'There's more to student life than Getting Pssst!', through the media of film, photography, Facebook and YouTube, and the student radio.
>
> The campaign itself involved the launch of a 'chill-out cabin' in the city centre on nights popular with students. The cabin offered a non-alcoholic experience within the students' usual drinking environment. Visitors were offered mocktails (non-alcoholic cocktails) and could listen to music, play games and enjoy massages and beauty treatments.
>
> The cabin was supported by an integrated communications campaign targeting students as they moved between venues on a night out. This included alcohol 'wheels' to illustrate alcohol units by type of drink so students could see how much they had drunk compared to what is 'healthy'. Interaction with staff, who were from a similar age group, allowed students to discuss their drinking habits in an informal manner. Such discussions helped break down social norms, where visitors may have found that other students weren't drinking as much as they perceived.
>
> A broadcast and print media advertising campaign to convey health messages was also run, featuring advertising on buses and phone kiosks, building projections, and Bluetooth messages.
>
> ### Evaluation and results
>
> Three hundred street interviews were conducted with students during and after the intervention, including 100 interviews in the 'chill-out cabin' and in-depth interviews at the end of the programme.
>
> The 'chill-out cabin' received over 3,000 visitors over the 19 nights it was open, and served over 2,500 mocktails. Of 100 interview respondents:
>
> - 99% of visitors felt the cabin was an appropriate way to promote sensible drinking;
> - 84% felt it had an impact on their own drinking behaviours;
> - 41% of visitors said they drank less that evening, following their visit to the cabin;
> - 70% stated that they were likely to look for other non-alcoholic options in the future.
>
> Research three months after the programme found positive trends in the drinking behaviours of cabin visitors compared to the general student population. Sixty per cent of cabin visitors still felt that the cabin had had some impact upon their drinking behaviours and stated that they would like to see the cabin open more frequently and in more locations across the city centre. Trends suggested that cabin visitors were drinking slightly less and on fewer occasions than the general student population.

Liverpool PCT committed to invest £10 million in the period until 2010 to tackle alcohol misuse in the city. Initiatives included education in schools, intervention in the workplace, improved access to treatment and raising awareness on the dangers of alcohol misuse.

Conclusion

Targeting students to promote sensible drinking messages is a difficult task. Students, living away from home for the first time, tend to experiment with alcohol and drink in excess. This behaviour often drops away after the end of their degrees, when other priorities, such as careers and relationships, take over. This intervention saw relatively small numbers of students and the evaluation claims success, thanks to its intense, non-prescriptive model. Students are unlikely to be receptive to long-term health messages, so on-the-spot interventions are likely to be a more appropriate option, although long-term behaviour change would be hard to measure.

Source: http://www.nsmcentre.org.uk/public/CSView.aspx?casestudy=89#top

Summary

Social norms and group influences are important for social marketers. In general, people seriously underestimate the extent to which they are influenced by others around them. The concepts of social influence should probably be more widely deployed within social marketing.

Repositioning social marketing as a technique that can *work with groups*, rather than just *target individuals,* is important for its future growth. Recently, Andreasen (2006) made the point that social marketing is sometimes criticised by other professionals as being too 'downstream' and too much focused on individuals.[13] Perhaps these critics have a point – social marketing can be pigeonholed as rather tactical as a result. Social marketing also has a reputation for sometimes deploying manipulative techniques and this is partly down again to the perception that it is aimed at isolated individuals. In this chapter we have presented a broad set of theory-rich frameworks for public workers to organise their marketing strategies around communities and groups.

The English Jacobean poet John Donne wrote his historic meditation 'No Man is an Island' in the early 1600s. He understood clearly that society is fundamentally interdependent:

> Any man's death diminishes me, for I am involved in mankind. And therefore never send to know for whom the bell tolls. It tolls for thee.[14]

If Donne were alive today, perhaps he would have had sympathy for social marketers, trying to re-educate policy makers about the need for social cohesion. In an individualistic age, social marketing is often upheld as a consumer's answer to a consumerist culture. But in this chapter we offer a set of principles that we hope suggest a more connected vision for the discipline.

CHAPTER REVIEW QUESTIONS

1 Think about a range of products you have purchased recently. To what extent was your purchase decision influenced by others? Then think about behaviours such as decisions to smoke or not, types of healthy or unhealthy foods to eat or how much/what type of exercise you take. Contrast the group influences on these behaviours with your product purchases. What actions would you recommend be taken to influence behaviour change for your age group?

2 How important do you believe conformity to perceived group norms is for behaviours such as smoking, safe drinking or safe driving? How do you recommend this conformity should be taken into account in developing interventions aimed at changing behaviours?

3 Interview five friends about their attitudes and behaviours in regard to cycling. What group influences appear to exist and how might they be addressed in developing interventions aimed at changing behaviours?

4 Review the literature regarding social marketing interventions focused on changing social norms: some have been successful, others not.

   (a) What do the key success factors appear to be in these types of intervention?

   (b) What do the main reasons appear to have been for some interventions being less successful than expected?

5 Given the strength of reactance effects, especially among young people, how would you determine likely reactions to government-sponsored social marketing interventions versus those that originate from commercial or non-commercial sources (such as charities)?

6 How would you determine which of the three routes for social influence should be used for:
   - smoking cessation;
   - sexual health;
   - alcohol moderation;
   - increasing physical activity?

Justify your recommendations.

Recommended reading

Cialdini, R.B. and Goldstein, N.J. (2012) Social Influence: Compliance and Conformity. *Annual Review of Psychology,* 55 (1), 591–621.

Gladwell, M. (2000) *The Tipping Point.* Boston: Little, Brown & Company.

Goldstein, N.J., Cialdini, R.B. and Griskevicius, V. (2008) A Room with a Viewpoint: Using Social Norms to Motivate Environmental Conservation in Hotels *Journal of Consumer Research,* 35 (3) (October 2008), 472–82.

Kotler, P., Roberto, N., Leisner, T. (2006) Alleviating Poverty: A Macro/Micro Marketing Perspective. *Journal of Macromarketing,* 26 (2) 233–9.

McKenzie-Mohr, D. (2011) *Fostering Sustainable Behavior* (3rd edn). Gabriola Island, BC: New Society Publishers.

Notes

1 Franzoi, S. (2000) *Social Psychology* (2nd edn). New York: McGraw Hill.

2 Asch, S.E. (1955) Opinions and Social Pressure. *Scientific American,* 193 (5), 31–5.

3 Franzoi, S. (2000) Op. cit.

4 McKenzie Mohr, D. and Smith, W. (1999) *Fostering Sustainable Behavior: An Introduction to Community-Based Social Marketing* (2nd edn). Gabriola Island, BC: New Society.

5 Cialdini, R. (2007) *Influence: The Psychology of Persuasion,* New York: HarperCollins.

6 Gladwell, M. (2000) *The Tipping Point.* Boston: Little, Brown & Company.

7 Berkowitz, A. (2004) *The Social Norms Approach: Theory, Research and Annotated Bibliography,* Higher Education Centre for Alcohol and Other Drug Abuse and Violence Prevention. Available from: www.higheredcenter.org/socialnorms

8 US National Institute on Alcoholism and Alcohol Abuse cited in Berkowitz, A., (2004) Op. cit.

9 See, for example, Franzoi, S. (2000) Op. cit.

10 McKenzie Mohr, D. and Smith, W. (1999) Op. cit.

11 Franzoi, S. (2000) Op. cit.

12 Cialdini, R. (2007) Op. cit.

13 Andreasen, A.R. (2006) *Social Marketing in the 21st Century.* Thousand Oaks, CA: Sage.

14 Donne, J. (1624) Meditation 17, from Devotions Upon Emergent Occasions. Available from: www.poetryfoundation.org/bio/john-donne

PART 3

Designing effective social marketing solutions

Designing social marketing interventions: products, branding, channels and places

Chapter objectives

On completing this chapter, you should be able to:

- identify different levels of products and apply these to the development of social marketing campaigns;
- critically discuss the role of branding in social marketing;
- apply and discuss appropriate branding strategies and develop a suitable brand image for your campaign;
- critically discuss the role of channels and distribution in social marketing product development.

Designing campaigns

At the core of social marketing campaigns is a focus on behaviour. In terms of 'tangible products', as we have seen in Chapter 3, this is often, though not always, related to a service. This chapter develops the understanding acquired in Chapter 3 and expands on the key concepts required to develop a potentially successful social marketing 'product' by looking at three components in detail: product development, branding and place/channel selection.

Developing products for social marketing campaigns

When starting to develop a social marketing campaign, it is often useful to think of the future campaign in terms of a product, which offers a unique value proposition to the prospective consumers. While the target of the social marketing campaign is most likely a new or changed behaviour, the surrounding activities may include several other product types: for example, services (such as a counselling service); ideas (such as living healthily); persons (such as family doctors); physical buildings or other property (such as health centres) or even tangible products (such as condoms). The products related to a specific campaign are often referred to as the product platform, i.e. all the products that help users to achieve the desired outcomes.

The product platform itself can be divided into three levels of products: a core product (or benefit/value proposition), the actual product (i.e. the desired behaviour) and one or several augmented products (related tangibles and services).

The *core product* is the perceived main benefit for the consumer – in other words, it is what makes adopting the actual product (behaviour) worthwhile for the target audience. For example, cycling to work (actual behaviour) for its own sake is not a good value proposition for most people; however, the benefits associated with regular, moderate exercise, such as weight loss, a better body, having more energy, saving fuel, etc. have the power to entice the target audience to adopt cycling to work regularly. Many behaviours have several outcomes; to identify the core product, it is necessary to make decisions based on the insights from the scoping process during the planning phase in order to show the relevance of adopting the behaviour by associating the behaviour with relevant benefits. For example, for a target audience that places a high value on environmental friendliness, emphasising saving fuel and lowering carbon emissions as a result of cycling to work as the core product will be more persuasive then focusing on weight loss.

The *actual product* builds upon the less-specific values (e.g. cutting carbon emissions) and shows a specific way of achieving these (e.g. cycling to work). Similar to commercial marketing, where a specific product is promoted, the actual product in social marketing also includes the brand, which we will cover in more detail later in the chapter.

Finally, the *augmented product* or products associated with a campaign include all the tangible objects and services that will help to perform the behaviour or support the promotion of the behaviour. So, cycle lanes would be an augmented product for a cycling to work campaign. Similarly, a website that shows cycle-friendly routes between two points would be a complementary augmented product for the same actual product (cycling). For example, the Barclays Cycle Hire Scheme in London fulfils the less specific values of cutting carbon emissions and overcrowding on the public transport network, using the specific way of providing a low-cost cycle hire scheme for short distances. The augmented product then consists of cycles and docking stations, the cycle 'superhighways' and support services enabling the rental of cycles.

As many social marketing campaigns are service-led, we briefly review the dimensions by which consumers assess perceived quality. The frequently used SERVQUAL model identifies five specific dimensions[1] particularly relevant when designing a social marketing-related service:

1 *Tangibles*: such as the physical facilities and the appearance of staff;
2 *Responsiveness*: willingness to provide prompt and knowledgeable service;
3 *Empathy*: caring attention and understanding provided;
4 *Reliability*: the ability to deliver the service as promised;
5 *Assurance*: the ability of staff to inspire trust.

By continuously reviewing the design of the product and evaluating the offering using these dimensions, social marketers can ensure that the offered product is perceived as a high-quality product, which is especially important when competing against commercial services. When designing social marketing campaigns, it is important to consider not only the other social marketing campaigns as competition, but also the behaviour that should be changed. For example, by creating a social marketing campaign to reduce smoking, not only are other smoking cessation campaigns direct competitors, but the most important competitors to consider are tobacco companies.

Brand development for social marketing

Brands are a powerful tool to communicate about the actual product – and apply to both upstream as well as downstream social marketing. A recognisable and consistent brand adds value to the product, by enhancing the relationship between target audience and products and by adding an emotional tie between them.

Branding can also unite different behaviours under a single, unified brand.[2] As many social marketing campaigns require complex behaviour changes – for instance in the case of nutrition changes – using branding can simplify the message and encourage the target audience to maintain behaviour changes. Another example is the branding of various forms of exercise under the 'Change4Life' brand or road safety under 'Think!'.

While in the commercial world many brands promote consumption of certain products, in social marketing, branding is more usually used to emphasise the core product by branding of actual or augmented products in order to establish a link between them. For example, a fruit salad can be branded with a 'Five A Day' logo to show that it contributes to the recommended fruit intake.

Relationship building, value adding and exchange have been identified as three mechanisms that underlie successful branding in social marketing.[3]

Relationship building is based on acquiring sophisticated knowledge of customers (or target audiences) and responding appropriately. The focus is not only on a single ad hoc transaction, but rather on maintaining and enhancing the relationship between a brand and the consumers, with the aim of achieving trust and commitment from the consumers towards the brand. The brand thus becomes a 'trusted friend' for the target audience, and services or products endorsed by the brand are also perceived as trusted friends.

By 'adding value', brands move beyond a purely functional perception of a product or service and build additional values into the consumption. For example, Abercrombie and Fitch don't just sell clothes to keep people warm, but rather they sell a lifestyle associated with their clothes. Similarly, in social marketing, campaigns like the VERB campaign don't 'just' sell physical activity, but rather add the 'coolness' factor to exercise.[4]

Lastly, successful brands need to create the perception of a beneficial exchange between consumers and brand (or producer) by delivering a product or service that is worth the money and time spent on it – or whatever other sacrifice the consumer is making. For example, the 'Truth' campaign identified independence, rebellion and a sense of 'coolness' with not smoking for young people,[5] values that made maintaining non-smoking an attractive 'exchange' for young adults.

Brand attributes

How consumers respond to brands depends to a large extent on the amount of favourable (or unfavourable) knowledge they have about a brand and its attributes. Brand attributes, in turn, are made up of brand awareness and brand image.

Brand awareness measures the salience of a brand by considering brand recognition, recall and dominance. In other words, will consumers recognise a brand as familiar (recognition); will they be able to name the brand, either aided or unaided (recall); which brand is top of the consumers' mind for a certain category (dominance) and which attributes are connected to a particular brand (knowledge)? Without brand awareness, a brand is meaningless as consumers would be unlikely to recognise it. The danger for many social marketing campaigns is that because of often limited budgets, they cannot achieve sufficient brand awareness for them to compete with other (often commercial) competing brands.

Brand image (or identity) represents the associations made by consumers for the overall perception of the brand. These include perceived quality when compared to competing brands; perceived value; the brand's personality and any association the consumers may make with the parent organisation. These are important constructs that help consumers to establish an emotional bond with the brand. For social marketing campaigns, developing a suitable brand image is especially important in cases where there are strong, but sometimes counterproductive, organisational associations. For example, as previously pointed out, many people mistrust government information. Creating a strong brand image reflecting organisational attachment to government bodies has the potential to influence brand image negatively.

Brand dimensions

When people choose between brands in a commercial context, a few key issues play a significant role in the outcome. This is because few people make choices based on a single characteristic, but equally few make choices based on a multitude of features, characteristics or values. Broadly speaking, the choices made are based on a combination of rational deliberation (e.g. I'm thirsty and therefore need some water) and emotional deliberation (e.g. I'm a sporty person and therefore like to be seen with a brand that represents these values). The ultimate choice is then an attempt to reconcile both rational and emotional deliberations – for example, by choosing a brand of water that is associated with a sporty lifestyle.

The de Chernatony-McWilliam matrix[6] encapsulates the key choices a consumer makes, and enables planners to concentrate on two independent dimensions: functionality and representation (Figure 10.1). Consumers choose between competing brands by balancing both dimensions with their own needs and wants.

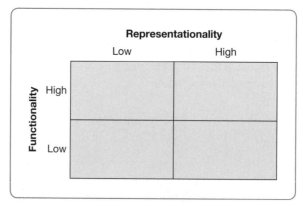

Figure 10.1 de Chernatony-McWilliam matrix

Many social marketing organisations have different, and sometime contradictory, missions, as a result of different audiences and gatekeepers. For example, a social marketing organisation promoting a smoking cessation programme has the government, other donors, employees, volunteers and service users as audiences. This complexity makes branding in a social marketing environment more complex than many commercial companies. Traditional marketing strives to achieve brand congruency; however, different levels of branding are recognised. The different levels are examined below.

Corporate-level branding

This branding is at the highest level, such as the 'DoH' branding on many Department of Health initiatives. It is the equivalent of, for example, Nestlé branding in the commercial world. Corporate-level brands are often not used dominantly on individual products or initiatives, but frequently serve as a 'quality assurance' label. So the DoH logo appears on some social marketing campaigns, which are funded by the Department of Health, just as Nestlé logos appear on most of their products (see Figure 10.2), even if they are not sold primarily under the Nestlé brand name.

Figure 10.2 KitKat with the Nestlé branding
Source: Alamy/SS Studios.

Family branding

This is sharing a brand across different products, although the brand may be distinct from the corporate-level brand. For example, the Mars brand is used consistently across different chocolate bars, drinks and ice cream. Similarly, the Change4Life campaign uses its '4life' brand across a range of products and services (see Figure 10.3), even those targeted at different behaviours (e.g. Walk4life). The main advantage of this approach is that it allows an organisation to develop different messages for some target audiences, and then leverage the synergies between several products being offered under the same family of brands.

Figure 10.3 Various 4life brand images
Source: NHS.

Product-level branding

Product-level branding involves developing brands for individual products or services. This approach offers a more individualised approach to branding, allowing an organisation to develop distinctive brands and target messages at specific groups. For example, the Chelsea and Westminster NHS Foundation Trust in the UK offers sexually transmitted infection screening services under the brand name '56 Dean Street' for the gay community (Figure 10.4).

Branding as a social/identity factor

Consumption has long been associated with identity, especially the consumption of branded products and services.[7] Using branded products or services was first associated with female emancipation, then black emancipation and lately with LGBT emancipation.[8] More recently, this consumption behaviour has been used more generally – i.e. not assuming that it is based on certain subcultures, but rather that it can be applied to all groups of people. These self-formed groups are then described as neo-tribes, who emerged as a movement as people searched for a community to which to anchor themselves, based on their consumption.[9]

For social marketing campaigns, the creation of a community can be very effective. For example, Rescue Social Change Group uses branded events to promote anti-tobacco messages. They developed several 'social brands,' targeting different tribes or communities, such as Verge (LGBT) and Commune (Young Adults who identify as 'Hipsters') (Figure 10.5). Under these brands they create events during which the non-smoking message is introduced and promoted as a desirable behaviour to be part of the 'in-crowd', rather than focusing on the health effects.

Place and distribution channel

Just as commercial marketers carefully design their distribution strategies in order to provide their customers with easy access to their products and services, the same is equally true for social marketing campaigns – especially those where the augmented product involves a service or requires physical access (e.g. a cycling path).

There are five factors that can help to reduce access barriers to services and products: proximity; target audience location; opening hours; point of decision-making; competitor access.

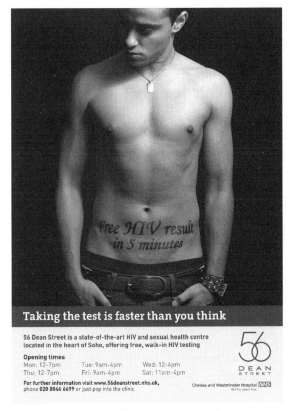

Figure 10.4 56 Dean Street branding, with NHS branding as a smaller, quality assurance-type branding

Source: 56 Dean Street.

Figure 10.5 Verge brand, targeting LGBT community and Commune, for young adults

Source: Rescuescg.com

Proximity

Physical proximity is an important factor when reducing access barriers. Fast and convenient access, for example by locating gyms near workplaces, reduces the time it takes for exercise – one of the most cited barriers for access.[10] Similarly, for blood donations, inconvenient access is a major barrier[11] with the use of mobile blood donation units making access fast, easy and convenient – especially if located in places where people work or spend some spare time.

Target audience location

In addition to the idea of proximity, it's also often useful to think about the locations where members of a specific target audience socialise, live or work. A good example of this is locating sexual health services specifically designed and branded for gay men in areas with a high concentration of gay bars or clubs – such as the previously mentioned 56 Dean Street Clinic, which is located in London's Soho area, and just a few minutes' walk away from most of the gay pubs and clubs in that area. This enables people to access the service in an area where many socialise and therefore visit frequently.

223

The idea of using settings where the target audience socialises has also been used to target black American women. In one case, which has been copied widely, the beauty salon was identified as a place where black American women could be targeted and educated about breast cancer prevention.[12]

Opening hours or extended hours

Being available and accessible when it is convenient for your target audience is another factor which may lead to an increase in service uptake. For example, by extending opening hours of general practitioners in the UK, the NHS is hoping to encourage more people to visit GPs.[13]

Being open and available when the target audience can access services is, logically, important. However, as with all the place attributes, it is not a magic bullet: extending the time period for voting brought only a modest increase in voting behaviour – especially amongst young people, who are more difficult to motivate to vote.[14]

POD – point of decision-making

A further relevant factor is *where* users are likely to make decisions about using a product or service. For example, while condoms are available for free from NHS sexual health clinics, they are not used 'on site'. This can create a barrier in so far as the condoms may not be available when sex takes place. In response, Terrence Higgins Trust initiated a scheme of distributing condoms and branding bars or premises where sex takes place as 'Play Zones' (Figure 10.6). Thus, condoms and lubricant are available for free to patrons of these bars, ensuring minimum barriers to engaging in safe sex.

Figure 10.6 Play Zone logo

Competitor access

A final point to consider when designing a social marketing product or offering is how it compares in terms of barriers to competing products or services – especially behaviours, products or services that are targeted to be changed (e.g. cigarettes, alcohol). The focus is on making access either easier than access to competitor products – or more difficult. For example, some authors claim that removing junk food from school vending machines (and thus making it more difficult to access) has a significant impact on the consumption of healthier alternatives.[15] This view has also been taken by the UK government, which banned junk food sales in schools in 2005.[16] However, as with other place factors, results are not always clear-cut. An evaluation of the smoking ban in Scotland (i.e. making access to 'smoking' as a behaviour to be avoided in public more difficult) found that, while the legislation resulted in a decrease of exposure to second-hand smoke, it did not result in a hypothesised reduction of smoking rates when compared to the rest of the UK.[17] Conversely, the smoking ban in England has been credited with a large reduction in smoking rates and smoking-related deaths.[18]

In decisions about the place – or distribution channels – of a social marketing product there is not one attribute that is the most decisive, but rather there is a combination of the five factors discussed above. In other words, it is important to identify which are the barriers for the product being used, the service being accessed or the desired behaviour. This can then be used to identify the optimal place strategy in order to achieve the desired outcomes.

CASE STUDY 10.1

Transport for London – CABWISE™: creating a brand to help prevent rapes

Introduction

Safer Travel at Night was a partnership between the Mayor of London, Transport for London (TfL), and the Metropolitan Police Service. It aimed to reduce the use of unlicensed minicabs by increasing public awareness of the dangers they present to unsuspecting passengers – in particular, the risk of being raped or sexually assaulted.

Until 2005, the Mayor of London and TfL ran a telephone service that people could call for the numbers of local taxi firms. In 2005, they automated the service and launched the UK's first text-based service to make safer minicab and taxi travel in London easier. Users texted the word 'HOME' to the number 60835; they were then sent the phone numbers of one black cab and two licensed minicab firms in the area from which they are texting.[19]

The objective

The Mayor of London and TfL have a history of effective advertising in promoting safer travel at night and decreasing the number of rapes and sexual assaults committed by illegal minicab drivers.

There has always, however, been a sizeable group of women who continue to use illegal minicabs, despite previous advertising making them aware of the dangers. The aim of developing CABWISE™ was to stop the majority of these women from using illegal minicabs in London, on a relatively modest media spend of only £671,000.

Table 10.1 The number of sexual assaults and rapes committed by illegal minicab drivers

	Sept–Dec. 2003	Sept–Dec. 2004	Sept–Dec. 2005	Sept–Dec. 2006
Number of serious sexual assaults and/or rapes committed by illegal minicab drivers in London	17	12	13	4

Source: Metropolitan Police/GLA State.

Case study 10.1 (*continued*)

The strategy

Historically, TfL advertising had been effective at dissuading women from using illegal minicabs. Despite seeing a decrease in intent to use illegal minicabs, there was no uplift in usage of the text service. As a result, there were still many 16–34-year-old women who went out late in Central London and continued to use illegal minicabs, despite having been exposed to warnings.

This called for a different approach: women needed to be scared away from illegal cabs while the text service needed to relaunch as the best alternative to an illegal minicab at the end of the night.

Scaring women away from illegal minicabs

Tracking research showed that there was a sizeable group of women who were persisting in using illegal minicabs despite being aware of TfL marketing activities. These women were from a wide demographic spectrum.[20] However, in-depth interviews showed that they were very similar attitudinally. They were united in their confidence and optimism. They had a belief that something as horrific as a sexual assault or rape would never happen to them because they simply would never *allow* it to happen.

This was because emotionally they felt that they could read and avoid a dangerous situation better than other women. They felt that they could judge the character of the driver through his voice, his looks and the kind of car he was driving. More rationally, they had all taken the same precautions when getting into illegal minicabs which, they believed, would save them from harm. First, they felt they would be OK if they got into a cab with their friends (even if they were being dropped off at different locations). Secondly, they saw their mobile phone as a lifeline. If they had their mobile in their hand or were talking on the phone during their journey, it would act as a deterrent to the driver and would make them feel safe.

Relaunching the text service

Qualitative research had shown that, late at night, the 'homing pigeon instinct' could override safety – especially if it was cold or raining and the tubes had stopped running. At the same time, getting these women to pre-book minicabs or taxis at the start of the evening was unrealistic as it would inhibit spontaneity.

All the investigations showed a real enthusiasm for a text service as it solved a real problem for young women, especially when they were out in an unfamiliar area without knowledge of local cab firms. However, the same research also showed three hurdles to overcome in converting intent into actual usage:

1 They didn't know or remember the number and didn't know what to name it when saving it to their phones.

2 The advertising to date had scared them, which they deemed inappropriate for a bar or club environment. Hence, they claimed to 'zone out' any threatening messaging at venues.

3 By the time it was getting close to going home time, some of these women were tired and others had had a few drinks and were not in a frame of mind to want to decode any complex advertising messages.

In other words, marketing activities needed to be memorable, useful and able to be decoded easily in the bar or club environment, scaring women but helping them take positive steps to get a legal cab home.

Figure 10.7 CABWISE™ logo

Turning the text service into a brand

The key to achieving the objectives and holding the activities together was turning the TfL text service into a brand in its own right. The brand that was developed was CABWISE™; a memorable brand name with a clearly stated purpose: be WISE about the CAB that takes you home. This brand name gave women a name to save into their mobile phones; it was a gentle reminder of the perils of choosing the 'wrong' cab and acted as the glue to hold the two strands of activity together.

Two strands of activity were developed to connect with the audiences at point of contact.

The fear side

Broadcast, print and digital activity designed to be seen at home, at work and at times when our diehard users might be thinking of and planning a night out, creating a sense of personal danger when it came to using illegal minicabs and to challenge their perceived 'safety nets'.

The functional side

Broadcast, outdoor and experiential activity designed to influence the audience when they were out and in a position to use the CABWISE™ service. Constructed to make sense to people whilst (potentially) under the influence of alcohol: clear, bold type style, simple layout and structure. This made CABWISE™ a useful part of the night out rather than being the 'killjoy'.

CABWISE™ developed an integrated media approach which focused on optimising all touch points to create a 'surround-sound' effect. The media plan contained over 32 individual activities, all honed to their environment (from dance clubs, pubs and music venues to student bars and venues frequented by shift nurses). All activities were designed to take women on a journey towards usage of the CABWISE™ service and away from the temptation of illegal minicabs.

Activity plan

There were three clear target audiences:

1 Diehard users of illegal minicabs: they'd ignored previous messages on the subject. These were confident young women who felt somewhat invincible. This was the hardest audience to reach and persuade.

2 The 'churn' audience: those new to London, students, new movers, etc. This was the audience least likely to be aware of the dangers of illegal minicabs and therefore more likely to be tempted by them.

3 Influencers: including boyfriends, parents, educational institutions and employers. These people could have a powerful influence on the actions of the primary target, in particular getting wives, girlfriends or daughters to store the CABWISE™ number on their mobile phones.

Case study 10.1 (*continued*)

The media strategy had three interdependent media strands to amplify and maximise efficiency.

The 'halo' strand was designed to use high-profile media such as TV to create talkability and deliver the 'fear' message to all audiences. TV advertising would have been vital to do the halo job. However, it was not affordable to divert a substantial part of the budget without having a detrimental impact on the rest of the campaign. CABWISE™ therefore maximised the budget by running the TV during the Christmas period only, as this was when nights out were more prevalent for all audiences; thereby delivering the 'fear' message more efficiently.

The 'discrete' strand used media that allowed the message to be focused for individual audiences. For the 'churn' audience, CABWISE™ chose student media, such as student union table tops, Sub TV, University six-sheet posters and also computer screens. The 'churn' audience was also captured in our wider outdoor and radio campaign. CABWISE™ utilised London press to target the influencers, and within this used a wide range of ethnic press (in a variety of languages) to ensure the message was reaching all areas of London. CABWISE™ also involved London businesses by offering to supply information packs to pass on to their employees, for which there was a strong uptake. A digital campaign involving two 'warning' emails (one from a victim's perspective and one from the Metropolitan Police) was also sent out virally to Oyster Card customers who used public transport late at night. These email warnings had a very high pass-on rate.

The final 'point of prey' strand concentrated on proximity-targeted media. Usage of proximity media was extensive. On a transport level, CABWISE™ identified London Underground stations which were hot spots and positioned six-sheets in prime spots in these areas. Targeted phone boxes close to clubs and nightspots allowed an on-street presence. Very importantly, female washrooms and screens in bars were used to reach the audience when they were actually in the bar environment.

These three strands all worked together to create the 'surround-sound' campaign on a budget of under £700,000.

As well as paid-for media, CABWISE™ was able to utilise Transport for London's position to present CABWISE™ alongside other permanent modes of transport, and to place the CABWISE™ logo permanently on Transport for London maps and leaflets. It even had a continuous presence on *Eastenders* – on posters in and around Walford Tube station.

All activity commenced in the third week of September 2006. Part of the creative work is shown in Figure 10.8. The current television advertisement can be viewed at: http://www.tfl.gov.uk/tfl/gettingaround/taxisandminicabs/taxis/default.aspx.

Results

Decreased cab-related rapes and sexual assaults

The number of sexual assaults and rapes committed by illegal minicab drivers dropped significantly from the very start of the activity. They fell from an average of 14 during the September–December period over the previous three years, to a total of four in September–December 2006. This is still four rapes and sexual assaults too many, but a significant drop nevertheless.[21]

CABWISE™ usage

This decrease in the number of cab-related rapes and sexual assaults coincided with the uplift in usage of CABWISE™ (Figure 10.9). Usage of the service increased from the very start of the campaign in September 2006. The 12 months following the campaign launch showed an average monthly increase of 52% versus the previous 12 months.

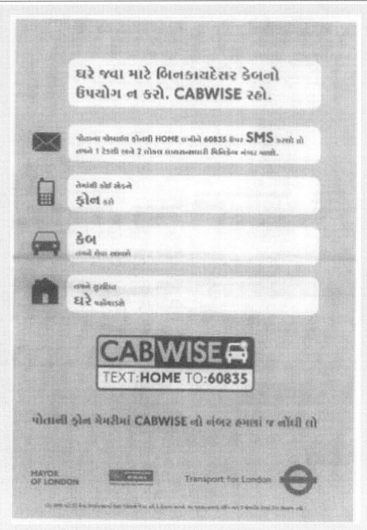

Figure 10.8 Press ad in the *Gujarat Samachar*

In fact, the number of individual users of the service almost doubled in the 12 months following the launch of CABWISE™ compared to the previous year and the number of regular users (using the service 10+ times) increased threefold (from 420 to 1280 users).

Advertising awareness

These results were linked to the marketing activity through a 36% increase in advertising awareness amongst 16–34-year-old females after the campaign launch and through greater reassurance being sought in the legal, licensed status of minicabs.

Despite such a limited spend and thanks to targeted media, over a quarter (27%) of all 16–34-year-old females[22] *spontaneously* cited CABWISE™ when asked the names of any schemes or initiatives in London that help people to travel home safely at night. When prompted, 80% of these women[23] recalled seeing advertising for CABWISE™. Of those women seeing the advertising, over 90% found the messages persuasive at encouraging them to take a safer method of transport.

Case study 10.1 (*continued*)

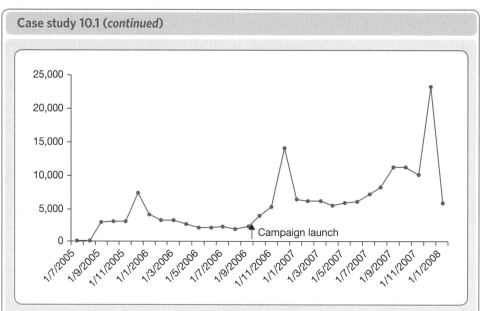

Figure 10.9 Monthly usage of CABWISE™ text service

Source: Incentivated actual usage data.

Intended behaviour towards illegal cabs

Following the advertising, those who had seen or heard the advertising were significantly less likely to use an unbooked minicab when leaving a bar late at night. This intention to avoid illegal cabs amongst those who have heard of the advertising is further substantiated by the fact that nearly 1 in 5 of these women[24] has the CABWISE™ number saved on their mobile phone. This difference was not caused by the 'Rosser Reeves effect'[25] as only 10% of those aware of the advertising had ever used the service – removing users from the data still left a significant difference in the data between those aware and not aware of the advertising (see Figure 10.10).

The percentage of young women who are likely to get an unbooked cab home is influenced significantly by whether they have seen CABWISE™ advertising or not.

Any changes to policing policies in Greater London over this time were clearly having little to no effect as all this was achieved with the same number of illegal cabs on the streets approaching women late at night.

Beyond ROI

This activity was about stopping rapes and sexual assaults in the most cost-effective way with only £671,000 to spend on media. The total marketing spend came to c.£1.2 million and the conservative estimate suggests that CABWISE™ helped prevent at least eight rapes and/or sexual assaults over the four-month launch period of marketing activity.

The value of a campaign like this goes beyond quantitative evaluation and return on investment calculations because these measurements can never account for the impact of rape on a woman's life. Each woman who is raped will respond differently, but support organisations like Rape Crisis (www.rapecrisis.org.uk) know that women they work with

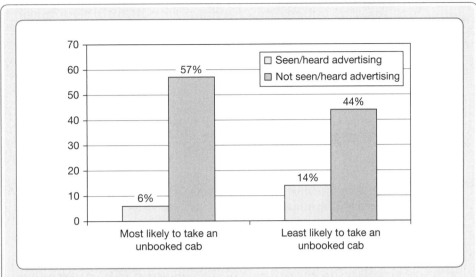

Figure 10.10 Persuasive ability of the advertising

frequently experience a range of reactions including: shock, disbelief, anxiety and panic attacks, nightmares, flashbacks and a sense of powerlessness to list just a few.

The value of sparing women the physical and emotional trauma of rape can never be calculated in monetary terms. However, the nature of our judicial process and legal system means that courts pass judgment on the level of compensation that should be paid to people who have been subjected to rape. On 14 November 2000, the High Court in London awarded £256,000 in damages to Amanda Lawson, who suffered a horrific ordeal at the hands of rapist Christopher Dawes. Nearly eight years after the event itself, the court accepted Miss Lawson's account of events and compensated her for the terrifying ordeal that she suffered.

Few rapes get as far as the High Court. Many are not even reported to the police as those subjected to this crime often fear that the investigation would be as painful and traumatic as the event itself. However, if the eight rapes and sexual assaults it is estimated that the campaign prevented were taken to the High Court, compensation payments could have been in the region of £2 million.

Source: Adapted from Okin, G., Sangster, V., Thurner, R., Adam, F., Leedham, M., Bowden, S., Cross, J. and Smart, P. *Transport for London – CABWISE™: creating a brand to help prevent rapes*. This case won the IPA Effectiveness Bronze Award in 2008.

Summary

This chapter reviewed product development, branding and place/channel selection. As behaviours usually are not strictly tangible, developing social marketing intervention with a tangible product in mind helps to reinforce the message. Social marketing products combine three types of 'product level': a core product (or benefit/value proposition), the actual product (i.e. the desired behaviour) and one or several augmented products (related tangibles and services). A recognisable and consistent brand adds value to the product, and branding can simplify complex messages for the target audience. This, in turn, is likely to encourage the target audience to maintain behaviour changes. Finally, easy access to services and tangible products, i.e. augmented products, related to a social marketing intervention is crucial, especially where the augmented product involves a service or requires physical access (e.g. a cycling path).

CHAPTER REVIEW QUESTIONS

1 What are the differences between core, actual and augmented product? What would be an example of an actual and an augmented product for
- reducing greenhouse gases?
- increasing longevity through obesity reduction?
- increasing recycling rates of newspapers?

2 What role does branding play in health-related social marketing campaigns? What do you see as the potential negative effects of using 'official brands', such as the NHS or Department of Health? What are the positive effects of using these?

3 What role do identity and tribe play when designing brands? Can you identify commercial brands that use these concepts to market their products? How can this be used to help social marketing campaigns?

4 Which of the five factors do you consider the most important in terms of designing a place/distribution strategy for your social marketing campaign?

Recommended reading

Evans, W.D., Blitstein, J., Hersey, J.C., Renaud, J. and Yaroch, A.L. (2008) Systematic Review of Public Health Branding. *Journal of Health Communication,* 13 (8), 721–41.

Evans, W.D. and Hastings, G. (2008) *Public Health Branding: Applying Marketing for Social Change.* Oxford: Oxford University Press.

Luca, N.R. and Suggs, L.S. (2010) Strategies for the Social Marketing Mix: a Systematic Review. *Social Marketing Quarterly,* 16 (4), 122–49.

Notes

1 Parasuraman, A., Zeithaml, V. and Berry, L. (1988) SERVQUAL: A Multiple-item Scale for Measuring Consumer Perceptions of Service Quality. *Journal of Retailing,* 64 (1), 12–40.

2 Evans, W.D. and Hastings, G. (2008) Public Health Branding: Recognition, Promise, and Delivery of Healthy Lifestyles. In *Public Health Branding: Applying Marketing for Social Change.* Oxford: Oxford University Press, pp. 3–25.

3 Ibid.

4 Wong, F., Huhman, M., Asbury, L., Bretthauer-Mueller, R., McCarthy, S. Londe, P., et al. (2004) VERB™ – A Social Marketing Campaign to Increase Physical Activity among Youth. *Preventing Chronic Disease,* 1 (3).

5 Evans, W.D., Renaud, J., Blitstein, J., Hersey, J., Ray, S., Schieber, B., et al. (2007) Prevention Effects of an Anti-tobacco Brand on Adolescent Smoking Initiation. *Social Marketing Quarterly,* 13 (2), 2–20.

6 De Chernatony, L. (1993) Categorizing Brands: Evolutionary Processes Underpinned by Two Key Dimensions. *Journal of Marketing Management*, 9 (2), 173–88.

7 Chasin, A. (2001) *Selling Out: The Gay and Lesbian Movement Goes to Market.* Basingstoke: Palgrave Macmillan.

8 Ibid.

9 McGee-Cooper, A. (2005) Tribalism: Culture wars at work. *Journal for Quality and Participation,* 28 (1), 12–15.

10 Booth, M.L., Bauman, A.E., Owen, N. and Gore, C. (1997) Physical Activity Preferences, Preferred Sources of Assistance, and Perceived Barriers to Increased Activity among Physically Inactive Australians. Available from: http://www.ingentaconnect.com/content/ap/pm/1997/00000026/00000001/art00116

11 Gillespie, T.W. and Hillyer, C.D. (2002) Blood Donors and Factors Impacting the Blood Donation Decision. *Transfusion Medicine Reviews*, 16 (2), 115–30.

12 Forte, D.A. (1995) Community-based Breast Cancer Intervention Program for Older African American Women in Beauty Salons. *Public Health Reports,* 110 (2), 179.

13 Carvel, J. (2007) GPs offered £150m for longer opening times. *The Guardian,* 20 December [accessed 1 May 2011]. Available from: http://www.guardian.co.uk/society/2007/dec/20/nhs.health

14 Blais, A., Dobrzynska A. and Loewen P. (2007) Potential Impacts of Extended Advance Voting on Voter Turnout [accessed 1 May 2011]. Available from: http://www.elections.ca/res/rec/fra/Potential_Impacts_e.pdf

15 Haskins, R., Paxson, C.H., Donahue, E., Fighting Obesity in the Public Schools. *The Future of Children Policy Brief.* Brookings Institution.

16 BBC News (28 September 2005) Junk food to be banned in schools. BBC Online [accessed 1 May 2011]. Available from: http://news.bbc.co.uk/1/hi/education/4287712.stm

17 Hyland, A., Hassan, L.M., Higbee, C., Boudreau, C., Fong, G.T., Borland R., et al. (2009) The impact of smokefree legislation in Scotland: results from the Scottish ITC: Scotland/UK longitudinal surveys. *The European Journal of Public Health,* 19 (2), 198.

18 Laurance, J. (2008) Smoking ban has saved 40,000 lives *The Independent,* 30 June [accessed 1 May 2011]. Available from: http://www.independent.co.uk/life-style/health-and-families/health-news/smoking-ban-has-saved-40000-lives-856885.html

19 Texts are charged at 35p per enquiry plus the standard cost of a text message from your mobile network. The service is not currently available on Virgin and 3 mobile networks.

20 'There do not appear to be any significant differences in the demographic profile of users and non-users.' (Synovate pre-advertising tracking)

21 The reason measurement was stopped at this stage is that the police changed their methodology for recording and reporting cab-related rapes and sexual assaults – making it impossible to provide properly comparative tracking after 2007.

22 Source: Synovate tracking

23 Source: Synovate tracking

24 19% of 16–34 females who have seen the advertising have the CABWISE™ number saved to their mobile phones.

25 Rosser Reeves effect: users of a product or service have a heightened awareness of that brand's advertising and can skew advertising measurements.

Chapter 11

Message framing

Chapter objectives

On completing this chapter, you should be able to

- understand the role of message framing in developing social marketing interventions;

- critically analyse the role of message framing in developing social marketing interventions;

- critically assess whether positive or negative framing may be effective for specific circumstances or population segments;

- critically assess whether rational or emotional messages may be effective for specific circumstances or population segments;

- assess and make reasoned recommendations regarding ways of evaluating framing alternatives for a specific intervention.

Introduction: types of framing

The issue of how to 'frame' persuasive messages has been debated extensively in the literature, with somewhat mixed results.[1, 2] Message framing has its origins in prospect theory,[3, 4] which developed from extensive research into responses to people's perceptions of the prospect of positive (gain) or negative (loss) outcomes stemming from specific behaviours.

Message framing in the context of social marketing generally refers to the way health (or socially relevant) messages should be structured. The message can either emphasise the advantages of doing a certain action (e.g. losing weight as a result of regular exercise) or it can emphasise the negative consequences of not taking a certain action (e.g. having a higher likelihood of cardiovascular disease as a result of not taking regular exercise). For example, the international '5 a Day' campaign promotes the consumption of fruit and vegetables as they can help reduce the risk of diseases like cancer, heart disease and obesity.[5] Conversely, during the 1980s, the 'Don't die of ignorance' campaign highlighted negative consequences (illness/death) as a result of not taking action (safer sex behaviour).[6]

However, research that has explored the effects of both positive and negative message framing has led to conflicting results.[7, 8] It is now usually recognised that no one single framing approach is applicable across all intervention types,[9, 10] with effectiveness being contingent on a number of factors. These include the level of personal motivation in relation to the behaviour, the level of certainty that undertaking the action will result in the desired outcome[11] and the presentation style of the message, such as using anecdotal messages or presenting statistical data.[12] There are also interactions between message framing and the credibility of the source. The latter includes the expertise, trustworthiness and reputation of the message sponsor and spokesperson.[13]

The **Elaboration Likelihood Model**[14] suggests that information is processed in one of two ways – centrally, where the information is deemed personally relevant and therefore warranting attention and thought, and peripherally, where attention is lower and impressions are formed on the basis of cues such as the attractiveness of people featured in advertisements. Credibility of spokespeople may therefore be a significant influence under peripheral processing.

Responses to risk information are not always rational and are influenced by several factors such as preferences for avoiding unpleasant information, or apathy.[15] People tend to underestimate their personal risk levels, a phenomenon referred to as self-positivity bias, influencing their motivation to process messages.[16] Further, different population segments may respond differently to the same message. For example, adolescent egocentrism and attitudes towards risk-taking and sensation-seeking have been found to be significant factors influencing the way that moderation messages are processed.[17]

However, even allowing for these complicating factors, we can identify situations where either positive or negative framing is likely to be more effective.

Positive framing

Positive framing emphasises the positive outcomes of a given action, for example losing weight as a result of exercise; being healthier after making better dietary choices, etc. Positively framed messages appear to be stronger for preventive behaviour and health-affirming messages (i.e. no risk in undertaking the behaviour), such as stopping smoking before the onset of ill health related to smoking. However, reviews of previously published studies suggest that this may not apply in all situations[18] and, in fact, the highly acclaimed and generally successful safer-sex campaigns of the 1980s noted above were largely negatively framed despite promoting a prevention message.

This may potentially be explained by the findings that positively framed messages will not be effective if the recipient is unsure about behavioural norms.[19] For example, if the use of condoms is not considered a behavioural norm, then a positively framed preventive health message may be confusing, as the recipient may question why, if the solution to the problem is simple (e.g. using a condom), this is not done all the time.

Additional factors potentially impacting on intervention effectiveness include whether new behaviour is being promoted or ceasing current behaviour is targeted.[20] Additionally, it has been argued that positive framing fosters a greater self-efficacy, which, in turn, is a major factor in compliance behaviour[21] and therefore long-term behaviour change. Self-efficacy has been identified as a factor that should be stressed more strongly by health professionals during their discussions with patients[22] and expectations regarding self-efficacy have long been proved to be a major factor in the outcomes of health behaviour change interventions.[23]

Using a different approach to which type of framing is more effective, it has been argued[24] that in low-involvement conditions positive messages are more effective, whereas the reverse is true for high-involvement conditions. Again, this may support why, for example, positive framing appears to have been effective in the past for sunscreen use, i.e. that messages framed as:

'If you use sunscreen with SPF or higher, you increase your chances of keeping your skin healthy and your life long.'

'Using sunscreen decreases your risk for skin cancer and prematurely aged skin.'

were more effective than:

'If you don't use sunscreen with SPF 15 or higher you increase your chances of damaging your skin and bringing on an early death.'

'Not using sunscreen increases your risk for skin cancer and prematurely aged skin.'[25]

A further reason why positive framing seems to be effective for sunscreen use is that these interventions tend to be particularly directed at a younger target audience who are unlikely to have much experience in the effects and consequences of cancer.

However, others[26] caution that positive message framing may have a boomerang effect if the message conflicts with pre-existing knowledge, attitudes and beliefs or with behavioural norms.[27] For example, some anti-smoking interventions have not only been ineffective, but have also apparently strengthened young smokers' determination to continue to smoke.[28] Similar effects have been found in relation to anti-drug interventions, such as a 1980s American campaign featuring posters of a 'wasted' heroin addict which had no effect other than to make the posters a collectable item.[29] At times, message effects have differed across genders, such as anti-speeding interventions which have revealed boomerang effects among young males but not females, due to reactance effects (see page 245).[30]

Until recently, it would, have been reasonable to assume that positively framed messages would be more effective than negatively framed messages in relation to the adoption of sensible sun protection strategies, i.e. no risk, reasonably certain outcome of avoiding sunburn, maintaining health etc. However, the complications introduced by the vitamin D debate[31] mean that the application of sunscreen may now be perceived as a risky behaviour, therefore a rider should be added to any messages, clarifying this point.

Negative framing

Conversely to positive message framing, negative message framing has been found to be more effective for illness-detecting behaviour,[32] where there is uncertainty about the outcome of the behaviour, but awareness of the danger of not getting a problem detected early. An example of this is screening programmes which prevent a more serious outcome, such as regular mammography for older women or cholesterol checks. However, there is also evidence of significant barriers to such negative message framing among adolescents and

Figure 11.1 A negatively framed advertisement
Source: AIDES (HIV awareness – France).

young adults, with the message not only being rejected, but resulting in reinforcement of behaviours being targeted if the behaviour is consistent with perceived norms within a desirable social group.[33]

Often, negative framing relies heavily on the use of fear appeal, such as the fear of dying from a specific cause. As argued by some authors,[34] if such a condition is high-involvement, for example in a case where a close relative has died from stroke attributed to high-blood pressure, the fear and high-involvement of also dying from the same cause may have a highly motivating and behaviour-changing effect. Negatively framed safer-sex messages were highly successful in communities that had many AIDS victims, such as the gay population particularly in larger cities.[35] The personal experience of many gay men seeing friends and partners die of AIDS in the 1980s would have increased involvement and thus negatively framed messages were effective (see Figure 11.1).

CASE STUDY 11.1

'Under the skin': campaign aimed at hardened smokers

(Gold winner 2004 IPA Effectiveness Award)

The campaign was part of ongoing activity which had used a range of messages and message frames, as shown by the illustrations overleaf.

Case study 11.1 (*continued*)

Source: Advertising Archives.

The strategy chosen reflected the constant and multifaceted challenge to reduce the number of UK smokers and drew on the combined forces of the government, the British Heart Foundation and all other related charities working constantly towards minimising the number of people who start and maximising the number of people who successfully stop.

The British Heart Foundation's part in this was the now infamous 'fatty cigarette' campaign which dramatically bought to life the arterial damage caused by smoking. This case documents how the efforts of multiple advertisers produced a powerful combined effect, helping to reduce the number of smokers by over a million. Iconic imagery of the fat dripping from the cigarette created a powerful visceral response of revulsion in the smoker, and successfully pushed many of its target over the tipping point to quitting.

Source: Advertising Archives.

Given its enormous success, the British Heart Foundation could easily have opted to run 'fatty cigarette' again and again. But instead they chose to try to create the same impact, but with a new tactic. Those who resisted the 'fatty cigarette' message were now sufficiently desensitised to suggest its impact was abating. The law of diminishing returns had kicked in. A new and unexpected way to increase the determination of the hardened smoker to successfully quit was needed, one that positioned BHF as a friend of the smoker, a place to seek the help and support so vitally needed.

The primary target was seen as 'multi-quitters'. These are hardened smokers, aged 30–50, C1C2D, that have tried, but failed, to give up three times or more. They are open to cessation communication. They hear all these messages, but don't necessarily listen. Listening is on another level to hearing, because it implies a level of processing and thought. We had to help them to listen.

A secondary target was identified as influencers and medical professionals and, beyond that, the rest of the smoking population.

In order to put together the strategic battle plan, we needed an understanding of the mindset of our core target, what they were expecting and how they could be 'caught' unawares.

Research had identified the following characteristics:

- Expecting to be lectured and made to feel like socially unacceptable outcasts.
- Expecting huge scary statistics, most of which they know already and can repeat back to you word for word.
- Expecting to be made to feel like pariahs, when in fact the cigarette is the real enemy.
- An amazing capacity to defer the effects of smoking into the future on the basis that they'll stop 'tomorrow' or convince themselves that the worst-case scenario won't happen to them.

The strategy was to take a feel-good, popular song about love and longing, and cruelly twist it to refer to heart damage. However, this realisation would hit people only after they had begun humming along.

> *I've got you under my skin*
> *I've got you deep in the heart of me.*
> *So deep in my heart, that you're really a part of me.*
> *I've got you under my skin . . .*
> *I'd sacrifice anything come what might.*
> *For the sake of having you near.*
> *In spite of a warning voice that comes in the night.*
> *And repeats, repeats in my ear:*
> *Don't you know you fool, you never can win?*
> *Use your mentality, wake up to reality.*
> *But each time I do, just the thought of you.*
> *Makes me stop before I begin.*
> *'Cause I've got you under my skin.*

The campaign did not portray someone on their deathbed, but instead just regular people, seemingly healthy (beautiful even), in regular everyday smoking scenarios that every smoker can relate to. It is the cigarette that is vilified, as the smoker is seen to be unaware of the clot that moves under their skin, moving ever nearer to the heart . . . and a heart attack.

The creative focused on communicating the ever-present danger of breakaway blood clots that can cause a heart attack any time, anywhere. The statistic 'A blood clot kills another smoker every 35 minutes' was a perfect fit to purpose. The statistic wasn't the biggest heart-stopping fact when researched, but was the one that best elicited a reaction of sufficiently alarm, without being so dramatic as to permanently remove all hope (and therefore reason to stop). Through making the cigarette the enemy, not the smoker, and by adopting a tone of helpful ally rather than disdainful judge, the BHF aimed to give people hope.

TV launched the campaign with a 60-second message, which was further developed through national press and outdoor executions. Radio was employed to catch people first thing in the morning, when they are lighting up. Posters showed the sinister ripple moving through arteries as people travel up and down the escalators.

Media placement targeted people when they had smoking front of mind – just coming out of the station ready to light up or having just put one out on their way into the station. Getting on and off the tube in Zone 1 is stressful in anyone's estimation . . .

Case study 11.1 (*continued*)

Having beer mats in pubs was too good an opportunity to miss, catching people who had a pint in one hand and a fag in the other. An online strategy reached smokers at work. Here they could look in more detail at what they had heard or seen in other media the same day, while the initial message was still fresh.

Results

Sixty-three per cent of the core target strongly engaged with the TV, with a third 'completely drawn into it'. A large proportion of these people would have switched off instantly to traditional shock-based anti-smoking communications. We reached people previous campaigns couldn't.

The campaign was reported in detail, and at length, in most of the major national daily and weekly newspapers. More than four out of five of the core targets saw some element of the campaign. The campaign achieved very high cross-over, with over half the target seeing three or more parts of it. This compares to one in ten for the 'fatty cigarette' campaign.

People who saw three or more channels were 70% more likely to set a date to quit. Setting a date is recognised by the experts to be a serious step towards quitting. Over and above this, 18% of the target that saw three or more channels actually gave up versus 16% that saw just a single channel.

Seventeen per cent of the core target who saw the campaign stopped smoking. Of the core target that missed the campaign, only 11% stopped smoking. The difference is large enough to assert that the campaign didn't just make people more determined to quit, it nudged them over the quit line. The figure rose to 20% for people who strongly agreed that the ad told them 'smoking causes blood clots'.

These people could lapse; they had in the past. However, the average smoker takes six attempts at quitting before they finally make it. At the very least this was one more towards the final, successful, attempt. For many, it was that attempt.

The campaign's grand purpose was ultimately to improve the health, and therefore life expectancy, of the people we targeted. If the campaign is measured against the value of a life, it needs to save nine lives to warrant its £3 million investment. In these terms the campaign massively over-exceeded its objectives by contributing towards saving over 5,400 lives. For every £1 invested, £600 of value was retained within the economy.

The property of the song will live on beyond the campaign. People who saw the campaign will hear it again and again, and it will continue to remind these people not of falling in love, but of blood clots heading to the heart. Betty McBride, Policy and Communications Director at the BHF, summed it up: 'Thanks to Sinatra, every time they hear that song the smoker will bring to mind the unseen damage.'

Source: Case material taken from Institute of Practitioners in Advertising IPA Effectiveness Award Submission, 2004.

There appear also to be cultural,[36] context and situation variations, and additional confounding factors, including whether new behaviour is being promoted or whether ceasing current behaviour is targeted.[37] Table 11.1 summarises the existing state of knowledge regarding the situations in which positively or negatively framed messages have been found to be most effective.

Table 11.1 Summary of positive/negative framing

Positively framed messages more effective	Negatively framed messages more effective
• Low motivation • High perceived efficacy • No risk in behaviours • Certain outcomes • Acceptable in relation to perceived behavioural norms • Prevention focus (maintaining good health, appearance)	• High motivation • Low or uncertain perceived efficacy • Uncertain outcomes • Detection/early diagnosis

Fear appeals

Fear-based appeals are a subset of negative framing. Theory may help explain the impact of fear appeals, though these, too, have been found not always to achieve their objectives. Early studies suggested that fear appeals had the potential to influence attitude change and subsequent behaviour.[38, 39] However, more recent research presents a less optimistic outlook. Most studies which suggest effectiveness of these appeals have been laboratory-based, often with methodological shortcomings, and focused on short-term effects. It is suggested that real-world effects are weaker – and are least effective with people with low self-efficacy, which in turn is less likely to be positively affected by negatively framed messages.[40]

Many unintended effects of health communication campaigns are directly, but not exclusively, attributable to fear appeals, i.e. dissonance, discomfort and distress, boomerang effects, epidemics of apprehension and desensitisation.[41] Additionally, strong fear appeals are more likely to be regarded as unethical if the target populations do not believe they can readily undertake the recommended behaviour or that the behaviour will be effective in minimising the perceived threat.[42]

The **Extended Parallel Process Model**, shown in Figure 11.2, may offer an explanation for the fact that some fear appeals are effective and others not.

Some authors[43] have suggested that fear appeals are only appropriate in a situation where the solution to a fairly critical problem is relatively easy. For example, in the case of the sexually transmitted infection chlamydia, the solution is often reasonably straightforward (usage of condoms/regular screening and easy treatment in case of infection) and thus a fear appeal may be appropriate in this case, as shown by the 2008 campaign run by THT on the London Underground, which played on the fear of losing attractiveness because of an STI (see Figure 11.3).

However, conversely, when they are used with low-efficacy messages – i.e. messages that don't offer an easy and convincing solution – fear appeals tend to create a defensive response, and thus may be ineffective.[44] This may explain why campaigns which involve complex, less well-defined and long-term behaviour change, such as physical activity campaigns or healthy eating campaigns, have more negative outcomes when relying on fear appeals rather than supportive and positive messages.

Another aspect of the use of fear appeals is the possible erosion of their effectiveness over time. The ongoing use of fear appeals can, in fact, lead to complacency, as people start to respond no longer with fear, but rather with indifference to social marketing campaigns.[45]

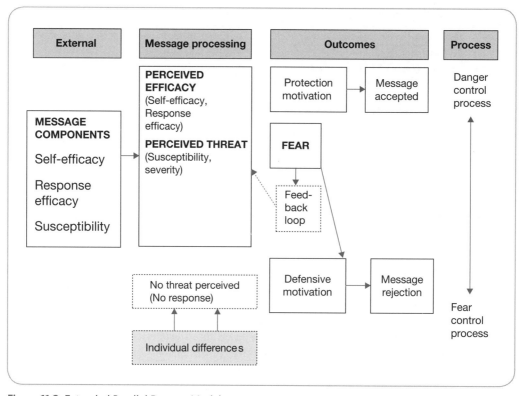

Figure 11.2 Extended Parallel Process Model

Source: Witte, K. (1994) Fear Control and Danger Control: A Test of the Extended Parallel Process Model (EPPM). *Communication Monographs, 61* (1).

Other authors have suggested that fear appeals can evoke self-protection and inaction rather than the desired behaviour change.[46] Conversely, the use of fear appeals may well lead to heightened anxiety in some individuals, which in turn may cause an additional burden on the health system which has to deal with them. A well-known example of this are 'worried well' patients, who believe that they have contracted HIV, and, despite not being infected, continue to use healthcare system funds by repeatedly retesting, sometimes over 50 times in a year,[47] thereby putting considerable strain on the health system.[48]

Rational versus emotional appeals

Many social marketing campaigns have tended to rely more heavily on rational appeals, rather than evoking emotional appeals (other than fear appeals).[49] However, using a variety of (positive) emotional appeals can, in fact, enhance social marketing communication campaigns significantly, especially by gaining the attention of those that consider themselves already familiar with a campaign. It may also encourage those who don't consider a campaign's message to be personally relevant to engage with the message.[50] More recent research[51] supports the move from the rational appeals and scare tactics traditionally used towards more positive emotional appeals for promoting health and social marketing objectives.

Figure 11.3 STI Advertising by the NHS 'Condom Essential Wear'
Source: NHS branding.

Cross-cultural issues in message framing

An almost totally neglected aspect of message framing relates to **culture**. There is evidence that there are significant differences in terms of emotional and attitudinal responses to appeals in advertising, even in culturally close countries.[52, 53] Any intervention that is intended to be used across cultural groups needs to be thoroughly tested with all significant segments of the target population to ensure that the message is framed in a way that is acceptable to the intended recipients.

Fear appeals have been found to be interpreted differently across cultures,[54] while other studies have highlighted different responses to social obligation as a motivational factor across cultures.[55] One of the few studies that used cross-cultural concepts linked to appeals used in smoking cessation advertising found that loss-framed messages were more favourably perceived in a high uncertainty avoidance culture, whereas individuals from a low uncertainty avoidance background perceived gain-framed messages more favourably.[56]

Other research suggests that cultural differences in responses to framing can be linked to regulatory focus theory.[57] Regulatory focus theory posits that individuals are either promotion-focused – i.e. they wish to attain gains and achieve positive outcomes – or prevention-focused, wishing to avoid losses and negative consequences and driven by a need for security. In a study of Chinese and (white-) British students,[58] Chinese students responded more favourably towards loss-framed dental health-related messages, while British students showed a more positive attitude after being exposed to gain-framed messages. This would suggest that gain-framed messages are preferred in individualist cultures, while loss-framed messages are more persuasive for collectivist cultures. However, this distinction does not seem entirely straightforward: in a different study of gay men from Portugal (a highly collectivist country) and Britain (a highly individualist country), both preferred gain-framed messages. The effect was true for both smoking as well as safer-sex messages, suggesting that the gain-framed/loss-framed link may be mediated by culture but is not directly linked.[59]

Individuals in collectivist societies tend to take greater responsibility for the welfare of the group, thus framing messages with shared or common responsibility have been seen as appropriate for collectivist societies.[60] Equally, there is evidence that messages relating to private behaviours (such as safer-sex campaigns) are less culture-bound than those relating to publicly visible behaviours (such as smoking), though both are mediated by culture.

Given the limited – and often confusing – evidence, different messages and different framing strategies are likely to be needed for different segments. Pre-testing possible framing options with members of the intended target segment will guide the selection of appropriate strategies. The challenge is not to apply our own perspectives to what strategies might be effective, but to ensure that the views, preferences and norms of the various target segments are considered. A way to avoid this is the use of co-creation and seeking extensive group feedback.

Considerations should include not just the messages themselves, but the entire delivery of an intervention, including content and how, when and where it is to be delivered, as well as what means of contact and communication are most likely to be accepted and potentially effective.

Personal relevance/tailored interventions

Many studies have shown that relevance for the targeted groups is a major success factor in campaigns, as it creates more involvement with the campaign objectives.[61] However, there is no single factor that creates relevance in a target audience, but rather a myriad of different factors. Some of the more frequently cited ones include the message content itself; perceived self-identity by the target group (often in contrast to the senders' identity); communication source and communication channel as well as a perceived awareness of everyday life for members of the targeted group.[62] Personalisation of messages has been suggested as a possible way to create more personal relevance, meaning that interventions are tailored to individuals' communication preferences, rather than standardised messages being delivered to a large target audience.

This theory has been tested in the Smoking Termination with Computerised Personalisation (STOP) programme, where participants were asked to complete a short questionnaire about their smoking habits, and then were sent either a personalised (or tailored) letter giving them advice on how to stop smoking based on their responses, or a standard letter. However, while recall of the personalised letter was much higher than the standard letter, the smoking cessation rate was similar in both groups, possibly suggesting that tailoring approaches may improve recall but not outcome.[63] Similarly, for physical activity, a computer-generated tailored intervention has resulted in increased recall, but not increased physical activity over the standardised intervention,[64] thus suggesting that, although tailored interventions may be more effective in theory, it is hard to make them work in a practical setting.

Reactance effects

The theory of psychological **reactance** originated in the 1960s.[65, 66] It states that direct or potential perceived threats to personal freedom, such as consumption of specific products or engaging in particular behaviours, may be resisted. Further, people may then become motivated by the perceived threat itself, rather than the actual consequences of the threat, to assert their freedom and regain control of their own decision-making and thereby of their threatened freedom. Engaging in the threatened behaviour is one means of re-establishing this freedom.[67] Reactance effects appear to be strongest when the threatened freedom is perceived as important and the affected individual considers that their 'counterforce' efforts will achieve personal control. Conversely, if an individual does not perceive that their actions will be effective in countering the threat, reactance will be minimal.[68]

In terms of persuasive communication, such as mass media public health intervention programmes, reactance may generate actions that resist or are the opposite of those desired by the individuals or organisations seeking to influence both attitudes and behaviours. Reactance effects explain not only why some public health interventions may not be effective, but also why they may produce effects contrary to those intended.[69]

CASE STUDY 11.2

Road safety campaign: 'Pay attention, or pay the price'

Road Safety Authority (Republic of Ireland) and the Department of the Environment (Northern Ireland)

David Lyle, Julie Anne Bailie, Dawn McCartney, Robert Lyle and David Martin

Context/background

Overall, Northern Ireland's road death rate is the highest in the United Kingdom. Extensive analysis of road casualty statistics identified pedestrians as the second-highest road user group being killed on the roads. In Northern Ireland between 1995 and 2000, pedestrians made up 19.1% of all road deaths and serious injuries (see Figure 11.4).

The pedestrian safety campaign launched in November 2002. That year, 33 pedestrians died on Northern Ireland's roads and 86 died on the roads in the Republic of Ireland.

Analysis provided a breakdown by age and gender of pedestrians being killed and seriously injured. A political decision was taken to focus on the younger people over-represented, with a specific aim of the Northern Ireland Road Safety Strategy 2002–12 being to reduce the number of children being killed and seriously injured on Northern Ireland's roads by 50% each year. The Republic of Ireland Road Safety Strategy, 1998–2002, highlighted collisions as being the biggest killer of 15–24-year-olds. The younger focus was a priority throughout Ireland.

During analysis of the cause of pedestrian deaths and serious injuries, drivers were identified as the problem in 24% of cases in Northern Ireland. While this data was not recorded in the Republic of Ireland it was clear that if pedestrian deaths and serious injuries were to be reduced, drivers could not be ignored as a contributor.

Case study 11.2 (*continued*)

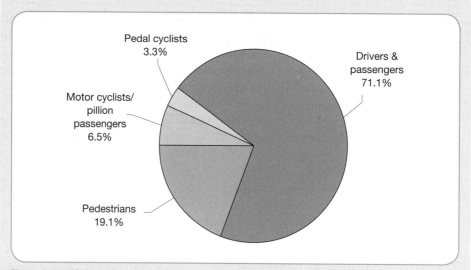

Pedal cyclists
3.3%

Motor cyclists/
pillion
passengers
6.5%

Drivers &
passengers
71.1%

Pedestrians
19.1%

Figure 11.4 Where is the problem? Road users killed and seriously injured in Northern Ireland 1995–2000

Source: Road Safety Authority, Republic of Ireland.

The campaign had to transform pedestrian safety from a boring, irrelevant issue to one that mattered and was important to all road users. This was going to be difficult given the climate of opinion – 'It's not relevant to me.' In other words, it had to be pushed up the public agenda and made personally relevant.

The campaign had the opportunity to make pedestrian safety relevant to all road users. It had to demonstrate that drivers, as well as pedestrians, can be to blame for collisions involving pedestrians and, as a result, have equal responsibility in preventing them.

During the strategy development research it became clear that the advertising faced steep challenges, including teenage pedestrians' lack of responsibility and young drivers' dismissiveness of pedestrians.

Objectives

- To raise awareness generally of the number of pedestrians being killed and seriously injured on the roads.

- To make pedestrians and drivers more aware of their personal responsibility for avoiding road traffic collisions involving pedestrians.

- To reduce the number of pedestrian road deaths and serious injuries.

The solution

Independent qualitative research was conducted as part of the strategy development by Millward Brown (formerly known as Irish Marketing Surveys Group). The research revealed that, while there is high spontaneous awareness of the dangers faced by pedestrians, it is not an emotive issue. It is viewed as the responsibility of others but 'not me'.

The campaign needed to make road users sit up and take notice. It had to shock them out of complacency. Pedestrian safety needed to be shown as everyone's responsibility. Drivers and pedestrians can both be responsible for a collision and this needed to be demonstrated in order for them to take personal responsibility.

A behavioural-focused campaign was thought to be the best method of engaging, involving and changing the target audiences. The Northern Ireland data was useful for this. Examination of pedestrian fatality data 1996–2000 revealed that:

- 'Heedlessness of traffic' is a major pedestrian killer, responsible for 28% of pedestrian road deaths and 7.1% of all road deaths. This is the single biggest killer of child pedestrians under 16 years – responsible for 36% of child pedestrian deaths.
- Driver behaviour is the next most serious pedestrian killer, responsible for 22% of pedestrian road deaths, with the top three causes being inattention, excessive speed and driver alcohol. However, driver behaviour is the second-biggest killer of child pedestrians – responsible for 29% of child pedestrian deaths.

The strategy pointed to two executions: one execution focused on pedestrian culpability ('Texting') with the other focusing on driver culpability ('Home'). This avoided any confusion regarding who was to blame, therefore removing any 'out' for either the driver or the pedestrian.

The message 'Pay Attention – or Pay the Price' was used to make road users take personal responsibility and demonstrate that irresponsible behaviour would have consequences both for themselves and, more importantly, others.

It was evident from the research that the target audiences overestimated their ability to cope with risk. The campaign had to show them that, although they think it will not happen to them, it could happen to them.

The idea

'Texting'

This execution targeted the teenage pedestrian audience. It used the hooks of: after-school liberation, boy/girl relationships and the status symbol of the mobile phone. The school bell turns into tragedy as teenagers text each other. Due to his inattention while texting, the young male steps into the path of an oncoming van.

'Home'

This execution targeted drivers. A mother collects her little boy from school, but they never make it home. A young driver focusing his attention on an attractive female turns the corner and strikes the mother and her young son as they cross the road. His inattention meant he could not avoid the collision. The endline 'Pay Attention – or Pay the Price' encapsulated the fact that inattention costs lives.

Psychological triggers built into the campaign include:

1 Self-identification – start in *their* world, *their* mindset.

2 Personal relevance – see themselves in it.

3 Anticipated regret – dramatise the consequences.

4 Induction of cognitive dissonance:

   – 'I want to be free' in conflict with the reality that road inattention destroys personal freedom.

   – Therefore modification of the cause of their dissonance: *'Pay Attention or Pay the Price'*.

   – Engage them personally in the inner debate.

Case study 11.2 (*continued*)

5 Integrate rational and emotional approaches – using post-9pm 'bolt-out-of-the-blue' shock tactics.

6 Integrate with enforcement by involving the police arrest scene to dramatise what is an arrestable offence.

The activity

TV was used in the launch phase for the campaign in both Northern Ireland and the Republic of Ireland for its ability to generate mass awareness amongst the target audience: young adults aged 15–34. Across the launch phase in Northern Ireland 90% 1+ and 75% 3+ coverage was achieved. In the Republic of Ireland, 83% 1+ and 62% 3+ coverage was achieved across the launch burst. TV activity was timed to coincide with months that were over-represented in terms of pedestrian fatalities and also to build awareness during key times in the young adults' calendar, such as the back-to-school period in September.

The school calendar formed an important backdrop to the timing of awareness-building activity. Across the campaign period, key holiday periods (Easter and summer) were targeted, with reminder interventions at danger times when the target audience was likely to be out travelling on foot. The onset of darker evenings, when visibility began to decline, was also targeted, with TV activity as part of a 'clocks back' awareness campaign.

All commercially available stations in each marketplace were used to reach the target audience. Key youth-oriented programming, such as *Big Brother,* and cult teen shows, such as *Pimp My Ride* and *Cribs,* were used to interrupt the teen audience with the reality of carelessness on the road.

Once high levels of awareness had been generated through TV, point-of-danger, out-of-home media interventions were deployed. Reaching the target audience through the use of outdoor formats was crucial to transfer the message and impact of the ad to reach the youth audience as they travelled on their daily journeys. Outdoor formats such as Adshel were targeted within 30 metres of key youth locations. Sites were placed near schools, cinemas, fast-food outlets and other entertainment locations where large numbers of the target audience were likely to congregate. This included six-sheets at Northern Ireland's largest entertainments complex – the Odyssey Arena. Bus rears were also deployed to reach drivers, warning of the dangers posed by inattention on the road and the potential to kill a pedestrian.

This theme was continued in a series of radio edits which ran during the key morning and afternoon school drive-time periods. A rotation of edits intervened with drivers on the road at the point of danger.

The campaign media budget 2002–7 was €3,191,070. In 2005 the competitive automotive sector had an expenditure of €70 million.

The results

Evaluation of the campaign was independently conducted by Millward Brown, formerly the Irish Marketing Surveys Group, via a quantitative survey.

Awareness

Awareness of 'Texting' peaked at 91% in Northern Ireland and 90% in the Republic of Ireland. Awareness of 'Home' peaked at 87% in Northern Ireland and 88% in the Republic of Ireland (see Figures 11.7 and 11.8). These scores are extremely impressive, given the Millward Brown norm for TV advertising of 49%. This norm is based on the tracking of 1,979 TV ads.

Figure 11.5 Bus advertising

Figure 11.6 Press advertising

Attitude improvements

The campaign forced the majority of the population (96% in Northern Ireland and 95% in the Republic of Ireland) to acknowledge that drivers and pedestrians have a shared responsibility to avoid road traffic collisions involving themselves. As a result of the campaign, over 90% of the population agreed all road users are at risk.

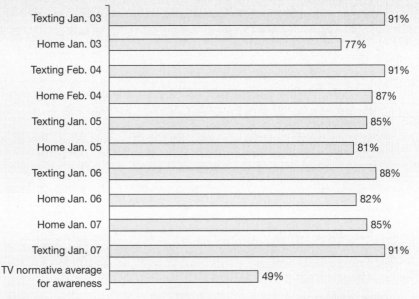

Texting Jan. 03	91%
Home Jan. 03	77%
Texting Feb. 04	91%
Home Feb. 04	87%
Texting Jan. 05	85%
Home Jan. 05	81%
Texting Jan. 06	88%
Home Jan. 06	82%
Home Jan. 07	85%
Texting Jan. 07	91%
TV normative average for awareness	49%

Figure 11.7 Northern Ireland – Pedestrians' historical awareness – all respondents

Source: Irish Marketing Surveys Group/Millward Brown Ulster Omnibus.

Case study 11.2 (*continued*)

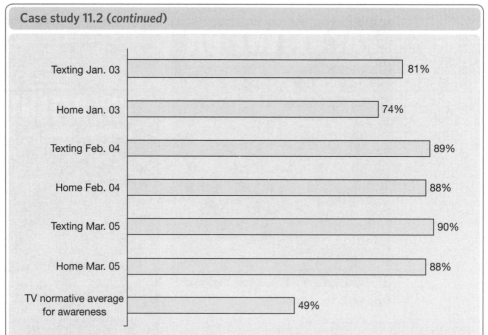

Figure 11.8 Republic of Ireland 'Texting' and 'Home' historical awareness – all respondents
Source: IMS/Millward Brown.

Reported behaviour change

Those aware of the campaign, 80% in Northern Ireland and 86% in the Republic of Ireland, agreed they changed their behaviour as a result. This behaviour change included – paying more attention to the road as a pedestrian, paying more attention to pedestrians when driving, talking about it with friends or family, encouraging someone to pay more attention when a pedestrian and encouraging someone to pay more attention to pedestrians when driving (see Figure 11.9)

Lives saved – evidence of behaviour change

In Northern Ireland, comparing the three years before 'Texting' and 'Home' with the three years since, we find that pedestrians killed or seriously injured were down by 234 – a reduction of 26%.

In the Republic of Ireland, comparing the three years before 'Texting' and 'Home' with the three years since, we find that pedestrians killed and seriously injured were down by 173 – a reduction of 25% in pedestrian tragedy.

Influence

Advertising's role in driving attitude and behaviour improvements is revealed in the post-campaign research. The question: 'To what extent does this advertisement influence you or not influence you?' engendered a high response (see Figures 11.10 and 11.11). These influence scores overshadow the normative TV ad score as rated in Northern Ireland at 41% influential and the Republic of Ireland as 50% influential.

Further evidence isolating the importance of the advertising as the key factor influencing change was established when the Northern Ireland Department of the Environment's

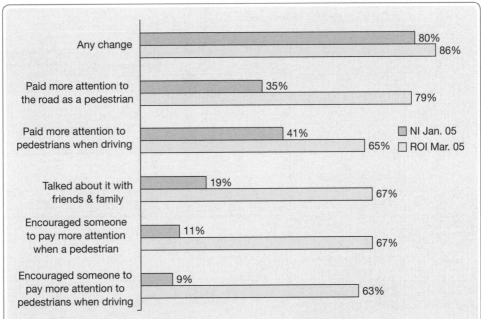

Figure 11.9 Reported behaviour changes

TV ads emerged, in the public's perception, as the most influential in saving lives on the roads. In the Republic of Ireland, road safety TV ads came second to new road traffic laws. While penalty points were introduced in 2003, 2006 saw the high-profile introduction of 31 more offences that could attract penalty points (see Figures 11.12 and 11.13).

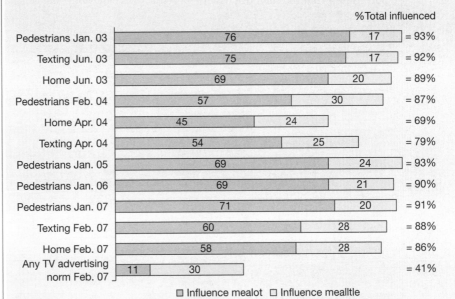

Figure 11.10 Northern Ireland – Pedestrians' historical influence – all respondents

Source: Irish Marketing Surveys Group/Millward Brown Ulster Omnibus.

Case study 11.2 (*continued*)

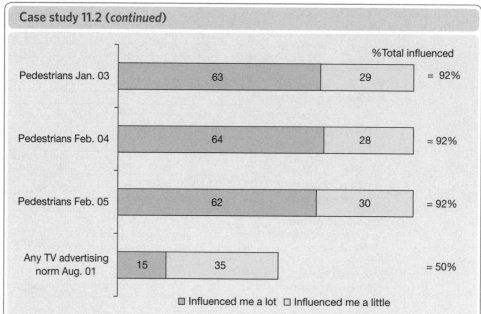

Figure 11.11 'Texting' and 'Home' historical influence – all respondents
Source: IMS/Millward Brown IMS Omnibus.

Payback

Northern Ireland

In the three years following the launch of the campaign in Northern Ireland, 234 pedestrians were saved from death or serious injury, compared to the previous three-year trend (see Table 11.2).

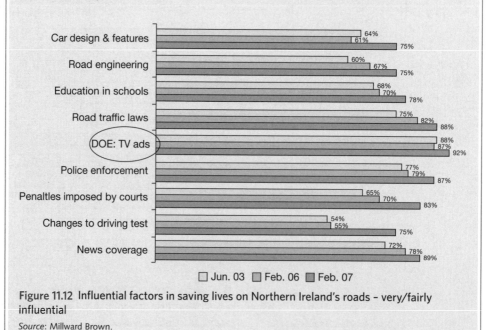

Figure 11.12 Influential factors in saving lives on Northern Ireland's roads – very/fairly influential
Source: Millward Brown.

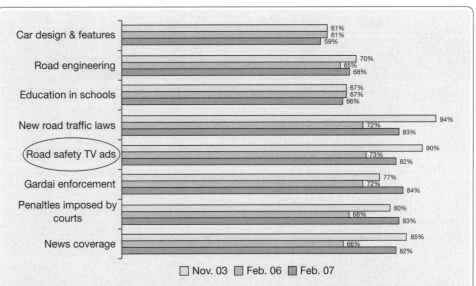

Figure 11.13 Influential factors in saving lives on the Republic of Ireland's roads – very/fairly influential

Source: Millward Brown.

In 2005, the Department for Transport estimated the cost of a road fatality in the UK at £1.4 million and the cost of a serious injury at £0.160 million. Given these cost estimates, the economic saving of these 234 pedestrians alive and uninjured equates to a massive £59.76 million.

Sterling saving:

- 18 fewer killed @ £1.4 million per death = £25.2 million
- 216 fewer seriously injured @ £0.160 million per serious injury = £34.56 million
- 3-year saving £59.76 million
- 234 fewer killed/seriously injured
  - 0.19 fatalities per 10,000 population
  - 0.15 fatalities per 10,000 population

Table 11.2 Payback

Year	Pedestrian road deaths	Pedestrian serious injuries	Pedestrians killed or seriously injured	Pedestrians killed per 10,000 population	Pedestrians killed or seriously injured per 10,000 population	NI Population
2000	32	292	324	0.19	1.93	1,682,944
2001	32	268	300	0.19	1.78	1,689,319
2002	33	244	277	0.19	1.63	1,696,641
Total	97	804	901	0.19	1.78	5,068,904
2003	28	222	250	0.16	1.47	1,702,628
2004	23	190	213	0.13	1.25	1,710,322
2005	28	176	204	0.16	1.18	1,724,408
Total	79	588	667	0.15	1.30	5,137,358

- 3 years – down 21%
  - 1.78 fatalities or serious injuries per 10,000 population
  - 1.30 fatalities or serious injuries per 10,000 population
- 3 years – down 27%

Republic of Ireland

In the three years following the launch of the campaign in the Republic of Ireland, 173 pedestrians were saved from death or serious injury, compared to the previous three-year trend (see Table 11.3).

Table 11.3 Payback

Year	Pedestrian road deaths	Pedestrians seriously injured	Pedestrians killed and seriously injured	Pedestrians killed per 10,000 population	Pedestrian killed and seriously injured per 10,000 population	Republic of Ireland population
2000	85	215	300	0.22	0.79	3,789,200
2001	89	167	256	0.23	0.67	3,847,200
2002	86	179	265	0.22	0.68	3,917,203
Total	260	561	821	0.23	0.71	11,553,603
2003	64	153	217	0.16	0.55	3,978,862
2004	70	130	200	0.17	0.49	4,043,763
2005	74	157	231	0.18	0.56	4,130,700
Total	208	440	648	0.17	0.53	12,153,325

In 2004, Goodbody Economic Consultants in its *Parameter Values for Use in Cost-Benefit Analysis of Transport Projects* estimated the cost of a road fatality in the Republic of Ireland at €2,018,126 and the cost of a serious injury at €226,757. Given these cost estimates, the economic saving of these 173 pedestrians alive and uninjured equates to a massive €104,969,990.
Euro saving:

- 52 fewer killed @ €2,018,126 per death = €104,942,552
- 121 fewer seriously injured @ €226,757 per serious injury = €27,437,597
- 3-year saving = 132,380,149
- 2000–2 0.23 fatalities per 10,000 population
- 2003–5 0.17 fatalities per 10,000 population
- 3 year – down 26%
- 2000–2 0.71 fatalities or serious injuries per 10,000 population
- 2003–5 0.53 fatalities or serious injuries per 10,000 population
- 3 years – down 25%

Summary

This pedestrian safety campaign was introduced in November 2002 with the following objectives:

- To raise the awareness generally of the number of pedestrians being killed and seriously injured on our roads.

- To make pedestrians and drivers more aware of their personal responsibility for avoiding road traffic collisions involving pedestrians.

- To reduce the number of pedestrian road deaths and serious injuries.

Campaign achievements

- Awareness of the campaign peaked at 90% and over.

- Over 90% of the population is now taking personal responsibility for avoiding road traffic collisions.

- Over 90% agree all road users are at risk.

- 80% and over have changed their behaviour following the introduction of the campaign.

- 234 pedestrians in Northern Ireland and 173 in the Republic of Ireland are alive and uninjured today as a result of the campaign.

- Campaign influence levels peaked at over 90%. This level of influence is more than double the norm rating for any TV advertising in Northern Ireland and almost double the rating in the Republic of Ireland.

- The public isolated road safety TV ads as one of the most influential factors in saving lives.

- The economic payback of the campaign was £60 million in NI and €132 million in ROI.

Source: Condensed from Institute of Practitioners in Advertising: IPA Effectiveness Awards, 2007.

Summary

The way messages are framed is an important aspect of social marketing campaigns. Messages can either be framed positively (emphasising a gain) or negatively (emphasising a loss). There is lively debate surrounding appropriate framing, though current research suggests that positive framing is more effective in a low-motivation environment and when linked to high levels of self-efficacy and certain (positive) outcomes. Conversely, negative framing is more effective if the motivation for the desired behaviour (change) is high, but linked to uncertain outcomes and/or low levels of self-efficacy. Further, positive framing is most effective for prevention-promoting messages, while negative framing is more effective in the case of detection and early diagnosis-related messages.

However, different message frames are perceived differently across cultures and target groups. For example, research suggests that, in collectivist cultures, negative message framing is more effective than in individualistic cultures. Careful testing of appropriateness and effectiveness of message frames used is therefore crucial for a successful social marketing campaign.

CHAPTER REVIEW QUESTIONS

1 You are involved in the development of a social marketing intervention aimed at encouraging responsible driving among young people of both genders. Would you recommend using positively or negatively framed messages? Justify your answer.

2 How would you test the effectiveness of framing alternatives for this intervention?

3 You are involved in the development of a social marketing intervention aimed at reducing domestic violence across all sectors of the community. Would you recommend using positively or negatively framed messages? Justify your answer.

4 You are involved in the development of a social marketing intervention aimed at encouraging health screening among women, including those from minority groups. How would you determine whether positively or negatively framed messages would be effective? Justify your answer.

5 You are involved in the development of a social marketing intervention aimed at encouraging healthier lifestyles, including both diet and exercise. You are to pilot the intervention in a large city which has a diverse population, including several ethnic minority communities. How will you develop and test the type of message that is likely to maximise communication effectiveness across all segments of the community?

6 If you find that your proposed communication programme for the intervention in question 5 above is effective only in some segments of the population and not others, what courses of action must you then consider?

Recommended reading

Block, L.G. and Keller, P.A. (1995) When to Accentuate the Negative: The Effects of Perceived Efficacy and Message Framing on Intentions to Perform a Health-Related Behavior. *Journal of Marketing Research,* 32 (2), 192–203.

Hastings, G., Stead, M. and Webb, J. (2004) Fear Appeals in Social Marketing: Strategic and Ethical Reasons for Concern. *Psychology & Marketing,* 21 (11), 961–86.

Orth, U.R., Koenig, H.F. and Firbasova, Z. (2007) Cross-national Differences in Consumer Response to the Framing of Advertising Messages. *European Journal of Marketing,* 41 (3/4), 327–48.

Notes

1 Arora, R. and Arora, A. (2004) The Impact of Message Framing and Credibility: Findings for Nutritional Guidelines. *Service Marketing Quarterly,* 26 (1), 35–53.

2 Block, L.G. and Keller, P.A. (1995) When to Accentuate the Negative: The Effects of Perceived Efficacy and Message Framing on Intentions to Perform a Health-Related Behavior. *Journal of Marketing Research,* 32 (2), 192–203.

3 Rothman, A.J. and Salovey, P. (1997) Shaping Perceptions to Motivate Healthy Behavior: The Role of Message Framing. *Psychological Bulletin,* 121 (1), 3–19.

4 Gerend, M.A. and Cullen, M. (2008) Effects of Message Framing and Temporal Context on College Student Drinking Behavior. *Journal of Experimental Social Psychology,* 44 (4), 1167–73.

5 Blanchard, C.M., Fisher, J., Sparling, P.B., Shanks, T.H., Nehl, E., Rhodes, R.E., et al. (2009) Understanding Adherence to 5 Servings of Fruits and Vegetables per Day: A Theory of Planned Behavior Perspective. *Journal of Nutrition Education and Behavior,* 41 (1), 3–10.

6 Holland, J., Ramazanoglu, C., Scott, S., Sharpe, S. and Thomson, R. (1990) Sex, Gender and Power: Young Women's Sexuality in the Shadow of AIDS. *Sociology of Health & Illness* 12 (3), 336–50.

7 Maheswaran, D. and Meyers-Levy, J. (1990) The Influence of Message Framing and Issue Involvement. *Journal of Marketing Research,* XXVII, 361–7.

8 Homer, P.M. and Yoon, S.-G. (1992) Message Framing and the Interrelationships Among Ad-Based Feelings, Affect, and Cognition. *Journal of Advertising,* XXI (1), 19–31.

9 Rothman, A.J. and Salovey, P. (1997) Op. cit.

10 Block, L.G. and Keller, P.A. (1995) Op. cit.

11 Ibid.

12 Cox, D. and Cox, A.D. (2001) Communicating the Consequences of Early Detection: The Role of Evidence and Framing. *Journal of Marketing,* 65 (3), 91–103.

13 Rucker, D.D. and Petty, R.E. (2006) Increasing the Effectiveness of Communications to Consumers: Recommendations Based on Elaboration Likelihood and Attitude Certainty Perspectives. *Journal of Public Policy & Marketing,* 25 (1), 39–52.

14 Cacioppo, J.T. and Petty, R.E. (1984) The Elaboration Likelihood Model of Persuasion. *Advances in Consumer Research,* 11 (1), 673–5.

15 Alaszewski, A. (2005) Risk Communication: Identifying the Importance of Social Context. *Health, Risk & Society,* 7 (2), 101–5.

16 Menon, G., Block, L.G. and Suresh, R. (2002) We're at as Much Risk as We Are Led to Believe: Effects of Message Cues on Judgments of Health Risk. *Journal of Consumer Research,* 28, 533–49.

17 Greene, K., Krcmar, M., Rubin, D.I., Walters, L.H. and Hale, J.L. (2002) Elaboration in Processing Adolescent Health Messages: The Impact of Egocentrism and Sensation Seeking on Message Processing. *Journal of Communication,* 52 (4), 812.

18 Van Assema, P., Martens, M., Ruiter, R.A.C. and Brug, J. (2001) Framing of Nutrition Education Messages in Persuading Consumers of the Advantages of a Healthy Diet. *Journal of Human Nutrition and Dietetics,* 14 (6), 435–42.

19 Stuart, A.E. and Blanton, H. (2003) The Effects of Message Framing on Behavioral Prevalence Assumptions. *European Journal of Social Psychology,* 33, 93–102.

20 Snyder, L.B., Hamilton, M.A., Mitchell, E.W., Kiwanuka-Tondo, J., Fleming-Milici, F. and Proctor, D. (2004) A Meta-Analysis of the Effect of Mediated Health Communication Campaigns on Behavior Change in the United States. *Journal of Health Communication,* 9 (1), 71–96.

21 Jayanti, R.K. and Burns, A.C. (1998) The Antecedents of Preventive Health Care Behavior: An Empirical Study. *Journal of the Academy of Marketing Science,* 26 (1), 6–15.

22 Holloway, A. and Watson, H.E. (2002) Role of Self-efficacy and Behaviour Change. *International Journal of Nursing Practice,* 8 (2), 106–15.

23 Strecher, V.J., De Vellis, B.M., Becker, M.H. and Rosenstock, I.M. (1986) The Role of Self-Efficacy in Achieving Health Behavior Change. *Health Education Quarterly,* 13 (1), 73–91.

24 Donovan, R.J. and Jalleh, G. (1999) Positively versus Negatively Framed Product Attributes: The Influence of Involvement. *Psychology & Marketing,* 16 (7), 613–30.

25 Detweiler, J.B., Bedell, B.T., Salovey, P., Pronin, E. and Rothman, A.J. (1999) Message Framing and Sunscreen Use: Gain-Framed Messages Motivate Beach-goers. *Health Psychology: Official Journal of the Division of Health Psychology, American Psychological Association,* 18 (2), 189–96.

26 Cox, D. and Cox, A.D. (2001) Op. cit.

27 Stuart, A.E. and Blanton, H. (2003) Op. cit.

28 Wolburg, J.M. (2006) College Students' Responses to Antismoking Messages: Denial, Defiance, and Other Boomerang Effects. *Journal of Consumer Affairs,* 40 (2), 294–323.

29 Bird, S. and Tapp, A. (2008) Social Marketing and the Meaning of Cool. *Social Marketing Quarterly,* 14 (1), 18–29.

30 Goldenbeld, C., Twisk, D. and Houwing, S. (2008) Effects of Persuasive Communication and Group Discussions on Acceptability of Anti-speeding Policies for Male and Female Drivers. *Transportation Research: Part F,* 11 (3), 207–20.

31 Youl, P., Janda, M. and Kimlin, M. (2009) Vitamin D and Sun Protection: The Impact of Mixed Public Health Messages in Australia. *International Journal of Cancer,* 124 (8), 1963–70.

32 Rothman, A.J., Martino, S.C., Bedell, B.T., Detweiler, J.B. and Salovey, P. (1999) The Systematic Influence of Gain- and Loss-Framed Messages on Interest in and Use of Different Types of Health Behavior. *Personality and Social Psychology Bulletin* 25 (11), 1355–69.

33 Hellman, C.M. and McMillin, W.L. (1997) The Relationship Between Psychological Reactance and Self-Esteem. *Journal of Social Psychology,* 137 (1), 135–8.

34 Donovan, R.J. and Jalleh, G. (1999) Op. cit.

35 Struckman-Johnson, C., Struckman-Johnson, D., Gilliland, R.C. and Ausman, A. (1994) Effect of Persuasive Appeals in AIDS PSAs and Condom Commercials on Intentions to use Condoms. *Journal of Applied Social Psychology,* 24 (24), 2223–44.

36 Orth, U.R., Koenig, H.F. and Firbasova, Z. (2007) Cross-national Differences in Consumer Response to the Framing of Advertising Messages. *European Journal of Marketing,* 41 (3/4), 327–48.

37 Snyder, L.B., Hamilton, M.A., Mitchell, E.W., Kiwanuka-Tondo, J., Fleming-Milici, F. and Proctor, D. (2004) Op. cit.

38 Ray, M.L. and Wilkie, W.L. (1970) Fear: The Potential of an Appeal Neglected by Marketing. *Journal of Marketing,* 34 (1), 54.

39 Strong, J.T. and Dubas, K.M. (1993) The Optimal Level of Fear-Arousal in Advertising: An Empirical Study. *Journal of Current Issues & Research in Advertising,* 15 (2), 93.

40 Hastings, G., Stead, M. and Webb, J. (2004) Fear Appeals in Social Marketing: Strategic and Ethical Reasons for Concern. *Psychology & Marketing,* 21 (11), 961–86.

41 Witte, K. and Allen, M. (2000) A Meta-Analysis of Fear Appeals: Implications for Effective Public Health Campaigns. *Health Education & Behavior,* 27 (5), 591–615.

42 Snipes, R.L., LaTour, M.S. and Bliss, S.J. (1999) A Model of the Effects of Self-efficacy on the Perceived Ethicality and Performance of Fear Appeals in Advertising. *Journal of Business Ethics,* 19 (3), 273–85.

43 Witte, K. and Allen, M (2000) Op. cit.

44 Ibid.

45 Hastings, G., Stead, M. and Webb, J. (2004) Op. cit.

46 Brennan, L. and Binney, W. (2010) Fear, Guilt and Shame Appeals in Social Marketing, *Journal of Business Research,* 63 (2), 140–46.

47 Bor, R, Perry, L., Miller, R. and Jackson, J. (1989) Strategies for Counselling the 'Worried Well' in Relation to AIDS: Discussion Paper. *Journal of the Royal Society of Medicine,* 82 (4), 218.

48 Reynolds, B. and Seeger, M.W. (2005) Crisis and Emergency Risk Communication as an Integrative Model. *Journal of Health Communication,* 10, 43–55.

49 Freimuth, V., Hammond, S., Edgar T. and Monahan, J. (1990) Reaching those at Risk. *Communication Research,* 17 (6), 775–91.

50 Monahan, J.L. (1995) Thinking Positively: Using Positive Effect when Designing Health Messages. In E. Maibach and R.L. Parrott (eds) *Designing Health Messages: Approaches from Communication Theory and Public Health Practice.* Buckingham: Sage, pp. 81–98.

51 Lewis, I.M., Watson, B., White, K.M. and Tay, R. (2007) Promoting Public Health Messages: Should We Move Beyond Fear-Evoking Appeals in Road Safety? *Qualitative Health Research* 17 (1), 61–74.

52 Orth, U.R., Oppenheim, P.P. and Firbasova, Z. (2005) Measuring Message Framing Effects Across Europe. *Journal of Targeting, Measurement and Analysis for Marketing,* 13 (4), 313–26.

53 Orth, U.R., Koenig, H.F. and Firbasova, Z. (2007) Op. cit.

54 Sheer, V. and Chen, L. (2008) Fear Appeals in Chinese Print OTC Ads: Extending the Four-component Message Structure. *International Journal of Communication,* 2, 936–58.

55 Barrett, D.W., Wosinska, W., Butner J., Petrova, P., Gornik-Durose, M. and Cialdini, R.B. (2004) Individual Differences in the Motivation to Comply across Cultures: The Impact of Social Obligation. *Personality and Individual Differences*, 31 (1), 19–31.

56 Reardon, J., Miller, C., Foubert, B., Vida, I. and Rybina, L. (2006) Antismoking Messages for the International Teenage Segment: The Effectiveness of Message Valence and Intensity across Different Cultures. *Journal of International Marketing*, 3 (14), 115–38.

57 Higgins, E. (1998) Promotion and Prevention: Regulatory Focus as a Motivational Principle. *Advances in Experimental Social Psychology*, 30, 1–46.

58 Uskul, A., Sherman, D. and Fitzgibbon J. (2009) The Cultural Congruency Effect: Culture, Regulatory Focus, and the Effectiveness of Gain- vs. Loss-framed Health Messages. *Journal of Experimental Social Psychology*, 45 (3), 535–41.

59 Dahl, S. (2010) Message Framing Across Cultures, proceedings of ISM Open, Milton Keynes: Open University.

60 Ibid.

61 Aldoory, L. (2001) Making Health Communications Meaningful for Women: Factors That Influence Involvement, *Journal of Public Relations Research,* 13 (2), 163–85.

62 Ibid.

63 Reiter, E., Robertson, R., Osman, L.M. (2003) Lessons from a Failure: Generating Tailored Smoking Cessation Letters, *Artificial Intelligence,* 144 (1–2), 41–58.

64 Spittaels, H., Bourdeaudhuij, I., Brug, J. and Vandelanotte, C. (2007) Effectiveness of an Online Computer-tailored Physical Activity Intervention in a Real-life Setting, *Health Education Research,* 22 (3), 385–96.

65 Ringold, D.J. (2002) Boomerang Effect: In Response to Public Health Interventions: Some Unintended Consequences in the Alcoholic Beverage Market. *Journal of Consumer Policy,* 25 (1), 27–63.

66 Brehm, S. and Brehm, J.W. (1981) *Psychological Reactance*. New York: Academic Press.

67 Rummel, A., Howard, J., Swinton, J.M. and Seymour, D.B. (2000) You Can't Have That! A Study of Reactance Effects and Children's Consumer Behavior. *Journal of Marketing Theory and Practice,* 8 (1), 38–44.

68 Hellman, C.M. and McMillin, W.L. (1997) The Relationship Between Psychological Reactance and Self-Esteem. *Journal of Social Psychology,* 137 (1), 135–8.

69 Buller, D.B., Borland, R. and Burgon, M. (1998) Impact of Behavioral Intention on Effectiveness of Message Features: Evidence from the Family Sun Safety Project. *Human Communication Research,* 24 (3), 433–53.

Chapter 12

Creativity in social marketing

Chapter objectives

On successfully completing this chapter, you should be able to:

- discuss the role of creativity in social marketing interventions;
- discuss how creative strategy evolves from scoping stages and the identification of insights into possible behaviour change options;
- develop a creative brief for the design of material;
- discuss how the needs of disadvantaged groups should be taken into account when designing interventions;
- discuss the influence of different media on the development of material;
- discuss the unique features of designing material for new media forms and social media.

Note: The design principles section is based on Eagle, L., Kemp, G. and Jones, S. (2009) *Design Principles – Social Marketing Intervention Material.* Report prepared for the South West Public Health Observatory Bristol.

Creativity

Let's start with what creativity is. Your initial thoughts may be that it refers to some form of 'artistic' measure,[1] but it is far more than this. It is not just about designing interesting or novel advertising or printed material; it encompasses every part of an intervention design and implementation.[2] It is the ability to look at a problem from different, often new, perspectives and to develop new relationships between concepts[3] and factors in people's lives that may hinder or help behaviour change. It has been described as drawing on:

> Knowledge, imagination, intuition, logic, accidental occurrences, and constructive evaluation to discover new connections between ideas and objects.[4]

Consider the following example. In the USA, African-American women have been reluctant to use conventional health services for advice on issues such as smoking cessation or other aspects of healthier lifestyles, including cancer screening. The team working on the problem were encouraged to think beyond obvious forms of distribution. Their solution was to use hair and beauty salon staff as conduits – training them in providing basic information, encouraging women to get further advice from sources they felt comfortable in using.[5]

Think about whether and how such activity could be tailored for other sectors of the population, whether this activity takes resources away from interventions with wider focus, and who should decide on behalf of each population segment what information sources might be effective.

An example discussed earlier in the text was the British Heart Foundation's 'Under your skin' intervention (see Chapter 11). Research had shown that the target group expected to be lectured and made to feel like socially unacceptable outcasts – so the decision was made to show the cigarette as the real enemy and BHF as providing a helpful and non-judgemental ally in the fight against it.

Another example of creative thinking can be seen in a Swedish intervention that aimed to encourage people to use the stairs rather than the escalators at the Odenplan subway station in Stockholm. Overnight, the stairs were transformed into a fully functioning keyboard. As people walked on each step, a different musical note was heard. People soon experimented with making actual music and videos of their attempts were posted on YouTube: http://www.youtube.com/watch?v=2lXh2n0aPyw.

Most importantly, 66% more people used the stairs than before the 'keyboard' was installed.[6]

As can be seen from the above examples, creatively approaching a behaviour change – i.e. linking behaviour change and intervention by using imagination to design interventions informed by knowledge about the target audience and their attitudes – can be highly successful. Very few of the readers of this text will actually develop creative material – most will commission or evaluate creative work. A range of creative people may be involved, such as copywriters, art directors, designers or specialist internet web designers. This chapter is not intended to turn you into a 'creative' but to help you to be confident in briefing creative people who will develop the material, and, importantly, to help you evaluate whether their material is consistent with the objectives for the intervention. You should also be confident about realistic and affordable ways of evaluating whether the chosen approach and the proposed creative material works with the intended targets.

The starting point for creativity is the starting point for overall intervention development discussed in the earlier chapters, particularly Chapter 3. The initial scoping phase helps with understanding the problem being addressed and possible solutions – but from the target's perspective.

In this phase, the way the targeted behaviour fits in with the individual's and social group's life and potential barriers to, or enablers of, behaviour change should be identified along with the impact of competition. This phase should also be linked to the use of appropriate behavioural theories. For example, identifying whether behaviour is driven primarily by norms or by self-efficacy will provide an indication of the type of creative approach that may be effective, as the following quotes from leading behavioural theorists remind us:

> The relative importance of these psychosocial variables as determinants of intention will depend upon both the behaviour and the population being considered.

And:

> one behaviour may be primarily determined by attitudinal considerations, whereas another may be primarily influenced by self-efficacy. Similarly, a behaviour that is attitudinally driven in one population or culture may be normatively driven in another.[7]

Consider the following examples:

1 Sun protection behaviours differ by population segment. For example, adolescents and young adults are overwhelmingly motivated by social norms; outdoor workers believe that their job prevents them from being able to take effective precautions and mothers of young children take care to protect their children from the sun – but do not always protect themselves, as they see value in being seen by their social contacts as having a suntan.[8]

2 Similarly, age differences play a role as a motivating factor for exercise and physical activity. While younger adults tend to be motivated to exercise mostly by non-health-related messages, such as weight loss and increased attractiveness, people in later life are more motivated by the immediate health benefits and remaining young and active.[9]

An analysis of the creative approach used by competitors may also provide a useful starting point. This was effective in the American 'Truth' anti-smoking initiative[10, 11] which analysed the creative strategies of the tobacco industry – and of successful youth-oriented marketers – as part of their initial intervention design phase.

The link between creativity and effectiveness is not clear-cut; a large amount of literature has focused only on perceptions within the marketing communications industry, such as the relative importance of 'creative' awards rather than marketplace performance[12] (which *is* captured in the IPA-sponsored effectiveness awards). The key is to remember that creativity is not an end in itself – along with originality, innovation and other factors that may help gain attention, the intervention must be relevant for the target[13] and it must be persuasive.[14]

In the remainder of the chapter we will now focus on how to develop, evaluate and implement creative strategy.

Creative strategy formation

Despite many attempts to try to classify persuasive communications, particularly advertising, on a standardised creativity scale,[15] no such scale has yet been developed. We can, however, share recognised good practice and useful checklists to help you evaluate material.

Creativity checklists

Table 12.1 should provide you with a useful checklist to refer to when evaluating creativity. Variations of this type of checklist have been used in commercial marketing for several decades.

The type of appeal to be used in all communications is important – whether to phrase material in rational or emotional, positive or negative terms. This is discussed in more detail in Chapter 11.

Table 12.1 The nine-point creative strategy format

1	***What are we really selling?*** It seems deceptively simple but deserves some serious consideration. For example, in our work with regional health organisations, a senior staff member exclaimed during a discussion of this point in relation to cancer screening – 'We have been selling cancer – we should be selling hope!'
2	***Who is our target and what makes them different from others?*** Do we really understand the factors that drive their current behaviour and the things that might encourage or inhibit sustained behaviour change?
3	***What is our target's problem – and do they recognise their behaviour as being problematic?*** If they don't, what are the implications for our intervention? How are we intending to help them 'solve' the problem? Is this solution likely to be acceptable to them? Refer back to using hair salon staff to encourage health-related behaviours for an example of the application of this type of thinking.
4	***Do we face competitive pressure?*** This may be the activity of commercial marketers or it may be attitudes and beliefs among our target groups. If they do not accept what we are saying – or are even hostile towards us – the challenge of breaking through their barriers will be difficult.
5	***What is our most important benefit?*** It is important to look at this from the perspective of the target, not from those who are designing or delivering the intervention. There may not be shared views – and it is the views of the target that really matter.
6	***What parts or features of our intervention offer the benefits most likely to be valued by the target?*** These should be stressed in communications.
7	***What is our personality?*** Are we seen in the way we would like to be seen? Again, refer back to the BHF 'Under Your Skin' intervention, where previous interventions had led smokers to expect authoritarian nagging and preaching, therefore the decision was made to position BHF as a non-judgemental ally.
8	***What else can help encourage sustained behaviour change?*** Keep this as short as possible – if there are numerous secondary points, we are likely to confuse people – there should be a simple and persuasive primary benefit with some supporting features.
9	***What do we want our target to do and have we made it easy for them to do it?***

Source: Adapted from Berkman, H.W. and Gilson, C. (1980) *Advertising: Concepts and Strategies* (2nd edn). New York: Random House.

Patriotism

Another option to think about when considering alternative ways of approaching an issue may be linking it to patriotism. Take the example of the highly successful 'Don't mess with Texas' campaign. The anti-littering campaign appealed to the sense of patriotism and pride of Texans to motivate them not to throw rubbish onto the local roadside. The campaign was extremely successful: after the original advertising campaign along the highways of Texas and on radio and television, the slogan (Figure 12.1) became so popular that it is now featured on a variety of gadgets and in several television series (including *The Simpsons*), and is even the official motto of a USS submarine (the USS *Texas*).

Cultural norms

Cultural norms, discussed in Chapter 11, can also give important impetus as how to devise a creative campaign. For example, the Hombres Sanos campaign[16] targeting Latino men who have sex with both males and females uses the slogan: 'No one knows . . . and with a condom, no one will' to convince the target audience, who traditionally see themselves as predominantly heterosexual and are strongly motivated to hide sexual encounters with

Figure 12.1 Example of the 'Don't mess with Texas' slogan
Source: Alamy/Gabbro.

men, to use condoms. This slogan might appear offensive for a white LGBT (lesbian, gay, bisexual or transgender) audience, who might prefer an open discussion on safe-sex practices and sexuality. However, the campaign was very effective because it appealed to cultural sensitivities and combined these creatively in a campaign.

Testimonials

Using testimonials can often be an effective way of engaging an audience. Testimonials involve showing target audience members speaking directly to the audience, and explaining the positives of the behaviour change targeted. Using vivid clues, especially in the form of testimonials, has been shown to be particularly effective for lower socio-economic groups, as it advances reward perception and increases the likelihood of taking action.[17]

Needs of low-literacy consumers

Despite awareness of the problem, health information materials continue to be produced at a level well above the average reading level,[18] placing patients at risk of problems due to incorrect or inappropriate usage. For example, people with low literacy levels are more anxious about the possibility of developing cancer, yet, due to lack of accessible information, are often not diagnosed until cancers are advanced.[19]

Though varying definitions of literacy make cross-study comparisons difficult, some findings indicate that some 20% of the population of most developed countries have severe literacy problems and a further 20% have limited literacy.[20, 21] There also exists an additional group that could be classed as 'aliterate', in that they are able to read but choose not to, and rely on television rather than print media for news. More importantly, they learn through trial and error rather than by reading instructions.[22] The specific needs of these groups must be taken into account, acknowledging their difficulties but avoiding appearing to condescend in the design and delivery of appropriate interventions.[23]

The average adult reading skill level is 3–5 grades below the level expected at the end of formal education.[24] Relating this to the UK national curriculum levels, a person who left secondary school at age 16 (reading skill 12, national curriculum 5) can be expected to have a post-education reading skill level of 7–9; national curriculum level 3. The Basic Skills Agency's report (May 2000) indicated that almost four out of every ten adults in some parts of the UK are functionally illiterate.[25] The Commons Public Accounts Committee (2006) reported that up to 16 million adults – nearly half the UK workforce – have reading skills no better than that of children leaving primary school.[26]

Table 12.2 presents the adult reading skill levels for the UK in relation to the primarily American literature[27, 28] and the national standards for literacy. The *Skills for Life* adult basic skills strategy, launched by the UK government in 2001, developed national standards for literacy. The literacy framework outlines what an adult should be able to achieve at entry level (divided into three sub-levels), level 1 and level 2 or above. The framework recognises that an adult may be classified at an overall level of literacy but have higher or lower levels of ability in different aspects of that skill. Furthermore, within this framework, the skills levels and tests for literacy pertain primarily to reading skills, rather than writing.

While this is not an easy issue to address, there are some basic principles that can be used. Try to balance writing at a level that allows material to be understood without the risk of appearing patronising. Focus on practical advice that is based on an understanding of how people live their lives and the actual and perceived barriers they may face in changing behaviours.

Avoid:

- words with more than two syllables;
- words that may not be familiar to the target groups, including medical and technical terms or acronyms;
- appearing judgemental;
- telling people what may seem obvious or already known.

Table 12.2 Reading skill level by age cohort as indicated in the literature and the national standards for literacy

School level	Approximate age	Approximate grade/ reading skill level expected	UK National Curriculum Level	UK adult literacy level	UK population %
Nursery Junior/ primary school	3–5	1	1	Entry level 1	3
	6	2	1		
	7	3	2	Entry level 2	2
	8	4	2		
	9	5	2		
	10	6	2		
Secondary school	11	7	3	Entry level 3	11
	12	8	3		
	13	9	3		
	14	10	3		
	15	11	4		
Further education	16	12	5	Level 1 Upper secondary attainment	40
	17	13	5		
Higher education (college/university)	18	14	6 to 8	Level 2 or above	44
	19	15			

Be careful with:

- statistics;
- images that may scare.

Use a readability test (SMOG,[29] REALM[30]) or any validated and widely used tool to assess the readability of your material against the data in Table 12.2. For an online SMOG calculator, see http://www.harrymclaughlin.com/SMOG.htm.

Presentation of strategy

The next stage is to decide how to present the chosen creative across a range of communication channels in ways that will ensure consistency of the message: integration of all elements of the intervention so that each element reinforces the others. A key question at this stage is whether the material will attract attention and be seen as relevant, meaningful and persuasive.

After identifying the core messages, ensure all parts of the plan synergise. It is best to create a strategic overview at this stage and then carefully check how the various media forms contribute to the identified objectives. Refer to Chapter 13 on media planning for more details on how to plan the tactical steps for the campaign, but it is important to remember not to lose sight of the main message and strategy.

Creativity for print: leaflets, posters, newspapers, magazines etc.

In all print-based activity, there are some fundamental design principles that should be followed. These are based on an understanding of the function of different parts of any material. Generally, a concept layout will be produced by whoever is designing the creative material. This is either a rough sketch or a computer-generated outline of the way the material should be presented, including positioning of the key elements discussed in the next section.

Design principles

Headlines should state benefits, and entice people to read more to solve a problem or gain knowledge.

Subheadings are then used to help break up material into sections that each give specific information on a topic area. Subheadings should be attention-getting in their own right – and aimed at signalling where information can be found.

Visuals such as photographs, drawings or diagrams can attract attention and illustrate particular points. Ask yourself what role a visual plays in enhancing the presentation and value of your material.

In evaluating layouts, questions that you should ask are:

1 Is it appealing and does it invite potential readers to read on for more details?
2 Does it talk to them in language they will understand and relate to?
3 Does it communicate the key messages as simply as possible?

4 Do the illustrations work with or against the text material?

5 Does it provide what will interest the target group rather than what an expert thinks they should know?

Copy

Generally, people start at the top left of material and work across the headline, then down, often diagonally, through the rest of the material, but numerous studies have shown that few people read all the material unless they have a strong personal motivation to do so.

Keep the text simple – think of the information needs and information processing abilities of those who struggle with literacy – avoid wrapping text around illustrations, tables or figures – consider how easily the example below is to read.

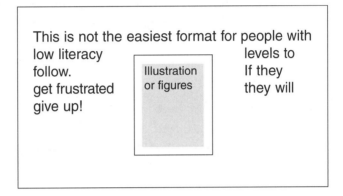

Avoid:

- Long sentences – break them up to make the information easier to read – people process information in small chunks at a time.
- Printing over illustrations if it limits contrast with the text.
- Transparent paper – text showing through from the other side makes reading difficult.
- Patterned background if it makes the type difficult to read.
- Glossy paper – it is difficult to read due to reflections of light from the paper.
- Yellow ink – it presents major problems for visually impaired people.

Use:

- Headings – they make it easy for people to find key information. Number headings if information is sequential and specific steps are to be taken.
- White space – don't fill everything up to the point where the material is jammed together.
- Illustrations – position these at the end of a paragraph rather than in the middle. They must be relevant, illustrating important points or providing visual guides for poor readers.

Typefaces

Think of your target and the environment in which they will see the material – make sure that the type size selected is large enough to be readable. Generally, do not use less than a 12-point font for leaflets – use larger font sizes for older people.[31]

For posters, a quick review of existing posters in shopping malls or train stations will show you how difficult much of this material is to read unless you are very close to it.

Avoid:

- Reverse fonts (light type on dark or coloured backgrounds – they might look creative, but they are less easy to read than dark type on light backgrounds, as the following example shows:

> This is an example of a reverse font on a darker background

> Compare the above to this – dark font on a light background – which is easier to read?

- Using all capitals or fancy fonts, as the following illustrates:

> Fancy fonts might look creative, but they can be difficult to read
> Fancy fonts might look creative, but they can be difficult to read
> Fancy fonts might look creative, but they can be difficult to read

Also be careful with colour combinations – do not use red and green together as those with colour blindness will struggle to read it. Blue/yellow colour blindness is rare, but again, try not to put any barriers in the way of readers. Dyslexia can make comprehension difficult – there are specialist websites that provide guides for those who face this challenge, e.g. the British Dyslexia Association's site at http://www.bdadyslexia.org.uk/about-dyslexia/further-information/dyslexia-style-guide.html.

Evaluation/copy testing

All material should be pre-tested with a sample of the target group to ensure that the message you are trying to send is what is being received. This will include comprehension and readability measures such as those discussed above. You may find it valuable to check what media channels these people use and how they expect your material to be conveyed through them.

Creativity in outdoor activity

Outdoor messages are notoriously hard to convey, as often there is a lot of clutter competing for the attention of motorists and other road users, for example in the form of posters and roadside advertising. However, one of the challenges in road safety activity is to take messages to where the behaviour occurs, despite the clutter. A creative approach was an example from a 2008 Philadelphia anti-speeding intervention. It used a 3-D illusion that appeared to be actual speed bumps but which were simply 2-dimensional images made from plastic and burned into the road surface. The aim was to use a novel approach to slow traffic.

Short-term results were reported to be encouraging, with speeds dropping from 38 mph (13 above the speed limit) to 23 mph.[32]

A more recent, and extremely controversial, intervention using a similar strategy, nicknamed 'Pavement Patty', was one part of a multi-component Canadian intervention aimed at reducing preventable accidents. (Other activity included reducing drowning and increasing safety helmet usage.) The 3-D illusion, positioned for one week outside a primary school, featured what appeared to be a young girl running across the road to catch a ball. Nearby signage stated:

You're probably not expecting kids to run out on the road.

The intervention was developed to try to reduce child pedestrian injuries by making drivers more aware of the possibility of children on roads, and to encourage speed reduction and greater driver vigilance. Reaction was mixed, with some posts on the intervention website suggesting that effects would be short term only or that it might be a distraction and actually cause accidents. Unfortunately, within the social marketing academic community, the issue moved from whether or not the intervention would be effective in the longer term to whether or not it was actually social marketing! (Georgetown University e-list: soc-mktg@georgetown.edu)

Questions for you to consider are:

1 Do you believe it will be effective in the longer term?

2 If so, will behaviour in streets where the signs are not located also improve?

3 What 'exchange' assumptions underlie the intervention?

Creativity for television, radio and cinema

Scripts and storyboards

The electronic equivalent of a concept layout for electronic media is a script. This is exactly what it seems – it gives the words – and visuals if television or cinema are being used. Often people overestimate the amount of information that can be provided – as a rough rule of thumb, a 30-second commercial should contain about 75 words. It is quite an art distilling the key messages down into both time and word quota!

The script will be divided vertically in two, with the left half giving the words and sound effects; the right half describes the corresponding visuals that will be shown.

In evaluating initial scripts, the questions that you should ask are similar to those for print media:

1 Is it appealing and does it invite potential viewers/listeners to focus on the message for more details?

2 Does it talk to them in language they will understand and relate to?

3 Does it communicate the key messages as simply as possible?

4 Do the visuals work with or against the text material?

5 Does it provide what will interest the target group rather than what an expert thinks they should know?

Evaluation/pre-testing

Once the scripts are at a finished point, pre-testing should be undertaken, as outlined earlier for print media. An added complication with electronic media is whether, if scripts alone are used, people will be able to visualise exactly what is intended. If you mock up a rough version of the commercial, it will be much closer to the finished version, but there will be additional costs involved in the production. A decision therefore needs to be made about at what point to test – and what the trade-offs in testing concepts rather than rough commercials or completed versions may mean in judging the potential impact of the material when it is aired.

Creativity for new/electronic media

New media, from traditional websites to **social media**, offer many avenues of synergistically using several media channels to convey a message. For example, the Barbados-based *Island Queen* series uses its established television programme to raise HIV/Aids awareness – but supplements this by the use of a traditional website (http://www.islandqueen.tv/), Facebook groups (http://www.facebook.com/IslandQueenTV), Twitter (http://twitter.com/islandqueenbim) and a dedicated YouTube channel (http://www.youtube.com/islandqueentv).

Using YouTube supported by other online media is central to the Los Angeles-based *In the Moment* (http://www.inthemoment.tv/). The campaign was developed by the LA Gay and Lesbian Center, and focuses on key points of sexual decision-making including barriers for proactive (safer) sexual choices. The episodes, released on YouTube, feature fictional characters, as well as community members, thus breaking down barriers between the 'fictional' soap and real life. The YouTube campaign is supplemented by appropriate offline campaigns, such as posters and events to promote the main campaign.

While many current social marketing campaigns focus on social media, traditional websites, especially when designed interactively, can still play a vital role in developing creative social marketing campaigns. For example, the British Heart Foundation used an interactive online game as the major vehicle for its campaign to reduce childhood obesity. In the Yoobot versus Yoonot game (http://www.yoobot.co.uk/) children make nutritional choices as part of the game.

However, bear in mind that this kind of intervention has a tendency to be used by people who are already motivated and will therefore go out of their way to go online to play a game. Online tools are unlikely to be successful for non-motivated audiences. Those audiences could simply not visit websites, upload or share comments. They are likely to ignore communications received, no matter how creatively these are executed.

On the basis of these assumptions, a suitable online tool for a highly motivated audience could consist of a traditional website (education intervention). More elaborate, online social marketing campaigns may be useful for individuals who are motivated, but do not have the opportunity and/or ability to carry out a behaviour change. They can provide guidance and support in making proactive choices – or act as virtual role models.[33]

Regulation

We noted in Chapter 1 that some social marketing interventions had been found to breach the codes of advertising administered by the Advertising Standards Authority in the UK (the 'fishhook' campaign). Striking a balance between potentially alarmist or frightening interventions and the importance of 'cutting through the clutter' is a significant point when considering campaigns. Note that the ASA in the UK is no longer restricted to regulating only paid-for advertising, but also regulates internet and new media content. For the UK, the codes for both broadcasting and non-broadcasting media can be found at http://www.cap.org.uk/.

CASE STUDY 12.1

TV ad: Fire Safety Ireland – Escape Plan

Introduction

Northern Ireland has one of the highest ratios of smoke alarm ownership in Europe and yet, in a majority of home fires that result in fatalities, indications are that, even if a smoke alarm is fitted, it fails to operate.

This case study demonstrates how advertising succeeded in educating the public to think about fire safety behaviour, how it moved people to make positive changes in the home to prevent fire, and how lives can be saved by ensuring that *working* smoke alarms, if properly fitted and maintained, will alert people in the event of fire.

The study demonstrates how sequential advertising messages – crafted in response to researched consumer insights – effected significant change through a structured longer-term campaign that set itself four overarching phased principles:

1 Raise perceived levels of personal responsibility for self and others through education.

2 Challenge behavioural attitudes through raising awareness and knowledge of personal risk.

3 Focus on the key cause of death in domestic dwellings and how to mitigate the risk.

4 Challenge attitudes to highlight responsibility, accountability and behaviour.

The campaign had a single goal: **save lives and property**.

This case study also sets out to isolate the advertising effectiveness – in human and financial terms – over the campaign period 2004–8.

LONG-TERM STRATEGY

Over a sustained four-year period, the four overarching phased principles were gradually honed creatively in line with awareness of strengths or deficits in people's attitudes raised in the immediately preceding campaigns and in the targeted communications channels.

Objectives

- Raise public awareness on causes of fire.
- Raise awareness of safety practices and routines.

Case study 12.1 (*continued*)

- Reduce fire incidents by over 20%.
- Effect behavioural change – specifically, habitual checking of smoke alarms.
- Reduce death and injury by over 20%.
- Make significant savings to the public purse – no fiscal target set.

It was crucial to use several campaigns to move from a broad causation awareness strategy to the key life-saving tactic of regularly ensuring your smoke alarm is working, properly fitted and maintained.

PHASED RESEARCH MECHANISM

Every phase underwent a formal review programme to understand response to the previous advertisements and was conducted uniformly with:

1 Serving officers – interviews
2 General public – interviews and groups.

This was backed up by intense scrutiny of fire incident reporting data and biannual government research on awareness levels of publicly funded advertising. Analysis of this identified:

1 Awareness and recall
2 Attitudinal and behavioural responses to campaigns
3 Gaps or opportunities in public psyche regarding fire issues.

These disciplines informed each evolution in the phased approach.

Phase 1 – Raise perceived levels of personal responsibility for self and others through education

Campaign title: 'Writing on the wall'
Phase period: 2004–5

Reason for change
Previous advertising campaigns had established Mondays as the day to check smoke alarms; it was decided to build on this established habit. Other main hazards causing fires, injury and death were analysed, identifying that our audience initially needed to be educated across five key areas:

1 Candle safety – in 2003–4, candles were the fastest-rising cause of fire in the UK.
2 Escape plan – the need for a viable and rehearsed escape route to navigate in zero visibility.
3 Chip pan safety – unattended pans accounted for over 90% of such fires.
4 Door safety – an ordinary household door can contain fire and smoke for up to 15 minutes.
5 Battery maintenance in smoke alarms – failed smoke alarms can be fatal if any other precautions have been overlooked.

Creative dynamic

As part of the new learning process, we felt that it was important to understand the human experience of being in a fire.

The brand team underwent real fire training and viewed forensic footage which revealed horrific post-fire scenarios including a prevalent tragic feature: handprints strewn across walls by those desperately seeking a way out.

This informed the core of the campaign – developing a series of pleas left by the dying, with finger-written messages scratched desperately into charred walls.

It would be the first of a series of four campaign phases designed to create the 'nudge on the sofa' – that moment where people watching television together are pricked and inspired to action under the scrutiny of others.

Touch for life/Mondays

Rather than abandon the firm franchise built around weekly testing of smoke alarms, a completely separate, more benign advertisement was created that ran first in break during every local UTV news report, every Monday for two years. Potent images were used of a baby touching a parent's finger, fully trusting – a finger that could on this day, just test a smoke alarm.

Phase 2 – Challenge behavioural attitudes through raising awareness and knowledge of personal risk

Campaign title: 'Waiting room'
Phase period: 2005–6

Reason for change

The groups showed that Phase 1 had strong recall and that there were significant increases in the awareness of the causes of fire along with preventive action, and a strong sense of the need to take responsibility for others. Improvements in incident statistics and, most importantly, fire death figures were beginning to be seen.

The following were now addressed:

- a clear deficit in the feelings of personal vulnerability
- the potential that you yourself could die in a fire
- further enhancing knowledge of the main causes of fire.

Creative dynamic

In order to demonstrate that death spares no one, an afterlife waiting room was created, run by a matronly Anne Robinson type, allocating places in the afterlife, dependent on how a wide spectrum of people had variously died in their own house fires.

A precision blend of dark humour and menacing educational messages delivered the key messages in 60 seconds with 30-second edits produced addressing specific risks and allowing us to start concentrating on **working smoke alarms**.

The 30-second advert that dealt with this rotated into 75% of all 30-second slots with upweights in risk-specific 30-second slots when responding to current or recent incidents as they occurred. The content of the adverts was designed to emphasise the consequences of bad practice without actually demonstrating (and thereby reinforcing) it.

Case study 12.1 (*continued*)

Phase 3 – Focus on the key cause of death in domestic dwellings and how to mitigate the risk

Campaign title: 'Smoke kills'
Phase period: 2006–7

Reason for change

Tracking research and focus groups in key at-risk groupings revealed a high awareness of the causes of fire and preventive action. However, people also felt that smoke and noise would waken them and that they could then exit the house as characters do in films and TV dramas. They would not and could not.

Analysis of fire incident statistics showed a significant number of people did not test their alarm regularly and in 50% of fatal house fires NIFRS had recorded that a smoke alarm had been fitted . . . but failed. People were not maintaining, or testing their smoke alarms.

Creative dynamic

> *In a house fire heat and flames don't kill people, the smoke does.*
> (Assistant Chief Fire Officer, Peter Craig)

Clearly there was a need to demonstrate the stealth and vigour of smoke moving through your house and straight into your lungs, killing occupants almost instantly if a smoke alarm fails to operate. The theme of a message from the dead was sustained – but concentrated on the impossibility of escape without a working smoke alarm.

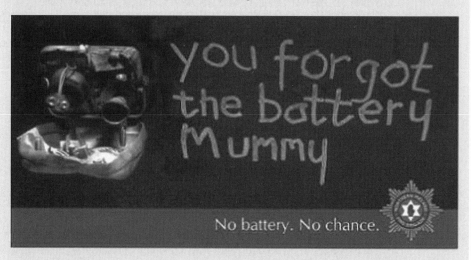

Phase 4 – Challenge attitudes to highlight responsibility, accountability and behaviour

Campaign title: 'Love the things that matter'
Phase period: 2007–8

Reason for change

Through formulated research mechanics, people's perceptions of risk and of cause of death were understood. Furthermore, examining what people valued and protected highlighted that people regularly take precautionary action to protect possessions by locking cars, securing valuables, etc., rather than risk losing them. However, they did not perform this same programmed behaviour when protecting their family from fire.

While fire incidents and deaths were still decreasing as a result of previous phases, data still showed that, in 50% of fatal house fires, a smoke alarm had been fitted but failed.

Creative dynamic

We needed to reprogramme people's attitudes to normal precautions taken in the home and position them in the context of the most important valuable they have – their family. Checking your smoke alarm should be as fundamental as locking your car.

From a dead child's perspective, the question was posed why her parents loved their possessions so much, but clearly mustn't have loved her sufficiently to regularly check the smoke alarm.

COMMUNICATIONS STRATEGY

The strategy devised to reach the identified target audiences included strategic and integrated media planning to ensure optimum coverage of, and connection with, the mass Northern Ireland audience.

Message relevance

Client data showed a propensity for certain of the original five key hazards to occur in specific geographical regions/demographic groups. This allowed us to target selected audiences with the most prevalent risk they and their neighbours faced.

As the phases evolved into more generic, mass targeting smoke alarm messaging, upweighting in higher-risk areas was still achieved and identified through NIFRS hotspot data.

Similarly, following specific incidents in localised areas, they were targeted with media and home leafleting derived from the campaign, with the most pertinent relevant creative message.

Campaign timing

According to CLG national fire statistics and NIFRS historical data, the highest-risk period is September – February because winter means people stay in more and more electrical appliances – heaters, fires, etc. – are on. Christmas time accounts for a significant amount of incidents resulting from overloaded plugs.

When the public smoking ban came into effect, some radio advertising was amended to cover increased risks from smoking in the home under the influence of alcohol.

Case study 12.1 (*continued*)

Candidate media

Television

The targeting of each individual fire safety message to a specific audience was facilitated through extensive programme research and daypart analysis. For example, the chip pan safety message was upweighted at dinner time and late night to target those returning hungry from pubs and clubs.

The television activity provided a constant presence throughout the high-risk period. In recognition of the strength of local news, an initiative/partnership was deployed with UTV for two years (across Phases 1 and 2). This consisted of a 30-second commercial running in each of the three local news breaks every Monday for 104 weeks, providing much-needed repetition of the 'check your battery' message.

Key efficiency: The station partnership was negotiated at over 50% discount, achieving repetition of the battery message three times every Monday, and further sponsorship was secured from Allianz due to the commercial's benign tone. Sixty-eight per cent of Northern Ireland's population would have watched this ad at least once over a three-month period, with 31% watching the ad at least four times over the same period.[34]

Radio

Radio ads delivered repetition of the campaign messages to the target audience whilst in the home. Activity was planned to run in creative contrast to the upbeat Christmas and January sale retail activity, maximising recall by catching the audience off-guard with an incongruous sombre creative. The creative concentrated on risk-specific executions throughout all phases.

Key efficiency: 64% of radio listening in Ireland takes place at home, with an average listening time of 3.5 hours each day. Forty-six per cent of all adults in NI listen to commercial radio at least once a week, with 24% being medium to heavy listeners.[35] The creative treatment for each spot was precisely planned to ensure that the individual creative treatments were placed in the most relevant parts of the day – e.g. the bedtime routine message was only aired after 8pm.

Press

NIFRS was able to work in partnership with *The Belfast Telegraph,* Northern Ireland's only indigenous evening title, to heavily discount a rotation of creative sites throughout the paper across the year.

Key efficiency:

- Cost-effective initiative to provide 104-week press campaign on specially created ad sites.
- Press ads allowed more detail on best practice.
- Monday title corners were secured in support of the Monday TV messaging.

Outdoor

Outdoor ads delivered all the emotive fire safety images and precise geographical targeting – upweighted with Adshel – providing coverage of the main population arteries throughout winter.

Key efficiency:

- 72% of people questioned recall outdoor advertising campaigns one week later.

- Sites were strategically bought where each creative would appear in the most relevant risk-group catchment areas by postcode.

- 43% of all adults in Northern Ireland can recall 48-sheet advertising from the previous week[36]

Transit

The 'Smoke kills' campaign was deployed on four fully wrapped buses, ensuring high-impact secondary messages in specified geographic areas.

Key efficiency:

- The double-deckers deployed in Greater Belfast offered exposure to its residents but also its 300,000 commuters from further afield. Routes outside Belfast were tactically chosen and, where possible, the buses carrying the ads were deployed as school buses in the winter months.

- 42% of all adults in Northern Ireland can recall external bus advertising from the previous week[37]

Ambient

This offered us the opportunity again to segment the market by risk, lifestyle and even gender, with researched relevant creative executions.

EFFECTIVENESS – HOW THE ADVERTISING WORKED

The campaign consistently delivered advertising awareness when independently researched, prompted action and, more importantly, saved lives. See Figure 12.3 for the reduction in numbers of accidental fires. After Phase 1: 2004–5 alone, the campaign showed extraordinary results:

- 14% decrease in the total number of household fires year on year

- 12% decrease of overall fire injuries year on year

Case study 12.1 (*continued*)

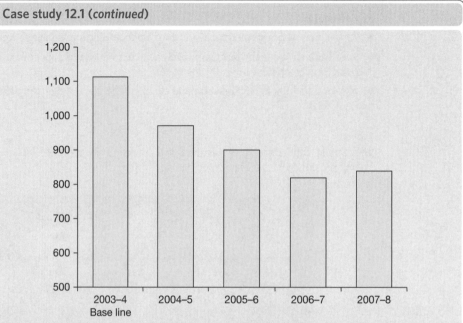

Figure 12.3 Accidental fires in the home, Northern Ireland, 2003–8
Source: NIFRS data.

Sixty per cent of respondents were influenced to take action and do something practical to prevent fire in the home as a direct result of the advertising. The research clearly evidenced an awareness of the five fire hazards advertised and a change in behaviour.

1 Candle safety – 39% decrease in fires caused by candles.

2 Escape plan – 18% of respondents had prepared a fire safety plan.

3 Chip pan safety – 18% decrease in chip pan-related fires.

4 Door safety – 38% of respondents said that they now closed their doors before going to bed at night, an 11% increase on the previous year.

5 Battery maintenance – as a result of seeing the campaign, 17% said they fitted a smoke alarm and 42% said they tested their smoke alarm.

Phases 1–4

With only Phase 2 addressing these risk awareness levels, taking all four phases spanning 2004 to 2008 into account, the following results were achieved:

- 24% reduction in number of fires in dwellings – down from 1110 in 2003 to 847 by end of 2008
- 23% reduction in serious injuries from accidental fires – down from 174 in 2004 to 134 by end of 2008

Fire deaths

There is a ongoing downward trend in fire deaths in NIFRS's long-term strategy. However, three cases of multiple deaths occurring from single incidents in 2006 and 2007 are reflected in Figure 12.4.

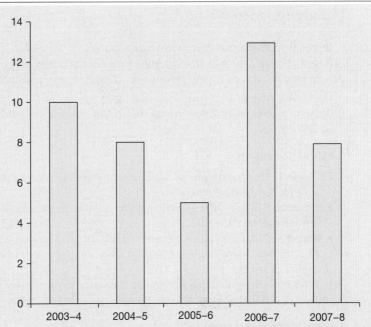

Figure 12.4 Accidental fire deaths in dwellings, Northern Ireland, 2003-8
Source: NIFRS data.

This should be counterbalanced with a real incident reduction of 24%, which more accurately reflects the targeted behaviours.

There is no 'competitor' factor in this instance other than apathy and this has been significantly eroded.

It is worth noting that there is a general decrease in both dwelling fires and fire injuries in the UK, with a generic fire safety advertising campaign running sporadically throughout. However, the tactical approach taken in Northern Ireland focusing on specific fire hazards and actions was clearly more effective; both measurements show that the decrease in Northern Ireland was more than double the national rate.

Focus on the habitual checking of smoke alarms:

- Smoke alarm ownership in the accounting period has risen from a base line of 93% to now exceed 98% – unequalled in the UK or Ireland.

- A third of respondents (32%) checked their smoke alarms 'every week' with a further 20% checking alarms 'every 2–3 weeks' and monthly.

Client objectives
Client objective 1: To raise public awareness on the causes of fire.
Result: 57% of respondents said that they remembered fire safety advertising campaigns in the last year.

Client objective 2: To raise awareness of safety practices and routine.
Result: 83% said the campaign resulted in improved awareness of fire safety issues, including the causes of fires.

Client objective 3: Reduce fire incidents by over 20%.
Result: Reduction of 24%, 13% higher than the national figure.

Case study 12.1 (*continued*)

Client objective 4: To effect behavioural change.
Result: 71% said the advertising resulted in a change in how they thought about fire safety. 60% were influenced to take precautions. Over 50% now regularly check smoke alarms.

Client objective 5: To reduce death and injury by over 20%.
Result: Injuries down 23%. Deaths well below government set target of 28 per annum (only 8 deaths).

NEW LEARNINGS

- **Phase 1:** That handprints on walls could be used to create a message to those responsible for the death of others.
- **Phase 2:** Feelings of invincibility meant we had to personalise the vulnerability that anyone may be the victim.
- **Phase 3:** Consumer misconceptions of how fire and smoke perform drawn from fictitious dramas were redressed with graphic images to demonstrate the reality of no chance of escape.
- **Phase 4:** Reprogramming people that the safety of your family was **far** more important than ensuring the safety of mere possessions.

RETURN ON INVESTMENT

Value of lives saved
Table 12.3 indicates the notional savings that the lives saved are worth £132.9 million – assuming a monetary value of £1.357 million per life saved[38] and a government set target of diminishing 28 deaths per annum.

Table 12.3

Year	Fatalities	Total monetary value of human life
2004/2005	8	£27.1 million
2005/2006	5	£31.2 million
2006/2007	13	£20.4 million
2007/2008	8	£27.1 million
2008/2009	8	£27.1 million
Total		**£132.9 million**

Value of services saved
Table 12.4 indicates the actual savings of £3.9 million delivered by not having to mobilise NIFRS services using an average incident cost of £2184.[39]

Table 12.4

Year	Accidental dwellings fires	Savings to NIFRS
2003/04	1110	N/A
2004/05	969	£775,320
2005/06	899	£982,800
2006/07	825	£1,089,816
2007/08	837	£1,063,608
Total		**£3,911,544**

Value of property saved

Table 12.5 demonstrates actual value in average damage to property saved amounting to £44 million.

Table 12.5

Year	Accidental dwellings fires	Savings against damage to domestic property
2003/04	1110	N/A
2004/05	969	£8,875,000
2005/06	899	£10,625,000
2006/07	825	£12,475,000
2007/08	837	£12,175,000
Total		**£44,150,000**

Overall, the campaign achieved an 80.4:1 rate of return on investment, i.e. for the £2.25 million spent, total savings of lives, property and economical costs achieved amounted to around £181 million (Table 12.6).

Table 12.6 Return on investment summary

Total savings to life + property + economy	Total marketing investment phases 1–4	Return on investment
£181 million	£2.25 million	80.4 : 1

Source: Stephen Roycroft – Ardmore Advertising; Institute of Practitioners in Advertising: IPA Effectiveness Awards 2009; Creative from Xtreme Information.

Summary

This chapter has focused on the role that creativity plays when developing social marketing campaigns. Creativity is important to cut through the clutter – but the need to stand out (perhaps through being overly creative) needs to be balanced with the strategic goals and objectives of a campaign. In this context, it is important to consider that various campaign elements should work together synergistically. Special consideration must also be given to the target audience; taking into account their motivational stage, typical media usage, cultural context and education level. Ultimately, expert knowledge (especially through careful scoping when planning the intervention), imagination, intuition and logic will help to strike a careful balance when connecting ideas and objectives.

CHAPTER REVIEW QUESTIONS

1 Define 'creativity' in social marketing. How important do you believe it is in communication effectiveness? Justify your response.

2 Locate three examples of social marketing intervention creativity other than those discussed in this text. Critique them in terms of their creative approaches. What suggestions can you make to improve their creativity in future?

3 Locate three leaflets or pamphlets encouraging health-related behaviours. Analyse their readability. What advice can you give to their designers?

4 What challenges do you believe new media present and how should social marketers overcome them?

5 Visit at least two of the social media sites noted in the chapter. Critique their content. What improvements would you recommend making?

Recommended reading

Ang, S.H. and Low, S.Y.M. (2000) Exploring the Dimensions of Ad Creativity. *Psychology and Marketing,* 17 (10), 835–54.

Davies, M. (2000) Using an Analytic Hierarchy Process in Advertising Creativity. *Creativity and Innovation Management,* 9 (2), 100–8.

Haberland, G.S. and Dacin, P.A. (1992) The Development of a Measure to Assess Viewers' Judgments of the Creativity of an Advertisement. *Advances in Consumer Research,* 19 (1), 817.

Hicks, J.J. (2001) The Strategy Behind Florida's 'Truth' Campaign. *Tobacco Control,* 10 (1), 3–5.

Rothschild, M.L., Mastin, B. and Miller, T.W. (2006) Reducing Alcohol-impaired Driving Crashes through the Use of Social Marketing. *Accident Analysis & Prevention,* 38 (6), 1218–30.

Shimp, T.E. (2007) *Advertising, Promotion and Supplemental Aspects of IMC* (7th edn). Mason, OH: Thomson South-Western.

White, A.W. (2007) *Advertising Design and Typography*. New York: Allworth Press.

Whittingham, J.R.D., Ruiter, R.A.C., Castermans, D., Huiberts, A. and Kok, G. (2007) Designing Effective Health Education Materials: Experimental Pre-testing of a Theory-based Brochure to Increase Knowledge. *Health Education Research,* 23 (3), 414–26.

Websites

British Dyslexia Association: http://www.bdadyslexia.org.uk/about-dyslexia/further-information/dyslexia-style-guide.html

European Blind Union: http://www.euroblind.org/search/search.pl?terms=clear+print+guidelines&Realm=euroblind.org&set%3Alang=english

Royal National Institute for the Blind: http://www.rnib.org.uk/professionals/accessibleinformation/printedmaterials/Pages/printed_material.aspx

Plain English Campaign: http://www.plainenglish.co.uk/

Notes

1 Koslow, S., Sasser, S.L. and Riordan, E.A. (2003) What Is Creative to Whom and Why? Perceptions in Advertising Agencies. *Journal of Advertising Research,* 43 (1), 96–110.

2 El-Murad, J. and West, D.C. (2003) Risk and Creativity in Advertising. *Journal of Marketing Management,* 19 (5/6), 657–73.

3 Shipp, S., Lamb Jr, C.W. and Mokwa, M.P. (1993) Developing and Enhancing Marketing Students' Skills: Written and Oral Communication, Intuition, Creativity, and Computer Usage. *Marketing Education Review,* 3 (3), 2–8.

4 Evans, 1991, cited in Shipp et al. (1993) above.

5 Linnan, L.A. and Ferguson, Y.O. (2007) Beauty Salons: A Promising Health Promotion Setting for Reaching and Promoting Health Among African American Women. *Health Education & Behavior,* 34 (3), 517–30.

6 Bates, C. (2009) Scaling New Heights: Piano Stairway Encourages Commuters to Ditch the Escalators. MailOnline, 12 October. Accessed from: http://www.dailymail.co.uk

7 Fishbein, M. and Cappella, J. (2006) The Role of Theory in Developing Effective Health Communications. *Journal of Communication,* 56 (August Supplement), S1–S17.

8 Jones, S., Eagle, L.C., Kemp, G. and Hughes, R. (2009) Social Marketing-Based Strategy for Sun Protection Interventions: Supplementary Document – Quantitative Benchmark: Cornwall PCT Region. Report Prepared for South West Public Health Observatory, and Eagle, L.C., Kemp, G.A. and Jones, S. (2008) Social Marketing-Based Sun Protection Intervention Strategy for Cornwall PCT – A Pilot. Report for South West Public Health Observatory, Bristol.

9 Dahl, S. and Ebrahimjee, M. (2011) Golden Moves, Proceedings of the 14th IRSPM Conference, Dublin: Trinity College, 11–13 April, 2011.

10 Sly, D.F., Heald, G.R. and Ray, S. (2001) The Florida 'Truth' Anti-tobacco Media Evaluation: Design, First Year Results, and Implications for Planning Future State Media Evaluations. *Tobacco Control,* 10 (1), 9–15.

11 Niederdeppe, J., Farrelly, M.C. and Haviland, M.L. (2004) Confirming 'Truth': More Evidence of a Successful Tobacco Countermarketing Campaign in Florida. *American Journal of Public Health,* 94 (2), 255–7.

12 Till, B.D. and Baack, D.W. (2005) Recall and Persuasion: Does Creative Advertising Matter? *Journal of Advertising,* 34 (3), 47–57.

13 West, D.C., Kover, A.J. and Caruana, A. (2008) Practitioner and Customer Views of Advertising Creativity. *Journal of Advertising,* 37 (4), 35–45.

14 Dahlen, M., Rosengren, S. and Torn, F. (2008) Advertising Creativity Matters. *Journal of Advertising Research,* 48 (3), 392–403.

15 Kover, A.J., Goldberg, S.M. and James, W.L. (1995) Creativity vs. Effectiveness? An Integrating Classification for Advertising. *Journal of Advertising Research,* 35 (6), 29–40.

16 Martinez-Donate, A.P., Zellner, J.A., Sañudo, F., Fernandez-Cerdeño, A., Hovell, M.F., Sipan, C.L., Engleberg M. and Carrillo, H. (2010) Hombres Sanos : Evaluation of a Social Marketing Campaign for Heterosexually Identified Latino Men Who Have Sex with Men and Women, *American Journal of Public Health,* 100 (12, December), 2532–40.

17 Dahl, S. and Ebrahimjee, M. (2011) Visceral Clues: Are we too Good to do Good? Proceedings of the 15th Academy of Marketing Conference, 5–7 July 2011, Liverpool: University of Liverpool.

18 Eagle, L.C., Hawkins, J.C., Styles, E. and Reid, J. (2006) Breaking Through the Invisible Barrier of Low Functional Literacy: Implications for Health Communication. *Studies in Communication Sciences,* 5 (2), 29–55.

19 Friedman, D. and Hoffman-Goetz, L. (2006) A Systematic Reivew of Readability and Comprehension Instruments Used for Print and Web-Based Cancer Information. *Health Education & Behavior,* 33 (3), 352–73.

20 Adkins, N.R. and Ozanne, J.L. (2005) The Low Literate Consumer. *Journal of Consumer Research,* 32 (1), 93–105.

21 Office for National Statistics (2000) International Adult Literacy Survey 2007, from http://www.statistics.gov.uk/ssd/surveys/european_adult_literacy_review_survey.asp

22 Wallendorf, M. (2001) Literally Literacy. *Journal of Consumer Research,* 27 (4), 505–11.

23 Guttman, N. and Salmon, C.T. (2004) Guilt, Fear, Stigma and Knowledge Gaps: Ethical Issues in Public Health Communication Interventions. *Bioethics,* 18 (6), 531–52.

24 Shea, J., Beers, B., McDonald, V., Quistberg, D.A., Ravenell, K., Asch, D., et al. (2004) Assessing Health Literacy in African American and Caucasian Adults: Disparities in Rapid Estimate of Adult Literacy in Medicine (REALM) Scores. *Family Medicine,* 36 (8), 575–81.

25 Basic Skills Agency (2000) data accessed from: http://www.literacytrust.org.uk/Database/adultres.html

26 The Commons Public Accounts Committee (May 2006) Employer's perspective on improving skills for employment. Accessed 18 February 2008 http://www.publications.parliament.uk/pa/cm200506/cmselect/cmpubacc/cmpubacc.htm

27 Hoffman, T., McKenna, K., Worrall, L. and Read, S. (2004) Evaluating Current Practice in the Provision of Written Information to Stroke Patients and Their Carers. *International Journal of Therapy and Rehabilitation,* 11 (7), 303–9.

28 Wallace, L. and Lemon, E. (2004) American Academy of Family Physicians Patient Education Materials: Can Patients Read Them? *Family Medicine Journal,* 36 (8), 571–5.

29 McLaughlin, G.H. (1969) SMOG Grading: A New Readability Formula. *Journal of Reading,* 12 (8), 639–46.

30 Shea, J., Beers, B., McDonald, V., Quistberg, D.A., Ravenell, K., Asch, D., et al. (2004) Op. cit.

31 Chubaty, A., Sadowski, C.A. and Carrie, A.G. (2009) Typeface legibility of patient information leaflets intended for community-dwelling seniors. *Age and Ageing,* 38 (4), 441–7.

32 Hamil, S.D. (2008) To Slow Speeders, Philadelphia Tries Make-Believe. New York Times, July 12. Accessed from http://www.nytimes.com

33 Dahl, S. (2010) Social Media for the Social Good, Middlesex University Discussion Paper, London: Middlesex University, available at SSRN: http://ssrn.com/abstract=1624522

34 Barb Infosys, based on the delivery of 360 TVRs over this period.

35 TGI survey: http://www.tgisurveys.com.

36 Ibid.

37 Ibid.

38 *The Economic Cost of Fire: Estimates for 2004* (2006) Office of the Deputy Prime Minister.

39 Northern Ireland Fire and Rescue Service finance department.

Chapter 13

Media planning

Chapter objectives

On completing this chapter, you should be able to:

- explain the principles of planning traditional mass media such as television, radio, newspapers or magazines;
- discuss the issue of advertising weight versus duration of an advertising schedule across a budget period;
- critically review the enduring debate over whether advertising (and, by extension, all forms of marketing communication in the current era) is a strong or weak force;
- discuss the strengths and weaknesses of major media;
- review qualitative factors that should also be considered in planning media.

Basic media planning principles

Media planning is the process by which advertising budgets are allocated to different types of media such as television, radio or newspapers, and to specific vehicles (television programmes or publications) over a budget period. Media planning does not operate in isolation; it is part of the overall marketing strategy process and is developed at the same time as programmes are developed for all other marketing activity, especially other promotional activity such as sales promotions and public relations.[1] Planning is based on simple principles:

- *What are the objectives?* What goals should be set and what exactly do we want each part of the media programme to do? For example, is the task primarily to build a specific image or to provide detailed product information?
- *What alternatives are there?* In which ways could the objectives be achieved? What are their relative strengths and weaknesses?

- *Which alternative offers the best chance of achieving the objectives?* Consider here the resources available in terms of budget, existing material such as television advertisements or magazine advertisements, timing and the availability of media time and space.

In evaluating different media options, the standard measurement tools available focus on the following:

- The number or percentage of the target group reached with an advertising message or group of messages in a specific time frame (rating points, or target audience rating points: 'TARPS').

- The average number of times (frequency) that a member of the target group is likely to see these messages, and the frequency distribution (i.e. what percentage will see only one message, two, three, etc.).

- The cost of achieving this, usually measured either in terms of cost per percentage of the target group reached (generally referred to as 'cost per rating point', 'cost per TARP' or 'CPT') or in terms of cost per thousand (the latter is usually shown as CPM, M being the Latin numeral for 1000, to avoid confusion with CPT) of the target group reached. However, while it may be possible to compare the cost-efficiency of advertisements across different media through comparing CPT or CPM measures, these measures do not allow an objective assessment of the communication effectiveness of different media.[2]

Terms such as 'TARPS', 'reach' and 'frequency' themselves appear to be straightforward, but disguise the complexity of the media environment. The media planning literature reveals an ongoing debate centred on 'How much is enough?'[3,4] For example, while reach × frequency = total TARPS, schedules with the same number of TARPS may achieve a very different balance of reach and frequency, depending on the type of media purchased:

- A schedule of 210 TARPS that is entirely made up of advertisements in high-rating prime-time television shows may reach 70% of the target group, an average of three times ($70 \times 3 = 210$).

- A schedule of 210 TARPS that is made up of off-peak time may reach 30% of the target group, but will be seen an average of seven times ($30 \times 7 = 210$).

Which schedule is likely to be more effective depends on what is being advertised, the brand equity and the budget available for the advertising programme. In terms of cost and effectiveness, advertising can vary widely and decisions are often complex – for example, a full-page advertisement in the *Telegraph* costs around £46,000,[5] similar to a full-page advertisement in *The Sun*[6] – despite largely different audiences and numbers. Similarly, television advertising varies by region and station – as well as by time when the advertisement is being shown (e.g. evenings are more expensive than daytime).

How much is enough?

The next question that has occupied academics and practitioners for almost 50 years is what level of exposure (frequency) is optimum over a specific period of time (usually a week or a product purchase cycle). A considerable body of literature has built up debating this.[7, 8, 9] There appears to be a widely held belief in commercial marketing that a frequency of less than three is ineffective and a frequency of more than 10 will lead to 'wear-out' (exposure fatigue)[10] which may lead to irritation on the part of those 'exposed' to the advertising.

Marketers are, or should be, aware of the implications of excessive spending. These implications include questions as to whether advertisements that are frequently repeated send positive signals about product quality and the marketer's commitment, or negative signals that excessive advertising equates to lower brand quality – or even a sense of desperation to sell the product.[11]

This 'wisdom' is based on research conducted during a period when there were far fewer media options than there are now and thus the relevance of such indicators to current media planning must be questioned. For example, a landmark study which investigated whether intense concentrations (bursts) of advertising were more effective than spreading the advertising over more weeks but using fewer exposures per week was based on mailing reprints of a newspaper advertisement for a household product to women selected from a telephone directory in the 1950s.[12]

Opinion remains divided, with some suggesting continuity of exposure to ensure that advertisements reach potential purchasers as close to the purchase decision time as possible rather than adhering to the minimum number of exposures suggested above.[13] The debate has long occupied marketing communication theorists and practitioners alike, with considerable discussion of aspects such as the trade-off between reach and frequency;[14] exposure distributions;[15, 16] continuity;[17] and the use of models to estimate the effectiveness of media schedules.[18] The debate centres on very different perceptions of the persuasive power of advertising.

Advertising as a strongly persuasive force

The impact of advertising has historically been viewed[19, 20] as following a 'hierarchy of effects', a concept that originated a century ago in personal selling literature, in which consumers move through a series of stages from initial awareness of a product (A) through exposure to its advertising, to interest in the product (I), desire for the product (D) and finally action (A) in terms of purchase behaviour (the AIDA model).

The view of advertising as a strongly persuasive force in all market sectors remains a major theme in both academic and practitioner literature, particularly that originating from the USA. It has maintained its dominance in spite of challenges launched over more than 30 years by a number of, mostly British, academics who worked primarily, but not exclusively, on frequently purchased goods in mature markets.[21, 22] This lengthy battle to gain acknowledgement that the 'strong force' does not apply to all market sectors is well documented[23] and can be summed up as follows:

> The assumption that advertising equals persuasion is so ingrained in the USA that to challenge it elicits much the same reaction as questioning your partner's parentage.[24]

Advertising as a weaker, primarily repurchase reminder force

There is a body of evidence that supports claims that a great deal of advertising for routine products and services has much weaker impact on consumers than for products that have higher consumer involvement.[25] For low-involvement products, there is an expectation that familiar brands in a product category will be similar in performance to each other and that there is therefore minimal incentive for consumers to pay attention to advertising for these brands.[26]

Further support for the concept of a weak force theory of advertising's influence is provided by product preferences often being formed after an initial trial. In low-involvement purchasing, experience with a product is a stronger influence on future purchasing decisions than is advertising, which is regarded as primarily reinforcing existing preferences and helping to defend consumers' perceptions of a brand.[27]

It is suggested that consumers make one of three choices: distinguish between optimising choice on the basis of proven brand performance superiority; satisficing with the first 'acceptable' brand in a brand repertoire being selected; or indifference. This latter choice mechanism operates in low-involvement purchasing when the only search for information undertaken is restricted to identification of a brand and the purchase choice is based on buying the first brand out of a set they like.

For social marketing, the task is much more complex. While we would like to think that those we target would become highly involved in the interventions we design, as we have noted in earlier chapters, social marketers are often faced with target groups that display lack of interest and apathy and believe that they are unlikely to be affected by health and lifestyle risks. Communications have to work hard to break through the barriers and to generate interest in the topic – especially when it involves getting people to do things they don't want to do – or to stop doing things they would rather continue doing.

The reality is that the strength of advertising is situation-specific; at times it can be strongly persuasive, at other times it fulfils a much weaker, primarily reminder role.

So how much should we spend?

It is suggested that marketers who view advertising as an investment will spend to the level necessary to maximise the return on investment.[28] However, this may lead to levels of investment that, at first sight, often cause disbelief,

> The overriding consensus is that there are no willing advertisers. Each time the decision is made to spend money on advertising it is only because the manufacturer or retailer does not know of a more efficient, more economical way of generating sales of his product.[29]

In the case of fast-moving consumer goods (FMCG) that rely on distribution via major supermarket chains, advertising may be a means by which distribution/shelf space is maintained.[30] An additional factor that impacts on the weight of advertising is the need to keep a presence in the market as brand images and awareness levels decline over time. Not only do people forget advertising over time, but competitive advertising activity may negatively impact on a brand's perceptions,[31] although this latter interference may impact less on familiar brands than on unfamiliar ones.[32]

Again, social marketing faces very different market dynamics – spending the same as commercial competitors is often beyond the resources available. However, maintaining a level of advertising repetition relative to competitive advertising is important, as a reinforcement of brand associations which need to be easily recalled by the target groups at the point of behaviour change and of action.[33]

Thus, there are no simple checklists that can be provided regarding the relative importance of reach versus frequency or whether advertising should be concentrated at heavy levels of TARPS or spread over more weeks at lower levels.

Media choices

Obvious factors to consider in deciding on which media to include and how much of the available budget to allocate to each one are:

- A thorough understanding of the target groups for the advertising – and specifically an understanding of their media usage habits – is absolutely vital to ensure appropriate media channel selection and to deliver precisely targeted advertising activity.

- The overall marketing objectives for the product or service and the way all elements of the marketing mix may work together. It would be futile to plan for a media schedule centred on television advertising that enabled an up-market image to be portrayed if there are plans to discount the product heavily or to undertake major price discount-based sales promotion activity. The planned creative approach intended may also influence the type of media that may be considered, such as whether a detailed product demonstration is recommended, or whether the creative approach will be based on the portrayal of emotional or rational appeals.

- A detailed analysis of past competitive activity in order to predict likely future activity and to decide whether to match their activity in terms of media options or to find channels with lower levels of competitive activity. The latter may reduce the risk on potential effectiveness being adversely impacted by the 'clutter' of other messages.[34]

- The resources available. There is no point in planning a substantial multimedia programme with heavy weights (in terms of TARPS) of advertising if there is insufficient funding available to sustain the programme.

Each type of media has specific strengths and weaknesses. For example, television has credibility with both consumers and retailers, and reaches substantial audiences. It also enables product demonstration. However, advertising time is expensive and commercial production costs high, so TV advertising is often beyond the budgets of small and many not-for-profit organisations.

To highlight more examples of the strengths and weaknesses of other media in a far from exhaustive list:

- Radio offers more regional, demographic and psychographic selectivity but can often be a passive 'background' medium.

- Newspapers lack the high-colour reproduction qualities of magazines (other than via pre-printed inserts) but can communicate a large amount of detail that is not possible via short (usually 30-second duration) radio or television advertisements. (Remember: in 30 seconds, only some 75 words are possible.)

You should be able to draw up an extensive list of the strengths and weaknesses of all media under consideration, with different items taking on more or less importance according to the nature of the product or service for which the advertising programme is being developed. Each selected medium should complement other media selected so that the cumulative effect is greater than their individual contributions.[35, 36]

Consider how the various media can be used individually or in combination for a company providing holidays to tropical locations. Television might enable a range of locations, such as beautiful beaches and waving palm trees, to be shown, together with a range of water sports. Radio, using the soundtrack of the television commercial, may be used for 'imagery transfer', to recall the television advertisement and extend activity between or beyond more expensive television flights. Radio may be concentrated only in selected areas which are deemed to be the most important markets. Magazines may feature a visual from the television commercial and give summary details of the travel agency outlets, or provide website details. Newspapers may provide specific details of local travel agency branches, including street addresses and telephone numbers as well as website details, and may also provide more details about specific prices and packages than is possible in other media. Cinema might complement media such as television.[37] How might the choice of media alter if the primary target audience was families with young children, young singles, or older but unconfident holiday makers?

An additional aspect of media use that has also been largely ignored in much of the academic literature is the issue of simultaneous use, in which consumers may be using several media forms such as the internet and either television or radio at the same time.[38] For instance, research has shown that, in the USA, 32.7 % of males and 36.4% of females watch television while they are online, with the two media becoming either foreground or background depending on the task and interest.[39] There is no data available on simultaneous

Figure 13.1 Simultaneous media use
Source: Alamy/MBI.

media use in other markets, and the way in which messages across these media may interact and reinforce each other is totally unresearched.

In addition to these factors, other, more subtle factors need to be considered, including the impact of media context on communication effectiveness.

Media context

Imagine the way an advertisement for an airline would be perceived within a television programme or a magazine feature on romantic overseas holidays as compared to a programme or feature on the dangers of travel, including accidents, risk of illness, robbery or violence. An advertisement for cake mixes is likely to be perceived very differently within an environment centred on the benefits of cooking than in an environment which shows graphic images of reconstructive surgery as a result of accidents. However, the latter may be a very effective environment into which road safety or alcohol moderation messages could be placed.

Where there is low involvement in a product category, but advertisements for the product are embedded in a context that is similar ('congruent'), attitudes towards the advertisement have been found to be more positive than when they appear in an environment that sharply contrasts with the tone of the advertisement.[40] Positive contexts appear to lead to more positive attitudes to advertisements placed within them, although different effects may occur for familiar versus unfamiliar brands.[41]

There may be some very pragmatic reasons for avoiding placing advertisements within a movie or television programme containing high levels of violence, as there is evidence that communication effectiveness may be compromised. Advertisements shown in this type of environment achieve less favourable reported attitudes both towards the specific advertisement and the advertised brand than when the same commercial is used in an environment that does not contain violence.[42]

The rational hierarchy of effects models reviewed earlier reflects a very positivist view of 'what advertising does' to apparently passive receivers.[43] In fact, people are far from passive and may construct their own realities and meanings from the combinations of communications to which they choose to pay attention. Social contexts may also influence the effects of advertisements. For example, in group interactions when people discuss the interpretation of advertising, or its creative executions, those individuals who are not familiar with specific advertisements may be excluded from group interactions.[44]

What is becoming increasingly clear is that social marketers must adopt a very different mindset from that of the past and consider what people do with the range of marketing communications they use[45] – which may not be conventional advertising. In today's volatile and rapidly changing marketplace, 'the communication challenge is to consider all contact points with customers and thus every channel of communication is a medium'.[46] This becomes particularly important when considering new, primarily electronic media forms in which people may co-create the context of the media, as evident with social media sites. The implications of new media for effective communication strategies are the focus of the rest of this chapter.

Planning for new media

New media have added significant opportunities and additional contact points with customers. Particular advantages over traditional media are the advanced metrics and targeting options that are available for most modern media forms. For example, website users can be targeted not only by the website they are using, but also on the basis of their location (i.e. the location of the computer they are using) – and each display of an advertisement can be counted and click-through rates recorded and tracked. However, while there is an active debate about which measures should be used – and indeed if traditional measures are adequate to evaluate new media,[47] measurement data is easily available and generally accessible.

A more important barrier to effective communication remains the challenge of maintaining a coherent message across different media forms, and integrating messages in both traditional and new media, i.e. achieving what could be called 'interactive integrated media communications' – or 'interactive IMC'.[48] Finding an appropriate mix of new and traditional media forms and comparing effectiveness is a difficult task, especially given the often different consumption environment.

Some new media, for example websites, could be argued to be similar in terms of consumption environment to traditional media. While superior in terms of measurement, websites share many similarities with traditional print media, i.e. visitors tend to visit websites because of the content – and advertising placed on these websites is perceived only peripherally: the visitor is seen as mostly passive in terms of advertising consumption.

Other new media types offer more diverse forms of media opportunities, and a very different consumption environment. For example, in the case of in-game advertising, where adverts are placed inside games, the players are often immersed in the game action. This immersion in the action has been linked with decreased persuasion knowledge and reactance potential.[49] Advertising can then be part of the surroundings, i.e. as part of the games background – or indeed it can be a more active part of the game, as when individual objects are placed inside the game and become part of the game narrative (e.g. the Best Buy store in the CityVille game).

While placing advertisements or objects within games is attractive because it allows the advertiser to buy into the existing user-base of the games, sometimes developing own games

Figure 13.2 QR code for http://stephan.dahl.at/

can be beneficial. For instance, online games can be a fun, effective and interactive way to teach children, or to educate consumers about safer sex.[50]

Online content can be used to enhance messages in traditional media by providing additional information and/or interactive content, as previously discussed. QR (or quick response) codes, which can be scanned by smart phones and direct the phones to further information online, or applications to download etc. (see Figure 13.2), can provide a way to link offline advertising with online content, which is easier and more convenient and flexible to navigate than traditional websites.

Social media

Social media represent a different media platform that needs to be integrated into the overall communication plan. Because the content is largely consumer-generated, planning is less straightforward and involves more complex scenarios than traditional media planning. While for traditional media (and purchased advertising on websites and in games) the media vehicle, the message and the timing can be accurately planned, all of these are less predictable in a social media environment.

As the consumers are in control of both creating the message and passing the message on, much of the planning focuses on creating a message that is engaging and that offers the potential to 'go viral'. Once a message has been created, internet metrics can be used to determine the success of the campaign. Commercial tools can track topics discussed through social networks, such as blogs (e.g. blogpulse.com) or mentions and repeats of messages can be measured on social networks such as Twitter.

Summary

Planning the media campaign is an important and integral part of the campaign planning. Once core messages have been identified, tasks have to be distributed across different media classes (e.g. traditional, online, social). After prioritising the cost-effectiveness of each media platform, appropriate choices can be made in order to maximise effectiveness and impact. For this, the planner needs to understand the relative strengths and weaknesses of the various media choices – as metrics alone are inadequate as a guide to how effective a media campaign is likely to be. An effectively planned campaign combines different media choices synergistically in order to avoid clutter and engages audiences – for example, by combining traditional advertising campaigns, linked via QR codes to online games where the content of the advertising campaign can be illustrated as part of an online game experience.

CHAPTER REVIEW QUESTIONS

1 How important do you believe traditional media are in the current environment relative to newer communication options?

2 How might you determine the impact of simultaneous media usage among adolescents?

3 You are considering purchasing advertising time in a newly released movie showing in cinemas. The movie has received severe criticism for gratuitous violence. Does this affect your decision as to whether to buy advertising or not? Would your decision change once the movie is released for screening on television?

4 You are considering purchasing television advertising in a US-originated programme which rates well against your primary target group but which is known to contain product placements for a competing brand. Discuss your options.

5 How might creative factors affect media objectives and strategies? Give examples to illustrate your answer.

6 Draw up a table of the strengths and weaknesses of:

Television

Radio

Newspapers

Magazines

Cinema

Outdoor advertising (posters, hoardings etc.)

The internet

as advertising media.

Now critically discuss how the importance of any factors you listed might change for:

Fast-moving consumer goods

Durable goods such as washing machines

Cars

Overseas holidays

Charity fund-raising

Social marketing for energy conservation and for sun protection.

7 Using examples you are familiar with, discuss how you can use social media. What are the strengths and weaknesses of using new media?

8 How can you maintain message consistency amongst traditional media and new media, especially social media?

Recommended reading

Ambler, T. (2000) Persuasion, Pride and Prejudice: How Ads Work. *International Journal of Advertising*, 19 (3), 299–315.

Donnelly, W.J. (1996) *Planning Media Strategy*. Upper Saddle River, NJ: Prentice Hall.

Heath, R. and Feldwick, P. (2008) Fifty Years Using the Wrong Model of Advertising. *International Journal of Market Research*, 50 (1), 29–59.

Pilotta, J.J. and Schultz, D. (2005) Simultaneous Media Experience and Synesthesia. *Journal of Advertising Research*, 45 (1), 19–26.

Pilotta, J.J., Schultz, D.E., Drenik, G. and Rist, P. (2005) Simultaneous Media Usage: A Critical Consumer Orientation to Media Planning. *Journal of Consumer Behavior*, 3 (3), 285–92.

Notes

1 Parente, D. (2004) *Advertising Campaign Planning: A Guide to Marketing Communication Plans* (3rd edn). Mason, OH: Thomson South-Western.

2 Shimp, T.E. (2003) *Advertising, Promotion and Supplemental Aspects of IMC* (6th edn). Mason, OH: Thomson South-Western.

3 Krugman, H.E. (2000) Memory Without Recall, Exposure Without Perception. *Journal of Advertising Research,* 40 (6), 49–54.

4 Naples, M.J. (1979) *Effective Frequency.* New York: Association of National Advertisers.

5 http://i.telegraph.co.uk/telegraph/multimedia/archive/01790/Rate_Card_1790821a.pdf

6 http://nicommercial.com/assets/pdfs/NGN%20Display%20Rate%20Card%20Oct-2010.pdf

7 Krugman, H.E. (1984) Why Three Exposures May Be Enough. *Journal of Advertising Research,* 24 (4), 15–18.

8 Boivin, Y. and Coulombe, D. (1990) Are Exposure Distributions Really Necessary? *Current Issues & Research in Advertising,* 13 (1), 227.

9 Sissors, J.Z. and Surmanek, J. (1986) *Advertising Media Planning.* Lincolnwood, IL: NTC Business Books.

10 Blair, M.H. (2000) An Empirical Investigation of Advertising Wearin and Wearout. *Journal of Advertising Research,* 40 (6), 95–100.

11 Kirmani, A. (1997) Advertising Repetition as a Signal of Quality: If It's Advertised So Much, Something Must Be Wrong. *Journal of Advertising,* 26 (3), 77–86.

12 Zielske, H.A. (1959) The Remembering and Forgetting of Advertising. *Journal of Marketing,* 23 (3), 239–43.

13 Ephron, E. (1995) More Weeks, Less Weight: The Shelf-space Model of Advertising. *Journal of Advertising Research,* 35 (3), 18–23.

14 Percy, L., Rossiter, J.R. and Elliott, R. (2001) Media Strategy. In *Strategic Advertising Management.* Oxford: Oxford University Press.

15 Boivin, Y. and Coulombe, D. (1990) Op. cit.

16 Cannon, H.M., Leckenby, J.D. and Abernethy, A. (2002) Beyond Effective Frequency: Evaluating Media Schedules Using Frequency Value Planning. *Journal of Advertising Research,* 42 (6), 33–47.

17 Ephron, E. (1995) Op. cit.

18 Ha, L. (1995) Media Models and Advertising Effects: Conceptualization and Theoretical Implications. *Journal of Current Issues & Research in Advertising,* 17 (2), 1–15.

19 Barry, T.E. (1987) The Development of the Hierarchy of Effects: A Historical Perspective. *Journal of Current Issues & Research In Advertising,* 10 (2), 251–95.

20 Barry, T.F. and Howard, D.J. (1990) A Review and Critique of the Hierarchy of Effects in Advertising. *International Journal of Advertising,* 9 (2), 121–35.

21 Ehrenberg, A.S.C. (1974) Repetitive Advertising and the Consumer. *Journal of Advertising Research,* 14 (2), 25.

22 Ehrenberg, A.S.C., Barnard, N. and Scriven, J.A. (1997) Justifying Our Advertising Budgets. *Marketing and Research Today,* 25 (1), 38–44.

23 Jones, J.P. (1990) Advertising: Strong Force or Weak Force? Two Views an Ocean Apart. *International Journal of Advertising,* 9 (3), 233–46.

24 Ambler, T. (2000) Persuasion, Pride and Prejudice: How Ads Work. *International Journal of Advertising,* 19 (3), 299.

25 Helgesen, T. (1992) The Rationality of Advertising Decisions: Conceptual Issues and Some Empirical Findings From a Norwegian Study. *Journal of Advertising Research,* 32 (6), 22–30.

26 Heath, R. (2001) Low Involvement Processing – A New Model of Brand Communication. *Journal of Marketing Communications,* 7 (1), 27–33.

27 Vakratas, D. and Ambler, T. (1999) 'How Advertising Works: What Do We really Know?' *Journal of Marketing,* 63 (1), 26–43.

28 Danaher, P.J. and Rust, R.T. (1994) Determining the Optimal Level of Media Spending. *Journal of Advertising Research,* 34 (1), 28–34.

29 Flandin, M.P., Martin, E. and Simkin, L.P. (1992) Advertising Effectiveness Research: A Survey of Agencies, Clients and Conflicts. *International Journal of Advertising,* 11 (3), 204.

30 Schultz, D.E. (2001) Ehrenberg's FMCG Ad Analysis Background is Showing. *Marketing Research,* 13 (3), 38–9.

31 Burke, R.R. and Srull, T.K. (1988) Competitive Interference and Consumer Memory for Advertising. *Journal of Consumer Research,* 15 (1), 55–68.

32 Kent, R.J. and Allen, C.T. (1994) Competitive Interference Effects in Consumer Memory for Advertising: The Role of Brand Familiarity. *Journal of Marketing,* 58 (3), 97–105.

33 D'Souza, G. and Rao, R.C. (1995) Can Repeating an Advertisement More Frequently than the Competition Affect Brand Preference? *Journal of Marketing,* 59 (2), 32.

34 Ha, L. and Litman, B.R. (1997) Does Advertising Clutter Have Diminishing and Negative Returns? *Journal of Advertising,* 26 (1), 31–42.

35 Naik, P.A. and Raman, K. (2003) Understanding the Impact of Synergy in Multimedia Communications. *Journal of Marketing Research,* 40 (4), 375–88.

36 Kliatchko, J. (2005) Towards a New Definition of Integrated Marketing Communications (IMC). *International Journal of Advertising,* 24 (1), 7–34.

37 Ewing, M.T., du Plessis, E. and Foster, C. (2001) Cinema Advertising Re-Considered. *Journal of Advertising Research,* 41 (1), 78–85.

38 Pilotta, J.J. and Schultz, D. (2005) Simultaneous Media Experience and Synesthesia. *Journal of Advertising Research,* 45 (1), 19–26.

39 Pilotta, J.J., Schultz, D.E., Drenik, G. and Rist, P. (2005) Simultaneous Media Usage: A Critical Consumer Orientation to Media Planning. *Journal of Consumer Behavior,* 3 (3), 285–92.

40 De Pelsmacker, P., Geuens, M. and Anckaert, P. (2002) Media Context and Advertising Effectiveness: The Role of Context Appreciation and Context/Ad Similarity. *Journal of Advertising,* 31 (2), 49–61.

41 Janssens, W. and De Pelsmacker, P. (2005) Advertising for New and Existing Brands: The Impact of Media Context and Type of Advertisement. *Journal of Marketing Communications,* 11 (2), 113–28.

42 Prasad, V.K. and Smith, L.J. (1994) Television Commercials in Violent Programming: An Experimental Evaluation of Their Effects on Children. *Journal of the Academy of Marketing Science,* 22 (4), 340–51.

43 Heath, R. and Feldwick, P. (2008) Fifty Years Using the Wrong Model of Advertising. *International Journal of Market Research,* 50 (1), 29–59.

44 Ritson, M. and Elliott, R. (1999) The Social Uses of Advertising: An Ethnographic Study of Adolescent Advertising Audiences. *Journal of Consumer Research,* 26 (3), 260–77.

45 Shankar, A. (1999) Advertising's Imbroglio. *Journal of Marketing Communications*, 5 (1), 1–15.

46 Jenkinson, A. (2006) Planning and Evaluating Communications in an Integrated Organisation. *Journal of Targeting, Measurement and Analysis for Marketing,* 15 (1), 51.

47 Stewart, D.W. and Pavlou, P.A. (2002) From Consumer Response to Active Consumer: Measuring the Effectiveness of Interactive Media. *Journal of the Academy of Marketing Science,* 30 (4), 376–96.

48 Peltier, J.W., Schibrowsky, J.A. and Schultz, D.E. (2003) Interactive Integrated Marketing Communication: Combining the Power of IMC, the New Media and Database Marketing. *International Journal of Advertising,* 22 (1), 93–116.

49 An, S. and Stern, S. (2011) Mitigating the Effects of Advergames on Children. *Journal of Advertising,* 40 (1), 43–56.

50 http://www.marketingmagazine.co.uk/news/1012285/

Chapter 14

The challenges of evaluation

Chapter objectives

On completing this chapter, you should be able to:

- critically discuss why evaluations should occur, what should be evaluated and when evaluations should occur;
- justify the contribution of evaluation processes at all stages of an intervention programme;
- critically evaluate formal and informal evaluative processes;
- develop and justify evaluation programmes for a range of social marketing interventions;
- discuss the specific challenges involved in evaluating multi-component interventions and multi-partner interventions;
- critically discuss the way in which the effect of competition on interventions can be evaluated.

Why evaluate?

Not everything that can be counted counts, and not everything that counts can be counted

(Albert Einstein)

Evaluation (and even more scary, audits) have a negative image and people are understandably nervous about possibly being 'held to account' for activity over which they may not have had total control. A recurring myth is that many organisations cannot afford to evaluate. We argue that no organisation can afford **not** to. Evaluation should be seen as an integral part of all phases of activity, including the planning and implementation phases. As such, its purpose is to help refine activity and to ensure that interventions are as effective as possible. It should not be a 'one-off' exercise when the intervention has finished.

At every stage of an intervention development, these questions should be asked:

- Do we fully understand the attitudes and beliefs underpinning actual behaviours?
- Do we understand how the behaviour is situated within the lives of our targets?
- Do we fully understand the barriers to and potential enablers of sustained behaviour change?
- What environmental and or socio-economic factors may act as barriers?
- Are the proposed intervention strategies and methods appropriate for all target groups?
- Are there any risks for communities or individuals (both staff delivering the intervention and those who are the target of it)?
- Are the strategies and methods proposed or in use ethical?
- For written material, including websites and printed material, is the message we think we are sending the one that is actually being received by the target groups?
- Do all segments of the target group comprehend the material (have we catered for the needs of those with learning difficulties including dyslexia and low literacy levels)?

Evaluation also provides an ongoing check that the chosen strategies and tactics are working as anticipated. Are all segments of the target being reached? Are they responding? Is the behavioural goal being reached? If not, what changes can be made to make the intervention more effective?

Pragmatically, evaluation that demonstrates success provides evidence to justify the continuing funding of an intervention programme and continuing or future partnership participation. An often-overlooked aspect of end-of-intervention evaluation is that it provides a valuable reward for those who actually implemented the intervention – to know that they have achieved positive results is a great motivator for continuing the momentum or commencing new interventions. At the post-intervention phase, the evaluation is not only a measure of how the intervention performed, but also a planning aid to help design and implement future activity.

There may be multiple organisations involved in an intervention, each with slightly different expectations of what should be evaluated and at what point. For example, a government body may provide overall funding and will be looking for evidence of the impact of the intervention (i.e. outcomes) in terms of specific behaviour changes, such as the number of smokers successfully quitting as the result of a smoking cessation intervention. Increasingly, government funding is dependent on proof of past impact.[1, 2]

A regional organisation charged with co-ordinating the implementation of an intervention will also want to know how different access points such as health clinics, pharmacies, libraries or community centres are working throughout the duration of the intervention (process evaluation).

Where multiple community partners are involved, evaluation of how each organisation is meeting the agreed objectives, working with other partners and meeting the needs of their specific target groups allows fine-tuning of elements of the intervention while it is still active. The mechanisms by which partnerships can be evaluated at all stages of an intervention are discussed in more detail below.

Often omitted is evaluation by the target group themselves. How well will a proposed intervention meet their needs? What would they change to improve the intervention? What is their experience of working with the social marketing team?

> **VIGNETTE 14.1**
>
> ### Lose the Fags[3]
>
> 'Lose the Fags' was a co-created social marketing project aimed at increasing the smoking quit rate for contemplators in a deprived ward of Stockport, Greater Manchester. The programme involved several stages of consultation and consumer research. Initial research indicated that both low awareness and psycho-social issues were causing the quit attempt rate to be very low. There were service delivery problems with current services and also quitting was not socially acceptable, whereas smoking was. There was a 54% smoking rate in the area.
>
> A group of local residents (both smokers and quitters), health professionals and community group members and organisers was convened to lead the programme. Research was fed back to them and workshops run to generate ideas. These workshops led to the development of the 'Lose the Fags' brand, by creative agency The Hub. The workshops also led to the ideas for the new services: one at the local children's centre targeting women, and one at the local gym targeting men. Workers who lived locally and were already trusted by residents of the area were trained in smoking cessation to deliver the intervention. A text support service was also set up. No 'new' staff or outsiders were involved in the daily running of the project; it was run and managed by residents.
>
> The result has been an increase in quit attempts and also a change in quit culture. The 'Lose the Fags' brand has become synonymous in the area with quitting, and people of all ages use the phrase as well as wear the t-shirts and hoodies or carry the bags which formed part of the communications programme.
>
> **Questions to consider**
>
> 1 *Discuss the benefits of co-creation for this case.*
> 2 *How would you evaluate the acceptance of the two venues used?*
> 3 *What challenges might exist in evaluating all components of this intervention?*

What to evaluate

The decision as to what to evaluate should have been made at the initial planning stage. Being clear on the intervention's specific behavioural goals should guide the planning of the evaluation. Behavioural goals should be set which allow the measurement of actual achievements against those intended. This careful planning should also enable the identification of specific activities that have performed better or worse than expected and reasons for the variance which will allow appropriate action to be taken in the future. It is vital to identify and agree on who has the right to set priorities for a community. To take the case of family planning for teenage girls – should the behavioural goal be to avoid pregnancy, to use condoms or to abstain from sex? These behavioural goals will have very different evaluation criteria. Which do you think would be relatively easy to evaluate and which more difficult?

To evaluate the effectiveness of your intervention, it is important to have a **baseline** against which changes can be measured. Often this can be gained from data already in the public domain, such as road accident statistics, hospital admissions, accident and emergency unit data, rates of sexually transmitted diseases or cancer incidence. In some instances, some additional research may be needed to gain sufficient data in a local region. The perceived urgency of a specific problem or tight deadlines imposed by funders can lead to interventions being implemented without adequate research either to provide a benchmark or to guide the development of an intervention through provision of meaningful insights into the actual drivers of current behaviours.[4]

An often-neglected aspect of evaluation at the initial planning stage is a systematic **cost-efficiency** analysis of different types of intervention structures. This can be done by complex **econometric modelling**[5] or by drawing up simple tables with both quantitative dimensions (e.g. cost of additional staff or staff training, cost of printed material, etc.) and qualitative dimensions (judgement of how the intervention will fit with existing activity such as staff workloads, likely effectiveness in reaching segments who have been hard to reach or motivate in the past, etc.). This allows projected costs to be compared for different alternatives and judgements made about the strengths and weaknesses of each option. Judgement and past experience are valuable commodities. Remember Einstein's quote at the beginning of this chapter!

One of the more difficult judgements relates to **equity assessment**. How well do different intervention options address the needs of disadvantaged segments of the target groups? Are any options likely to widen existing inequalities or upset any specific segment of the population that feels it is either being ignored or unfairly singled out? The cost of reaching some segments may be higher than others; it requires judgement as well as hard data to decide whether the additional costs for one segment are justified or whether they will result in resources being unfairly taken from other segments which might be more responsive to the intervention. You may find rereading Chapter 5 (Ethical issues in social marketing) useful for a more detailed discussion of some of the issues.

Another aspect of evaluation which is difficult to judge is when the impact of a specific intervention can be measured and by what means. Figure 14.1 illustrates different levels of effectiveness that may be chosen at different times.[6] It is not always possible to measure directly the ideal outcomes due to the time delay between intervention and desired outcomes. For example, given the lengthy time period between adoption of behaviours and potential impact on health issues, such as in the case of obesity-related illnesses, skin cancer, etc., well-being may be something to aspire to, but more pragmatic interim measures may be needed. Focus, particularly at the local community level, is likely to be on the three lower levels in the initial stages of an intervention.

Changes in **social norms** may occur over time, as they appear to be doing in relation to tobacco products, but it will be many years before any impact in other areas can be determined. For example, an intervention may seek to decrease current high levels of social norms regarding the desirability of a suntan in order to reduce skin cancer rates, which are currently increasing at 8% per year.[7] As there is a considerable time lag between skin damage and subsequent development of skin cancers, interim measures of intervention effects and effectiveness must be used.

The following material has been drawn from one of the few papers that specifically focuses on the evaluation of the effectiveness of social marketing interventions.[8] It shows a hierarchy of effects, progressing from awareness through to, ultimately, an improvement in overall societal or environmental well-being.

Table 14.1 provides a guide to the types of changes that should be sought at each of the preceding levels. It is worth noting, however, that, according to the commonly received

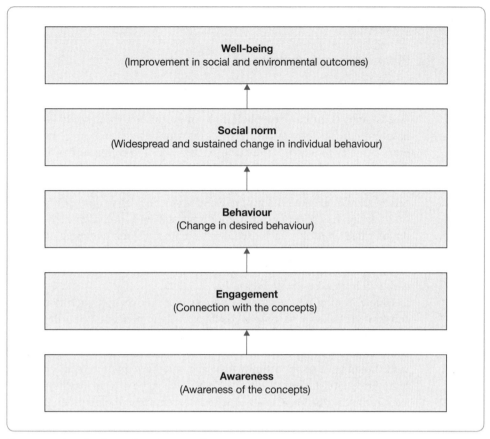

Figure 14.1 Levels of social marketing effectiveness

definition of social marketing, the goal of interventions has to be behaviour change rather than simply awareness.[9]

Ideally, evaluations should occur at all phases of an intervention, with different focus at each point.

Table 14.1 Changes sought at each level of effectiveness

Level	Key changes sought	Result level
Awareness	Increase in awareness of issue	Individual changes in awareness
Engagement	A change of attitude and contemplation of behaviour change. Behavioural responses to individual programmes	Individual changes in attitude and responses to programmes
Behaviour	Individual behaviour change	Individual changes in behaviour
Social norm	The desired behaviour change has permeated widely and sustainably and is therefore maintained	Normative changes in attitude and behaviour
Well-being	The desired behaviour change has resulted in an improvement in quality of life for individuals and society	Changes in social and environmental outcomes

Source: 'Assessing the Effectiveness of Social Marketing', paper presented at the ESOMAR conference, Berlin (Varcoe, J., 2004), ESOMAR.

When to evaluate

Planning/scoping phase

As we have noted earlier, setting measurable objectives should happen at the initial stage of development. At the scoping stage, which is the first stage of the planning process (see Chapter 3 for more on planning), an evaluation plan should be drawn up. Here, the baseline criteria for evaluating the intervention's success must be decided; all parties must agree as to who has the right to assess risks to communities and individuals,[10] who decides on norms, standards or goals; what incentives or rewards might be necessary to attract or enable under-represented groups to participate in a partnership[11] and what action should be taken if a group disagrees or decides to opt out after development of an intervention has commenced.[12] If an intervention is not supported or perceived as legitimate, those who have been excluded from its development and planning may undermine it.[13] As part of this negotiation, agreement needs to be gained as to what will be evaluated, when, by whom, who will analyse the data, to what use the findings will be put and who will have access to the data.

A new form of intervention or a particularly novel approach to delivering it may be a substantial challenge to those who will actually implement it. It is important for them to be involved at the initial planning stage so that they understand why the chosen approach has been selected and support it – a process which forms a part of **internal marketing**.[14] These staff should have an opportunity to discuss and have input into any changes that may be required to established work activity. They will also be extremely valuable in reporting, however informally, on initial impact of an intervention and indentifying potential problems as the intervention progresses.

Developing intervention materials/pre-testing

There are many ways in which your intervention may reach the target audience; whether it is via mass media (social advertising), posters, leaflets, websites, social media, face-to-face contact or any other method. The materials used should be pre-tested to help fine-tune the messages and the medium through which the message will be sent. This should include consulting those who will actually deliver the message – by whatever means. If those intermediaries feel that the message is not suitable for the intended target, or that, based on past experience, there are better ways of delivering it, the effectiveness of your delivery may be hindered. Most importantly, test the material with those who are the intended target. Among the things to check with them are:

- **Media preferences** – is the intended medium one that is used and valued by them (be it face-to-face advice from a health visitor or printed material)?

- **Message sources** – is the source of the material one that is trusted by the target? If not, consider why there is a lack of trust and what this means for your intervention.

- **Comprehension**/understanding[15]/health literacy – as we have noted earlier, a large amount of printed material is written in language that is too complex for the average person. Check whether the message being sent is what is being received. If it is not, what do you need to change to ensure that people do understand the message? Understanding does not equate to persuasion: we have known for a considerable period of time that there is a disconnect between awareness and actual behaviour.[16] Not only does your message need to be understood, it has to be persuasive.

- Cross-cultural issues: the methods by which you interact with your target group may need to change according to what is culturally acceptable to different segments of the population.

- Potential for boomerang effects/possible offence: unfortunately, some interventions have succeeded in reinforcing existing behaviours rather than making any positive change.[17] This is often due to not fully understanding the factors that underpin behaviour and potential barriers to change. It is possible that a well-designed and well-implemented intervention may be effective with its intended target but offend another group that is not the target. You may want to refer back to the discussion of these aspects in Chapter 5.

Implementation processes

In Chapter 4 we discussed the challenges presented by partnerships. Participants must be able to feel their contribution is valued and that their input results in real rather than illusory power to make a positive difference to the communities they represent.[18] Some examples of the diversity of successful partnerships are summarised below. As you read them, think about how the partnerships would have been put together and what you would have suggested the role of each partner should be. Then think about how you would ensure that each partner's input was what had been agreed and how their input should be evaluated.

Box 14.1 Examples of successful partnerships

Multiple community collaborations combating drug and alcohol-related problems USA

The Fighting Back Initiative funded 15 communities across 11 US states to combat drug and alcohol-related problems. Partners included schools, police, courts and correctional facilities, health care organisations, the alcohol industry (including retailers), workplaces, faith-based organisations and neighbourhood associations.

The inclusion of faith-based organisations was seen as particularly important for reaching cultural minority groups, but also to build on existing local networks to reach into affiliated communities and involve families in the programme.

Activities included education in schools, assistance programmes for students and employees, together with the hosting of recovery groups by a range of community-based organisations.[19, 20]

Healthy food choices and physical activity – USA

Involvement of employers in combating problems associated with obesity and lack of physical activity via provision of healthier food offerings, providing discounted membership of fitness clubs and supporting physical activity programmes has been shown to both reduce health care costs and increase productivity. Such programmes are not likely to achieve major changes in targeted behaviours, but the study authors observe that increasing the average level of physical activity and healthy eating by only 5 – 10% is predicted to 'dramatically reduce future cases of diabetes, heart disease and many other chronic diseases'.[21]

> **Box 14.1** (*continued*)
>
> For this case, think specifically about how you would respond to critics who suggest that the level of change being achieved is too small to warrant continuing with this type of intervention.
>
> **Non-conventional partnerships – USA**
>
> Thinking beyond conventional approaches to community partnerships can also be successful. In the USA, the use of hair salons and beauty salons to help disseminate information regarding smoking cessation, breast cancer screening and other health-related topics has prove effective in reaching low-income women from ethnic minority groups, particularly those unwilling or unable to access advice and support through mainstream medical channels.[22, 23, 24]
>
> For this type of intervention, think about how you would evaluate the effectiveness of this type of activity – what would count as success?

Wherever possible, individual intervention components should be evaluated, either formally or informally. For example, a multi-component intervention may have included group meetings with the target, but you have been advised that these meetings have been poorly attended. This information enables you to assess several things:

1 Why is attendance poor? If the group meetings are not seen as useful to the target, should you continue to offer them?

2 It may be that the target likes the idea but finds the time or location of the meetings difficult. What times and/or venues would better meet their needs?

3 If you decide to discontinue the meetings, how will that impact on those who did attend and what else can you offer them?

Intervention outcomes – effects and effectiveness

Holistic evaluation versus contribution of components

A key part of evaluation is trying to determine whether the intervention worked as intended. Even taking into account the issues discussed above and agreement in advance as to what is to be measured, this is not a simple task. For example, if your intervention has multiple components, how can you identify the impact of each individual component? How can you determine what external factors such as other related interventions or significant media coverage of an issue may have helped or hindered the intervention?[25]

There is evidence that integrated campaigns are more effective than those whose components are not integrated.[26] When all elements of an intervention are integrated, it is possible that the results will be greater than the contribution of each individual component, due to synergy.[27, 28] However, this makes identifying particularly successful or less successful sections even harder.

Difficulties with evaluating parts of an integrated intervention

Lag times

Few interventions have immediate impact – there will generally be a delay, or lag time, between the intervention and people's actual behaviours. This may be short, such as deciding whether to visit a smoking cessation help centre you have seen advertised or making a phone call to ask for an appointment to get help with improving diet. The time delay between seeking advice, taking action and noticeable results, such as successfully quitting smoking for a specific period, or improving blood pressure, cholesterol or weight measures, may be considerably longer. In the case of sun protection, the ultimate aim is to reduce the growing rates of skin cancer – but this impact will not be evident for a number of years as skin cancers can take several years to become visible. In this latter instance, there needs to be agreement on what intermediate measures are appropriate to evaluate the impact of any intervention.

Variations across groups

You may find that some segments of your target are responding well to the interventions and others are not. You will then need to try to determine why some are not responding and how you can alter the intervention components to connect more effectively with them. This highlights the importance of evaluation throughout all stages of an intervention rather than leaving it until the end, only to find that the intervention has not been effective for all segments.

How to evaluate – techniques for different phases, components and media

There is no single method of evaluation. It is dependent on the type of activity and, of course, the resources available. An overview of some of the most commonly used methods is provided below.

Randomised controlled trials

The 'gold standard' for medical research has been **randomised controlled trials** (RCTs), where a group is given a treatment, with measurements taken before and after the treatment. These measurements are compared with those for at least one other group who may receive a different intervention – or no intervention at all (a 'control' group). The allocation of people to the different intervention or to the control group is totally random, with participants (and often those administering the intervention) having no idea which group individuals are in. RCTs are not feasible for all types of interventions.

The complexity and dynamic nature of communities means that community-based interventions will differ across a number of important factors. Firstly, it is extremely difficult to find communities that are identical in all respects, to be given different interventions or to act as a control group. There are also numerous uncontrollable factors such as media coverage within each community, different forms of dissemination or support for the intervention or interactions between the communities.

Touchpoints

A useful concept that is not yet widely used in social marketing is that of **touchpoints** – consideration of all the ways in which any component of an intervention – or any staff involved in its delivery – can meet with the intended target.[29] Valuable feedback on the acceptability of an intervention – and on how to improve it – can be fed back from front-line staff.

Affordable and achievable impact evaluation

The UK government signalled in mid-2010 that they would require publically funded interventions to demonstrate 'unequivocal evidence' of measureable benefits.[30] Evidence of success has been provided for some campaigns, for example a 2008 anti-tobacco campaign cost £26 million but the Central Office of Information (COI) claimed 171,000 people stopped smoking as a result, saving the NHS £113 million.[31] The health secretary has, however, stated that some campaigns have been a waste of money,[32] suggesting that return on investment measures will be given greater prominence in future. Although no details have been released about proposed methodology for this, a paper published by the COI[33] offers a framework for a financially-based evaluation of public sector communication. Undertaking this kind of evaluation, as the authors point out, is no easy matter. Whereas commercial marketers are trying to influence normally simple purchasing-based behaviours that add shareholder value within a year or two, governments are attempting to influence health or social behaviours that shift slowly over much longer time frames and involve a multitude of cross-cutting factors. Consequently, this kind of evaluation is complex and often expensive to complete.

Smaller interventions present more of a challenge in that they may lack both the funding and the expertise to conduct evaluations. Where possible, all members of intervention delivery teams should be taught how to collect both qualitative and quantitative data[34] and, more importantly, how to interpret it and make informed decisions based on the findings. Vignette 14.2: Evaluating Lose the Fags gives an example of how this small-budget intervention used both quantitative and qualitative evaluation to gain a full picture of the effectiveness of the different parts of the intervention.

VIGNETTE 14.2

Evaluating 'Lose the Fags'[35]

The evaluation plan for 'Lose the Fags' has five strands, each described below.

Pre- and post-intervention service registration rates

Access rates of the local stop smoking services were the primary evaluation data required. However, the standard measure for NHS-supported quit attempts (the four-week measure) was used to compare the intervention with other smoking cessation interventions. The percentage of quits that were successful at four weeks were compared with data from before the 'Lose the Fags' project was launched to gauge any change.

➡

Pre- and post-qualitative

Qualitative research was undertaken after 'Lose the Fags' had been in place for 12 months to explore how the intervention had impacted Brinnington's smokers.

Service use questionnaire

At the end of the 12-month implementation stage, a brief two-page questionnaire was developed and issued to a small purposive sample of service users to capture functional data about their experience of using each service that came under the 'Lose the Fags' umbrella: GP; 'Quit for Life' drop-in group; children's centre one-to-one clinic; and Lapwing Centre drop-in access. These were used to help guide future changes to the services.

Pre- and post-quantitative: awareness and experiences of quitting in Brinnington

A quantitative market research company was commissioned to deliver a statistically significant pre–post survey questionnaire. The questionnaire, delivered in Brinnington (the target area) and a control area, captured the impact of the 'Lose the Fags' work, plus detailed smoking and demographic data.

Qualitative service delivery evaluation

For internal use only, a two-stage qualitative research programme was also implemented to gather implementation evaluation data. Service delivery staff were interviewed halfway through the first 12 months and also at the end of the first 12 months. The purpose was to feed back to the PCT comments from the service delivery teams, key partners and stakeholders which were used to improve the sustainability of the intervention.

Some of the more commonly used means of measuring the effects and effectiveness of interventions are shown in Table 14.2.

Table 14.2 Possible indicators of success at each level of effectiveness

	Indicators	Means of measurement
Awareness	X% aware of issue	Surveys (formal/informal – think about how to administer questionnaires/who, where, when) Interviews, focus groups, incorporation into language and discourse
Engagement	X% contemplating changing behaviour X% discussing/responding/participating	Surveys Behavioural data (e.g. website hits, requests for brochures, calls to helplines, etc.) Interviews, focus groups Engagement with social media
Behaviour	X% self-report behaviour X% behaviour changes recorded	Self-report (diaries, video diaries), observation Behavioural data (e.g. participating in sports clubs, road speed data)
Social norms	X% positive attitudes/positive media coverage Anecdotal feedback/observation Political environment	Surveys Media and political tracking Anecdotal feedback Observation
Well-being	X% increase in social outcome X% increase in environmental outcome	Social reports (annual compilations of indicators of well-being) Epidemiological data Environmental data

Social advertising and communication

Mass media

Commonly, one of the most substantial costs of any intervention is paid **mass media** advertising via television, radio, newspapers or magazines. It is important to evaluate this activity in several ways. In assessing the effects of mass media some aspects can be quantified, others are far more subjective. These latter include: the ability of mass media to reach budget holders and policy makers, not just those who are specifically targeted. Thus mass media can help keep a specific topic 'on the radar screen' for future funding. It can also provide a sense of legitimacy and reassurance for those delivering the intervention at community level.[36] It is impossible to quantify the effect of mass media on these factors.

Paid advertising

In evaluating **paid advertising**, the first question to ask is quite simply whether you got what you paid for. Did all scheduled advertisements appear as planned? Individual electronic media such as television or radio will be able to verify this. Print media will, of course, be able to provide you with a copy of the publication in which the advertisement appeared or a 'tear sheet' – a copy of the page on which it appeared. The second question is whether the advertising performed as expected. Print media readership data is provided only on an annual basis, therefore advertisements are placed on the basis of historical data. Only when the next readership study is completed are advertisers able to evaluate whether there have been any significant positive or negative changes in readership levels and profiles that should be considered in planning future activity.

The third question is how your message might have been impacted by the environment in which it appeared, such as surrounding editorial, programme content or competitive messages (this issue is reviewed in depth below). Remember that mass media advertising can be useful for raising awareness but on its own does not lead to long-term behaviour change in areas such as diet, physical activity and sun protection.[37, 38] Measuring the number of people who were aware of the advertising and who can recall key messages, prompted or unprompted (you may want to refer back to Chapter 7, Conducting research in social marketing) is therefore useful as one indicator of the impact of the advertising.

PR/publicity and sponsorship

Many of the benefits of PR/publicity campaigns or sponsorship of an event are often seen as being intangible, and therefore difficult to measure. However, it is just as important to measure and research the effect a PR or sponsorship campaign had as that of any other form of communication with target groups.

A common evaluation technique is to simply 'count' the space an article devotes to discussing a company's new product (favourably) and then converting this into a measurable output by calculating how much it would have cost to buy this space if it had been purchased as paid advertising. It is also possible to calculate other measures, such as how many people have potentially been exposed to the message through readership or viewing data.

Other (face-to-face, leaflets, etc.)

Production of leaflets and other printed material has long been a mainstay of health education and patient information,[39] evolving in response to evidence over the last 40 years that patients forget or misunderstand the majority of the content of verbal discussions with health professionals.[40] This assumes that when people are given written material they will read it, understand the information and act on it – yet there is evidence that these assumptions are not valid.[41] The bulk of research in this area has been done from the perspective of health information providers, i.e. those who produce the material.[42]

We are unable to locate studies that have evaluated the development of print-based material from the perspective of meeting the end-users' information needs or how relevant and useful existing material is. Some studies[43] have found evidence that material compiled from an expert-led, paternalistic perspective is perceived by end-users as patronising. There is little evidence of consideration of how this material is expected to change behaviour, such as influencing cognitions.[44]

Monitoring 'noise'/upstream factors

As well as monitoring your own intervention's activity, you should also try to monitor the effect of any activity that may directly or indirectly impact on your intervention.

Competition/unexpected confusion

Your intervention is not going to occur in isolation. It will be impacted by competing messages, such as fast-food advertising versus healthy eating or exercise messages. Sometimes,

Figure 14.2 Example of unexpected competition through nearby media space
Source: Lynne Eagle.

the impact is more direct than could normally be expected. Consider the photo in Figure 14.2, taken by one of the authors. How do you think the planners for either the fast food or the social marketing communications activity would have reacted to these two posters being placed side by side? What would you advise both parties to do?

While this may be somewhat amusing, the implications can be potentially serious. Consider the impact of alcohol advertising on responsible drinking interventions, sunbed advertising on sun protection interventions, or car manufacturers whose advertisements show speeding cars on anti-speeding interventions. This activity cannot be banned, but its potential impact on social marketing interventions should be recognised. While the example in the photo is, we hope, a relatively isolated occurrence, sometimes a crisis of confidence can be generated with little warning. Imagine that you are the manager in charge of an intervention to increase the measles, mumps and rubella vaccination rates among children. What are the major barriers that might impact on your intervention, both positively and negatively? Now assume you were that manager but back in the late 1990s. Consider the situation outlined in Box 14.2.

Box 14.2 MMR vaccine

Immunisation for measles, mumps and rubella using a combined vaccine (MMR) fell sharply after a widely reported medical study suggested a link between the vaccine and autism and inflammatory bowel disease.[45] As a result of news media reports of the paper, the percentage of UK children being vaccinated with the MMR vaccine fell sharply, from 92% to around 80%, but as low as 50% in some metropolitan areas.[46, 47] The media also reported that GPs were advising parents not to have their children vaccinated with MMR, further reinforcing perceptions that there were problems with the vaccine and leading to an overall loss of confidence in both the vaccine's safety and the credibility of government advice.[48]

Subsequent studies refuted the speculative causal link made by Wakefield and his team[49] but were not reported in the mass media, which continued to portray a controversy for several years. The level of public confusion can best be summarised in an extract from a major Economic and Social Research Council report (Table 14.3) which shows that, in addition to evidence of uncertainty as to whether or not there was a link between the MMR vaccine and autism, there was an increase in belief that there was equal weight of evidence on both sides of the MMR debate over the period April–October 2002.

Table 14.3 ESRC analysis of public understanding of the safety of the MMR vaccine*

'Which of the following statements is true?'	April %	October %
The weight of scientific evidence currently suggests a link between MMR vaccine and autism	25	20
The weight of scientific evidence currently suggests no link between MMR vaccine and autism	30	23
There is equal evidence on both sides of the debate	39	53
Not answered	6	4

*This table is taken from 'two nationwide surveys (both with representative samples of over 1,000), conducted in April and October 2002'.

Source: Hargreaves, I., Lewis, J. and Speers, T. (2003) Towards a Better Map: Science, the Public and the Media. London: Economic & Social Research Council.

VIGNETTE 14.3

Conflicting advice on sun protection

Now consider the impact of mass media editorial on a lower-profile health issue – skin cancer, which is closely linked to sun exposure. However, some sun exposure is recommended in order to generate vitamin D in the body. There is a lack of clear expert advice as to how much sun exposure is necessary to generate adequate vitamin D, primarily because the amounts vary from person to person. This fact has been used by some writers to generate controversy around whether current sun protection advice is correct. For example, official sun protection messages are directly challenged in some popular media, as illustrated by the following from an article in *Psychology Today* entitled 'The Great Sunlight Standoff':

> Hold the sunscreen – at least for a few minutes. Evidence is emerging that some unfiltered sun exposure repels ills from heart disease to cancer to multiple sclerosis, not to mention depression – enough to add seven years to your life. Are you ready for a more nuanced view of sunshine?[50]

There is a growing perception in Australia that sun protection may result in not having enough vitamin D, potentially undermining the effectiveness of long-running sun protection campaigns.[51] We have been unable to identify studies in other countries. The news media claims made for vitamin D with regard to its significant health protection and disease prevention properties continue to have a high profile. In the absence of clear advice from official sources that recognises the claims made in the media and offers responses that acknowledge both speculative and potential benefits of vitamin D, consumers are likely to base their behaviour on the media material.

In the UK, there has not been sufficient funding to enable mass media sun protection information and education activity to run. Official information is therefore restricted to information on health websites such as the NHS and individual primary care trusts, as well as Cancer Research UK's SunSmart website, which includes downloadable leaflets and posters http://publications.cancerresearchuk.org/epages/. This should be viewed against some £13.2 million in advertising undertaken by sun care advertisers.[52]

Information about sun protection and skin cancer – and many other health and lifestyle issues – is largely passively acquired via consumer media, with active searching occurring only when it is needed to resolve a specific problem.[53] Consistent with the Elaboration Likelihood Model,[54] when involvement is low, peripheral effects, such as perceived quality of presentation, and source effects become important.[55] Peripheral cues may influence thoughts and confidence in judgements made,[56] especially when thoughts in response to messages are positive.[57]

With low-involvement processing, decisions will be made to simply accept or reject the message without any investment of thought or deliberation.[58] Commercial sources, such as sun care advertising, reinforce the prevailing perception of a suntan being sexy.[59] Messages that appear to conflict with prevailing norms, such as covering up or staying out of the sun, are likely to be disparaged and therefore are unlikely to be persuasive,[60] even if actively sought from official health sites.

Question to consider

If you were advising the people involved in planning, implementing and evaluating the effectiveness of sun protection initiatives, what advice would you give them?

Consider other forms of 'risky' behaviour, such as excess alcohol consumption or reckless driving. Analyse how the issue is portrayed in popular media and how this coverage may impact on any social marketing interventions aimed at trying to change that behaviour.

Environmental competitive factors

Consider how environmental issues may compete with interventions to reduce target group engagement. For example, an intervention aimed at encouraging people to become more physically active may fail because of fear of crime in the neighbourhood.[61] Think of a range of possible intervention areas and what social or environmental factors might be barriers to an intervention. Then think about how you might be able to minimise the barriers.

Special circumstances

There are several forms of evaluation that should be considered that do not involve actual or potential end-users of an intervention.

Internal versus external satisfaction

Consider, for example, an intervention that appears to be working well for your target group, but which is not popular with the front-line staff who are tasked with delivering it. This problem may occur when an intervention is considerably different from previous activity. Concepts from **diffusion of innovations theory**[62] can be useful here. Staff will need to be convinced of the relative advantage of the intervention over what may have been done in the past. They may need support in adjusting to activity that is more complex than, or is not seen as compatible with, previous ways of working, but which does offer advantages for the target groups.[63] Sometimes there simply needs to be an adjustment period while staff get used to new ways of working, with benefits from being able to observe or discuss new interventions with those who have been successful in adapting to it. At other times, being involved in the intervention development, understanding the reasons for it and being able to suggest ways of modifying delivery without compromising the intervention itself may improve staff satisfaction levels. Co-creating an intervention with staff and using internal marketing effectively can be a useful way of building important relationships with key stakeholders like front-line staff. (See Chapter 4 for more on co-creation.)

Dealing with unintended effects

Specific intervention areas, such as sexual health, may offend some cultural or religious groups who, while they may not be directly targeted, may still receive material relating to the topic. As noted earlier, it is possible for harm to occur as a result of well-intentioned actions. For example, concerns have been identified over the appropriateness of fear appeals in communicating health risks,[64] but there are also issues relating to how competing wants might be judged and what information it is reasonable to seek from people in order to develop effective health interventions.[65] It is therefore important not only to involve as many relevant sectors of the community in initial research and intervention concept development as possible, but also to test proposed material for factors such as comprehension, cultural acceptability, etc., before the material is developed into the format in which it will be delivered.

Evaluating partnerships[66]

Not every partnership will require formal evaluation – local organisations or retailers assisting in providing display space do so as a contribution to the community in which they operate rather than because they see the action as a formal requirement.

Depending on the nature of the partnership and the level of inter-partner trust, the checklist provided at the end of Chapter 4 should form the basis for discussions about the objectives and governance of the partnership prior to development activity commencing. Having evaluated each of the partners individually, it should be useful then to evaluate the partnership as a whole using the same checklist.

In addition, the evaluation process should enable the partnership to discuss possible unforeseen or negative consequences of activity and other factors that may require action to be taken that was not anticipated. Contingency planning involves thinking of 'worst case' scenarios and then evaluating possible courses of action that would be available. It involves weighing up the pros and cons of each option, together with how decisions will be made as to whether or when this action might be needed, and how it will be conveyed to stakeholders, including the affected community. A factor that should also be considered at this time is who will liaise with media organisations – who has the right to speak on behalf of the partnership overall.

In working with partners it is important to gain agreement on what will count as success (or otherwise) for components over which you may not have direct control. Where interventions are largely based in a community, the resources and techniques by which data can be collected need to be determined and agreed by all parties – and contingency measures put in place to ensure that data can be collected as agreed if participating organisations or individuals within them become unable to continue to collect the data over time.

Evaluation of procedures may include partners themselves evaluating whether they believe progress is being made and whether they believe their involvement is a positive experience.

Evaluation of service delivery by the partnership may involve counts of the number of users of the services and other quantitative measures. There is the opportunity to gain valuable insights as to how well services meet the client's expectations and needs through questions such as the following:

- Do participants feel as though they are making progress?
- Are no, or few, negative side effects reported by participants?
- Do participants report that they like involvement with the programme?
- Do participants recommend it to others?
- Do those people around the participants (e.g. family and friends) report that participants are making progress and are satisfied with their involvement?
- Do participants feel that they are included in the development process? Do they feel that they have a voice in programme improvement?[67]

Collection and analysis of data can be problematic, as Vignette 14.4 shows.

VIGNETTE 14.4

UK Community Alcohol Prevention Programme (UKCAPP)

A number of community partnerships have been formed in the UK to reduce alcohol-related harm through community-based interventions focusing not on specific target groups but rather on changing community structures or environments.[68] Partnerships in individual areas involved partners such as 'health authorities, community safety partnerships, alcohol and/or drugs teams, police, licensing forums, the news media, the licensed trade and groups representing sections of the general public'.[69]

Initial analysis of the impact of these programmes focused on the challenges of developing and maintaining positive relationships between partners, managing time and resources as well as reconciling differing agendas. More recent analyses highlighted difficulties in sourcing and interpreting data intended to measure the impact of programmes. Problems were evident in data collection due to different methods used by partners such as the police, ambulance and hospital/A&E departments, together with the impact of subjective judgement by analysts as to classification of data:

'As one analyst explained: "I could call up data that could prove anything I wanted to. If I wanted to make a case that it's really good . . . using proper data I can manipulate it to make it look pretty. Similarly, if I wanted to put pressure on the Home Office to support us with an initiative I could put my hands on data that would do just that. So, it's whatever you want . . . All partnerships do that."'[70]

This has led to calls for funding not only of interventions but also of evaluation strategies that will allow valid and reliable data to be applied across regions and over time.[71]

Questions to consider

1 How do you recommend the challenges of 'selective' and subjective data strategies be rectified?

2 How would you overcome the differences in data collection methods used by different partners?

3 How would you evaluate the impact of the activity undertaken by each of the parties listed?

From the perspective of those providing funding for services that may be offered by partnerships, there will be an expectation of the impact of the partnership's activity on the wider community, including cost-effectiveness or return on investment data

Summary

Evaluations and audits should not be seen as negative experiences. They are an integral part of intervention activity and can provide valuable data to aid planning and implementing future activity. Evaluation can be more complex when multiple partners are involved, but can help ensure the needs of all partners – and the groups they represent – are met. Involvement of the groups targeted by an intervention can also help ensure future interventions continue to meet their needs.

You need to decide what to evaluate and how at each stage of an intervention's development and implementation. There are many techniques that can be used individually or in tandem. As well as evaluating your own intervention, the impact of competition, the media or other organisations' activity that may help, hinder or simply confuse the recipients of your intervention should also be included.

While evaluation can be time-consuming and complex, its benefits are significant for both current and future activity.

CHAPTER REVIEW QUESTIONS

1 How should you respond to comments that evaluation costs too much and therefore it should only be done at the end of an intervention?

2 You have been asked to critique an intervention that received very high awareness levels but no significant change in behaviour. How would you go about determining why this has occurred and what changes should be made to the intervention before it is considered for future use?

3 How would you respond to extreme dissatisfaction among intervention delivery staff about the complexity of record keeping for an otherwise successful intervention? What are the implications of not taking action?

4 Assume there are multiple partners delivering an intervention and negative feedback is traceable to the performance of one particular partner. What action do you recommend is taken to rectify the situation?

5 How would you recommend evaluating the impact of the media coverage of issues such as vitamin D and swine flu?

Recommended reading

Evaluation

Agha, S. (2002) An Evaluation of the Effectiveness of a Peer Sexual Health Intervention Among Secondary Students in Zambia. *AIDS Education and Prevention Prev,* 14, 269–81.

Austin, E.W., Pinkleton, B.E., Hust, S.J.T. and Cohen, M. (2005) Evaluation of an American Legacy Foundation/Washington State Department of Health Media Literacy Pilot Study. *Health Communications,* 18 (1), 75–95.

Bastuji-Garin, S., Grob, J.-J., Grognard, C., Grosjean, F. and Guillaume, J.-C. (1999) Melanoma Prevention. Evaluation of a Health Education Campaign for Primary Schools. *Archives of Dermatology,* 135 (8), 936–40.

Bloor, M., Frankland, J., Langdon, N.P., Robinson, M., Allerston, S., Catherine, A., et al. (1999) A Controlled Evaluation of an Intensive, Peer-led, Schools-based, Anti-smoking Programme. *Health Education Journal,* 58 (1), 17–25.

Bryant, C.A., Brown, K.R.M., McDermott, R.J., Debate, R.D., Alfonso, M.L., Baldwin, J.A., et al. (2009) Community-based Prevention Marketing: A New Framework for Health Promotion Interventions. In R.J. DiClimente, R.A. Crosby and M. Kegler (eds), *Emerging Theories in Health Promotion Practice and Research*. San Francisco: John Wiley & Sons.

Butterfoss, F.D. (2006) Process Evaluation for Community Participation. *Annual Review of Public Health,* 27, 323–40.

Butterfoss, F.D., Francisco, V. and Capwell, E.M. (2000) Choosing Effective Evaluation Methods. *Health Promotion Practice,* 1 (4), 307–13.

Drummond, M.F., Torrance, G.W., O'Brien, B.J. and Sculpher, M.J. (2005) *Methods for the Economic Evaluation of Health Care*. Oxford: Oxford University Press.

Fossum, B., Arborelius, E. and Bremberg, S. (2004) Evaluation of a Counseling Method for the Prevention of Child Exposure to Tobacco Smoke: An Example of Client-Centered Communication. *Preventive Medicine,* 38 (3), 295–301.

Francisco, V.T., Butterfoss, F.D. and Capwell, E.M. (2001) Key Issues in Evaluation: Quantitative and Qualitative Methods and Research Design. *Health Promotion Practice,* 2 (1), 20–3.

Groner, J., French, G., Ahijevych, K. and Wewers, M.E. (2005) Process Evaluation of a Nurse-delivered Smoking Relapse Prevention Program for New Mothers. *Journal Of Community Health Nursing,* 22 (3), 157–67.

Huhman, M., Heitzler, C. and Wong, F. (2004) The VERB Campaign Logic Model: a Tool for Planning and Evaluation. *Preventing Chronic Disease,* 1 (3), A11.

Jibaja-Weiss, M.L., Volk, R.J., Granchi, T.S., Neff, N.E., Spann, S.J., Aoki, N., et al. (2006) Entertainment Education for Informed Breast Cancer Treatment Decisions in Low-literate Women: Development and Initial Evaluation of a Patient Decision Aid. *Journal of Cancer Education,* 21 (3), 133–9.

Krahe, B., Abraham, C. and Scheinberger-Olwig, R. (2005) Can Safer-sex Promotion Leaflets Change Cognitive Antecedents of Condom Use? An Experimental Evaluation. *British Journal of Health Psychology,* 10 (2), 203–20.

Nilsen, P. (2005) Evaluation of Community-based Injury Prevention Programmes: Methodological Issues and Challenges. *International Journal of Injury Control and Safety Promotion,* 12 (3), 143–56.

Sahota, P., Rudolf, M.C.J., Dixey, R., Hill, A.J., Barth, J.H. and Cade, J. (2001) Evaluation of Implementation and Effect of Primary School-based Intervention to Reduce Risk Factors for Obesity. *British Medical Journal,* 323, (7320), 1027–9.

Wimbush, E. and Watson, J. (2000) An Evaluation Framework for Health Promotion: Theory, Quality and Effectiveness. *Evaluation,* 6 (3), 301–21.

Evaluating sponsorships

John-Leader, F., Van Beurden, E., Barnett, L., Hughes, K., Newman, B., Sternberg, J., et al. (2008) Multimedia Campaign on a Shoestring: Promoting 'Stay Active – Stay Independent' among Seniors. *Health Promotion Journal of Australia,* 19 (1), 22–8.

Madill, J. and O'Reilly, N. (2010) Investigating Social Marketing Sponsorships: Terminology, Stakeholders, and Objectives. *Journal of Business Research,* 63 (2), 133–9.

O'Reilly, N.J. and Madill, J.J. (2007) Evaluating Social Marketing Elements in Sponsorship. *Social Marketing Quarterly,* 13 (4), 1–25.

Notes

1 Fernandez, J. (2010) COI Warns that Government Ad Budget could Shrink by 50%. *Marketing Week,* online edition 3 June. Accessed 15 July from http://www.marketingweek.co.uk

2 Tylee, J. (2010) Can Payment by Results Work for COI? *Brand Republic.* 7 May. Accessed from: http://www.brandrepublic.com/Analysis/1003120/Close-Up-payment-results-work-COI/?DCMP=ILC-SEARCH

3 French, J., Merritt, R. and Reynolds, L. (eds) (2011) *Social Marketing Case Book*. London: Sage Publications.

4 Nutbeam, D. (1998) Evaluating Health Promotion – Progress, Problems and Solutions. *Health Promotion International,* 13 (1), 27–44.

5 Pinkerton, S.D., Johnson-Masotti, A.P., Derse, A. and Layde, P.M. (2002) Ethical issues in Cost-effectiveness Analysis. *Evaluation and Program Planning,* 25 (1), 71–83.

6 Varcoe, J. (2004) *Assessing the Effectiveness of Social Marketing.* Paper presented at the ESOMAR Conference, Berlin.

7 National Institute for Health and Clinical Excellence (2006) Press Release: NICE Issues Guidance to Improve Healthcare Services for Skin Cancers, 21 February 2006.

8 Varcoe, J. (2004) Op. cit.

9 Andreasen, A. (1994) Social Marketing: Its Definition and Domain. *Journal of Public Policy and Marketing,* 13 (1), 108–14.

10 Minkler, M. (2004) Ethical Challenges for the 'Outside' Researcher in Community-Based Participatory Research. *Health Education & Behavior,* 31 (6), 684–97.

11 Himmelman, A.T. (1996) On the Theory and Practice of Transformational Collaboration. In Huxham, C. (ed.) *Creating Collaborative Advantage.* London: Sage Publications, pp. 19–43.

12 Roberts, M.J. and Reich, M.R. (2002) Ethical Analysis in Public Health. *The Lancet,* 359 (23 March), 1055–9.

13 Gray, B. (1996) Cross-sectorial Partners: Collaborative Alliances. In Huxham, C. (ed.) *Creating Collaborative Advantage.* London: Sage Publications.

14 Greene, W.E., Walls, G.D. and Schrest, L.J. (1994) Internal Marketing: The Key to External Marketing Success. *Journal of Services Marketing,* 8 (4), 5–13.

15 Wellings, K. and Macdowall, W. (2000) Evaluating Mass Media Approaches to Health Promotion: A Review of Methods. *Health Education,* 100 (1), 23–32.

16 Weinstock, J. and Rossi, J.S. (1998) The Rhode Island Sun Smart Project: A Scientific Approach to Skin Cancer Prevention, *Clinics in Dermatology,* 16 (4), 411–13

17 Fishbein, M., Hall-Jamieson, D., Zimmer, E., Haeften, I.V. and Nabi, R. (2002) Avoiding the Boomerang: Testing the Relative Effectiveness of Antidrug Public Service Announcements Before a National Campaign. *American Journal of Public Health,* 92 (2), 238–45.

18 Francisco, V.T. and Butterfoss, F.D. (2007) Social Validation of Goals, Procedures, and Effects in Public Health. *Health Promotion Practice,* 8 (2), 128–33.

19 Zakocs, R.C. and Guckenburg, S. (2007) What Coalition Factors Foster Community Capacity? Lessons Learned From the Fighting Back Initiative. *Health Education & Behavior,* 34 (2), 354–75.

20 Stevenson, J.E. and Mitchell, R.E. (2003) Community-Level Collaboration for Substance Abuse Prevention. *Journal of Primary Prevention,* 23 (3), 371.

21 Simon, P.A. and Fielding, J.E. (2006) Public Health and Business: A Partnership that Makes Cents. *Health Affairs,* 25 (4), 1032.

22 Wilson, T.E., Fraser-White, M., Feldman, J., Homel, P., Wright, S., King, G., et al. (2008) Hair Salon Stylists as Breast Cancer Prevention Lay Health Advisors for African-American and Afro-Caribbean Women. *Journal of Health Care for the Poor and Underserved,* 19 (1), 216–26.

23 Linnan, L.A. and Ferguson, Y.O. (2007) Beauty Salons: A Promising Health Promotion Setting for Reaching and Promoting Health Among African American Women. *Health Education & Behavior,* 34 (3), 517–30.

24 Linnan, L.A., Emmons, K.M. and Abrams, D.B. (2002) Beauty and the Beast: Results of the Rhode Island Smokefree Shop Initiative. *American Journal of Public Health,* 92 (1), 27–8.

25 Abbatangelo-Gray, J., Cole, G.E. and Kennedy, M.G. (2007) Guidance for Evaluating Mass Communication Health Initiatives: Summary of an Expert Panel Discussion Sponsored by the Centers for Disease Control and Prevention. *Evaluation & the Health Professions,* 30 (3), 229–53

26 Reid, M., Luxton, S. and Mavondo, F. (2005) The Relationship between Integrated Marketing Communication, Market Orientation, and Brand Orientation. *Journal of Advertising,* 34 (4), 11–23.

27 Naik, P.A. and Raman, K. (2003) Understanding the Impact of Synergy in Multimedia Communications. *Journal of Marketing Research,* 40 (4), 375–88.

28 Naik, P.A., Schultz, D.E. and Srinivasan, S. (2007) Perils of Using OLS to Estimate Multimedia Communications Effects. *Journal of Advertising Research,* 47 (3), 257–69.

29 Davis, S. (2005) Marketers Challenged to Respond to Changing Nature of Brand Building. *Journal of Advertising Research,* 45 (2), 198–200.

30 Fernandez, J. (2010) Op. cit.

31 Spanier, G. (2010) Mark Lund's COI: From 'Lifeblood of Ad Industry' to Political Football. *London Evening Standard,* online edition 8 February. Accessed 15 July from http://www.thisislondon.co.uk

32 Sweney, M. (2010) Coalition Government Freezes Advertising Budget. *The Guardian,* online edition, 24 May. Accessed 15 July from http://www.guardian.co.uk

33 Central Office of Information (2009) *Payback and Return on Marketing Investment (ROMI) in the Public Sector: How to Evaluate the Financial Effectiveness and Efficiency of Government Marketing Communication.* London: Central Office of Information.

34 Bryant, C.A., Brown, K.R.M., McDermott, R.J., Debate, R.D., Alfonso, M.L., Baldwin, J.A., et al. (2009) Community-based Prevention Marketing: A New Framework for Health Promotion Interventions. In R.J. DiClimente, R.A. Crosby and M. Kegler (eds), *Emerging Theories in Health Promotion Practice and Research.* San Francisco: John Wiley & Sons.

35 French, J., Merritt, R. and Reynolds, L. (eds) (2011) Op. cit.

36 Green, W.E., Walls, G.D. and Schrest, L.J. (1994) Op. cit.

37 Marcus, B.H., Owen, N., Forsyth, L.H., Cavill, N.A. and Fridinger, F. (1998) Physical Activity Interventions Using Mass Media, Print Media, and Information Technology. *American Journal of Preventive Medicine,* 15 (4), 362–78.

38 Weinstock, J. and Rossi, J.S. (1998) Op. cit.

39 Murphy, S. and Smith, C. (1993) Crutches, Confetti or Useful Tools? Professionals' Views on and Use of Health Education Leaflets. *Health Education Research,* 8 (2), 205–15.

40 Kenny, T., Wilson, R.G., Purves, I.N., Clark J., Sr., Newton, L.D., Newton, D.P., et al. (1998) A PIL for Every Ill? Patient Information Leaflets (PILs): A Review of Past, Present and Future Use. *Family Practice,* 15 (5), 471–9.

41 Krahe, B., Abraham, C. and Scheinberger-Olwig, R. (2005) Can Safer-sex Promotion Leaflets Change Cognitive Antecedents of Condom Use? An Experimental Evaluation. *British Journal of Health Psychology,* 10 (2), 203–20.

42 Entwistle, V.A. and Watt, I.S. (1998) Disseminating Information about Healthcare Effectiveness: A Survey of Consumer Health Information Services. *Quality in Health Care,* 7 (3), 124–9.

43 Meredith, P., Emberton, M. and Wood, C. (1995) New Directions in Information for Patients. *British Medical Journal,* 311 (6996), 4–5.

44 Dijkstra, A. and De Vries, H. (2001) Do Self-help Interventions in Health Education Lead to Cognitive Changes, and Do Cognitive Changes Lead to Behavioural Change? *British Journal of Health Psychology,* 6 (2), 121–34.

45 Wakefield, A.J., Murch, S.H., Anthony, A., Linnel, J., Casson, D., Malik, M., et al. (1998) Ileal-lymphoid-nodular Hyperplasia, Non-specific Colitis, and Pervasive Development Disorder in Children. *The Lancet,* 351, 637–41.

46 Speers, T. and Lewis, J. (2004) Journalism and Jabs: Media Coverage of the MMR Vaccine. *Communication & Medicine,* 1 (2), 171–81.

47 Wood-Harper, J. (2005) Informing Education Policy on MMR: Balancing Individual Freedoms and Collective Responsibilities for the Promotion of Public Health. *Nursing Ethics,* 12 (1), 43–58.

48 Salisbury, D.M., Beverley, P.C.L. and Miller, E. (2002) Vaccine Programmes and Policies. *British Medical Bulletin,* 62 (1), 201–11.

49 McMurray, R., Cheater, F., Weighall, A., Nelson, C., Schweiger, M. and Mukherjee, S. (2004) Managing Controversy Through Consultation: A Qualitative Study of Communication and Trust Around MMR Vaccination Decisions. *British Journal of General Practice*, July, 520–25.

50 Ackerman, J. (2007) The Great Sunlight Standoff. *Psychology Today,* 40 (6), 97.

51 Janda, M., Kimlin, M.G., Whiteman, D.C., Aitken, J.F. and Neale, R.E. (2007) Sun Protection Messages, Vitamin D and Skin Cancer: Out of the Frying Pan and Into the Fire? *Medical Journal of Australia,* 186 (2), 52–4.

52 Bainbridge, J. (2009) Safety First, Glowing Results. *Marketing, 11 March,* 28–9.

53 Eadie, D. and MacAskill, S. (2007) Results from an Exploratory Study of Sun Protection Practice. *Health Education,* 107 (3), 250–60.

54 Petty, R.E. and Cacioppo, J.T. (1984) Source Factors and the Elaboration Likelihood Model of Persuasion. *Advances in Consumer Research,* 11 (1), 668–72.

55 Buda, R. and Zhang, Y. (2000) Consumer Product Evaluation: The Interactive Effect of Message Framing, Presentation Order, and Source Credibility. *Journal of Product & Brand Management,* 9 (4), 229–42.

56 Brinol, P. and Petty, R.E. (2009) Source Factors in Persuasion: A Self-validation Approach. *European Review of Social Psychology,* 20, 49–96.

57 Tormala, Z.L., Briñol, P. and Petty, R.E. (2006) When Credibility Attacks: The Reverse Impact of Source Credibility on Persuasion. *Journal of Experimental Social Psychology,* 42 (5), 684–91.

58 Mazursky, D. and Schul, Y. (1992) Learning from the Ad or Relying on Related Attitudes: The Moderating Role of Involvement. *Journal of Business Research,* 25 (1), 81–93.

59 Lowe, J.B., Borland, R., Stanton, W.R., Baade, P., White, V. and Balanda, K.P. (2000) Sun-safe Behaviour among Secondary School Students in Australia. *Health Education Research,* 15 (3), 271–81.

60 Jessop, D.C., Simmonds, L.V. and Sparks, P. (2009) Motivational and Behavioural Consequences of Self-affirmation Interventions: A Study of Sunscreen Use Among Women. *Psychology & Health,* 24 (5), 529–44.

61 Loukaitou-Sideris, A. and Eck, J.E. (2007) Crime Prevention and Active Living. *American Journal of Health Promotion,* 21 (4, Suppl), 380.

62 Rogers, E.M. (1962) *Diffusion of Innovations.* London: Simon & Schuster.

63 Greenhalgh, T., Robert, G., Macfarlane, F., Bate, P. and Kyriakidou, O. (2004) Diffusion of Innovations in Service Organizations: Systematic Review and Recommendations. *Milbank Quarterly,* 82 (4), 581–629.

64 Jones, S.C. and Owen, N. (2006) Using Fear Appeals to Promote Cancer Screening – Are We Scaring the Wrong People? *International Journal of Nonprofit and Voluntary Sector Marketing,* 11 (2), 93–103.

65 Murphy, P.E. and Bloom, P N. (1992) Ethical Issues in Social Marketing. In S.H. Fine, *Marketing the Public Sector Promoting the Causes of Public and Nonprofit Agencies* Piscataway, NJ: Transaction Publishers, pp. 68–78.

66 This material has been adapted from Eagle, L.C. (2009) *Health Partnerships: Guide to the Ethics of Local Partnerships for Health:* Report Prepared for the Department of Health via Oxford Strategic Marketing.

67 Francisco, V.T. and Butterfoss, F.D. (2007) Op. cit., 131.

68 Holder, H.D. (2000) Community Prevention of Alcohol Problems. *Addictive Behaviors,* 25 (6), 843–59.

69 Mastache, C., Mistral, W., Velleman, R. and Templeton, L. (2008) Partnership Working in Community Alcohol Prevention Programmes. *Drugs: Education, Prevention & Policy,* 15, 4–14.

70 Mistral, W., Velleman, R., Mastache, C. and Templeton, L. (2008) The Challenge of Evaluating Community Partnerships – A Little Local Difficulty or Endemic National Problem? *Drugs: Education, Prevention & Policy,* 15, 50–60.

71 Ibid.

Glossary of terms

above-the-line A term originally used to describe advertising in traditional mass media such as television, radio or newspapers, for which commission was paid by the media, compared to activities such as public relations or direct mail for which a fee was changed to the client – a line being drawn on invoices to separate out commission-bearing activity from fee-based activity.

acceptability How acceptable people find an idea or intervention, ethically and practically.

acceptance Agreement with or approval of an idea or message.

actual norms Values or beliefs that actually exist within a population, segment or social group. See also **norms** and **perceived norms.**

advergames Electronic (computer or video) games which contain advertising embedded within the games and which may include signage or the use of products or services by the characters within a specific game.

adverse event A specific situation or occurrence, such as illness, accident, etc., in which the health or well-being of an individual or their family is harmed.

advertising Communication of persuasive messages about goods, services or concepts via channels such as mass media (e.g. television, magazines, etc.) with the source (advertiser) identified and paying for the placement of the messages within the medium.

anxiety Uneasiness or worry about the possible occurrence of an event (such as a specific illness or road accident) and its potential consequences for an individual, their family, etc.

apathy Absence of interest or enthusiasm for a concept or idea (e.g. regular exercise or healthy eating), regardless of whether persuasive communication has been undertaken or not.

attention Concentration, either by watching, observing, reading or listening to a specific message or demonstration.

attitude A learned tendency to respond or behave in a consistent (favourable or unfavourable) manner towards a product, service or idea (e.g. liking, preference). Consists of three components: affective (feelings), cognitive (knowledge) and behavioural (buying intentions).

attitudes, interests and opinions (AIO) Psychographic factors within an individual's lifestyle that are combined to provide a composite measure of how people live and how they are likely to respond to different types of interventions aimed at changing behaviour.

audit An examination of records, usually financial, to verify they are correct. For media spending, the audit would cover proof of appearance of all material.

awareness A mental state where a targeted individual has heard, seen or noticed in some way at least one part of an intervention. Awareness is necessary, but rarely of itself sufficient to change behaviour.

baseline An initial measurement of attitudes, behaviours, etc. taken before an intervention commences and used to plan an intervention and/or measure the impact the intervention has on changing these factors.

behaviour Response to marketing activity such as purchase of a product or service or adoption of a particular behaviour – for example, stopping smoking.

behaviour adoption The act of commencing a new or modified behaviour. See **behaviour maintenance**.

behavioural change Changing an individual or group's behaviours to behaviour that is positive, i.e. less risky or more beneficial to individuals, the environment or overall health and well-being – for example, reducing alcohol consumption, stopping smoking, or exercising regularly.

behavioural economics A field of study in which social, cognitive and emotional aspects of behaviour are studied, including deviations from choices that would be considered to have been made purely on rational grounds.

behavioural goals Aims or targets in behaviour such as deciding to try to exercise for at least 30 minutes five times per week in order to improve health and fitness or lose weight.

behavioural influences A range of factors that may directly or indirectly influence actual behaviours, such as those identified in the discussion of behavioural theories.

behavioural intentions Stated intention to purchase a product or service, or change behaviour. Usually measured through research, but not necessarily leading to actual behaviour.

behavioural problem Behaviour that may lead to negative outcomes for an individual or society. Perceptions of whether behaviour is problematic may not be shared by those observing rather than performing the behaviour.

behavioural theory Theory of the inter-relationship between a number of intrinsic (internal) or extrinsic (external) factors that influence behaviours. See also **theory**.

behaviour maintenance Continuing in a new or modified behaviour over time following successful adoption of the behaviour. See **behaviour adoption**.

beliefs Internal or explicitly stated (verbally or in writing) reflections of knowledge, attitudes or assessments about an aspect of life, society or factors that influence individual behaviours.

below-the-line See above-the-line.

beneficence Actions performed for the good of others, including reducing potential harm or improving the situation of others.

Body Mass Index A measure of an individual's weight in relation to height. It is calculated by multiplying a person's weight in kilos and dividing that by the square of their height in metres. Underweight is indicated by a BMI of less than 18.5, normal is between 18.5 and 25, overweight is a BMI greater than 25 but less than 30 and obese is a BMI greater than 30.

brand A product or service that is clearly identifiable via words or symbols and differentiated from other products or services – for example, Coca-Cola, or Virgin; in social marketing, road safety in the UK is branded under Think!. Another example is the VERB campaign (see Chapter 6).

brand equity A term whose meanings vary according to different disciplines, e.g. marketing and accounting. For example, financial-based brand equity may reflect the difference between balance-sheet valuations and the specific value of tangible assets such as factories or equipment. Marketing-based brand equity refers to individuals' loyalty to a brand or its perceived benefits relative to competitors.

building blocks Concepts, theories, techniques or strategies used in the development of an intervention.

capacity to understand The ability of an individual to understand communication directed at them; limited by intelligence, language fluency and literacy.

case study A detailed study of an individual, organisation, group or event, describing, explaining or investigating causes for specific behaviours or outcomes.

causal processing Thought processes that relate to the cause of an observed phenomenon.

causal research Research undertaken to identify the specific causes of a behaviour or what behaviour changes occur as a result of a change in a particular intervention or policy implementation.

causation In research, investigation into what factors directly or indirectly resulted in a specific behaviour being investigated.

cause-related marketing Co-operative marketing between a commercial (for-profit) organisation and a not-for-profit organisation, such as a charity. It does not involve direct donation of funds.

choice architecture Study of how behaviours are influenced by the way in which choices are presented (such as giving more prominent positions to healthy foods in order to increase their uptake). Term used extensively in Thaler, R.H. and Sunstein, C.R. (2008) *Nudge: Improving Decisions About Health, Wealth and Happiness,* New Haven: Yale University Press.

classical conditioning In marketing communication, the repeated pairing of a message (including music) that aims to produce positive feelings or emotions (unconditioned response) with a product, brand name or slogan (conditioned stimulus). The aim is for the conditioned stimulus eventually to be able to produce the positive feelings without the message being used.

cluster analysis A set of statistical analysis techniques that sorts people into groups or 'clusters' in which members of each cluster share similar characteristics.

co-creation The process by which creation of (marketing) material involves both marketers and users.

code of ethics Written set of principles or rules setting out conduct and behaviour expected of people working in a specific occupational area.

coercion In social marketing, compelling people to change behaviour without considering their wishes or personal circumstances.

cognition Process in which knowledge is acquired. Includes perception and reasoning.

cognitive development Development of skills and abilities such as information processing, conceptual resources, perceptual skill, language development or understanding.

commercial marketing Marketing of products or services by organisations whose primary goal is to profit from the sales – for example, soft drinks, sweets, cars, airline travel. See also **non-commercial activity**.

communication The sending of a message (such as attempts to influence behaviour change) from a source, such as an organisation implementing a social marketing intervention, to its targets.

communication mix The combination of ways in which an organisation may communicate with a range of targets. This may involve the use of mass media, internet-based technologies, reports, leaflets or face-to-face communication.

communication strategy The selected ways in which a message will be structured and sent to target groups. There are usually multiple strategies that may be considered. The selected strategy will be the one judged most likely to be successful within the resources available – for example, the use of posters and print advertising for a low-budget intervention.

communication tactics The specific details of how a selected strategy will be implemented – for example, the specific media in which, and the dates when, a message may appear.

communication technologies All forms of communication through which a message may be sent to a target. Usually refers to electronic technologies such as the internet.

competing ideas Ideas that may compete with one being promoted. For example, the idea that suntans make people more attractive may compete with ideas that excess exposure to sun or sunbeds may cause skin cancer.

competing messages Messages from any of a range of sources such as advertising, media content, peers, family or social groups whose views or statements conflict with a message being sent. For example, alcohol moderation messages may face competition from peers who believe that drinking to excess is fun and acceptable behaviour.

competition Organisations, activities, or other social influences that may either vie for attention or resources, such as time or money, or which present messages that contradict or confuse those being sent in order to influence behaviour change.

complacency Belief that one's current actions or behaviours do not place an individual at risk of adverse consequences and that there is no need even to consider behaviour change. It results in messages about potential risks being disregarded as not being relevant to the individual.

compliance Behaviour in response to a direct request (e.g. to take medication, to decrease consumption of fatty foods, etc.).

comprehension Ability to understand the meaning or importance of something, including written information.

concept See **theory**.

conformity Behaving in the same way as others, such as family or social groups.

construct An abstract, complex idea about an object or attribute, made up of a synthesis of simpler ideas (for example, healthy eating). Often used as the basis for theory development.

consumer-focused/consumer-centric An approach to the promotion of products, services, concepts or ideas that starts with developing an understanding of the wants and needs of the target population or specific segments within the population and which then develops products and/or services to meet those wants and needs.

content analysis Research technique in which material (e.g. printed material or other intervention resources) are analysed to identify key messages being sent, together with underlying assumptions, strategies and tactics used.

context-dependent (behaviours) Behaviours that may vary according to the social, family or social environment in which an individual undertakes the behaviours.

contingency planning Planning for unlikely, but still possible, future events that may have negative or unintended effects on elements of an intervention. Planning should take the form of 'what if?' analyses to identify possible events and decide on the best course of action to prevent their occurrence or to minimise their impact if they occur.

control group Used in market research, medication trials, etc. The treatment group is given a specific 'treatment' and the success, change (or lack of it) observed. The control group will be selected on the basis of similar characteristics to the treatment group, but will not be given the 'treatment'. See also **treatment group**.

convergent A social marketer who tends to use techniques from not just marketing but also a range of other disciplines, and who may adapt or reject certain commercial marketing techniques, for social marketing.

corporate social responsibility (CSR) A concept that organisations, especially (but not only) corporations, have an obligation to consider the interests of customers, employees, shareholders, communities, and the environment in all aspects of their operation. This obligation is seen to extend beyond their statutory obligation to comply with legislation. CSR is closely linked with the principles of sustainable development, which argues that enterprises should make decisions based not only on financial factors, such as profits or dividends, but also on the immediate and long-term social and environmental consequences of their activities.

correlation Statistical measurement of the relationship between two variables.

cost efficiency A measure of the effects of an intervention in relation to the resources used to develop and implement it; usually calculated in financial terms. Effects may be the savings to individuals and health systems as the result of a smoking cessation programme, or in terms of accidents not occurring and therefore medical treatments not performed and disability/ deaths not occurring as the result of road safety interventions.

counter marketing Marketing and marketing communication undertaken deliberately to contradict and thus minimise the effects of a competitor. The American 'Truth' smoking cessation programme deliberately sought to counter the marketing efforts of the tobacco industry.

culture Set of shared and learned attitudes, beliefs, knowledge, customs and values within a particular society that make up the foundation for acceptable behaviour. Culture may impact on the acceptability of particular products and on the way promotional activity is perceived.

customise Alter an intervention or part of it to meet the preferences or needs of an individual or specific population segment.

decency Behaviour that meets accepted standards. In relation to communications regulation, the ASA Codes include decency as one of the criteria to be met.

demographics Characteristics of a population, including gender, age, marital status, income, occupation and education. Often used for market segmentation.

deontology In social marketing, ethical reasoning focused on the aims or objectives of an intervention, i.e. trying to do good or improve health and well-being, but accepting that some negative consequences may occur. See also **teleology**.

depth interviews A research strategy in which interviews are conducted by a trained moderator with individuals, rather than with groups. Data captured may be qualitative, quantitative or a combination of the two.

descriptive research Research activity in which the characteristics of a population being studied are summarised, using relatively simply statistical techniques such as frequencies and chi-square tests.

desk research Research conducted using available data rather than conducting new research to obtain data.

diffusion theory The Diffusion of Innovations theory describes how ideas and new technologies spread through cultures. Everett Rogers (1962) was the principal proponent of this influential theory (*The Diffusion of Innovations*, 5th edn, 2003, New York: The Free Press).

discipline Specific area of knowledge, research, concepts or theories, such as marketing, economics or psychology.

dissonance Cognitive conflict or anxiety resulting from an inconsistency between personal beliefs and actions.

downstream Intervention activity that occurs within the population group specifically targeted for behaviour change, as opposed to focusing on policy, regulatory or environmental (**upstream**) factors that may reinforce existing behaviours or act as barriers to behaviour change.

econometric modelling Use of mathematical statistical models in which the statistical relationship that is believed to hold between variables is stated and tested.

economic factors Factors within an economy that may affect employment, personal or social resources, health or well-being.

economy The combination of activities, usually examined on a global, national or regional basis, that relate to production, distribution and consumption or use of products and services. Money supply, availability of credit and interest rates are also included in economic analysis.

effectiveness Producing the results intended.

efficacy Whether a behaviour or intervention has the capacity to achieve the intended goal.

efficiency Producing results with the minimum (or least waste) of resources.

egoism Concern only for one's own personal or family/social group interests and welfare and not those of others in society.

elaboration Cognitive effort invested in processing a message; usually occurs when the message is perceived by its receiver as being highly relevant or important to them.

Elaboration Likelihood Model A persuasion model which identifies two routes through which persuasive messages are processed – i.e. either through a central route, where the recipient of the message engages with and elaborates on the message content, or a peripheral route, where the recipient engages with the message at a less conscious level.

electronic media A broad term used most commonly to refer to relatively new media forms such as the internet (and electronic mail, electronic shopping, etc.) rather than media such as newspapers, magazines, leaflets or other material distributed via traditional postal services.

empirical Produced using an experiment or observation, as opposed to being purely conceptual.

engagement State where an individual who has been exposed to an intervention understands the key messages being sent and the personal relevance of the issue to their own lifestyle, health and well-being.

entertainment media Media forms whose primary purpose is to entertain rather than inform (e.g. news media) or educate.

environmental factors/constraints Factors within the external environment that may impact positively or negatively on behaviour. For example, a person may agree with messages encouraging greater physical activity, but perceive fitness centres as too expensive and local parks as unsafe.

epidemiology A branch of medical science/public health that studies the occurrence, distribution and severity of diseases in a population, together with the effects and effectiveness of treatments and control efforts (for example, vaccinations).

equity assessment Evaluation of an intervention to determine whether it has been fairly implemented across all relevant sections of the population and whether it has improved rather than worsened conditions for socially, economically or health-disadvantaged groups.

ethical dilemma Situation where choices of action may result in undesirable results such as discrimination, disadvantage to some groups, or harm (e.g. anxiety or fear). Actions may not be illegal and may involve choices between different options, none of which can guarantee absence of negative effects across all segments of society.

ethical issues (in social marketing) Factors that should be considered in planning and implementing interventions that may result in ethical dilemmas.

ethics Moral (as opposed to legal) rules, principles and expectations or codes of behaviour (written or unwritten). There are substantial differences between cultures as to what types of behaviours are considered to be ethical.

ethnography Observational research in which a researcher gains direct experience with the social, cultural or working environment of the population being studied.

evaluation A systematic review of all parts of an intervention – development, implementation, effects and effectiveness – using criteria such as a set of standards or benchmark data.

exchange theory A central theory within social marketing that behaviours involve individuals giving up something (e.g. by stopping smoking) in return for improvements to health, well-being or the overall environment.

exclusion (in social marketing) Omitting access for individuals or specific population segments to an intervention.

experience survey A survey in which participants have specific knowledge or experience of the problem under investigation, or expertise with prior interventions.

expert knowledge Knowledge about a particular issue or problem, usually gained from those who work closely with those affected by it or within a specific community.

exploratory research A type of research usually conducted to help define a problem and explore potential causes, severity, etc. Usually followed by more focused research to help develop insights into what types of interventions might motivate people to change behaviours.

extended parallel process model A persuasion model which ascertains the critical role of fear in forming attitudes, especially the positive relationship between attitude formation and fear appeals when recipients of a message are highly engaged in an issue.

Facebook An internet-based social networking site launched in 2004; used by individuals to communicate with friends and share information.

face-to-face research Research in which an interviewer meets directly with a respondent, asks questions and records answers as given.

facilitation Activities or resources that assist individuals to act or change behaviours.

false consensus Incorrect beliefs about agreement between members of groups about specific ideas or topics.

fatalism Belief that all events are predetermined or beyond the control of individuals, who are therefore powerless to act (for instance, to change behaviours).

fear-based appeals Communication based on generating distress, alarm or apprehension in order to draw attention to a specific message by showing the consequences of not taking action (for example, the consequences of a road crash or house fire).

feedback Responses to a promotional message or product/service offering from the target population indicating agreement or non-agreement with the message, satisfaction or non-satisfaction with a particular product or service delivery, or other factors that enable the marketer to gain insights into the acceptance of their offering and to be able to use this to fine-tune future activity.

focus groups A research technique that uses small groups selected from a wider population of interest. Guided discussions draw on members' experiences, beliefs or opinions about specific issues, including factors that may encourage or inhibit behaviour change.

four Ps A concept, originating from mainstream marketing activity, which divides marketing activity into decisions relating to the product (or service) to be offered, the price to be set, the promotional strategy to be used and the 'place' or means of distribution. Service marketers expand the concept to include factors such as the importance of people in the marketing mix. Considerable debate has been generated within social marketing as to how literally the 4Ps can be applied to social marketing activity.

framing In advertising and marketing, the way a particular point is expressed (e.g. glass half-full/half-empty). Positive framing is where behaviours are presented in terms of potential gains (e.g. remain healthy through exercise), whereas negative framing present behaviours in terms of negative consequences (e.g. health problems through lack of exercise).

free choice Decisions made by individuals without actual or perceived influence of others (such as family members, social groups or authority figures).

functional literacy The ability to read or write simple sentences needed for everyday life.

generalisable Able to be applied from a specific intervention or situation to other situations, population segments, etc. (for example, an intervention that is successful in changing behaviour in one geographic region, or with a specific population segment, that has been identified as potentially successful in other areas and with other groups).

genetic predisposition Hereditary factors, i.e. passed from parents to children, that make a child vulnerable or susceptible to illness or disease.

geodemographics Segmentation based on a combination of demographic characteristics and geographical location – based on the fact that people with similar demographic characteristics tend to live in similar locations.

goal A target, aim, action or objective for which there will be a measurable outcome, such as losing a specific amount of weight, or ceasing smoking by a particular time period.

grey literature Articles and reports that have been made available through sources that have not necessarily involved independent editorial review (such as journals that use independent reviewers to evaluate the quality of articles). Grey literature may involve organisational reports, opinion pieces and commentary posted on internet sites.

group influences Influences of activities, perceived or actual norms by a group on the behaviour of individuals. Influences may be positive, where the individual tries to conform or copy behaviour. They may also be negative, where the individual tries deliberately to behave in ways that would not meet with group approval.

habitual behaviour Behaviour that is routine and conducted without conscious thought about it – usually this behaviour has been repeated frequently and has become non-conscious habit.

health education The process by which individuals and groups of people learn, via teaching, advice or the distribution of information, to behave in a manner that is intended to lead to the promotion, maintenance or restoration of health or healthy lifestyles.

health inequality Difference in health outcomes – such as illness and disease prevalence. Most commonly used to refer to poorer health of low socio-economic groups compared to those who have greater affluence.

health literacy The level of skill needed to obtain, process and use basic health information and services and to make decisions about health issues affecting the individual or their family.

health promotion Officially defined by the World Health Organization as 'the process of enabling people to increase control over, and to improve, their health'. In the USA, health promotion is much more narrowly conceived as 'the science and art of helping people change their lifestyle to move toward a state of optimal health'.

health-related behaviours Individual or group behaviours that may impact positively (such as healthy lifestyles and diets) or negatively (such as smoking) on people's health and well-being.

high involvement A high degree of interest in a product, service or behaviour, potentially likely to lead to close attention being paid to relevant marketing communication activity and messages. See also **low involvement**.

hybrid communication forms Forms of communication that involve multiple objectives, such as those that seek to both entertain and persuade (see **advergames** for an example).

impact Impression made by an intervention or component of it – positive impact should lead to behaviour change.

impression management A form of **socially desirable responding** in which research responses attempt to give a positive or favourable description of an attribute or behaviour. If this is incorrect, data collected may be distorted and not be a true reflection of the population being studied.

incentive An influence that motivates people to change behaviour, such as financial rewards for ceasing smoking or free pedometers to enable people to track their physical exercise levels.

indifference Lack of interest or concern regarding an issue, and thus lack of action by an individual.

individual differences Physical and psychological differences between people that lead to differences in understanding or attitudes – such as different levels of risk acceptability – and thus ultimately to differences in behaviours.

influences Anything affecting the attitudes, beliefs or behaviours of a person or group of people.

infodemiology The study of the distribution and determinants of information and communication patterns regarding health, illness and health-related public policy.

information Provision of ideas or facts, either actively or passively. Active information-gathering may occur through sourcing material from the internet, reading books or other material on a specific topic, or talking to others. Passive information-gathering may occur through observing others or watching a television programme.

information processing Theories of human learning focusing on how information is stored and retrieved from human memory.

informed consent Agreement (often in writing) to participate in research after the objectives, methodologies and data use have been explained and a potential participant has confirmed they understand these.

infoveillance Uses infodemiology data for surveillance purposes, such as identifying a surge of misinformation or epidemics of fear, to enable communications to be targeted at countering possible negative effects.

insights Detailed understanding of the complex factors influencing individual or group behaviours, including the relationship between factors and their relative influence on current behaviours and potential barriers to, or enablers of, behaviour change.

integrated marketing communication (IMC) A strategic marketing planning approach that starts with an understanding of the needs of the target group and which takes into account all forms of communication and means of contact with the target group (not just mass media). It aims to achieve synergy by offsetting the strengths of each communication channel against potential weaknesses in others and to achieve a strong, consistent and unified image.

intelligence Capacity for understanding, including, for social marketing interventions, comprehending the meaning of intervention messages, personal risk and actions needed to reduce the risk.

intention An aim or goal (e.g. to change a specific behaviour in the future).

interdisciplinary approaches Social marketing approaches that draw on and integrate concepts, theories, techniques and expertise from a range of different branches of knowledge, such as marketing and psychology.

internal marketing Marketing communication aimed at an organisation's own staff in order to generate understanding of an intervention and to gain support and enthusiasm for it or acceptance of a major change to the way an organisation operates in order to implement it.

internet A network of interconnected networks that enables data exchanges amongst users in different networks or localities on a global basis, using a specifically designed standard for data exchange.

intervention A planned programme aimed at interrupting existing negative/risky behaviours (e.g. smoking, excess drinking), changing future behaviours or encouraging new behaviours (e.g. taking regular exercise).

involuntary disinclination Underlying factors (such as addiction to nicotine) that hinder conscious attempts to change behaviours (such as ceasing smoking).

invulnerability Concept that suggests individuals minimise or disregard their own personal risk from behaviours (for example, smoking, excessive alcohol consumption) in the apparent belief that health problems will occur to others and not to themselves. Invulnerability is known to be a factor in much 'risky' adolescent behaviour.

iteration (of theory) Development, extension or improvement of a concept or theory as the result of testing its applicability across a range of situations (see Chapter 6 for examples of theory development).

knowledge Facts, or perceived facts, gained by learning and observation, and experiences.

laboratory study A study (for example, showing different types of intervention message options) conducted in an artificial situation, such as a laboratory, where the environment is controlled, rather than in a real-world environment, where factors such as distractions, competing messages and social influences may affect responses to the messages.

lag times The time delay between an intervention and measurable effects. For example, sun protection behaviours may improve as the result of an intervention, but the impact on skin cancer rates will not be apparent for several years.

legislation Laws, i.e. rules, made by parliament and enforceable by law courts. The intention of laws is to regulate conduct and protect citizens.

legitimate Perceived as lawful, correct or acceptable by individuals or groups.

lifestyle A set of attitudes, beliefs, opinions and possessions determining how an individual or group of individuals lives. Influenced by individual characteristics and social interaction with others.

Likert scale A scale used to measure attitudes and their strength by rating statements in terms of how strongly the respondent agrees or disagrees with each individual statement.

literacy Ability to read and write; some 20% of the population of most developed countries have severe literacy problems; a further 20% can read and write to only basic levels. See also **functional literacy** and **health literacy**.

lobbying activity Attempts to influence legislation, regulation or public policy on behalf of a particular interest group. For example, marketers have actively lobbied against tightening existing restrictions on advertising to children.

logistics Planning and organising to ensure that all elements of an intervention are in place, accessible and functioning as planned.

'low-hanging fruit' Term used to describe the targeting of an intervention at the segments of the population most easily reached or most likely to respond positively, rather than targeting those who might need the intervention the most. The term derives, unsurprisingly, from fruit picking where the lowest branches are the most easily harvested.

low involvement A low degree of interest in a product, service or behaviour. Attention to marketing activity, especially marketing communications, is unlikely to be high, and it may be focused on peripheral factors, such as pleasant scenery or attractive presenters, rather than on the central message itself.

macro environment Aggregate factors affecting an overall economy, such as income, employment or investment. See also **micro environment**.

mail surveys Questionnaires distributed and returned via the postal system.

mainstream marketing See **commercial marketing**.

mall intercepts Research methodology where people are approached at shopping centres or similar venues to participate in a study. This may then be conducted face-to-face or respondents may be given a questionnaire to complete, a computer terminal at which to input responses at the venue or a weblink to connect to at some later point in time.

mandatory intervention/inclusion An intervention which reaches everyone, such as adding folic acid to bread even though only a small group within society (in this case, pregnant women) will benefit from it. Other groups have little chance of avoiding the intervention, even though it will do neither benefit nor harm.

marketing concept A concept long held to be a central foundation of marketing activity, based on the belief that achieving organisational goals depends on determining the needs and wants of target markets and delivering satisfactions more efficiently and effectively than competitors do.

marketing of social causes See **social causes**.

mass media Media that reach large numbers or percentages of the population at any one time, such as television or newspapers.

mechanisms (behavioural) Behaviours executed with little or minimal cognitive deliberation (i.e. mechanistically).

media/medium A means of communication or channels (e.g. television, radio, internet) through which persuasive messages may be sent to specific target groups.

media preferences Personal preferences for the media channel(s) through which people want to access information, send queries or enter into discussions or dialogue about a specific issue.

medication compliance/adherence Following the advice given for the treatment or management of a medical condition, such as changing diet, reducing alcohol or taking medications when and how prescribed.

memory The ability of an individual to store and recall prior learning and experiences.

message framing The phrasing of a persuasive message in positive, negative, rational or emotional terms.

message sources The channels, formal or informal, through which communication reaches a target; the identifiable organisation or individual conveying the communication and key messages within it.

message tailoring The design and delivery of messages prepared specifically for an individual or a homogeneous target group/population segment, using information that is the most pertinent or relevant to the target and the communication channels that are used and valued by the target.

micro environment Factors affecting communities, families or individuals, such as specific employment status, income levels and living conditions.

misperception Incorrect understanding or belief.

misplaced social norms Perceived social norms that are actually incorrect. See also **norms**.

mixed methods research Research activity involving a combination of both qualitative and quantitative methods.

moderation Management of a discussion or focus group, including introduction of topics, ensuring the smooth running of the discussion and managing group processes, interactions and dynamics.

moral choices Choices about what actions are right (acceptable to a society) or fair (i.e. do not result in discrimination or disadvantage for others).

moral judgements Decisions or judgements based on what is right, equitable or ethical, rather than just on what the law will allow.

motivation The underlying (internal) reason or force behind a specific behaviour, such as acting (changing behaviour) or resisting behaviour change.

multi-agency interventions Interventions that are developed or implemented by a number of different organisations who are independent of each other. For example, an intervention that aims to increase child vaccination rates may involve government health agencies and also community groups.

nanny state/nannyism A government or government agency perceived as having a high level of interest in and active interventions or control mechanisms relating to people's lives, particularly in the area of public health and safety. See also **paternalism**.

natural sciences Knowledge and study of the natural, physical world and the laws that govern it (for example, chemistry or physics).

netnography Use of ethnographic research techniques to study online communities.

network marketing A relationship marketing approach that also incorporates co-creation of interventions with participating target groups and other partners.

news media Media such as newspapers, radio or television whose content contains a proportion of coverage of news of events in the wider society. News may also cover research results or commentary on specific interventions or the organisations delivering the interventions.

noise External stimuli (not within the control of the sender of a persuasive message) that may distract from or interfere with the reception of the message as intended.

non-commercial activity Activity such as fund-raising or intervention delivery undertaken by organisations that are not motivated primarily by personal profit.

norms General expectations about a product, service, idea or behaviour that are considered acceptable within a specific population, culture or segment.

obedience Behaving in response to a direct order (such as wearing a seat belt).

objectives The object, goal or aims of a marketing programme. A weakness of many programmes is that objectives are stated in vague, generalised terms (for example, to increase awareness) that cannot then be used on completion of the programme to measure success or otherwise. A useful acronym from the 1950s from management guru Peter Drucker is that objectives should be SMART, i.e. specific, measurable, achievable, realistic and time-specific.

observational learning Behaviours learned by observing the behaviour of others – and approval or disapproval of it by other individuals or groups.

observational research Direct observation of behaviours and interactions between people in natural settings.

organisational policy Set of rules or guidelines within an organisation, governing both internal and external activity.

paid advertising Advertising time and space negotiated and paid for by an advertiser, as opposed to donated free by a media organisation such as community announcements. The advertiser has full control over where paid advertising appears but not over community announcements, which are usually made up of unsold space and time.

parental consent Written authorisation by a parent or guardian for a child to participate in research, such as providing data in a questionnaire, or take part in an intervention where individual activity and responses are monitored.

partner In social marketing interventions, any organisation that joins another to develop and/ or deliver an intervention.

paternalism Policies designed in the Belief that policy makers are acting in people's best interests, especially in the case of health and welfare, but which may restrict people's freedoms or right to make choices. See also **nanny state.**

perceived behavioural control Belief that behaviour/behaviour change is within the power or ability of an individual rather than determined by external forces.

perceived norms Beliefs about the prevailing norms within society or a specific group such as a family or social group. These may not be an accurate reflection of actual norms.

perceived power Beliefs about the ability of an individual or group to change behaviours or make an impact on health and well-being.

perceived severity Beliefs about the potential seriousness of an adverse event or occurrence, such as an accident or contracting a disease, and the consequences (e.g. disability, pain, loss of income or death) if the event does occur.

perceived susceptibility Belief about individual risk of adverse events such as accident or contracting an illness.

personalised communication Any form of communication directed at a specific individual and personally addressed and tailored to their specific needs and preferences for both the nature of information and the form of its delivery.

personality Internal psychological characteristics that mean an individual will respond to their environment or stimuli in specific ways.

persuasion Encouragement, urging or convincing, as in the case of the need for specific behaviour change.

persuasion resistance Theory that suggests that consumers tend to resist attempts they recognise as persuasive in nature, with reactions and subsequent behaviours depending on the perceived motives of the originator of the persuasion attempt.

persuasive messages/communication Any form of communication, whether via media channels or face to face, that has persuasion as its primary objective.

PEST analysis A systematic analysis conducted at the initial stage of an intervention's development that analyses the potential impact of political, economic, societal or technological factors on the intervention's delivery or potential acceptance.

phenomenon (in individual behaviour) Any activity that can be detected by any of the human senses (e.g. sight, smell, taste, hearing or touch).

physical harm In research, actual injuries that occur as the result of participating in a study.

pilot study A small trial of research activity designed to test ideas, fine-tune research instruments or other aspects of the research design.

place In commercial marketing, also known as *distribution*. The way in which an intervention will be made available to its target, such as venues, clinics, etc.

planned social change A term used in the 1970s to describe central and local government activities to achieve a wide range of objectives that would benefit society as a whole. The term encompassed some social marketing activity but also broader issues such as increasing higher education participation and support of government-endorsed projects and financial bonds.

planning Development of detailed strategies and tactics in order to achieve specific objectives. Includes evaluation of alternative strategies and tactics, selection of those most likely to succeed within the resources available and identification of additional resources, such as staff training, that may be required.

pluralistic ignorance Lack of correct knowledge about a specific issue that is shared across a group such as a family, social group, etc.

policy A plan of action developed by central or local government regarding resources, priorities and strategies to be made available to address a specific issue, such as harm reduction from excess alcohol consumption.

political factors Attitudes and priorities of government.

population health Measurement of incidents of illness, disease and mortality across an entire population, and strategies used to reduce them, thereby improving overall health and well-being.

population segments See **segmentation**.

practitioner A person who is active in a specific profession, such as a medical practitioner or a public health practitioner.

pragmatism In social marketing, ease of practical planning, implementation and evaluation of an intervention.

preliminary interviews **a.** Also known as screening interviews, interviews used to ensure that those included in a study do actually meet the criteria for inclusion. **b.** Interviews undertaken as part of a **pilot study**.

pre-post research Research that measures the attitudes, beliefs or behaviours of individuals or specific groups before an intervention and then re-tests them after an intervention has been delivered.

pre-testing A relatively small-scale test of a product, service, concept, idea or programme against part of the target group. Used to measure acceptance and to predict likely success (and to enable fine-tuning) before marketing to the full target group.

price In commercial marketing, the sum of money exchanged in order to purchase goods or services. In social marketing, the price may not be financial – it may be time, or the social costs of undertaking a behaviour.

primary research Original research that is carried out in order to answer specific questions, as opposed to secondary research which involves re-analysis of data already collected.

problem recognition The first stage in a decision that may lead to a specific behaviour; it results from recognition that there is a difference between a current or likely future state and a desired state (e.g. fitness levels or body weight).

process See **theory**.

product marketing The marketing of tangible items such as cars, foodstuffs, etc. which results in ownership (compared to the marketing of less tangible offerings such as airline travel).

product placement Featuring branded products in movies, television programmes, etc. as part of the content, either as active placement, where cast members are shown using and/or endorsing the product as part of the scripted activity, or passive placement, where the product simply appears as part of the 'background' or surroundings to a scene.

profession Occupation requiring specialist training, such as accountancy, law or medicine. Members are registered by a national organisation which sets and tests standards of competency and conduct, including ethical behaviour. Standards can be enforced, with serious breaches potentially resulting in loss of registration and therefore the right to work in the profession.

programme A schedule of events, activities, etc. that may be part of an intervention. It will identify what needs to be done, by whom and time, resource or financial parameters.

projective research techniques Tasks or games in which respondents can be asked to participate during an interview or group, where respondents can 'project' their own (potentially embarrassing) feelings or beliefs onto an imaginary other person or situation.

provider-driven Determined and controlled by the provider of an intervention without necessarily consulting with the recipients. See also **receiver-driven**.

psychographics Activities, interests and opinions that influence an individual's lifestyle (as opposed to demographics such as age and gender); used for market segmentation.

psychological factors See **psychology**.

psychological harm Emotional distress, such as that caused by participating in research that stirs painful memories.

psychology The study of the mind and its functions, particularly as these functions impact on behaviours.

psychosocial variables Variables, including social factors, that affect individual thoughts and behaviours.

public good The aim of policies, services or interventions to improve health or well-being. See also **social good.**

publicity Non-personal communication such as editorial or news coverage about an organisation and/or its products and services; not paid for by the organisation.

public policy Selected options or courses of action, legislation or regulation and associated funding resources concerning a given topic and determined/agreed by a governmental body, local authority, etc. See also **policy.**

public–private partnership In social marketing, an intervention developed and/or implemented jointly between non-profit organisations such as government agencies or publicly funded health providers and privately owned, often commercial (i.e. profit-making) organisations.

public relations In social marketing, communication with relevant internal and external people or organisations ('publics') aimed at explaining or promoting the benefits of a current or proposed chosen course of action and developing positive impressions, relationships, understanding or acceptance.

qualitative research Research techniques usually involving small numbers drawn from a target population who provide detailed descriptive information about their thoughts, beliefs, feelings, etc. Often difficult to generalise findings to the wider population.

quantitative research Research techniques involving relatively large numbers of respondents drawn from a target population, designed to collect data that can be subject to a range of statistical tests, the results of which can be generalised to the wider population.

randomised controlled trials Specific type of experiment where participants are usually either part of a treatment group or a placebo group in order to compare the isolated effect of the treatment received.

random sample Sampling method in which all members of a group (population or universe) have the same chance of being invited to participate in the study.

reactance/psychological reactance Theory suggesting that actual or potential perceived threats to personal freedom, such as recommended restrictions on consumption of specific products or engaging in particular behaviours, may be resisted as a means to regain control of that freedom. The perceived threat itself, rather than the actual consequences of the threat, may motivate individuals or groups to assert their freedom and regain control of their own decision-making and threatened freedom. Engaging in the threatened behaviour is one means of re-establishing this freedom

receiver-driven Developed with and possibly controlled by the preferences of those receiving the intervention. See also **provider-driven**.

regulation In marketing, a level of control below, and subject to, legislation, put in place to ensure conformity to a set of codes of practice or rules. Examples include the codes for advertising administered by the Advertising Standards Authority. Regulation can never overrule legislation.

reinforcement A positive message or other form of encouragement that increases the likelihood of a behaviour being continued or repeated in the future.

relationship (between behavioural factors) The way in which factors are connected and how changes in one factor may influence changes in others.

relationship marketing A form of marketing developed from direct-response marketing campaigns and emphasising customer retention and satisfaction, rather than immediate, short-term sales.

relativism Concepts, such as in ethics, that suggest moral standards and related norms of acceptable behaviour are not absolute or universal but instead defined by culture, context, or society.

relevance Importance or significance to the individual or target segment.

reliability The extent to which a measurement tool provides consistent results.

response (psychological) How a person or group of people react behaviourally or attitudinally to a stimulus.

safe sex Sexual activity that involves the use of contraception, condoms, etc. to prevent unplanned pregnancies or sexually transmitted diseases.

sanctions Penalties or restrictions imposed as a result of contravening laws, regulations or societal norms.

scepticism Mistrust of people's motives, persuasive messages or the promotion of specific ideas.

scoping The initial stage of planning an intervention, during which the nature and extent of the problem to be addressed are understood and deep insights are gained into the target groups and the role of the targeted behaviour within their lives.

secondary research Research which involves re-analysis of data already collected.

segmentation The division of a population into specific sub-groups; members of a segment will have characteristics in common, but these will be different from those of other segments. For segments to be viable in planning or implementing marketing programmes, each segment must be identifiable in terms of measurable characteristics that are appropriate to the behaviour being targeted and that differentiate one segment from another; the segments must be accessible and of sufficient size to warrant activity being customised to meet their specific needs.

self-deception A form of **socially desirable responding** in which answers to a question reflect aspirations rather than actual behaviours, even if respondents believe their answers to be true.

self-efficacy An individual's ability, or belief in their knowledge, skills or ability, to perform a specific behaviour competently.

self-interest Motivation for an individual's behaviour or decisions that considers only the impact on that person and not on others.

self-serving bias This occurs when people attribute their successes to their own internal or personal factors, or those of close family or social groups, but attribute their failures to situational factors or the actions of others beyond their control.

selling The transfer of ownership of goods or services in exchange for (usually) money or provision of other goods and services in exchange.

services marketing The marketing of activities or facilities that are less tangible than products that can be purchased and physically 'owned' (for example, frozen peas or refrigerators). Services may include fitness centres, legal advice, air travel.

situational influences External factors such as time pressures, presence or absence of others or pleasantness/unpleasantness of an environment that can assist or hinder a specific behaviour.

skills Ability, either natural or acquired through education or training in order to accomplish a task successfully.

snowballing A way of sampling participants from friends or acquaintances of current participants.

social advertising Advertising that focuses on changing attitudes, beliefs or behaviours in society without providing other elements of the marketing mix such as physical access to services. For an example of successful social advertising, see the Northern Ireland smoke alarms case study in Chapter II.

social change See **planned social change**.

social causes A term used in the 1950s to describe a wide range of issues that, if improved, would benefit society. These included individual responsibility for actions and their consequences and participating in communities, as well as issues that would nowadays be counted as social marketing.

social contract theory A theory that suggests an implied contract exists between individuals and government which guarantees minimum standards of health and well-being together with access to government services.

social discouragement Social values, peer pressure or views, opinions or advice from people whose views are important to an individual that may discourage individuals or groups from ceasing, changing or adopting behaviours.

social encouragement The opposite of social discouragement – active encouragement from peers, families, advisers or general media coverage that confirms or persuades individuals or groups to adopt a recommended behaviour such as exercising more, giving up smoking or not drinking to excess.

social factors Structures or influences in a population or segment of it (including community, family or social groups) that may impact positively or negatively on individual or group behaviour, health or well-being. For example, high unemployment or very low wages may impact on diet and lifestyles, leading to health problems.

social forces Influences from society or specific segments that impact on an individual's attitudes, beliefs, intentions or actual behaviours.

social good Activity that benefits the overall health or well-being of society as a whole rather than providing profit or advantage for individuals within it.

social idea See **social causes**.

socialisation Communication of values, cultural beliefs or norms to new members of a group or society (for example, children or new immigrants).

socially desirable responding A form of research bias in which responses are biased due to the tendency of respondents to reply in ways that will be viewed favourably by others. This usually takes the form of over-reporting positive attitudes or behaviour or under-reporting negative or harmful behaviours. See also **impression management** and **self-deception**.

social marketing (classification of incorrect definition) The term 'social marketing' itself has been hijacked by at least one commercial organisation: In 2006, Jupiter Media announced a 'social marketing' service, examining social media on behalf of corporate clients. The social marketing community protested over the hijacking of the term; however, Jupiter decided to stick with the name, despite this approach being more correctly (and commonly) referred to as 'social media optimisation'.

Note 1: 'Social media' describes the online technologies and practices that people use to share opinions, insights, experiences and perspectives. Social media can take many different forms, including texts, images, audio and videos. Sites typically use technologies such as blogs, message boards, podcasts, wikis and vlogs to allow users to interact.

Note 2: 'Social media optimisation (SMO)' is a way to optimise websites so that they would be more easily connected or interlaced with online communities and community websites, also called social media sites.

social marketing toolbox Range of resources, concepts, techniques and theories that help guide the development of an intervention.

social media Media forms such as Facebook, MySpace, etc. that are used by individuals or groups to interact with each other and share information. They are distinguished from other more traditional media forms in that the users of social media supply and monitor the content of the medium.

social norms See **norms**.

social network theory This theory describes the actors in a network (nodes) and how they are related (ties) and looks at how behaviours spread through networks, how problems are solved or goals achieved and how these networks operate.

social pressure Actual or perceived influence exerted by a formal or informal social group on attitudes, values, or behaviour in order to conform, or to be seen to conform to social norms.

social problems Issues that directly or indirectly affect society or specific groups within it and that are considered to be problems or controversies related to acceptable behaviour, health or well-being. Examples include excess alcohol consumption and resultant noise, violence, property damage, etc.

social psychology A branch of **psychology** involving the study of social influence, social perception and social interaction and how these impact on indivudal and collective behaviours.

societal marketing The idea that the organisation should determine the needs, wants and interests of target markets and deliver the desired satisfaction more effectively and efficiently than competitors, in a way that maintains or improves the consumer's and society's well-being.

socio-cultural factors Combination of both social and cultural factors that may influence attitudes, beliefs or actual behaviours.

socio-economic Combining of social and environmental factors such as low education, low income and poor living conditions which may impact on health, well-being or participation in some social activities.

source credibility The believability or trustworthiness of a person, group or organisation that is attempting to deliver a persuasive message. Often influenced by perceptions of the source's power, expertise and credibility, together with their attractiveness.

spiral of silence A political science and mass communication theory relating to the failure of people to give an opinion on a topic if they feel their views will not reflect those of the majority.

sponsorship Investment in an event, organisation, exhibition, etc. in order to raise awareness, increase an organisation's profile or generate positive links between the sponsor and the event itself and thereby gain a positive image for the sponsor and its products or services.

'squeaky wheels' A somewhat negative term used to describe groups who are assertive and visible in calling for action to address a specific problem. These groups may not be the ones who need – or would benefit the most from – action. The term comes from squeaks in mechanical equipment such as wheels that are silenced by the application of lubricants such as oil.

stages of change model (or transtheoretical model of behaviour change). A model which characterises actual behaviour as the result of an individual passing through several 'stages of change' before performing and maintaining the desired behaviour.

stakeholders Individuals or groups with either a financial interest in an organisation or who have an interest in, or could be affected by, its activities. Groups may include employees, service users, local communities, etc.

stakeholder mapping Identification of the linkages and relationships between individual stakeholder groups and their objectives, resources, expectations and relative importance.

stakeholder theory This theory argues that a company is morally and financially responsible not only to its investors (shareholders) but also to customers, employees, suppliers, management, the community and the wider public.

standard of conduct Explicit or implicit expectations about behaviours within society or a specific group within it.

statistical analysis A range of methods used to collect, process, analyse and interpret large amounts of data, such as that obtained from surveys.

stereotype A fixed, frequently negative perception of individuals, specific groups or population segments. For example, a negative stereotypical view of low socio-economic groups may be that they lack motivation to change behaviours that negatively impact on their health (such as smoking).

stimulus An influence, such as personal contact, a persuasive message or an incentive that results in changes to attitudes, beliefs or behaviour.

structural changes Changes in the environment or service delivery that may impact on the design, delivery or implementation of an intervention.

subjective norm Perceived rather than necessarily actual norms regarding specific behaviours and the potential consequences of not conforming to these norms.

surveys A range of techniques used to gather data from specific populations or segments in relation to specific issues or problems.

SWOT analysis Analysis of the **s**trengths and **w**eaknesses of an organisation or partnership, together with the **o**pportunities for and **t**hreats to activity.

tailored interventions Programmes, including the intervention itself and the way in which it is communicated, that have been specifically customised to meet the needs and wants of a specific target group or population segment.

target Individuals or groups who are the specific focus of an intervention.

TARPS target audience rating points – i.e. percentage value of the target audience that views an individual advert.

teleology Ethical reasoning in social marketing that focuses on actual outcome effects and does not accept that any adverse outcomes should occur, even if they were not actually what was intended. See also **deontology**.

telephone surveys/questionnaires Questionnaires administered by telephoning potential respondents and reading questions to them, recording their responses (usually directly into a computer-based system) for subsequent analysis.

theory A set of principles, factors or interrelationships developed in order to help describe, explain or predict phenomena such as behaviours. Ideally, theories should be tested in multiple situations and studies before becoming widely accepted. See also **behavioural theory**.

tipping point The point at which the adoption of an idea or behaviour accelerates and becomes widely accepted.

total process approach An approach to planning, developing, implementing and evaluating an intervention that sees the approach to an intervention as consisting of a series of specific planning and development stages that result in a logical, research theory-informed integrated programme.

touchpoints All points of contact, formal or informal, or interface between an intervention supplier and the population at which it is targeted.

traditionalist A social marketer who takes a neoclassical approach, using traditional marketing techniques in this relatively new discipline.

treatment group See also **control group**. Used in market research, medication trials, etc. The treatment group is given a specific 'treatment' and the success, change (or lack of it) observed. The control group will be selected on the basis of similar characteristics to the treatment group, but will not be given the 'treatment'.

treatment trials Research in which interventions are trialled by treating individuals or groups in specific ways and observing or measuring the effects.

tribe A social group who define themselves or who are defined by territory or behaviour.

unintended consequences Results from an intervention that were not intended or planned. These consequences are usually unpleasant or harmful, such as anxiety or distress.

upstream factors Economic, environmental or policy factors that may influence individual or group behaviour by either inhibiting or facilitating opportunities for behaviour change. See also **downstream factors**.

utilitarianism An ethical perspective based on achieving the greatest benefits for the greatest number of people from a course of action, while accepting that some people may not benefit – and may actually be harmed or disadvantaged.

validity The extent to which a research instrument measures what it is intended/designed to measure.

viral effects Effects on attitudes, beliefs or behaviours that have occurred as the result of individual person-to-person communications, including the use of social media such as Facebook.

web-based questionnaires Questionnaires placed on a website, with respondents inputting their own responses by either selecting an option from choices or typing in their own comments.

Index